Indo-European

and Its Closest Relatives

Volume 1. Grammar

Indo-European
and Its Closest Relatives

The Eurasiatic Language Family

Volume 1. Grammar

Joseph H. Greenberg

Stanford University Press

Stanford, California   2000

Stanford University Press
Stanford, California

©2000 by the Board of Trustees of the
Leland Stanford Junior University

Printed in the United States of America

CIP data appear at the end of the book

To my wife, Selma

Preface

The present work is the first volume of a projected two-volume work on the Eurasiatic language family. It is devoted to the grammatical evidence; the second volume will present the lexical items that are, in fact, every whit as extensive and cogent as the grammatical evidence.

This grammatical evidence is quite sufficient in itself to establish the validity of the Eurasiatic family. I have chosen to present it first for several reasons. One of these is that in spite of the frequent affirmation of the importance of such evidence, it is almost lacking in present-day attempts to delineate broader and deeper linguistic stocks. The second major reason is that, despite all the facts regarding the presentation of evidence for linguistic stocks in my previous work, the myth persists that I only take into account vocabulary evidence.

A third reason is the inherent interest and fascination of this type of linguistic evidence in its own right. In particular, grammatical comparison of related forms in stocks of chronological depth provides rich material for diachronic typological study, both of the earlier stages of grammaticalization and of the later stages of the history of categories. Here typological and genetic studies are mutually fruitful. The study of later stages, leading in many instances to functionless survival, lexicalization, and functional reinterpretation, at once informs diachronic typology and leads to the identification of related forms in only distantly related languages whose basic connection is reinforced by dynamic typological considerations.

In the course of the preparation of this work, which began at least twenty years ago, I accumulated many indebtednesses that I am pleased to acknowledge. First, I should mention the staff of the Green Library Reference section at Stanford, whose helpfulness and willingness to go to extraordinary lengths to excavate from the Stanford library itself, or to procure and often reproduce materials essential to the present study, I acknowledge with profound gratitude.

Of these I first mention the reference librarians proper. I note here only those who were present during a major portion or all of the time I was at work on the present volume. Without exception, the many others, whose names are omitted for practical reasons, were equally cheerful and helpful.

Special gratitude is owed to Richard Fitchen, the director of the Reference section. I should also like to thank, among others, Eric Heath, Barry Hinman, Elisabeth Green, Kathryn Kerns, Rose Adams, and Joanne Hoffman. Especially important was the great service rendered by the Interlibrary Borrowing division, especially Sonia Moss, its head, and Olga Katz. I am especially indebted to John Rawlings, the linguistic and anthropological bibliographer at Green Library, and to Wojciech Zalewski, who expended great effort to obtain, on his collecting trips to Eastern Europe, doctoral dissertations and other materials often very difficult or impossible to obtain in this country. I would also like to express my indebtedness to Norris Pope, the director of Stanford University Press, and Muriel Bell, the editor of the Social Science division, for their help and their facilitation of the publication of the present work.

A number of scholars read earlier drafts of particular chapters of this manuscript and made valuable comments and criticism that have been incorporated in the present volume. I mention here especially Vyacheslav Ivanov, Richard Dasher, Carol Justus, Allan Bomhard, and Paul Kiparsky.

Finally, I owe a special debt of gratitude to Merritt Ruhlen, who, with his unique combination of gifts, designed and typeset the present volume, provided many critical comments, made the maps, and saw it through the press.

J.H.G.

Contents

Tables

Maps

Indo-European
and Its Closest Relatives

Volume 1. Grammar

Chapter 1

The Historical Background

In this volume I will present the grammatical evidence for the validity of Eurasiatic as a linguistic stock. Lexical evidence for Eurasiatic will be presented in Volume 2. I believe that this evidence is quite sufficient to establish the Eurasiatic hypothesis since the numerous and interlocking resemblances among the various subgroups—including, in some instances, agreement in irregular alternations—can only be reasonably explained by descent from a common ancestor. The alternative explanations of borrowing, sound symbolism, and chance cannot explain these similarities.

The present chapter is devoted to the historical background of the Eurasiatic hypothesis, including its relationship to the proposals of the Nostratic school. With regard to the relationship between the Nostratic and Eurasiatic hypotheses there has been both theoretical confusion and factual errors in the recent literature. This chapter will also consider the validity of the most important alternative hypotheses that have been advanced. These concern especially the genetic position of Korean, Japanese, and Ainu, and the validity of an Altaic subgroup within the Eurasiatic family tree.

As presented here Eurasiatic is identical in membership to that indicated in Greenberg (1987: 332), namely, Indo-European, Uralic-Yukaghir, Altaic, Korean-Japanese-Ainu, Gilyak, Chukotian, and Eskimo-Aleut (see Maps 1 and 2). In Chapter 3, devoted to a set of

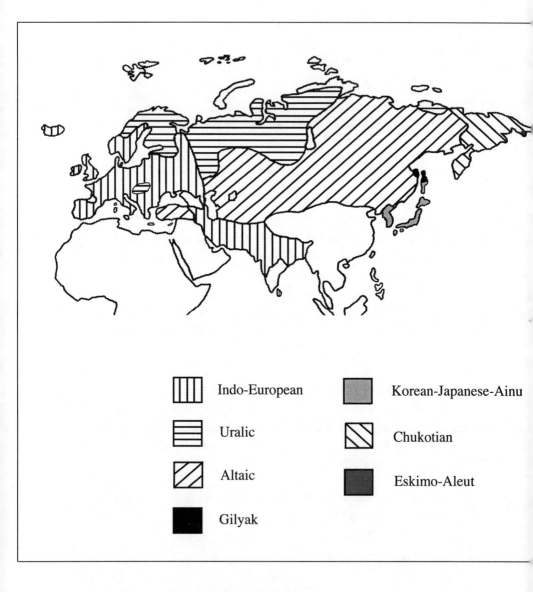

	Indo-European		Korean-Japanese-Ainu
	Uralic		Chukotian
	Altaic		Eskimo-Aleut
	Gilyak		

Map 1. The Eurasiatic Family

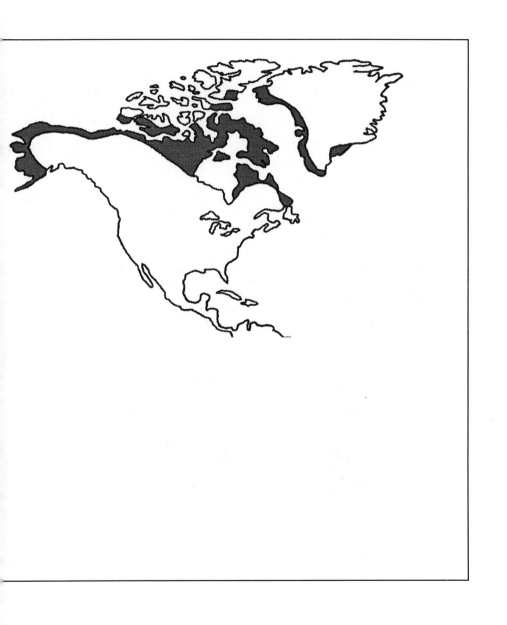

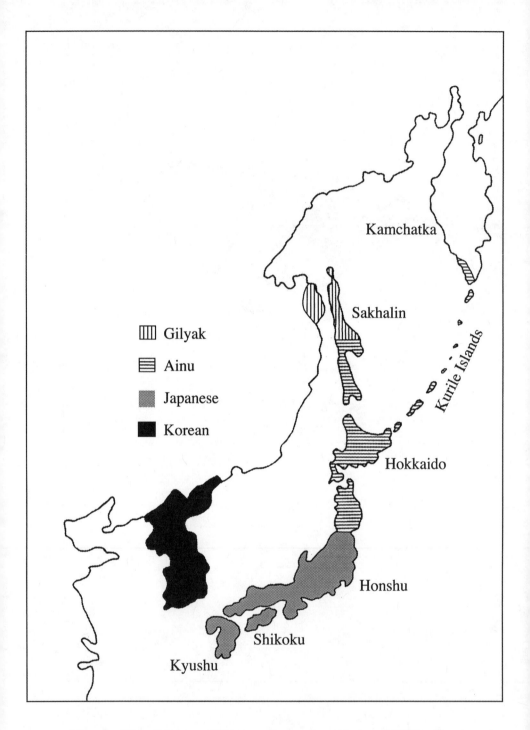

Map 2. Distribution of Korean, Japanese, Ainu, and Gilyak

Eurasiatic grammatical elements, this west to east order is followed in the exposition, except in a few instances in which other orders based on the convenience of exposition appear more suitable.

Eurasiatic and Nostratic

I first arrived at the Eurasiatic hypothesis some time in the mid 1960's in the context of my task of ascertaining the genetic affiliation of the native languages of the Americas, specifically that of Eskimo-Aleut, the third and northernmost of the three indigenous families in the Americas (Greenberg 1987).

At that time the Russian Nostratic school was hardly known in the United States and I arrived at my own results in complete independence of theirs. The Nostratic hypothesis, as formulated by Vladislav Illich-Svitych (1971–84), asserts the relationship of six families: Indo-European, Uralic, Altaic, Afro-Asiatic, Kartvelian, and Dravidian. Since Eurasiatic has much in common with Nostratic, along with major differences, the term Eurasiatic/Nostratic is sometimes found in the literature. The major differences have understandably led some historical linguists, such as the Indo-Europeanist Calvert Watkins (1990: 295), to shed doubt on both. He asks rhetorically whether he is being "nit-picky" in pointing them out. The answer, of course, is that he is not.

However, there have been significant changes in the views of Nostraticists in recent years, as the result of which the differences have been very greatly reduced. Of course the Nostraticists are a group of individual scholars who are not always in agreement with each other. For at least one prominent Nostraticist, Allan Bomhard (1994), there is almost no difference between his views and mine. A further point of significance is that the Nostratic family, as posited by Illich-Svitych, never corresponded to the actual views of early Nostraticists such as Holger Pedersen, the Indo-European scholar who first coined the term Nostratic.

Perhaps the best summary of the overall significance of recent developments is that of Lamb and Mitchell (1991: 123), namely, that in recent years Russian comparativists have revised their classification so that it is now closer to the Eurasiatic stock in two important respects. First, Afro-Asiatic (formerly Hamito-Semitic) is now generally viewed as a sister superstock to Eurasiatic, rather than part of it. Second, they have added additional stocks to the northeast extending as far as Eskimo-Aleut. They also note that an important question still to be resolved is that of Dravidian.

The exclusion of Afro-Asiatic from Nostratic had already been made by Sergei Starostin (1990), and is repeated in a number of subsequent publications. In 1989 he stated that Afro-Asiatic is a sister to, rather than a daughter of Nostratic and he thus in effect excluded it from Nostratic, to which it is only distantly related as a whole. He also noted that the relationship of Indo-European to Dravidian is more remote than that of Indo-European to Uralic and Altaic. He also reported a glottochronological study that gives the same taxonomic hierarchy: Nostratic proper, Dravidian at first remove, and Afro-Asiatic at second remove. Afro-Asiatic is essentially excluded from Nostratic since it involves a relationship to Nostratic as a whole at a deeper level.

Vitaly Shevoroshkin and Alexis Manaster Ramer (1991: 179) similarly note that Afro-Asiatic may be coordinate with Nostratic, a "sister" rather than a "daughter." They add that the Russian investigators A. N. Golovastikov and Aaron Dolgopolsky (1972), and Oleg Mudrak (1989a,b), have presented evidence for the Nostratic affiliations of Chukotian and Eskimo-Aleut, respectively.

The most comprehensive recent statements on this issue are from Bomhard and his collaborator, John Kerns (Bomhard 1992, Bomhard and Kerns 1994). In these works Eurasiatic is identical with mine, except for the omission of Japanese and Ainu. Korean, with some reservations, is included in Altaic so that the only real difference (aside from subgrouping) is the omission of Japanese and Ainu. Furthermore, Japanese is acknowledged to have Altaic elements, but in view of Paul Benedict's hypothesis connecting Japanese with Tai-Austronesian (Benedict 1990), judgement is reserved. Bomhard, however, now includes Japanese and Korean, while with regard to Ainu he suspends judgement because he has not yet himself investigated the problem in depth (personal communication). In addition, the Altaic affiliation of Japanese is accepted by Starostin, who has devoted a detailed monograph to the subject (Starostin 1991).

These recent changes in the views of Nostraticists have histori-cal antecedents, beginning with Pedersen, the founder of Nostratic theory. He introduced the term Nostratic in 1903 as a designation of languages and language families related to Indo-European; the term derives from Latin *nostrates* 'our countrymen.' In subsequent writings Pedersen emphasized certain points. First, Indo-European is more closely related to Finno-Ugric (part of Uralic) than it is to Semitic (part of Afro-Asiatic). At that time the relationship of Semitic to "Hamitic" was little explored and the concept of Afro-Asiatic (Greenberg 1963) as a family, of which Semitic is one branch, had not yet been formulated. Similarly, instead of Uralic, Pedersen refers to Finno-Ugric, which is today universally regarded as one of two branches of Uralic, Samoyed being the other.

With regard to similarities between Indo-European and Finno-Ugric pronouns, Pedersen noted that one will not find such a thor-ough agreement a second time (Pedersen 1933: 308). In view of the work of Wicklund (1906) and Paasonen (1907), it is no longer nec-essary to doubt the relationship, or, again, to deny it would be over-bold. In connection with the closer relationship of Indo-European to Finno-Ugric than to Semitic, Pedersen made the interesting remark (1933: 309) that Finno-Ugric is to be compared to Indo-European in its post-ablaut stage, but should be compared to Semitic in its pre-ablaut stage. He goes on to draw once more the conclusion that the separation of Indo-European and Semitic was at a more ancient period than that between Indo-European and Finno-Ugric. Peder-sen seems to be referring here to Indo-European qualitative ablaut $e \sim o$, but he gives no details. For a fuller discussion of this matter, see Greenberg (1990) and Chapter 2 of the present work.

Pedersen's second major conclusion was that Nostratic encom-passes a whole series of languages in northern Asia besides Finno-Ugric (1931: 337), including Turkish, Mongolian, Manchu, Yukaghir, and Eskimo. Indeed, as early as 1908, in his discussion of first-person *m* and second-person *t*, he cites Indo-European, Finno-Ugric, and Altaic (which he called Turkish-Mongol-Manchu), and then, refer-ring to Uhlenbeck's (1907) thesis of a relationship between Indo-European and Eskimo, he states that this same pronominal pattern is also found in Eskimo (Pedersen 1908: 342–43).

A new stage is reached in Nostratic theory in the work of Illich-Svitych, who is generally regarded as the founder of Nostratic in its modern version. His earliest comprehensive statement was published in 1967 in the form of a series of etymologies from the six families usually cited as "classical Nostratic." However, it is interesting to note that in a slightly earlier publication (1964), significantly called "Oldest Indo-European-Semitic Linguistic Contacts," he considered that the case for a relationship between Semitic and Indo-European was weak and that most of the resemblances were due to borrowing from Semitic by Indo-European. In the 1967 study Afro-Asiatic as a whole is considered, rather than just the Semitic branch. It is possible that the wider framework provided in this way for Semitic, and the extension to other non-Indo-European groups such as Uralic, modified his views by putting them in a broader perspective.

In 1971 there appeared the first volume of the Nostratic dictionary, which has become the basic source for Nostratic etymologies. It was edited by Vladimir Dybo after Illich-Svitych's untimely death in 1966. Although the dictionary follows the paper of 1967 in comparing just the six main groups, Korean is occasionally cited as a member of Altaic, following G. J. Ramstedt and Nikolaus Poppe. In the introduction Illich-Svitych (1971: 61) notes, with regard to Yukaghir, that the work of Björn Collinder (1940), Johannes Angere (1957), and Oliver Tailleur (1959b), though not allowing us to consider it a Uralic language, does allow us to consider its Nostratic character. In an editorial footnote Dybo added that the same remarks probably apply to Korean and Japanese in relation to Altaic.

About the same time that Illich-Svitych began to publish his Nostratic studies, Aaron Dolgopolsky (1964, 1965) independently developed a theory linking Indo-European with Afro-Asiatic, Kartvelian, and a series of languages in northern Asia including Uralic, Altaic, and Eskimo-Aleut. He called this group Sibero-European and criticized the name Nostratic because of its ethnocentric character. Nevertheless, he later adopted the more widely used term. In a later work on personal pronouns in Nostratic (Dolgopolsky 1984) he included Gilyak and Chukotian, as well as Elamite and Dravidian.

From the foregoing historical review it is clear that the Nostraticists, beginning with Pedersen, never restricted their notion of Nostratic to just the six groups usually mentioned. Moreover, the special, more distant position of Afro-Asiatic (to him, of course, Semitic) is already insisted on by Pedersen. Every group that I include in Eurasiatic, with the exception of Ainu, is included in some of their enumerations and even in their comparisons. Similarly, more recent developments have produced results virtually identical with mine. It is unfortunate, therefore, that Nostraticists, who are perfectly aware of these developments, continue in statements to the public media to enumerate the same six groups used in Illich-Svitych's dictionary, thus stressing a difference that is now almost non-existent and thereby providing, as we have seen in the case of Watkins, ammunition to all those opposed to any broader historical comparison of language groups. It should be added that Illich-Svitych's subgrouping of Nostratic into Western (Indo-European, Afro-Asiatic, and Kartvelian) and Eastern (Uralic, Altaic, and Dravidian) branches, which would make Indo-European closer to Afro-Asiatic than to Uralic and Altaic is, as far as can be seen, almost universally abandoned.

This alleged closeness of Indo-European to Afro-Asiatic, in violation of obvious facts, clearly has its roots in the earlier attempts of Hermann Møller (1906) and Albert Cuny (1937) to show the relationship of Indo-European to Semitic, to link, as it were, Homer and Shakespeare to the Bible and the Quran. These non-linguistic considerations are shown most vividly, in terms that could be characterized as racist, in Cuny (1937: 142) when he asserts that Pedersen "did not hide his faith in the single origin of the languages of the white race."

Since such languages and language groups as Yukaghir, Chukotian, and Eskimo-Aleut are, as we have seen, repeatedly mentioned as Nostratic, beginning with Pedersen, why were they not included in the Nostratic dictionary? The answer is given by two Nostraticists, M. Chejka and A. Lamprecht (1984: 86). After discussing Pedersen and Illich-Svitych they remark, regarding the six groups cited in the latter's comparative dictionary, "obviously this does not mean that the number of Nostratic families in the world is confined to the six mentioned. In his generalizations Illich-Svitych only used those language families for which the proto-linguistic bases have progressed to a satisfactory level."

Although the Nostraticists believe that by these restrictions they are employing the comparative method as practiced by Indo-Europeanists, this does not accord with actual Indo-European practice since, for example, the Indo-Europeanists have not hesitated to include in their comparisons such poorly attested languages as the extinct Phrygian of Asia Minor. The presence or absence of a reconstruction reflects the activities of linguists, not the properties of the languages themselves, and inevitably leads to the positing of incomplete and erroneously defined families.

In fact, in one important instance, that of Afro-Asiatic, it can hardly be asserted that Illich-Svitych had an adequately reconstructed protolanguage to compare with the other branches of Nostratic. His basic source at the time was Diakonov (1965). As Illich-Svitych (1971: 46ff) noted, "many important aspects of the reconstructed system have still not been explicated . . . [and] a general work on the comparative phonetics is absent." Igor Diakonov himself (1965: 23) states that "in the case of Cushitic and Chad as often as not we limit ourselves to a comparison of lexical and morphological elements consisting of acoustically similar phonemes, since the regularity of the correspondences cannot always be proved conclusively by a sufficient number of individual reflexes" and, in regard to the table of correspondences for the entire family, he says "thus, even between Semitic on the one hand, and Egyptian and Berber-Libyan on the other, many problems of phonetic correspondences are unsolved" (1965: 25).

Bilateral Comparisons

In additon to such multi-family stocks as Eurasiatic and Nostratic, there is a large literature—much larger than that for Nostratic and Eurasiatic—that consists of restricted, mostly bilateral, comparisons. With a few exceptons (e.g. Collinder, Ramstedt, Martin, Miller) in this literature the explanations of the observed similarities have been non-genetic. A favorite notion in this large literature is that of linguistic "strata"; so, for example, the numerous resemblances between Uralic and Yukaghir are attributed to the existence of a Uralic stratum in Yukaghir.

Another favorite alternative explanation is borrowing or a vague notion of influence. Of course borrowing is frequently a plausible explanation for certain specific resemblances, but its validity as an overall explanation becomes suspect in a wider context. One of the few who has realized this is Roy Andrew Miller, who notes that the occurrence of resemblances supposedly explained by borrowing between two Altaic language groups becomes inadequate when the same item reappears in one or more of Korean, Japanese, or Ainu.

This large literature of mostly bilateral comparisons contains many valuable etymological suggestions and is referred to at numerous points in Chapter 3. Nevertheless, as should be obvious, such bilateral comparisons cannot lead to a taxonomy of languages that reflects genuine linguistic history. The choice of languages to be compared is arbitrary, with important and well-documented languages being favored. It is for this reason that Eskimo figures in comparisons with Indo-European (e.g. in the work of Uhlenbeck), but Aleut, universally acknowledged to be the closest relative of Eskimo, is never compared with Indo-European or anything else (except, of course, Eskimo).

The authors of these comparisons fondly believe that in such restricted comparisons they are using the comparative method because they employ its superficial external apparatus. I have examined a large part of this literature. It has yielded, as might be expected, some valid grammatical and lexical comparisons that are helpful, but which, as noted above, require testing in a wider context.

The Altaic Problem

It will have been noted that in the enumeration of Eurasiatic languages at the beginning of this chapter languages such as Korean and Japanese were not included in Altaic proper as has been common in writings concerning these languages and can be seen in the very title of Miller's well-known book *Japanese and the Other Altaic Languages* (1971). However, it is obvious on the merest inspection that languages of Altaic proper (Turkic, Mongolian, and Tungusic) have much in common that is not shared by Korean or Japanese. This is recognized by Poppe (1960: 8) in his classical comparative work on Altaic in which he includes Korean, but considers it a separate branch distinct from conventional Altaic. It figures relatively infrequently in his etymologies. Moreover, languages like Korean and Japanese frequently show resemblances with other Eurasiatic languages which they do not share with Altaic in the restricted sense, as can be frequently noted in the grammatical comparisons in Chapter 3.

Facts such as these have led to the so-called Altaic problem. Since the writings of Gerhard Clauson, and more recently Gerhard Doerfer, it appears that most, if not all, of the younger specialists in one or more of the traditional three branches of Altaic (Turkic, Mongolian, and Tungusic) no longer believe that there is an Altaic family.

There are two separate questions involved here. Are the Altaic languages related to one another? This is to be distinguished from a second question. Do they form a valid genetic node, that is, a set of languages more closely related to each other than to any others? If so, they have a common ancestor, Proto-Altaic, which gave rise to the above-mentioned groups of languages and no others.

I believe that the answer to the first question, that of mere relationship, is overwhelmingly positive. The answer to the second is more difficult and some Nostraticists indeed believe that there is no Altaic node and that each of the three groups goes back separately to Proto-Nostratic.

In several publications Miller (1991b,c,d) has defended the traditional view. His arguments are largely phonological, especially the existence of two reconstructed pairs of liquid phonemes, l_1, l_2, r_1, and r_2, which within Altaic are only distinguishable in non-Chuvash Turkic. There is also a merging within Proto-Turkic of Proto-Altaic $dž$, j, n and nj, all represented by Proto-Turkic $*j$. In such instances, in order to maintain the usual anti-Altaicist interpretation in terms of borrowing, first from Turkic into Mongolian (with some reverse borrowing), and then from Mongolian into Tungusic, since it is Turkic that has carried out the wholesale phonetic mergers, the borrowing has to be pushed back to a time so early that it becomes indistinguishable from Proto-Altaic; that is, a time when Turkic still distinguished $dž$, j, n and nj, and all the Altaic languages outside of non-Chuvash Turkic still displayed a difference between l_1 and l_2, as well as r_1 and r_2. At such a time all the languages would have had a sound system that is identical to that reconstructed by Ramstedt, Poppe, and others for Proto-Altaic.

Miller also alludes to the cogency of the grammatical data regarding verb derivation in Ramstedt (1912) and Poppe (1973). I agree with him on all of this, except that, as will be seen in Chapter 3, most of these features are found in Eurasiatic languages outside of Altaic proper. I believe, however, that based on personal, demonstrative, and interrogative pronouns the relationship of Turkic, Mongolian, and Tungus is obvious. However, the anti-Altaicists have carefully avoided presenting this evidence in a coherent manner and, when they have alluded to it, they have sought to explain it away as language contact, or even sound symbolism, rather than accept the obvious hypothesis of genetic relationship.

Let us begin with the first- and second-person pronouns. In the first-person singular in non-Chuvash Turkic, some languages (e.g. Osmanli Turkish) have nominative singular *ben* and a stem *ben-* that, except for the widespread internal vowel variation in the dative (e.g. Osmanli *bana*) is found in all oblique cases. Most Turkic languages, however, have *me-n*, in which *-n* (often called pronominal *n* by Altaicists) had as its original function the marking of oblique cases, and is ultimately of genitive origin (see No. 25 in Chapter 3). In non-Chuvash Turkic, this *-n* has spread analogically to the nominative. However, in Chuvash, which groups separately as against all the rest of Turkic, this does not occur. The nominative case here is *e-pě*, in which *e-* is a deictic element, and the oblique stem is *man-* (e.g. genitive *man-ăn*).

The alternation between the nominative without *-n*, as found in Chuvash, and the oblique with *-n* recurs in Mongolian (e.g. Classical Mongolian nominative *bi*, genitive *min-u*) and Tungusic (e.g. Evenki nominative *bi*, genitive *min-i*). The forms *men* and *min* are not restricted to Altaic, but are found also in Uralic (e.g. Finnish *minä* 'I'), Indo-European, and even Etruscan (*mi* 'I,' *mini* 'me'). For Proto-Indo-European, on the basis of Baltic, Slavic, and Indic, Oswald Szemerényi (1990: 220) reconstructs Proto-Indo-European **mene* for the genitive. In Baltic and Slavic the form in *-n* has been extended to all oblique cases, as in Altaic (e.g. Old Church Slavic instrumental *mŭnojǫ*). Indo-European presents important confirming evidence for the original oblique case function of *n* as seen also in Indo-European *r/n* stems and a single *l/n* stem (*su̯el/su̯en* 'sun').

Returning to Altaic, it is clear that the chance of an irregular alternation *bi/men* arising independently three times is infinitesimal. That it should be borrowed twice is also utterly improbable. One has literally to scour the earth to find instances of a borrowed first- or second-person pronoun, much less the borrowing of an irregular alternation in these forms. These data by themselves are enough to show that the Altaic languages are related. Furthermore, the specific agreement in the nominative case in Chuvash *e-pĕ*, Mongolian *bi*, and Tungus *bi* is confined to Altaic. Therefore it can be considered to be a shared common innovation within Eurasiatic that contributes to the establishment of traditional Altaic as a valid genetic entity.

How is this evidence treated by Clauson and Doerfer, the two leading exponents of the anti-Altaic position? It is ignored when possible. In Clauson (1969), which applies glottochronology to the Altaic problem, discussion is unavoidable since 'I' is part of the glottochronological list. He seeks to argue away the threefold agreement among Old Turkish, Old Mongolian, and Manchu (a Tungusic language) as follows:

It is known (but has not been explained up to now) that there are phonetic resemblances between personal pronouns in languages which are completely unconnected with each other, for example, between English 'mine,' German *mein*, and the Turkish genitive *menin* (from *ben*) and Mongolian *minö* [sic!] (from *bi*; and between Latin *tu* and Mongolian *ci* (< *ti*). The phonetic resemblances between Turkish, Mongolian, and Tungus-Manchu in regard to these items cannot therefore be recognized as probative.

This kind of reasoning, which is very common, is to deny the significance of a resemblance because it is found somewhere else. In a similar manner Truman Michelson argued against Edward Sapir with regard to first-person *n* and second-person *m* in Algic because the same pattern occurs in so many other native American languages. It would be just as logical to deny the significance of the resemblance of English 'mine' to German *mein* because it also occurs in Mongolian. One must examine the full distribution of such forms. As soon as one gets to Sino-Tibetan or Nilo-Saharan, these forms—and many others characterizing Eurasiatic—are no longer found.

Furthermore, by using the nominative case for the glottochronological list, Clauson fails to consider the significance of the agreement
in the alternation *bi/min-*, which, as we have seen, occurs in Mongolian, Tungusic, and Chuvash. Since Chuvash is not included in
the comparison, the threefold agreement in this alternation does not
appear.

And what of the second-person pronouns? They are not discussed at all by Clauson. He unaccountably does not italicize as
resemblances Old Turkish *sen* and Manchu *si* (whose genitive *sinu*
does not figure at all because Clauson uses only the nominative).
In addition Old Mongolian *tere* 'this' and Manchu *tere* 'this' are
italicized as agreements, but passed over in silence.

In general, Doerfer fails to discuss grammatical resemblances,
but in his *Mongolo-Tungusica* (1985: 2), he says the following about
the first-person singular pronoun: "Indeed, even such an apparently
clear comparison as Mongolian *bi* with Tungus *bi* is not convincing on closer examination since the Mongolian form (on account of
the plural *bi-da*, cf. *e-de* 'these,' *te-de* 'those') goes back to *bï*. A
typical case of a sound symbolic (*Elementarverwandschaft*) surface
resemblance, but without the possibility of a connection by sound
correspondence."

What Doerfer is saying is that Mongolian *i*, with which *ï* had
earlier merged and therefore has two sources in a system of back-
front vowel harmony, must derive from a high *back* vowel, not a high
front vowel, because of the vowel of the second syllable *-da*, which
has a back vowel.

To begin with, deviations of this sort in languages with vowel
harmony are commonplace. For Finno-Ugric, Gyula Décsy (1969:
33) noted that after 80 years of research "we often cannot decide
among *a, o, u* (velar vowels) and *ä, e, i* (palatal vowels) in reconstruction" because of the numerous deviations, a situation reflected
in Redéi's (1988) standard Uralic comparative dictionary, in which
there is even a special symbol (*з*) for reconstructions in which the
issue of original front versus back harmony cannot be resolved.

Within Turkic itself Räsänen (1949: 57) notes that especially in
regard to Chuvash "one can conclude that a back vowel corresponds
to a front vowel in the rest of Turkic, and vice versa." To balk at
a comparison of Tungus *bi* with Mongolian *bi* (< *bï*) is therefore

absurdly pedantic, especially since they participate in the parallel alternation with *min-* found in Chuvash and Tungusic, a fact discretely omitted by Doerfer. To crown it all, Doerfer himself, in his description of Crimean Turkish (1972: 279), tells us about "frequent deviations in palatal harmony"!

What is more, Doerfer fails to point out that Mongolian *bida* is a first-person inclusive plural form. Now it is a worldwide typological fact that where there is a first-person inclusive/exclusive distinction in the plural, the exclusive, where analyzable, is usually the plural of the first-person singular, as it is in Mongolian where there is a perfect parallelism between the first-person exclusive plural and the second-person plural: *bi* : *ba* = *či* (< **ti*) : *ta*.

On the other hand, the first-person inclusive, if analyzable, is frequently a combination of first person plus second person, as in Tok Pisin *yu-mi*. Hence *bi-da* is very likely a compound of *bi* 'I' and *ta* 'you (plural).' In compounds vowel harmony need not apply anyway.

A parallel situaton exists in Tungusic, in which most languages have a first-person plural inclusive/exclusive distinction where the exclusive plural is based on the singular form with a vowel change (e.g. Evenki *bi* : *bu* = *si* : *su*). The first-person inclusive plural is here even more obviously a compound of first- and second-person forms (e.g. Evenki *mi-ti*, *mi-t*). This analysis of the Tungusic first-person inclusive is already found in Müller, and is endorsed by Menges (1952: 113).

Another one of the very few grammatical etymologies in Doerfer (1985: 27) is his No. 66, the interrogative stem *ya-* that is found in Mongolian and Tungusic. He admits that it "behaves like a genetically related word." Once more he resorts to "sound symbolism" as an explanation, and once again his only support is Indo-European, namely, **yo-*. But this is the widespread Eurasiatic interrogative **ya* (see No. 61 in Chapter 3). Once again we find an ad hoc resort to a sound symbolic explanation without any serious documentation.

Doerfer passes over the second-person pronouns in silence. Like Clauson, he believes that Mongolian borrowed massively from Turkic and Tungusic from Mongolian. Still he is clearly disturbed by the existence of certain etymologies common to Turkic and Tungusic, but not found in Mongolian (Doerfer 1985: 238–41), but he fails to mention the most glaring instance of all, the agreement of Turkic and Tungusic in a second-person stem in *s-*, as against Mongolian *t-*. Of course, if I am right in my analysis of the Mongolian and Tungusic first-person inclusive, *t* would also occur in Tungusic **mi-ti*, but in a different context.

Both *t* and *s* are widespread second-person markers in Eurasiatic (see Nos. 4 and 5 in Chapter 3). In general, there are a considerable number of other grammatical markers common to two or three Altaic branches. The number of these—as well as the lexical evidence—is sufficient to establish the validity of the Altaic family. In Chapter 3, Nos. 69–72 are devoted to grammatical items common to two or three branches of Altaic, but not found elsewhere in Eurasiatic. Of these, No. 70, reflexive *m* ~ *b* is admitted by Doerfer.

The distinctiveness of conventional Altaic as a separate node in Eurasiatic is supported most strongly by the *bi* ~ *min* alternation in the first-person singular pronoun, and by a few lexical items. That there have been a large number of lexical borrowings between various branches of Altaic is clearly true. The question of the separate genetic status of Altaic within Eurasiatic is not completely settled, though I am inclined to consider it valid. It is, of course, well known that outstanding subgrouping problems still exist in well studied and universally accepted families, for example, the validity of Balto-Slavic and the position of Anatolian in Indo-European, or that of Saami (=Lapp) in Uralic.

The Position of Japanese, Korean, and Ainu

As noted in the introduction to this chapter, the subclassification of Eurasiatic differs here from previous views in not placing Korean, Japanese, or Ainu within Altaic. I believe the distribution of grammatical elements, as well as vocabulary, within Eurasiatic shows no special affiliation of these languages to Altaic, as against, say, Indo-European, Uralic, or Eskimo-Aleut. Moreover, for reasons to be discussed below, I consider, though somewhat tentatively, that they form a distinct subgroup, although quite distantly related to one another, within Eurasiatic.

A rival hypothesis, or rather a somewhat differing set of similar hypotheses by various linguists, would connect one or more of these languages with languages of southeastern Asia and/or the Pacific. Of the three languages—Korean, Japanese, and Ainu—there is perhaps least dispute about Korean. Early on Ramstedt, in a whole series of studies, sought to demonstrate that Korean was Altaic and later Poppe, in his comparative grammar of Altaic, included Korean, though as a first branching from Proto-Altaic, thus assigning it a more distant position genetically (Poppe 1960). Following him, a number of Korean etymologies are to be found in the comparative Nostratic dictionary of Illich-Svitych under Altaic.

The position of Japanese is, however, more controversial. Ramstedt (1924b) initially adopted a fairly negative attitude towards the relationship of Japanese to Korean, and its consequent affiliation with Altaic, but later shifted to a positive opinion (see Lewin 1976: 392). In a series of studies, Miller (1967, 1971) argued for the affiliation of Japanese to Altaic, which for him did not exclude its relation to Korean. Samuel Martin (1966), in particular, presented a considerable body of Japanese-Korean etymologies and subsequently (Martin 1991) some grammatical evidence. Martin also considers both Japanese and Korean to be Altaic. More recently, Starostin (1991) published an extensive work which for all practical purposes demonstrates the Altaic affiliation of Japanese.

However, Evgenii Polivanov (1968) pointed to a number of resemblances between Japanese and the Austronesian languages. Polivanov's ideas influenced a number of Japanese linguists, most prominently Shichirō Murayama (1966, 1976), who had earlier been a strong adherent of the Altaic affiliation of Japanese. However, it is important to note that Murayama does not deny the existence of significant resemblances between Japanese and the Altaic languages. Rather he considers Japanese to be a mixed language, containing both Austronesian and Altaic components, while admitting the dubious nature of the whole notion of mixed languages. Miller (1974), in a review article concerning Murayama and Ōbayashi, expressed his belief that the Altaic and Austronesian theories can be reconciled by positing an Austronesian substratum. This would presumably make the assumption that people whose original language was Austronesian became speakers of an Altaic language, while maintaining some features of their earlier language. But he then notes (1974: 99) that the evidence for Austronesian influence was "still not impressive even after a careful reading of Murayama's new book."

One Japanese linguist, Nobuhiro Matsumoto (1928), has adopted a modernized version of Schmidt's Austric hypothesis. This would unite the Austroasiatic family of southeast Asia (known as Mon-Khmer in the earlier literature) with Austronesian in a single unit, Austric. Matsumoto then connects Austric with Japanese. Somewhat similar is the hypothesis of Paul Benedict (1990). In his view Japanese-Ryukyuan is most closely related to Austronesian and then, at successively deeper levels, to Kadai (a group containing Thai) and Miao-Yao, a group that some others have assigned to Sino-Tibetan. However, Austroasiatic is not included, so Schmidt's Austric is not involved.

In my view the best way to confront this problem is to compare Japanese simultaneously with both groups. I made such a comparison about 1990 on the basis of my own notebooks. More recently Alexander Vovin (1994), using the glottochronological 100 word list, compared Proto-Japanese with Proto-Altaic on the one hand (his Altaic consists of Turkic, Mongolian, Tungusic, and Korean), and with Austronesian on the other. In both cases the results are decisive, with a vastly greater resemblance of Japanese to Eurasiatic (or Altaic) than to Austronesian. In Vovin's list of 100 words no resemblant forms for the Proto-Japanese terms can be found for Proto-Altaic in 13 instances, but with Proto-Austronesian resemblant forms are lacking in 53 instances. A similar preponderance of Altaic (Eurasiatic) is found in grammatical markers. The greater resemblance of Japanese to Altaic pronouns is particularly striking: Japanese *ban 'I,' Proto-Altaic *bän 'I,' Japanese *si/sö 'you (singular),' Proto-Altaic *si 'you (singular),' and Japanese na 'you,' Korean ne 'you.'

There remains the question of Ainu. In general the Nostraticists have omitted Ainu in their comparisons and have considered its origins a mystery. The absence in Ainu of first-person m and second-person t and s, which are found everywhere else in Eurasiatic, has certainly contributed to this attitude. However, there is much else in both lexicon and grammar that indicates that the Ainu language belongs with Japanese and Korean. The view closest to that expressed here is that of James Patrie (1982), who has assembled a body of evidence—mainly lexical—to show that Ainu, Japanese, and Korean form a genetic group of fairly distantly related languages and that this family is in turn related to "conventional" Altaic (Turkic, Mongolian, and Tungusic). This general view is shared by Martin, while Miller (1983) states in a book note in *Language* that many of these etymologies are "solid and irrefutable" and that Patrie's monograph "is certain to become the point of departure for a new generation of significant work." Kirsten Refsing (1986: 57) is also generally positive, noting that Patrie has gone a long way in convincing us that Ainu is an Altaic language. In my view there are a number of unconvincing etymologies in Patrie (1982), but also a considerable number of highly probable ones. As discussed below, the broader Eurasiatic context supports a view similar to that of Patrie.

However, as is the case with Japanese, there are rival Southeast Asian or Pacific theories. John Bengtson has presented evidence for an Austronesian affiliation. In a reconstruction of Proto-Ainu, Vovin (1993) rejects any north Asiatic relationship of Ainu, severely criticizing Patrie, but unlike Bengtson he rejects an Austronesian connection and considers a tie with Austroasiatic promising, but far from conclusive.

Vovin considers that John Street's (1982) review of Patrie is so destructive of Patrie's book that his thesis can be forthwith rejected. A reasonably careful reading of Street's review shows, however, that this is far from the case. Although many of Patrie's etymologies are certainly to be rejected (I agree with Street in this regard), he finds (1982: 195) that of the Ainu-Altaic comparisons in Patrie's book, "thirty seven or so show such marked formal and semantic similarity between Ainu and Altaic as to require explanation." Regarding the other group of etymologies in Patrie's book, namely those connecting Ainu with Japanese and Korean, Street notes that these are far more numerous (226 as against 140 with Altaic) and that only one third is shared with Altaic. According to Street then, "it does seem clear that Ainu shares a considerable amount of vocabulary—not demonstrably Altaic in origin—with Korean, or Japanese, or both. Thus Street's review, while it does not accept Patrie's book as proof of his thesis, is far indeed from rejecting it out of hand. He notes further that the Ainu-Japanese-Korean etymologies are more persuasive than the Altaic-Ainu ones. All this of course is in general agreement with the present classification of Ainu-Japanese-Korean as a separate grouping, and its non-membership in Altaic in the narrow sense.

I believe the grammatical evidence presented here is in itself sufficient to show that Ainu is a member of Eurasiatic. Among the grammatical items discussed in Chapter 3, the following are particularly significant. The two most common interrogatives in Eurasiatic are *k* and *y* (Nos. 60 and 61). From the exposition in these sections it can not only be seen that both are well attested in Ainu, but that a usage shared only with Korean and Japanese occurs, namely, as sentence interrogatives in final position involving identical forms *ka* and *ya*. Furthermore, both occur as coordinators in all three languages (cf. Indo-European *-que*) and as indefinitizers (cf. Latin *quandocumque* 'whenever'). Ainu also has an interrogative *n* (No. 64), as in *ne-p* 'what?' and *ne-n* 'who?,' that occurs not only in Korean and Japanese, but in Turkic and Eskimo as well.

Another important item is the Ainu causative *-ke* ~ *-ki* (No. 51 in Chapter 3), which is derived by Ainu specialists from *ki* 'to make, to do' and which shows an exact parallel to Mongolian *ki* 'to make, to do' and the verbal derivational suffixes *-ke* ~ *-ki* in that language. As in Mongolian, *-ki* is used with onomatopoeic reduplicated forms. Ainu also has a locative *-ta* (No. 32 in Chapter 3). The existence in Ainu of reflexes of Eurasiatic dual **ki(n)* and plural **t(i)* (Nos. 14 and 15 in Chapter 3) is truly decisive since these items are, to my knowledge, found nowhere except in Eurasiatic.

A final cogent item is the third-person object *i-* ~ *e-* that is prefixed to verbs to indicate a third-person indefinite verb object (No. 8 in Chapter 3). Vovin notes the same element in Gilyak, with the same vowel variation, but in fact it is found, with the same vowel variation, in Indo-European, Uralic, Mongolian, and Tungusic. As described in detail in the Appendix, this is part of the Ainu system of vowel alternations that goes back to an old vowel harmony system whose Eurasiatic distribution is described in Chapter 3. In Ainu, where it has not previously been studied systematically, it is part of a system of alternations *i* ~ *e*, *u* ~ *o*, *e* ~ *a* that is virtually identical with the Gilyak, Chukotian, and other Eurasiatic vowel harmony systems, of which it is a relic. These are simply the most significant grammatical resemblances with other Eurasiatic languages and which hardly find a parallel in either Austronesian or Austroasiatic.

The Question of Kartvelian

Of the three groups—Afro-Asiatic, Dravidian, and Kartvelian—the last appears to be closest to Eurasiatic. However, I consider it not to be a member of Eurasiatic proper, in which I am in agreement with Bomhard and Kerns (1994). The most striking features of Kartvelian that agree with Eurasiatic are the first- and second-person pronouns, as seen in Georgian *men* 'I,' *šen* 'you (singular).' In other respects, however, such as lexicon, it seems closer to Afro-Asiatic. Illich-Svitych's comparative Nostratic dictionary shows a relatively small number of striking etymological agreements that are exclusively shared by Kartvelian and Afro-Asiatic. Etymologies that are restricted to just two of the six branches of Nostratic are quite infrequent, and therefore significant. A recent study by Václav Blažek (1992) on new Kartvelian etymologies in Nostratic strengthens this conclusion and, in fact, Blažek himself remarks that the priority of Afro-Asiatic cognates is evident. The position of Kartvelian remains an important problem for further research.

The Question of Etruscan

I had originally excluded Etruscan from this study as too little known. However, Bomhard, after reading the penultimate version of Chapter 3, suggested its inclusion. The evidence has, in my view, accumulated to the point where its inclusion in Eurasiatic, if not in Indo-European, seems highly probable. In particular, the first-person pronoun *mi*, and its objective form *mini*, are strongly diagnostic of Eurasiatic. However, as pointed out in Chapter 3, these forms point as much to other branches of Eurasiatic as to Indo-European. Similarly, Etruscan *tul* 'stone' is very similar to Korean *tol* 'stone' and has cognates in Turkic. Etruscan *tur-* 'to give' immediately suggests Greek *dōr(-on)* 'gift.' The Indo-European root is, of course, *dō-* ~ *də-*, with various extensions (e.g. *-n* in Latin *dōn-um* 'gift,' Sanskrit *dān-am* 'gift.' Once again Korean *tuli(-ta)* 'to give' offers the closest match with Etruscan. It is often the case that a poorly attested language can be assigned to a large group, even though its more precise genetic positon remains uncertain (e.g. Venetic in Indo-European). Vladimir Georgiev (1964), Francisco Adrados (1989), and Fred Woodhuizen (1991) have all suggested, with different variations, that Etruscan is an Anatolian language. In a broader framework, I find little to suggest Anatolian specifically. I hesitate between two solutions: (1) Etruscan as a separate branch of Eurasiatic, (2) Etruscan as a third branch of Indo-European, alongside of Anatolian and Indo-European proper. In the meantime I have cited Etruscan grammatical elements in Chapter 3, without committing myself to either of these theories, with the expectation that further study and new evidence will ultimately resolve the question.

Chapter 2

Some Aspects of the Comparative Phonology of Eurasiatic

In the present chapter I will discuss certain phonological phenomena whose import is broader than any single branch of Eurasiatic. I will be principally concerned with those phonological phenomena that have a bearing on—and will help justify—some of the interpretations of the Eurasiatic grammatical markers that are discussed in Chapter 3.

I will consider here four topics. The first of these is the existence, hitherto unnoticed, of an alternation (chiefly in word-final position) between stops and their corresponding nasals. This alternation is particularly conspicuous in Eskimo and it is possible, on the basis of the Eskimo data, to suggest a probable theory of the original phonetic conditions for this alternation. The identity of the basic alternant has, of course, a bearing on interfamily linguistic comparison. Finally, some sociolinguistic factors regarding men's and women's speech will help to explain the course of development within Eskimo.

The second topic to be discussed is the vowel system of Eurasiatic languages, especially a vowel harmony system that is probably reflected most clearly in Tungus, particularly Even (Lamut). This system involves the feature of normal versus retracted tongue root.

A preliminary discussion of this topic appeared in Greenberg (1990). As an integral part of this section on vowel harmony, a peculiarity in the distribution of the velar (k) and uvular series (q) in relation to adjacent vowels, is also discussed.

This Proto-Eurasiatic system is in one important respect similar, in another different, from the vowel harmonic systems found in Africa in the Niger-Kordofanian and Nilo-Saharan families. In both instances the vowels are divided into two series and a particular word contains vowels belonging to one series or the other. In both areas the differences between a particular pair of vowels—one in one harmonic series, the other in the other—tend to become simply matters of vowel height. However, in Eurasiatic the original contrast is between neutral and retracted tongue root, whereas in Africa it is between neutral and advanced tongue root ($\pm$ ATR). There are thus three positions of the tongue root: normal, retracted, and advanced. Ladefoged and Maddieson (1996; see also Lindau 1975), working in a binary feature framework, call the contrast between retracted and normal tongue root position $\pm$ pharyngeal, and that between advanced tongue root and normal position $\pm$ ATR. Since they provide no abbreviated symbolization for pharyngealized versus non-pharyngealized, I will symbolize this distinction as $\pm$ PH in what follows.

The third subject will be a phonetic phenomenon that is apparently confined to certain eastern subgroups of Eurasiatic. This is the existence of two r and two l phonemes, which have hitherto been studied exclusively in Altaic, with extensions to Japanese and Korean, especially in the work of Miller (1971). It will be shown here that, at least with regard to r_1 and r_2, the Chukotian family also preserves this distinction, or at least shows the phonetically expected reflexes of r_2. The final topic to be considered is the proposal to treat Indo-European post-vocalic word-final H, which appears there only as vowel length, as a reflex of a former velar or uvular stop, at least in this position.

Homorganic Stop/Nasal Alternations

In a number of branches of Eurasiatic there is alternation between a stop (usually final) and a homorganic nasal. Whether this alternation goes back to Proto-Eurasiatic—and whether all, some, or none of these phenomena are historically connected—is not entirely clear. Eskimo is considered first because it is a conspicuous and widely found phenomenon in this family and has been generally noted by Eskimologists. Furthermore, only in Eskimo can we find a plausible theory regarding the phonetic conditions under which the alternation arose. This topic is of importance for comparative Eurasiatic because for a number of grammatical markers (e.g. second-person *t*, plural *t*, ablative *t*; Nos. 4, 15, 33 in Chapter 3) the question becomes whether, for Proto-Eskimo, we are to reconstruct *t*, in agreement with evidence from other branches of Eurasiatic, or the nasal *n*, as has been done by some Eskimologists.

Except for a few nouns that have zero in the absolutive singular, all Eskimo "full words" have inflectional suffixes that end in a vowel or a single consonant. For the final consonants there is widespread variation between forms with a final stop or a homorganic nasal. For example, whereas in West Greenlandic the singular relative case of the noun ends in -*p*, in Kuskokwim (an Alaskan Yupik dialect) it ends in -*m*. In general, non-nasal forms are found in the east and nasal forms in the west. However, the distribution of nasal and non-nasals does not coincide with the main dialect division within Eskimo between Yupik (southern Alaska and Siberia) and Inuit (northern Alaska, Canada, and Greenland). Alaskan and western Canadian Inuit generally have nasal forms just like Yupik. Furthermore, the geographical distribution of nasal vs. non-nasal forms differs for different grammatical morphemes. Thus the nominal singular relative case marker *p*- is restricted to the extreme east (Greenland and Labrador), whereas for second person *t* ∼ *n*, the non-nasal alternant is much more widespread. In the case of second-person *t* ∼ *n*, even the same morpheme does not have a uniform distribution in all the forms in which it occurs. For example, in Central Alaskan Yupik we find -*n* as the mark of the second-person singular in the verb and nominal possessives, but in the independent second-person pronoun, which surely has the same suffix, we find *əɬpət*. However, in the Inuit of the Seward Peninsula of northwestern Alaska we find *ivlin* (a metathesized form) 'thou,' as well as the second-person -*n* just cited, in other forms in the same dialect.

Among those who have reconstructed Proto-Eskimo there is also a variety of opinion. In general, for those who have worked in the western area the tendency is to reconstruct final nasals, but with inconsistencies and differences among different linguists. For example, in the second-person singular independent pronoun, Marsh and Swadesh (1951) reconstruct *iɬvin, whereas Fortescue et al. (1994), in their monumental volume on comparative Eskimo, reconstruct alternate forms, *əlpət ~ *əɬvət, for the same word. In general, the earlier surveys of comparative Eskimo (Thalbitzer 1904, Uhlenbeck 1907) regarded the non-nasal variant as the original form. Thus, Uhlenbeck (1907: 12) notes that "in all Eskimo dialects k is a sign of the dual and t (-it) of the plural, but because of the widespread nasalization we find ŋ and n alongside of them." Similarly, Thalbitzer (1911: 985) talks of "the older g from which ŋ developed."

I believe that the key to the problem is to be found in the more easterly dialects. Here there was once a productive word sandhi that in recent times usually survives in only a few fixed phrases. The alternation is described by Boas, in an editor's footnote to Thalbitzer (1911: 988), as occurring on Baffin Island, where he did fieldwork. Boas describes it as involving three alternations: r (i.e. ʁ) > N, k > ŋ, and t > n. (It is traditional in Eskimo studies to use r to indicate a voiced uvular fricative.) The non-nasal is replaced in word-final position by its corresponding nasal if the following word begins with a vowel. In other accounts of this same rule it is often said that this only occurs if there is no pause before the initial vowel of the following word. For eighteenth-century West Greenlandic, Egede (1760) states that final b (phonemic p) is changed to m if the next word begins with a vowel; k becomes ng in the same environment; and t becomes n. In several Greenlandic religious publications (anonymous), published by the Moravian Brethren (unitas fratrum) at Barby, as cited in the Mithridates of Adelung and Vater (III.3: 435), we find in the titles with a relative case the alternation b ~ m, here construed as a genitive. For example, Jesusib Kristusim anausirsivta . . . (1778) illustrates this rule. A century later Theodor Bourquin (1891: 7) states in his grammar of Labrador Eskimo that "at the end of words hard consonants are often replaced by their homorganic nasals when a word beginning in a vowel follows without pause. Thus Jesup attingani 'In Jesus name' is often replaced by Jesum *attingani.*" In more recent times this change is often said to take place only in a few fixed phrases. Rasmussen (1888: 6) writes, with regard to Greenlandic, that "the change was once more general, but only occurs now with any frequency in certain fixed expressions, e.g. *suun-uku* 'who are these?' for *suut uku.*" The rule also exists further west in the Hudson Bay area, as attested by Spalding (1960: 8), who notes that usually words ending in -*t* change to -*n*, and -*k* to -*ng*, especially when closely followed by words beginning with a vowel: *tiguligit* 'take them,' *tiguligin ai* 'take them, won't you?' Indeed, Fortescue, who reconstructs nasals in many instances in his comparative volume on Eskimo, states in his own grammar of West Greenlandic (1984: 11) that "enclitic sandhi changes final *t* to *n*, for example, *sun-uku* 'who are these?'"

In all of these citations one may note that the non-nasal form is taken as basic, being replaced by the corresponding nasal in word sandhi. The language is usually ambiguous with regard to a synchronic replacement rule or a historical change, but of course the latter will have the former as a consequence. The reasons for the priority of the non-nasal are obvious. In sentence final only the nonnasal variant occurs and is even maintained within the sentence if the following word is not closely connected so that there is a pause. There are additional reasons. Where the rule is, or was, operative in all four positions, *p, t, k* and *q*, for the uvular position there is no reason to reconstruct a homorganic nasal *ŋ*, which appears in Eskimo only under these conditions and which has never been reconstructed for Proto-Eskimo by any of the scholars who have worked on comparative Eskimo. Although *ŋ* is sometimes reconstructed in final position, and occasionally in medial position, even Swadesh, who tends to reconstruct nasals (perhaps because of his own fieldwork in Alaska), notes in his joint work with Marsh on Proto-Eskimo (1951: 212) that "no cognates with final -*ŋ* are found." Since the alternation rule in Northwest Greenlandic affects all four points of articulation, a unitary solution is preferable.

There is an important sociolinguistic factor that led to the triumph of final nasal forms, with scattered exceptions, in the western area of Eskimo. Already in the eighteenth century, Egede noted in his *Relationer fra Grønland,* 1721–1736, that "nasal consonants particularly occurred among women" (Bobé 1925: 385). A century later

Kleinschmidt, in his classic grammar of West Greenlandic (1851: 5), stated the rule in the following manner: "A stop becomes a nasal when the next word begins with a vowel without pause, but only customarily, particularly with women." This sex difference is also described by Boas in his introduction to the *Handbook of American Indian Languages* (1911: 79) as follows: "Thus we find among some Eskimo tribes the men pronounce terminal *p*, *t*, *k* and *q* distinctly, while the women always transform the sounds into *m*, *n*, *ñ* and *ṇ̃*." Also, in an editorial note in Thalbitzer's grammar of Greenlandic Eskimo, Boas remarked that "in 1884 the old men from the east coast of Cumberland Sound used throughout oral stops, while women and young men used nasalized consonants. It seems that the nasalization in this case is due to the extension of the characteristic pronunciation of women to the male sex" (Thalbitzer 1911: 985). Boas also published a description of the language of Cumberland Sound (northern Baffin Island) in which this phenomenon is described in detail (Boas 1894).

There are a few instances of cross-dialectal variations of nasal and non-nasals in intervocalic word-interior position, all involving *k* ∼ *ŋ*. One example is the verb 'to lick,' reconstructed by Fortescue et al. (1994) as **aluɣ-*, which appears in Yupik as *aluŋə-*. Sirenik, however, here agrees with Inuit, having *aləɣ-*. Another example is Proto-Eskimo **alikə-* 'be afraid of,' which is also *aliŋa-* in some Yupik dialects, e.g. Chaplino in Siberia (Emeljanova 1982: 117). Fortescue et al. also reconstruct **taku-* 'see or check on,' which would seem to be a doublet of their **taŋəR-* 'see.' Both of these roots are found in Inuit and Yupik, the former always with a non-nasal, the latter with a nasal. In other instances Eskimo has *-ŋ* where Aleut has *ɣ* (e.g. Proto-Eskimo **təŋə-* 'fly up' is probably cognate with Aleut *taɣa-* 'bird alights'). The most conspicuous example of word-internal nasal/non-nasal alternation within Eskimo is the first-person possessive suffix of singular nouns in the absolutive case, where **-ŋa* must go back to a non-nasal, as we see from the corresponding dual and plural possessives *-ɣuk* 'of us (two)' and *-ɣut* 'of us.'

This latter example suggests that this alternation is at least as old as Proto-Eskimo, as proposed by Swadesh (1952: 171). Furthermore, as the variation in the verb 'to fly' cited above suggests, the alternation must go back to Proto-Eskimo-Aleut. Regarding Aleut second-person -*n*, Uhlenbeck (1907: 64) noted that it "could derive from *t*, just as in the plural *n* derives from *t*, since we have to do with the widespread nasalization which plays an important role in Western Eskimo." An important piece of evidence of this alternation in Aleut itself occurs in the Bering dialect, where G. A. Menovshchikov (1968) reports *čaŋ* 'five,' *čaχ* 'hand.' Aleut generally acts like an extreme western Eskimo dialect in preferring nasal to non-nasal forms, as seen in the nominal plural -*n* corresponding to -*t* in both Inuit and Yupik, and -*an* (ablative) corresponding to Inuit -*at*.

If this phenomenon is indeed of Proto-Eurasiatic origin it may help to resolve a longstanding historical problem within Uralic, namely, the existence of two forms for the second-person singular pronoun, *t* and *n*. As Péter Hajdú (1992: 228) says, "for linguists the double form in the second person has long been inexplicable."

The basic facts are the following. Whereas in most Uralic languages the second-person pronoun is *t*, and is considered by all Uralicists to derive from Proto-Uralic, in the Ob-Ugric languages (Vogul and Ostyak) the general second-person markers have *n* rather than *t*, without there being other instances of a *t/n* correspondence between Ob-Ugric and other Uralic languages. Thus, in Vogul we have *naŋ* 'thou,' -*n* 'thy,' and -*n* 'thou' (subject of intransitive verbs). There are almost identical forms in Ostyak. However, in some Ostyak dialects, alongside of dominant *n*, we find *t* in the possessive and in the second person dual and plural of the verb. In Vogul, which has the general Uralic nominal plural -*t*, agreeing with Eskimo and other Eurasiatic languages (see No. 15 in Chapter 3), this *t* is replaced by -*n* word internally (e.g. *kol-ət* 'house,' *kol-an-um* 'my houses.' This alternation is highly reminiscent of Eskimo.

Second-person forms in -*n* in Uralic are not confined to Ugric languages. In the Permian branch of Finnic, Komi-Zyrian has -*n* in the present, past, future, and in the negative auxiliary verb (e.g. *muna-n* 'thou goest,' *e-n vai* 'don't bring!'). However, the independent second-person pronoun is *te* 'thou,' *ti* 'you,' and the suffixed possessives are -*əd* 'thy,' -*nəd* 'your.' In Udmurt *t* forms are dominant; only in the negative auxiliary verb do we find -*n*.

The other main branch of Uralic—Samoyed—also has occurrences of second-person *n* (see Joki 1971). As discussed in Chapter 3, No. 6, in Yurak (a North Samoyed language) -*n* is the second-person singular ending of the subjective conjugation (e.g. *manzara-n* 'thou workest'). A probably distinct and unrelated phenomenon is the existence of variation between nasal and non-nasal in final position in Selkup (Ostyak Samoyed), the only surviving South Samoyed language. Selkup has three dialects: northern (Tāz), central (Ket), and southern (Tym). Ket has the nasals *m*, *n*; Tym, the non-nasals *p*, *t*; and Tāz has free variation between the two, for which I can discover no phonetic conditions. The case is strongest for two Proto-Uralic variants, *t* and *n*, in the second-person singular. An explanation of the variation as inherited, and corresponding to the Eskimo-Aleut alternation, is plausible. However, there is no evidence for this alternation occurring under the same phonetic conditions, i.e. a basic stop, with a nasal alternant when the next word begins with a vowel.

There are a few other scattered traces of a similar alternation elsewhere in Eurasiatic. In Yukaghir there are two instances in the only two surviving dialects, Kolyma and Tundra. The first is the *-k*, or *-l'e-k/-l'e-ŋ*, of the focus construction for the subject of intransitive verbs (No. 23 in Chapter 3), which consists of the verb *l'e* 'to be' plus an old demonstrative (stage III article) *-k*. This ending takes the form *-l'e-k* in Kolyma, but *-l'e-ŋ* in Tundra. Yukaghir also has a genitive (or general nominal dependency) marker that takes two forms, *d* and *n*. It is difficult to deduce a rule regarding this alternation; if anything, it reverses the rule with which we are familiar in Eskimo in that we usually find *d* before a vowel and *n* before a consonant (see No. 25 in Chapter 3).

In the Turkish of the Orkhon inscriptions, the earliest record on non-Chuvash Turkic that we possess, we find several instances of alternate forms with *-y* and *-ŋ* in word final postion, e.g. *süŋükün* ~ *süŋüküy* 'thy bones'; *bardiŋ* ~ *bardiy* 'thou didst go' (Tekin 1968: 7).

Finally, alternations of this sort occur in Chukotian. In Chukchi, with similar forms in the closely related Koryak group, we find *meŋin* 'who?' in the absolutive case, but *mik-* in the other cases. In the second-person singular pronoun *yət*, the oblique cases have, with a vowel always following, such forms as *yənək* 'in thee.' Here the phonetic conditions are similar to those in Eskimo. In Kamchadal, the western dialect has a nominal plural *-ʔn*, but *-t* or *-d* is found in the other dialects reported by Radliński and reappears even in some subdialects of the western dialect (for details, see No. 15 in Chapter 3). Another instance of sporadic alternation is that of Chukchi *-lyən*, which is a common suffix for the singular absolutive case and corresponds to Koryak *-lŋən*.

As should be clear from the preceding exposition, one can be reasonably certain that a nasal/non-nasal alternation occurred in Proto-Eskimo-Aleut under specifiable phonetic and sociolinguistic conditions. However, whether this alternation goes back as far as Proto-Eurasiatic is unclear. The most promising instances outside Eskimo-Aleut are the Uralic second-person pronominal form, a traditional crux in Uralic linguistics, and the alternation between word-final *-t* and word-interior *-n-* before vowels in Chukotian.

Vowel Harmony in Eurasiatic

I will begin with a discussion of the Proto-Indo-European system of vowel alternation, where I will be chiefly concerned with qualitative ablaut (Greenberg 1990). Although this system is well known to all Indo-Europeanists, and indeed to many comparativists who are not Indo-Europeanists, it will be convenient for purposes of discussion to set forth the essentials of the system, which are shown in Table 1.

Table 1. Proto-Indo-European Vowel Alternations

e-grade	o-grade	zero grade
e	o	zero
ey	oy	i ~ y
ew	ow	u ~ w
er	or	r̥ ~ r
el	ol	l̥ ~ l
en	on	n̥ ~ n
em	om	m̥ ~ m

Long vowels and long diphthongs are posited which parallel those in Table 1. For example, corresponding to *e, o,* zero we have *ē, ō, ə.* The vowel *ə* ("schwa") is represented by *i* in Indo-Iranian and by *a* elsewhere. The other series are long diphthongs, e.g. *ēy, ōy, ī,* and correspondingly with the other diphthongs. A great many long vowels are now attributed to sequences of short vowels followed by one or more of the laryngeals, the most common theory being that there were three of them, H_1, H_2, and H_3.

As we can see in Table 1, *i and *u are functionally in a totally different class from *e and *o. They are not true vowels since they occur only as the zero grade of diphthongs and belong with the sonants r, l, n, and m. Thus, we have $i : y$, $u : w$ just as $r̥ : r$, $n̥ : n$.

The relation between ey and oy, on the one hand, and $i \sim y$, on the other (with the variants depending on syllabic structure), is called quantitative Ablaut, as against $e : o$, $ey : oy$, etc., which is called qualitative Ablaut. Quantitative Ablaut is fairly well correlated with the position of the Proto-Indo-European accent and zero grade presumably arose from full vowels in non-accented position. I consider this to be more recent than qualitative Ablaut since its conditions can be reasonably stated within Indo-European and, furthermore, these conditions are phonetically plausible, namely, reduction or loss in unaccented position.

It should be noted that *a does not figure in Table 1. The peculiar typological position of what is conventionally reconstructed as Proto-Indo-European *a has long attracted attention. What is remarkable, considered in the context of directly attested vowel systems, is its basic lack of function within the Ablaut system and its low frequency, which becomes even more striking if we exclude those instances that can be accounted for in laryngeal theory as the modification of a full vowel adjacent to the laryngeal H_2. All this adds up to a marginal position for a vowel that on typological grounds would be expected to be highly frequent and to play an important functional role in the vowel system.

Let us begin with the first point, namely, the traditional treatment of i and u as sonants completely parallel to $r̥$, $l̥$, $n̥$, and $m̥$. Given this doctrine, it is no more conceivable that there should be an alternation between i and e, or between u and o, than between $r̥$ and e, or $n̥$ and o.

This is clearly stated in what is, to my knowledge, the first book-length discussion of the Proto-Indo-European vowel system as it developed in the work of Brugmann and others who worked on Proto-Indo-European comparative phonology in the 1870's and

1880's. The work in question is a monograph by Heinrich Hübsch-mann. In it he states unequivocally that "*i* and *u* are only conso-nants and cannot occur in any Ablaut series except with *y* and *w*. They can never be lost. Whenever they appear in any series as a vowel they have arisen by a secondary process" (Hübschmann 1885: 193–94).

The reason for this last statement was that, in fact, Hübschmann was aware of a fair number of instances in which *i* alternated with *e* and, less frequently, *u* with *o*, particularly in Greek, Slavic, and Baltic, but also in Indic and Latin. These include either instances in which one language had *e* and another *i* (and, correspondingly, *o* and *u*), or as interdialectal variants within a single language, or as doublets in the same dialect or language, sometimes with secondary semantic differentiation. Examples include Old Church Slavic *izŭ* < *jĭzŭ* < *ĭzŭ* 'out of,' Greek *eks* 'out of,' Latin *eks* 'out of'; Greek *núks* 'night,' Latin *noks* 'night'; within Greek, Attic *hestiá* 'hearth' corresponds to *histiá* in other dialects; and, within Slavic, Old Church Slavic shows a doublet, *večerŭ* 'evening' and *vĭčera* 'yes-terday' (cf. Russian *véčer* 'evening,' *včerá* 'yesterday').

There have been many statements of puzzlement regarding the *i* ~ *e* and *u* ~ *o* alternations, which are of course in contradiction with the basic assumption that *i* and *u* are merely sonants and not part of the basic Proto-Indo-European vowel system. Concerning the Greek forms in *i* and *u*, where *e* and *o* would be expected, Her-mann Güntert (1916: 28–29) says that "these words have always been a true dilemma (*eine wahre Crux*) for scientific linguistic in-vestigation." Paul Kretschmer (1891: 378) also noted, with regard to Greek, that we "find traces of unaccented vowels whose nature up to now has been completely puzzling (*rätselhaft*)." In the sec-ond edition of his *Grundriss* (1897, I: 119), Brugmann states, again with regard to Greek, that "in many forms *i* appears where we would expect *e* without it yet having been possible to explain *i* in a satisfac-tory way." In his standard comparative grammar of Greek, Eduart Schwyzer (1939, I: 135) not only admits the existence of *i* ~ *e* and *u* ~ *o* alternations in Greek, but also notes that these often corre-spond to the same alternations in Slavic. There have been various internally inconsistent or basically ad hoc attempts in etymological dictionaries of Classical Greek to explain away these inconvenient facts.

In regard to Slavic, Leskien, in the 1909 edition of his Old Church Slavic grammar, calls ǐ an Ablaut grade of e (p. 9) and gives a series of examples, whereas in the 1910 edition of the handbook (p. 17) the alternation between ŭ and o is noted but called unclear. In his comparative grammar of Lithuanian, Alfred Senn (1966: 78) states that "one of the commonest deviations (*Entgleisungen*) in Ablaut series I is the introduction of an -i-grade without the help of a liquid or nasal."

With regard to Indo-European *eĝhs* 'out of,' mentioned above, in which Greek and Latin e correspond to Slavic and Baltic i, Pokorny (1959, I: 28) refers to the Slavic and Baltic forms as having a "difficult *i*" (*mit schwierigem i*). Referring to the internal Slavic dialect variation in the numeral 'four,' *četyre* and *čǐtyre*, Meillet (1934: 48) declares that "it would be imprudent to affirm anything on this subject."

In Indo-Iranian there are instances of i alternating with a, which derives from *e and corresponds to i in other branches of Indo-European, e.g. Sanskrit *śiras* 'head' and Greek *keras* 'horn' (Pokorny 1959: 574–75), but Avestan *sarah-* (a < *e) agreeing with Greek. Note also Gamkrelidze and Ivanov (1984: 259), where the variant forms *śakvan* (< *śekvan) and *śikvan* 'intelligent' are cited as containing an "*i* of uncertain origin." Another Sanskrit example is *sama* 'same' and *sima* 'each.' Again, within Indo-Iranian, Avestan -*čina*, which forms indefinite generalizing pronouns, is cognate with Sanskrit *čana* (< *čena), which has similar functions.

However, in the more recent period, beginning, it would seem, with Kuryłowicz (1956), we find a number of well-known Indo-Europeanists who recognize an autonomous i and u apart from the zero grades of *ey* and *ew*. Such views are expressed in Szemerényi (1996), Gamkrelidze and Ivanov (1984), and Mayrhofer (1987). Szemerényi (1996: 136) points out that starting with the observation that i and u often represent the zero grade of *ey* and *ew*, the assumption is made that i and u always have this origin. This, of course, by no means follows. Moreover, as Szemerényi, Schmitt-Brandt (1973), and others have pointed out, many examples of *ey* involve an earlier independent i in which e has been introduced analogically, and the same would follow for u in relation to *ew*.

If, indeed, there were independent *i* and *u* phonemes in Proto-Indo-European, one would expect them to be reasonably frequent on typological grounds (especially *i*) and perhaps to participate in the system of qualitative alternation so that the apophonic alternation of *e* and *o* would have been, to begin with, but one set within a larger system, but one which had already in Proto-Indo-European times spread analogically at the expense of the others and had been partially grammaticized (e.g. present stem *e* versus perfect stem *o*), while the others only survived in a marginal and sporadic way. It is quite clear that this alternation would include *e* ∼ *i* and *o* ∼ *u*, of which we have already encountered examples that have proved puzzling to Indo-Europeanists. Before the period initiated by Kuryłowicz regarding the independent status of *i* and *u*, these alternations were treated in two ways. On the one hand, they were either ignored or explained away by ad hoc explanations in individual languages. Beginning, however, with Güntert (1916) some Indo-Europeanists posited an alternation between *i* and *e*, as well as *u* and *o*, considering such instances of *i* and *u* as reduced forms of *e* and *o*, respectively, in unaccented positions. They therefore assumed an additional reduced grade between full grade and zero. In Güntert's terminology these reduced members of the vowel series were called *schwa secundum,* distinct from the generally accepted schwa (*pace* Burrow 1979) that was the zero grade of the long vowels (Indo-Iranian *i*, but *a* elsewhere) and which was then called *schwa primum.* Thus the reduced grade of **er* was *ʋr*, whereas zero grade was *r̩*. The most prominent adherent of the theory of *schwa secundum* was Hermann Hirt, the leading Indo-Europeanist of his day, but many other Indo-Europeanists, including Antoine Meillet, assumed some form of reduced grade. The theory of *schwa secundum* is now generally abandoned, but the facts regarding the *e* ∼ *i* and *u* ∼ *o* alternations surely remain and should not be swept under the rug for the sake of assuming as simple a system of Proto-Indo-European vocalism as possible.

Finally, one may ask what evidence there is that in the alternation *i* ∼ *e* and *u* ∼ *o* are reduced vowels. First, it should be noted that, as Philip Baldi (1983: 16) states, "we are uncertain about the original position of the accent in many forms." There are clear instances, however, in which *i* is certain to have been accented. Therefore the most probable conclusion is that original *i* and *e* were simply indifferent to the Indo-European accent. Another possibility considered below is that in some instances *i* and *u* became zero when unaccented.

Among the instances in which accented *i* seems certain is the interrogative stem *$k^w i$- 'who?,' which alternates with *$k^w e$-. Another example is the first-person present of the verb *es 'to be,' which in West Slavic exhibits the reflexes of *is-mi. If the Indo-European accent is certain in any category, it is in the present active singular of -mi verbs. The view presented here is that there are not only independent phonemes *i* and *u*, but that they alternated with *e* and *o*, respectively. This view has now been fully accepted by a number of Indo-Europeanists (Mel'nichuk 1979, Palmaitis 1981, Speirs 1984). Regarding the *i* ~ *e* alternation, Speirs (1984: 39) notes that "it embraces many forms whose vocalism has consistently defied explanation in traditional theory." The *i* ~ *e* alternation is, of course, much more frequent than *u* ~ *o* on general typological grounds because it involves vowels that are, across languages, almost always statistically more common.

It follows from what was said above that some reconstructed *e* roots in Indo-European must go back to an *e* ~ *i* alternation rather than *e* ~ *o*. Certain of these can be identified and they tend not only to alternate with *i*, but to have few or even no forms with *o*. One of them is the root *es 'to be.' We noted above that the West Slavic form for the first-person singular reflects *is-mi. From the same root we find, in Old Church Slavic, istŭ 'true' and istina 'truth.' There is also the Greek second-person singular imperative ís-thi.

Outside Indo-European, Korean it- is a late development of isi- 'to be, exist, remain' (Ramstedt 1939: 71). In Kamchadal, a language which forms a genetic group distinct from the rest of Chukotian, there is an auxiliary verb is 'to be' (Bogoras 1922: 767–68), which, in the vowel height harmony system of the language, has the alternant form es. In Ainu, at least in the Hokkaido dialect reported in Batchelor (1905), there is a verb isu 'to be' (only found in Batchelor) and a negative existential isam 'there is not' (attested in other sources as well), which may contain the general Eurasiatic negative m (see No. 57 in Chapter 3).

Once we admit that the basic alternants of the stem are is, es and *s*, the problem of the Indo-European *s* aorist can receive a reasonably satisfactory and consistent solution. The formation of a past tense by suffixing a verb 'to be' is, of course, well known. In Latin the perfect indicative active second-person singular and plural suffixes, *-is-tī* and *-is-tis*, are generally admitted to contain the aorist *s* and to derive from *is*, which is also found in the perfect infinitive *dīx-isse*, the pluperfect *dīxeram* (in which *-er* derives from **is* by well-known rules of phonetic change), and the pluperfect subjunctive *dīx-issem*. However, they must, by current doctrine, be separated from forms of the verb 'to be,' *esse* 'to be,' *eram* 'I was,' *essem* 'I had been,' which go back to **es*. The Greek *ewéid-e(s)a* 'I knew,' traditionally a pluperfect, was already seen by Brugmann to be an *-es* aorist. The Sanskrit *-is* aorist cannot have its *i* from schwa because this would correspond to a elsewhere, which, as we have seen, it does not.

Another Eurasiatic root containing the *e ~ i* alternation is the Proto-Indo-European verb usually reconstructed as **deik-* 'to show, point out.' The basic meaning appears to have been 'index finger' and Latin *digitus* 'finger' is probably derived from this root. In addition to full grade *ei* and zero grade *i*, *e* survives in several Greek forms which cannot be explained away. The stem of the verb in the form *dek-* 'to point out' is well attested in literary Ionic, as well as epigraphically in Chios and Miletus (Bechtel 1921–24, III: 180). There have been various and obviously inadequate attempts to account for these forms. Hittite *tekuššami* is another example of *e* grade in this root. In cases like Sanskrit *diś* 'direction' and Latin *dicis causa* there is no reason to assume that *i* of the root is a reduced vowel. Indeed, as pointed out in Schmitt-Brandt (1973: 27), the vast majority of so-called *ei* and *eu* root stems have zero-grade stems, i.e. *i* and *u*, as in the instances just cited. In other Eurasiatic languages this root always appears as *tek* or *tik* and never as *teik*. In Eskimo we find West Greenlandic *tiki-q* 'index finger' (*-q* is the absolutive suffix), with similar forms in other dialects, both Yupik and Inuit. West Greenlandic also has a derived verb *tikkuagpaa* 'he points to it." Ainu has *tek* 'hand' (Hattori 1964: 11). From the original meaning 'finger' we also get 'one' because of its use in counting. In Turkic we find Osmanli Turkish *tek* 'odd (number), only, sole' and *teken* 'one by one,' Chuvash *tek* 'only, just,' and Old Turkish (Uighur) *tek* 'only, merely.'

A third Indo-European root in which there is both internal and external evidence for an e ~ i alternation is *bher- 'to carry,' which in Old Church Slavic gives both bĭrati 'to take' and berǫ 'I take.' This matches exactly the Chukchi verb 'to take,' which has the variants per ~ pir in a vowel harmony system based on height that will be discussed below. Probably the Old Turkish bir-, Osmanli ver- 'to give,' belongs here as well.

In a fourth example it is once again Slavic that agrees with non-Indo-European languages. Old Church Slavic shows the reflex ĭ in the dative-locative mĭně, but e in the genitive-accusative mene.

A parallel variation between stem forms in e and i is found in both Uralic and Altaic. Rédei and Erdélyi (1974: 199) reconstruct mi-nä and me-nä as variant Finno-Ugric forms of 'I.' In the Turkic branch of Altaic we find in Old Turkish (Gabain 1950: 91) ben, men, and min, and the same variations in the stem of the oblique cases.

There are two additional examples in basic items that are generally reconstructed for Proto-Indo-European. One is the interrogative pronoun, in which it is generally accepted that the nominative singular stem was *kʷi- (e.g. Latin qui-s), but in the singular oblique cases (except for the locative) the stem is *kʷe- (e.g. genitive *kʷe-syo; Szemerényi 1978: 270). Further details are given in No. 60 in Chapter 3.

The other important example of a reconstruction of an e ~ i alternation is the Proto-Indo-European demonstrative stem i ~ e (e.g. Latin is 'he,' eius 'his'). Szemerényi (1978: 268) reconstructs masculine nominative singular *is, accusative *im, but genitive *e-syo, and similarly with other oblique cases. The stem *ei- only occurs in the plural, where the -i is obviously the pronominal plural -i (e.g. Greek ho-i; see No. 16 in Chapter 3), a plural that has often spread to nouns (e.g. Greek -oi as the nominative plural of masculine thematic stems). Both kʷi ~ kʷe and i ~ e have related forms with similar alternations in other branches of Eurasiatic, in some instances as vowel harmonic alternants in systems with height harmony (Gilyak).

We shall now consider a number of such vowel harmonic systems that are found in various non-Indo-European branches of Eurasiatic. The first example comes from Chukotian. In some languages of the family this system has partially broken down, but its original form is clear and is fully functioning in a number of languages, including Chukchi proper, as shown in Table 2.

Table 2. The Chukchi Vowel Harmony System

High	i		e_1	u	
					ə
Low		e_2	a	o	

The general rule is that in every word all vowels must be high or ə, or all be low or ə. Thus ə is a neutral vowel. Of the two grades the low is dominant in that if any vowel of a word—whether in the stem or in an affix—is low, it will lower all high vowels to low. An example is the word for 'earth,' which, in the absolutive singular, is *nutenut* (a reduplicated form), whereas the allative is *not-ajpə*, in which the low vowel *a* of *-ajpə* has lowered the basic *u* of the stem *nut-* to its corresponding low vowel *o*. The neutral vowel ə, in some of its occurrences, is underlyingly low and hence lowers basic high vowels to low vowels in words in which it occurs. Irina Muravyova (1979: 56) believes that this "dominating" effect of the low vowels was a late occurrence in the prehistory of Proto-Chukotian, that is, that in forms like *notajpe* and *nutenut,* the first derives from an earlier *nutajpe* and that the *u* of the initial syllable was lowered by the influence of low vowel(s) in the same word.

Middle and Old Korean had a system of height harmony similar to that of Chukotian. In the present literary language, and in almost all dialects, it has broken down, but has left certain survivals to be discussed below. The old system of height harmony, as described for fifteenth-century Korean by Teruhiro Hayata (1975), is shown in Table 3.

Table 3. The Korean Vowel Harmony System

Feminine	e	y	u	
				i (neutral)
Masculine	a	ʌ	o	

The terminology 'feminine' and 'masculine,' or high and low, is found not only in grammatical traditions of literary languages in northeastern Asia, but in the sound-symbolic linguistic forms themselves (e.g. Manchu *erselen* 'female lion,' *arsalan* 'male lion'). This will be discussed below in some detail.

In Korean the modern literary language has one major survival in the verb system, the "combining form" (Lukoff 1982: 37–39). In addition, there are variant forms called isotopes in the dictionary of Martin, Lee, and Chang (1967). These are onomatopoeic, usually reduplicated adverbs (e.g. *solsol, sulsul* 'soft-flowing, softly, gently,' *mas, mes* 'taste, flavor,' and many others). There are also instances in which one dialect retains one variant and another dialect retains the other. For example, the present tense suffix in the North Korean dialect is -*ku*, but in the South Korean dialect it is -*ko* (Ramstedt 1952, I: 34).

All students of Gilyak agree that it once had a fully functioning system of height harmony. At present it survives in the Amur dialect in the variants of the third-person possessive and pronominal object prefix *i* ∼ *e*, the former with high vowels in the stem, the latter with low vowels. There are also survivals in the numeral classifier system. The Gilyak vowel harmony system is shown in Table 4.

Table 4. The Gilyak Vowel Harmony System

High	i	y	u
Low	e	a	o

As in Korean, Gilyak shows a considerable number of instances in which one dialect has selected the low vowel of a pair, and another dialect the high vowel. The two dialects shown in Table 5 are the Amur dialect and the main dialect of Sakhalin (east central), both of which are cited in the Saval'eva dictionary of Gilyak (1970). Not included in the table are the many cases in which Amur has *y* and Sakhalin *a* (e.g. Amur *tyf*, Sakhalin *taf* 'house'). There are, however, numerous instances in which both Amur and Sakhalin have *y*, or they both have *a*. Note also in Table 5 the words for 'only' and 'stick,' in which the exact opposite occurs, namely, Amur *a* corresponds to Sakhalin *y*. For other examples, see Panfilov (1962–65, I: 18–19).

In addition to this interdialectal variation there are instances of doublets within the same dialect with semantic differentiation. Examples from the Amur dialect, which is the best documented, include *ol* 'armpit of clothing,' *ul* 'bosom'; *tyf* 'house,' *raf* 'small cerimonial house' (*t*- and *r*- alternate in the Gilyak initial consonant mutation system); *lyx* 'rain,' *lax* 'cloud'; *vi-(d')* 'go, walk,' *ve-(d')* 'run (of animals)'; *kʻikr* 'above (in space),' *kʻekr* 'above a house on a higher level in the same village'; and *noɣ* 'be fragrant,' *nuɣnuɣ* 'smell' (transitive).

Table 5. Interdialectal Vowel Variation in Gilyak

Amur	Sakhalin	
mot	mut	'pillar'
-ju-	-jo-	'frequentative'
nik	nek	'now'
kis	kerš	'mud'
kip	kep	'handle'
park	pyrk	'only'
qʻas	kys	'stick'
vyt'	vat'	'iron'
rolo	rolu	'one another'
lax	lyx	'cloud/rain'
maɣ-d'	myɣ-d'	'put into port/land'

One purpose in citing these examples from Korean and Gilyak is to show the typical outcomes of a vowel harmonic system that has partially or completely broken down, including sporadic inter-dialectal or interlanguage variability and variations within the same language or dialect, frequently with semantic differentiation. We have seen in Chukotian, Korean, and Gilyak very similar systems of vowel height harmony consisting of three pairs of vowels contrasting in height, with or without an additional vowel.

In other cases where the vowel harmony system has broken down completely, very similar phenomena occur, for example, in Iranicized Uzbek, or in the south Mongolian group of languages spoken in China. Table 6 presents data from the four main languages of the south Mongolian group.

In Classical Mongolian and other Mongolian languages in which a vowel harmony system based on back vs. front vowels persists, a is a back vowel and the corresponding front vowel with which it alternates is *e*. What is noteworthy in Table 6 is the randomness of choice between the variants across languages, the variation within the same language (e.g. the causative in Dagur and Monguor), and most remarkably of all the occurrence in the same formative of *a* and *e* in the Baoan instrumental *-ga-le* and in the Dagur locative *-aare*, both of which violate the old vowel harmony rules in having both a back and front vowel in the same inflectional morpheme. We may compare this with the Sakhalin Gilyak form *rolu* 'one another, reciprocally,' which in an analogous manner breaks the rules of Gilyak height harmony within the same morpheme.

Table 6. Vowel Variation in South Mongolian Languages

	Baoan	Dagur	Dunsian	Monguor
Plural	le	—	la	—
Ablative	se	se	se	dza
Locative	re	aare	—	re
Instrumental	gale	gala	—	—
Comitative	—	—	le	la
Causative	ge	gaa, gee	ga	ga, ge
Past Participle	sang	sen	sen	dzan

It is clear from the preceding exposition that the Indo-European alternations *i* ~ *e*, *e* ~ *o*, *u* ~ *o* show the same characteristics of intradialectal variation, cross language variation, and occasional grammaticalization as that of a formerly functioning vowel harmony system. Moreover, two of the pairs, *i* ~ *e* and *u* ~ *o*, can be clearly recognized as exhibiting relative height differences. The typologically peculiar nature of what is usually reconstructed as Proto-Indo-European **a* was mentioned earlier. A number of Indo-Europeanists, considering this factor and also the fact that in most languages its reflexes are identical with those of Proto-Indo-European **o*, have suggested that the *e* ~ *o* alternation is to be reconstructed as *e* ~ *a*. If we accept this as a working hypothesis, then we may posit the pre-Proto-Indo-European vowel system as involving height harmony and taking the form shown in Table 7, which is identical, except for the reduced vowel, to that of Chukchi (and Proto-Chukotian) in Table 2.

Table 7. The Pre-Proto-Indo-European Vowel Harmony System

High	i	e	u
Low	e	a ($> o_1$)	o_2

We are making the assumption here, as have a number of Indo-Europeanists as early as Saussure (1879: 135), that there are a number of roots with "stable o" (here o_2), which do not alternate with e. These include such words as 'eight' (Latin *octō*), 'pig' (Latin *porcus*), and 'in front of' (Latin *prō*) that never seem to show an alternation with *e. In the last of these, *prō has an alternate with *u*, as in Greek *prúmn-ōs* 'the farthest' and *diaprúsios* 'going through, piercing,' which are often connected with *prō* (Pokorny 1959: 814).

A number of Indo-Europeanists have wished to eliminate traditional *a altogether, or consider it a late "hole-filling" development, deriving from expressive terms for defects (e.g. Latin *laevus* 'left-handed,' *caecus* 'blind'), or from *e adjacent to H_2, the "a-colored" laryngeal. I hesitate to eliminate it entirely. It may represent a neutral vowel resulting from the prehistoric merger of a fourth pair of formerly alternating vowels. There are several examples of Eurasiatic *a surviving in Indo-European. One example is Proto-Indo-European *al(i)- 'other,' which has cognate forms in other branches of Eurasiatic such as Aleut *ala-k* 'other, two' (in which -k is the dual suffix), Alaskan Yupik *alla-* 'another,' Ainu *ara* 'one of two' (Ainu has no *l*), Chukchi *aləm* 'one of a pair, paired thing,' *alvaŋ* 'otherwise,' and Amur Gilyak *alv-erq*, Sakhalin Gilyak *alyaf* 'behind, on the other side' (in the first Gilyak form -erq is the word for 'side' and in the second form -f is a common locative ending (see No. 28 in Chapter 3). Another example is Proto-Indo-European *anti 'in front of, opposite' (Pokorny 1959: 48–49), Hittite *ḫanti*, and Etruscan *hanθi*, with which we may compare Korean *antʰe* with the same meaning. The metathesis of aspiration, like that of glottalization, is a frequent phenomenon.

One might wonder whether there might not be actual survivals in Indo-European of the vowel harmony system proposed here. There are two instances that could be suggested. The first is the Hittite indefinite pronoun, in which a nominative *kuiš-ki* contrasts with a genitive *kuel-ka* and an ablative *kuets-ka*. This was considered to be a vowel harmonic alternation by Heinz Kronasser (1956: 48) and it would, of course, conform to the system proposed here. A second possible example is the contrast of the Indo-European reduplicative vowel *-i* in the present as against *e* in the perfect (e.g. Greek *gígnomai* 'I become,' *gégona* 'I have become'), for which no satisfactory explanation has, to my knowledge, been proposed. Here the present stem vowel *e* (zero grade in *gí-gn-omai*), contrasting with the *o* of the perfect, is in full agreement with the vowel harmonic system proposed here.

Let us now turn to other branches of Eurasiatic in which there is only fragmentary evidence for this system, or in which there is a functioning vowel harmony system based on front-back rather than high-low harmony. In Yukaghir there is evidence for an *e ~ i* alternation in the verbs *l'e* 'to be' and *l'i* 'to have,' whose relationship was pointed out by Krejnovich (1958: 40). He asserted that in the distant past they had a common genetic origin. In addition, the Tundra dialect (Krejnovich 1958: 130–31) has causative *re* and *ri*, with the choice between them lexical. There is also somewhat richer evidence for an *e ~ a* alternation. Krejnovich (1958: 14) also describes a rule in the Tundra dialect by which the negative *el'* (see No. 58 in Chapter 3) has its vowel lowered to *a* when there is an *a* in the stem (e.g. *al'-aj* 'don't shoot!'). This is of course identical with the Chukchi rule by which a low "strong vowel" lowers all high vowels in a word to their corresponding low partners. There is also in the same dialect free variation of *-t'eŋ* and *-t'aŋ*, a suffix meaning 'abounding in.' There is an interdialectal difference between Kolyma and Tundra in the locative case marker (Kolyma *ge*, Tundra *ɣa ~ ɣane*); in the prosecutive (Kolyma *gen*, Tundra *ɣan*); and in the ablative (Kolyma *get*, Tundra *ɣat*). All of these contain the same element, *ge ~ ɣa*, and are therefore a single instance. In the affix of the second-person singular of the conjugated form of verbs in logical focus, Tundra has *-mek* and Kolyma *-mik*, and in the diminutive-affective suffix, Tundra has *-tegie* (< **tegē*) and Kolyma, *-taga*. The distribution in these latter forms is the exact opposite of the locative forms, Kolyma *ge*, Tundra ɣa (see No. 26 in Chapter 3). A fuller discussion of vowel harmony in Yukaghir is given below.

I have not yet dealt with the fact that the Turkic and Mongolian branches of Altaic, as well as Uralic, have front-back rather than high-low vowel harmony. With regard to Turkic and Mongolian, already Wilhelm Schott (1849: 325) noted the existence of interlingual vowel variations based on height. Radloff (1882: 84) remarked on the variation in the vowel of the stem in Turkic languages "without any demonstrable cause." His examples include many of those cited below, but there are still others in inflections and pronominal forms that he does not mention. Poppe, the author of the standard work on Altaic and a strict adherent of regular sound laws, noted in his sketch of Yakut (1959), as had others before him, the appearance of *y* in Yakut in place of *a* and called this fairly frequent, but not reducible to rule (*regellos*). However, this alternation is by no means confined to Yakut, occurring with particular frequency in the northeastern part of the Turkic area, for example, in Tuvin *čyt* 'to lie,' compared with *jat* in other Turkic languages, or *yt* 'dog' for *at* elsewhere (Iskhakov and Pal′mbakh 1961: 224). There are also examples in which the exact opposite occurs; for example, the word for 'six' is generally *alty* in Turkic languages, but Yakut has *alta*. In Yakut one even finds an *a* ~ *y* alternation within the same paradigm (e.g. *aɣa-ta* 'his/her father' in the nominative, but *aɣa-ty-ɣa* 'to his/her father' in the dative). In Turkish we have *bir* 'one,' but *beraber* 'together.' The common Turkic verb 'to make' has alongside *et-*, a variant *it-*.

Other instances found in pronouns and inflectional affixes are rarely, if ever, cited by Turkologists, whose examples are almost exclusively lexical. The first-person singular independent pronoun is usually *men* or *ben* in the nominative case, but *min* occurs in a number of languages and similar variations occur in the second-person singular pronoun **sen*. Normally the first- and second-person singular pronouns have the same vowel, but in Yakut we have *min* 'I,' but *en* (< **hen* < **sen*) 'thou.' The interrogative pronoun 'who?' is usually *kim*, but is *kem* in Nogai, Karalkapak, Altai, and the Orkhon inscriptions. In addition to *u* ~ *o* alternations in the stems of nouns and verbs, we have in the near demonstrative (e.g. Turkish *bu* 'this') the variant *bo* in some languages (e.g. Tuvin *bo*, Shor *po*). Similarly, *ol* ~ *o* 'that, he/she' appears as *u* in Uighur and Uzbek.

Such variations also occur in Turkic inflections. One example is the ablative case marker, which is usually -dan, but appears as -dyn in some Turkic languages (e.g. Uighur -dyn). In Turkish the usual modern ending is -dan, but Hans Kissling (1960: 29) notes that earlier Turkish texts sometimes showed -dyn. A conspicuous example of variation between low and high vowels is seen in the so-called general tense, which is used to express timeless truths, habitual actions, and the future. This tense, sometimes also called the aorist in the Turkic linguistic literature, ends in -Vr after consonants. The choice between a low vowel and a high vowel is lexically determined and is usually indicated in dictionaries. In Turkish polysyllabic roots only statisical rules can be given, with numerous exceptions (e.g. ak-ar 'flows,' but al-yr 'takes'; bil-ir 'knows,' but bit-er 'ends.' The choice of the particular low or high vowel depends, of course, on back or front harmony and, in most Turkic languages, there is also agreement in lip rounding (so-called labial harmony) for high vowels. There is also considerable variation in the Turkic numeral 'two,' which is usually iki (e.g. Osmanli, Azerbaijani), but in a number of instances we find eki (e.g. Nogai, Karakalpak).

I would interpret these fairly numerous height variations within a system of front back harmony in Turkic languages as a survival of the older height harmony system that we have already encountered in Indo-European, Korean, Chukotian, Tungusic, and Gilyak. At least one Turkic specialist, M. A. Cherkasskij (1960), has arrived at this conclusion regarding these variations in Turkic, as well as similar variations in Mongolian languages. He states that "the best theory is that these alternations are relics of a previous stage. To this we may add that such systems based on height are found in Tungus" (Cherkasskij 1960: 59).

With regard to Mongolian, in addition to the numerous examples parallel to those from Turkic languages, Władysław Kotwicz (1936: 5) notes, in his discussion of pronouns in the Altaic languages, the alternation in the third-person pronoun and demonstrative i- 'he, she,' e-ne (plural e-re) 'this.' For more examples and further discussion of the near or unmarked demonstrative e ~ i, which appears in Indo-European, Uralic, Altaic, Gilyak, and Ainu with similar alternations, see No. 8 in Chapter 3.

In Uralic attempts to reconstruct the original vowel system have encountered numerous difficulties. There have been two main approaches, that of Wolfgang Steinitz (1950) and that of Erki Itkonen (1954). The former notes widespread vowel alternations and therefore assumes a whole series of such alternations in Proto-Uralic. Itkonen, however, assumes that with a few deviations Finnish has retained the Proto-Uralic vowel system. This is the view favored by most contemporary Uralicists.

Collinder, whose work forms the basis of present-day Uralic reconstructions, as found, for example, in Rédei (1988), stated, with regard to these two theories, in the very work containing the first reconstructions that specified the vowels of the initial sysllable—not merely whether the word as a whole had front or back harmony—that although his reconstructions are based on Itkonen's approach "it is quite legitimate to conclude (with Setälä, Lehtisalo and Steinitz) that there existed several vowel alternations. But, on the other hand, it is worthwhile to try (with Erki Itkonen) to get along without this hypothesis" (Collinder 1960: 151).

Both Collinder and Rédei admit height alternations in their reconstructions, including fundamental elements that we have already encountered in Indo-European and elsewhere. Thus Rédei (1988) reconstructs *ke (ki)* 'who?' since, alongside Finnish *ken*, Estonian *ke-s*, we find Hungarian *ki*. Rédei also notes the resemblance of these Uralic forms to Altaic *ke ~ ki* and Yukaghir *kin*. For the demonstrative he reconstructs **e*, but notes many *i* forms, including Hungarian *i-de* 'here, hither' alongside of *ez ~ e* 'this, the,' and Kamassian Samoyed *i-də* 'this, there.' For the first-person pronoun Rédei reconstructs *mย̆* 'I,' where *-ย̆* indicates a non-specified front vowel (cf. Finnish *minä ~ mä* with Komi-Zyrian *me*), and compares this with Turkic *min ~ men*. Collinder (1965b: 56–57) reconstructs the alternation *i ~ e* 'this' in Uralic and cites the agreement of this vowel alternation with Indo-European as supporting evidence for the genetic connection of the two families. For the Uralic interrogative pronoun Collinder (1960: 406) reconstructs *ke ~ ki*. We thus find alternations in three basic Uralic elements—the near demonstrative, the interrogative, and the first-person pronoun and parallel to it the second-person singular—that match similar alternations in the same elements in Indo-European, Altaic, and elsewhere.

A further instance that has not hitherto been noticed, except partially and with an incorrect historical explanation, is found in Vovin (1993). The alternations $i \sim e$, $u \sim o$, and $e \sim a$ are all found in Ainu. So as not to interrupt the discussion with a detailed account of Ainu vowel alternations, this material has been put in the Appendix. What is relevant to the present discussion is Vovin's (1993) recognition of the alternation $e \sim i$ in the third-person singular object prefix of the verb, a vocalic alternation whose occurrence he does not recognize anywhere else in Ainu (even though it is actually quite frequent). Furthermore, Vovin notes that it coincides with that of Gilyak, but he is apparently unaware of its wider occurrence.

We have now considered the vowel height alternations that might be interpreted as the survivals of a vowel height harmony system in all branches of Eurasiatic except Japanese and Eskimo-Aleut. The history of the vowel system of Japanese is the subject of a considerable literature. For discussions in Western languages, the reader is referred chiefly to Yoshitake (1934), Wenck (1954–59), Miller (1967, 1971), Lange (1973), Unger (1975), Starostin (1991), and Syromiatnikov (1981). Modern Japanese has five vowels, a, e, i, o and u, the last being unrounded (i.e. ɯ). This basic system seems to have been inherited from the system of the Heian period of more than a thousand years ago. However, in the preceding Nara period, from which we have our earliest written Japanese records, we find the first attempts to write Japanese in a system called Manyogana. Chinese characters were used to write Japanese words that had similar phonetic values. As early as the eighteenth century the Japanese scholar Norinaga noticed that three of the five Japanese vowels, e, i and o, were consistently represented in certain Japanese words by a certain set of Chinese characters, whereas in other words they were represented by others. The conclusion was that in this period an eight vowel system existed; the pairs of vowels were called kō 'primary' and otsu 'secondary.' The latter are conventionally represented by ë, ï and ö. (The use of two dots here has, of course, nothing to do phonetically with German umlaut.) Regarding the phonetic differences between the kō and otsu forms, there are differing opinions. One is that it was an opposition between vowels with and without a preceding palatal glide. Another, espoused by Yoshitake (1934) and others, is that the difference was one of vowel quality. The kō vowels

were *i, e, o*, whereas the *otsu* were *ɪ, ɛ, ɔ*, respectively. This latter interpretation, of course, accords well with what we have noted
so far, but even better with the Proto-Tungusic system discussed
below. There are, moreover, some vowel harmonic phenomena, the
most obvious and reliable being that *o* and *ö* may not occur in the
same root. Thus, there are words in Old Japanese like *tökörö* 'place'
(*tɔkɔrɔ* according to this interpretation) and *kökörö* 'heart,' but a
sequence like **kökoro* is not permissable. Furthermore, as noted by
Unger (1975: 23) and others, *u, o* and *a* do not as a rule occur with
ö, although there are a few exceptions (but none with *o*).

The Nara epoch system of eight vowels, namely, *a, e, ë, i, ï, o,
ö, u*, is commonly believed to have derived from an earlier system
that did not contain *e, ë*, and *ï*. This is because there are morphophonemic replacements for these vowels, namely, *e* arising from *i +
a, ë* from *a + i*, and *ï* from *u + i* or *ö + i*. However, even admitting
the correctness of these morphophonemic relationships, it does not
follow that one or more of the three resultants of these processes—*e,
ë*, and *ï*—did not already exist in the language and then merged
with the vowels arising from these contractions. Thus, the *ë* of *amë*
'rain' (but *ama-* in compounds) could have, and probably did, arise
from *a + i*, just as the *-ë* of transitive verbs (e.g. *tata-* 'to stand,'
tata-i- >*tatë-* 'to erect'). Both of these instances of **-i* are discussed
in No. 8 in Chapter 3. On the other hand, independent *ë* and *e* (as
well as *ï*) could have existed before the pre-Nara contractions and
this *e* or *ë* may be involved in the contrast *ani* 'older brother,' *ane*
'older sister.'

The only branch of Eurasiatic whose vowel system has not yet
been discussed is Eskimo-Aleut. Proto-Eskimo is reconstructed as
having had four vowel, *a, i, u*, and *e*; in Aleut there are just three,
a, i, and *u*. One may suspect here a complex history of mergers and
differentiations. As we shall see later, the distribution of the *k* velar
series and the *q* uvular series is relevant here and Eskimo-Aleut will
be cited below in that regard.

In summary, in a number of branches of Eurasiatic we find evidence of a vowel harmony system like that shown in Table 2 for
Chukchi. This system of height harmony is either fully functioning
(e.g. Chukchi), partly functioning (e.g. Gilyak), or in some languages
survives as a vowel alternation system (e.g. Indo-European Ablaut).

Moreover, certain fundamental roots (the interrogative, demonstrative, and personal pronouns) recur in different Eurasiatic branches with parallel alternations in accordance with this system.

However, as mentioned at the outset, I believe that this system of height harmony ultimately derives from a ±PH system such as we find in the Tungusic languages, especially in Even (Lamut), which retains it in its most archaic form. Synchronically all the Tungusic languages have either a system of cross-height harmony or a system derivable therefrom. As early as 1955 Johannes Benzing reconstructed four pairs of vowels, with the vowels of each pair differing in relative height. The series of grammatical sketches of Tungusic languages in *JNSSR* V (1979) are of great importance. In first reading this material I was forcibly reminded of the African languages belonging to the Niger-Kordofanian and Nilo-Saharan stocks that have a harmony system based on ±ATR. However, whereas in Africa it is based on advanced tongue root versus a neutral position, the active principle in Tungusic seems to be retracted tongue root versus a neutral position. The Russian investigators consistently reported voice quality distinctions between the sets of lower vowels, which they call "hard," and the higher members, which they call "soft." In the eastern dialect of Even, Novikova (1960: 7) notes that the hard vowels are pharyngealized. What happens here is that to produce +PH vowels the pharyngeal cavity is reduced to its minimum by (1) retraction of the tongue root, (2) raising of the larynx, and (3) pushing forward the pharyngeal wall, hence the pharyngealization noted by Novikova. For the phonetics of the tongue root feature the reader is referred especially to Ladefoged (1968) and Lindau (1975).

The scholar who has considered most carefully the synchronic and diachronic problems of the Tungusic system is Josh Ard (1981), who arrived at the conclusion that all Tungusic vowel systems derive from an original tongue root harmony system and he traced the changes they underwent in various Tungusic languages. He also concluded that "probably the ATR has no advancement and the important factor is retraction" (Ard 1981: 27). This is the same conclusion I arrived at about the same time, but did not publish until 1990.

We saw above that the +PH vowels of Tungusic languages are frequently called "hard" or "bright," whereas the −PH vowels are called "soft" or "dull." In a number of the eastern Eurasiatic languages we find that contrasts in ±PH, or its historical successor ±HIGH, are given sound symbolic value. The +PH, or low vowels are associated with masculinity, strength, and size, while the −PH, or high vowels are associated with their opposites. Where the distinction is one of relative height, the lower is the "strong" one and when, as in Mongolian, the system is synchronically based on a back-front distinction, the back vowels are strong and the front vowels weak.

The following are some examples of this widespread phenomenon. There are numerous examples in Manchu of the opposition a (masculine), e (feminine), in which a is both lower and further back than e. Representative instances include *ganggan* 'strong,' *genggen* 'weak'; *arsalan* 'male lion,' *erselen* 'female lion'; *haha* 'man,' *hehe* 'woman'; *habtaha* 'man's loin cloth,' *hebtehe* 'woman's petticoat'; and *wasi* 'ascend,' *wesi* 'descend.' These are but a few examples taken from Ōno (1970: 113). In Negidal, a north Tungusic language with a clear ±PH system, we have *exin* 'older sister,' *axɪn* 'older brother,' and similar examples can be found in other Tungusic languages. In Gilyak, which has a relative height system, there is a clear example in the Amur dialect (with corresponding forms in other dialects), namely, *iř* 'mother,' *eř* 'father.'

Ramstedt (1957, II: 183) discusses this phenomenon with examples from Manchu, Mongol, and Korean. The Korean examples include some in which there is a discernible difference of meaning between the low and high variants (e.g. *kęm* 'be black,' *kam* 'be coal black'; *pulgin* 'red,' *polgan* 'very red'), the strong variant being intensive in meaning. In his presentation of the Old Korean vowel harmony system, Kim Boo-Kyom (1959) calls the set of lower vowels 'strong' and the higher 'weak.' However, Martin (1962b) arrives at the opposite conclusion in his study of Korean vowel isotopes.

An effect on grammatical terminology is noted in Vladimirtsov (1929: 134), where it is reported that Mongolian grammars of the early eighteenth century call the back vowels and uvular consonants "masculine," the front vowels and velar consonants "feminine," and the neutral vowel *i* is called "bipolar." Vladimirtsov himself gives the Khalkha example *axxa* 'old man, older brother,' *exxe* 'old woman, mother.'

In Turkish the existence of vowel alternations has been discussed by Louis Bazin (1961: 14), who gives a number of examples of a y $\sim$ a alternation and notes that this opposition is well attested in Turkish, where y expresses an attenuation of the meaning of the forms in a. Instances include *par* 'vif éclat lumineux,' *pyr* 'faible éclat lumineux'; and *pat* 'fracas,' *pyt* 'bruit sourd.' Similar examples are found in other Turkic languages (e.g. Uighur *jar-t* 'split,' *jyr-t* 'tear').

To summarize, I have proposed that, as the comparative evidence of Ard (1981) convincingly shows, Proto-Tungusic had a ±PH system (pharyngealized versus normal vowels) in which the dynamic element included retraction of the tongue root from the normal position. Such systems, as shown most clearly in Nanai, are easily transformed into systems of height harmony, whereas the opposite development is not found. Furthermore, I have suggested, on the basis of numerous survivals in Turkic and Mongolian of the earlier stage, that the front-back harmony of these languages is secondary. For Uralic the main evidence of a former height system is the agreement in the $i \sim e$ alternation in the demonstrative, interrogative, and personal pronouns.

There is further evidence of the former existence of ±PH systems in non-Tungusic languages of Eurasiatic in the peculiar distribution of the velar and uvular series (referred to in the following discussion as simply k and q, respectively), whose contrast in most of these languages, if it exists at all, is non-phonemic, depending on vowel harmonic considerations. The normal and expected situation is found in Turkic and Mongolian languages, in which there are well established systems of vowel harmony based on an opposition of front and back vowels. In these languages there is often an allophonic distribution of the k and q series, with the former found in words with front vowels, and the latter in those with back vowels. Since k is farther forward, and q farther back, we may consider this a "natural" phonetic variation. In fact, in the older Osmanli Turkish orthography, which used the Arabic alphabet and was replaced in 1923 by the Latin alphabet in Kamal Ataturk's reform, the inadequate rendition of Turkish vowels in the Turkish orthography was to some extent remedied by writing the Arabic k in words with front vowel harmony, and q in words with back vowel harmony. In the traditional Mongolian orthography—a Nestorian Syriac derived alphabet—the same device is resorted to, namely, the writing of the Semitic k in words with front harmony and q in words with back harmony. In both Ottoman Turkish and Classical Mongolian there were phonetically distinct k and q series, whose difference, however, was non-phonemic since they could be predicted on the basis of whether the vowels were all front or all back.

In two non-Altaic languages, however, we have a distribution of k and q in which, although other back vowels are found with q, and front vowels with k, u is found with k even though it is a back vowel. One of these languages is Gilyak, whose high-low system of vowel harmony—though only partially functioning today—can easily be reconstructed. For the convenience of the reader, Table 4 is repeated here.

Table 4. The Gilyak Vowel Harmony System

High	i	y	u
Low	e	a	o

The rule in Gilyak is that k occurs before i, e, y and u, but q before a and o (see Krejnovich 1937: 87–95 and Hattori 1962: 86). Austerlitz (1990: 21) conjectured that k and q were once the same phoneme in Gilyak and that the key is the study of the adjacent vocalism.

A similar phenomenon is found in Yukaghir, where Krejnovich (1982: 11) also conjectures that this indicates that k and q were formerly a single phoneme. With regard to k he notes that it occurs most often with i, e and $ө$. This latter is a vowel of very limited distribution, found only in the Tundra dialect, and is phonetically a rounded form of e. In the same dialect q is found with a, o, and u. However, in the Kolyma dialect we find a distribution similar to that of Gilyak in which q occurs with o and k with u.

More generally in Yukaghir, as noted in Nikolaieva (1988: 78–80), the distribution of k and q in several constructions depends on the preceding vowels in both surviving dialects (e.g. the inchoative verbal suffix -$\bar{a}$ ~ -$\bar{e}$ and the diminutive suffix -$\bar{a}d\bar{e}$ ~ $\bar{e}d\bar{e}$). Here, once again, a front-back vowel harmony system is involved in which u and $\bar{u}$ are treated as front, not back vowels (e.g. *uneme* 'ear,' *unem-ēdē* 'small ear' in both the Kolyma and Tundra dialects, but *šorom-ādē* 'small man' in the Kolyma dialect. Nikolaieva (1988: 80) explicitly describes the Yukaghir vowel harmonic system as involving front versus back and notes the anomolous position of *u* and *ū*, phonetically back but generally to be classified as front in regard to the vowel harmony system.

In Eskimo and Aleut, although the phonemic status of *k* and *q* is well established and they contrast in all vocalic environments, in the widespread Eurasiatic interrogative in *k* ~ *q* both Eskimo and Aleut contrast the form for 'who?,' Proto-Eskimo **ki(-na)*, Aleut *kiin* (Fortescue et al. 1994: 173–74) with a stem in *qa-* for other interrogatives, such as Proto-Eskimo **qa-ku* 'when [in the future],' *qa-ŋa* 'when (in the past); Proto-Inuit **qa-nuq* 'how?'; Proto-Southern Yupik (i.e. non-Siberian Yupik) **qa-yuq* 'how?' Corresponding to these latter Eskimo forms we find the same stem *qa-* in Aleut, as illustrated by the following examples taken from the Atkan dialect: *qanan* 'which?, which one?,' *qanang* 'where?,' *qanaang* 'how many?' A virtually identical distribution of *k* and *q* is found in Yukaghir (where *x* derives from **q* in the Kolyma dialect): Tundra, Kolyma *kin* 'who?,' but Tundra *qabun* 'how many?,' *qada* 'where?,' *qadat* whence?,' *qaduŋun* 'which?,' *qaqun* 'how many?,' *qanin* 'when?'; Kolyma *xamun* 'how many?,' *xaŋide* 'whither?,' *xon* 'where?' The only discrepancy I have noted is Kolyma *xadi* 'who?,' in which the deviation is semantic, but not phonological, that is, *x* derives from **q* before *a*, but with the meaning 'who?'

What requires explanation is why *u*, which is a back vowel, occurs with *k* instead of *q*. As Ard (1981: 28) states in his general review of Tungusic vowel harmony, "in some Tungusic languages uvulars occur with 'hard' [i.e. −PH] vowels and velars with 'soft' ones, e.g. in Even." However, as the system breaks down and becomes one of vowel height, we find that the distribution of *k* and *q* becomes more sensitive to height and frontness. The advancement of the tongue root raises and fronts vowels. Hence, the high vowel *u* tends to occur with *k* rather than with *q*. Thus, in Negidal uvulars occur with *a, o, ɔ* and *e*, but not with *u* because of its height (Kolesnikova and Konstantinova, 1968, III: 19). It is for this reason that *o* occurs with *k*, but *u* with *q*. Similar distributions are found in Ulch (uvulars before *a* and *o*, but not *u*); in Orok, uvulars occur before *a*, *o*, and *ü*, but not before *u*. Here *ü* indicates a −ATR vowel and *u* indicates a +ATR one. In Udihe *k* occurs before *a* and *o*, but not *u*.

If the conjecture voiced here is correct, an originally allophonic distribution of *k* and *q* has persisted even after ±ATR was replaced by a height system. In these systems *u* is generally the outcome of earlier +ATR and is therefore fronted, occurring with *k* rather than *q*. This survival of a former allophonic distribution is, of course, remarkable, but I cannot see any other explanation for the peculiar distribution in Gilyak and Yukaghir of a phonetically paradoxical distribution of *k* before *o* and *q* before *u*.

Another possible phonetic survival occurs in Chukchi. Once more, for the convenience of the reader, Table 2 is repeated below.

Table 2. The Chukchi Vowel Harmony System

High	i	e_1	u	
				ə
Low	e_2	a	o	

Note that *e* occurs here in a twofold role. Is there any phonetic difference between e_1 and e_2? According to Skorik (1961–77, I: 23), *e* "has two basic variants depending on vowel harmony. The first [e_1 in Table 2] is more front and higher. . . . The second [e_2 in Table 2] is farther back and lower." In her reconstruction of the Proto-Chukotian vowel system, Muravjova (1979) makes the assumption of two original *e* vowels for the family as a whole. A similar conclusion may be drawn from Bogoras (1934: 14), where e_1 is *e* and e_2 is *æ*. This, of course, fits in well with what we have noted up to now. The inheritor of −PH is higher and more fronted than that of +PH. On the other hand, it is possible that this is the result of an assimilatory effect of other vowels in the words in which e_1 and e_2 occur, that is, the height of the other vowels in words in which e_1 occurs (*i* and *u*) and the lowness of *a* and *o*, the vowels with which e_2 occurs. However, this would not account for the relative frontness of e_1 and the frequent occurrence of both e_1 and e_2 in words whose only other vowel is the quite frequent neutral vowel ə. I have not found these variants of *e* in those languages of the Koryak group with intact vowel harmony systems.

The Contrast between Simple and Palatalized *r* (and *l*)

The next phonological phenomenon with which we will be concerned has to do with the existence of two varieties of *r*, and two of *l*, in Altaic languages, with reflexes, according to Miller (1971), in Japanese also. I will present here evidence that the contrast between at least r_1 (non-palatalized) and r_2 (palatalized) also existed in Chukotian.

The basis for positing a distinction between two forms of *r* and *l*—a contrast restricted to word-medial position in Altaic—is the following. The *r* in this position in Altaic languages has two different correspondences. In Chuvash, which we have noted constitutes a group by itself as against all the rest of Turkic, as well as in Mongolian and Tungus, the *r* found in these languages has two correspondences in non-Chuvash Turkic, namely, *r* and *z*. To *l* in these other languages non-Chuvash Turkic sometimes shows *l*, and sometimes *š*. It is generally assumed that non-Chuvash Turkic *z* (which derives from Proto-Altaic $*r_2$) is a palatalized form arising from a following *i*, and that non-Chuvash Turkic *š* (which derives from Proto-Altaic $*l_2$) similarly arose in a palatal environment.

We should expect instances in which, in non-Chuvash Turkic, morphophonemic alternations between r_1 and r_2, as well as l_1 and l_2, occur. I have, in fact, found two examples of $r_1 \sim r_2$, and one of $l_1 \sim l_2$. One is the existence in non-Chuvash Turkic of a noun *göz* 'eye' alongside of a verbal root *gör-* 'to see' (e.g. Turkish *göz* 'eye,' *gör-mek* 'to see'). Chuvash, interestingly, shows the same variation.

The second example of a $r_1 \sim r_2$ morphophonemic alternation is inflectional. The "aorist" or general tense of Turkic -*Vr*, which we saw earlier has both high and low variants, forms its negative in -*maz* ~ -*mez*. For example, Turkish *git-mek* 'to go' has as its positive aorist third-person singular *gid-er* 'he/she goes,' and as its negative, *git-mez* 'he/she does not go.' Regarding the $l \sim š$ alternation, Tenishev (1984, III: 482) points to the Turkic denominative suffix for verbs, which has variants -*la* and -*ša*. Thus we find Old Turkish *kary* 'old,' *kary-la-* 'to consider old,' and *qur* 'belt, girdle,' *qur-ša* 'to put on a belt, gird.' We also have Middle Turkish *tüš* 'dream' (noun) and Yakut *tūl* 'dream' (noun), *tüš-ā* 'to dream.' With these forms we may compare Mongolian *töl-ge* 'prophecy.'

It is possible that reflexes of $*r_1$ and $*r_2$ also exist in Chukotian. Chukchi r figures in two sets of correspondences in the Koryak group. In the first, we find t in some Koryak dialects (e.g. Palana) and in Aliutor, which is probably better considered a distinct language within the Koryak group. I am not yet certain of the Kamchadal correspondence, although it may be z (Golovastikov and Dolgopolsky 1972). The other correspondence to Chukchi r is Kerek j (Kerek is probably also a separate language in the Koryak group), but Palana r. For both, $*r_1$ and $*r_2$, Chavchuven, the basis of the Koryak standard language, has j. The obvious candidate for $*r_2$, because it is palatalized, is this second correspondence. It occurs in the Eurasiatic plural -r-i (see No. 17 in Chapter 3), for example, Chukchi mu-r-i 'we,' tu-r-i 'you,' but Chavchuven mu-j-i 'we two,' tu-j-i 'you two,' and Kerek məə-j 'we,' təə-j 'you.' In Chavchuven, as in Koryak in general, the dual clearly corresponds to the plural of Chukchi.

In extinct Kamchadal dialects we find Northern Kamchadal buzhe, Southern Kamchadal mush 'we' (Krasheninnikov 1755: 446 [1972]), with phonetic reflexes of $*r_2$ very similar to Turkic biz 'we.' Jonathan Bobaljik (personal communication) has noted in his fieldwork on Kamchadal that the z of modern Western Kamchadal is apparently the same sound as Czech ř, described in Ladefoged and Maddieson (1996: 228) as a trill made with the laminal surface of the tongue against the alveolar ridge, and only occurring as a regular speech sound in Czech. If the identification with Kamchadal z is correct, this would be the second attested occurrence of this rare sound.

The known historical origin and development of this sound in Czech, and as we shall see Polish, parallels in a remarkable way that of the Kamchadal sound. In Czech it arises from a palatalized r and in Polish this same palatalized r, written rz in Polish orthography, has become a ž sound (cf. Northern Kamchadal buzhe). Hence it has merged with Polish ż, which arose from the first Slavic palatalization of g, but is still orthographically distinct (i.e. both ż and rz are pronounced [ž]).

Further, as noted in Chapter 3 (No. 17), the plural oblique in r preceding case markers in nouns of the second or definite declension (identified there with plural $*r_2$) shows the same reflexes in Chukotian (Chavchuven Koryak -jə-).

That $*l_2$ may exist in Chukotian is indicated by the Chukchi alternation between *l* and *č*. Bogoras (1922: 834) notes that these two sounds are intimately related and frequently replace each other with a slight change of meaning. He asserts that the *l* forms indicate generalized or completed action, whereas *č* expresses special meaning or momentaneous action, but this does not account for many instances. An example from Moll (1957) is *lejvek* 'to wander, walk,' but *čejvek* 'go a great distance.' Although *l* is automatically palatalized (there is no unpalatalized *l* in Chukchi), *l* is here the obvious candidate for $*l_1$ and *č* for $*l_2$. It should be noted that there is no *s* or *š* in Chukchi.

Word-Final Laryngeals in Indo-European and Eurasiatic

According to the usual view of Indo-Europeanists a short vowel followed by a laryngeal results in the lengthening of the vowel in non-Anatolian languages. Of the three laryngeals H_1 is lost in the Anatolian languages, but H_2 and H_3 survive as *ḫ*. However, *ḫ* never occurs in word-final position, whereas long final vowels appear in non-Anatolian languages, a specially conspicuous example being the nominative of feminine *ā-* and *ī-*stems. The former is commonly reconstructed as -*eH*₂ with a colored laryngeal and the latter as -*iH*, with a non-specified laryngeal.

Now it is a remarkable, but little-noted fact about Indo-European that, although the frequency of velar consonants in roots is quite high, so that one might estimate that something like one third of Indo-European roots contains at least one velar, velars never seem to occur in grammatical formatives.

That there is some relationship between velars and laryngeals is well known. There are a number of roots which require proto-forms with *k* alongside of *H* (e.g. Latin *costa* 'rib' and Russian *kost'* 'bone' correspond to Greek *ostoûs* 'bone' and Hittite *ḫastai* 'bone'). Within Anatolian, Hittite *akuwanzi* 'they drink' corresponds to Palaic *aḫuwanti* with the same meaning. As stated by Schmitt-Brandt (1973: 106–7), the parallels are too numerous and striking to simply be dismissed.

All this suggests that Indo-European final long vowels might derive from forms with final -*k*, which, as has been seen, is strangely missing in Indo-European grammatical formatives. In No. 36 of Chapter 3 the final long vowel of the Indo-European feminine is connected to the widespread -*k* diminutive of both Indo-European and non-Indo-European branches of Eurasiatic; for example, Japanese -*ko* 'small' has as one of its main uses the formation of feminine proper names such as Michiko and Masako. Similarly, the long vowel of the Proto-Indo-European dual may be connected with the widespread *k* dual of Eurasiatic (No. 14 in Chapter 3).

Chapter 3

Grammatical Evidence for Eurasiatic

In this chapter I will present grammatical evidence for the Eurasiatic family. Seventy-two grammatical formatives are discussed, with a general organization as follows: pronouns, demonstratives, substantivizers, dual/plural, collective, personal, absolutive, accusative, genitive, dative, locative, ablative, comitative, vocative, diminutive, instrumental, nominalizer, possessive, participles, imperative, hortatory, denominative, causative, future, conative, reflexive, incompletive, negative, interrogative, ordinal, indefinite, and reduplication. Numbers 69–72 appear to be restricted to the Altaic branch and are therefore listed last.

1. First-Person M

The most widespread first-person pronoun in the Eurasiatic family is *m*. It seems to be fundamentally singular but is often found in the dual and plural, and in such instances it is usually combined with markers of non-singular number. It is often found in the singular with a final -*n*. This -*n* occurs less often with the second-person singular pronoun. Altaicists call it pronominal *n*, but the interpretation presented here (see No. 25) is that it is a genitival-oblique marker (also found in nouns) that has spread to the nominative, leading to an analysis of it as belonging to the stem. This same development occurs in nouns, though somewhat less frequently.

Although m is the basic indicator of first person, and is found in every subgroup except Ainu, it is also specialized in that it originally expressed the active in contrast to stative k (see No. 2). The contrast between m and k, where it occurs, varies in function, but m is always on the active, transitive, and ergative side in contrast to k as middle, intransitive, or absolutive.

In Indo-European -m is the first person singular of the non-thematic conjugation, e.g. Sanskrit *ád-mi* 'I eat' (-i here marks the present active indicative). It also occurs in the thematic imperfect and the root aorist, e.g. Sanskrit *ábhavam* 'I was' (imperfect), *ábhūm* 'I was' (aorist), as well as in other verbal moods than the indicative.

It combines with plural markers to indicate the first-person plural subject in verbs, e.g. Vedic -*mas*, -*masi* (present active indicative), Classical Greek -*men* (Attic), -*mes* (Doric), etc. It occurs likewise in the non-nominative case forms of the independent pronoun, e.g. in the enclitics *me* (accusative) and *moi* (dative) in Classical Greek. The Indo-European genitive singular is reconstructed as **mene*. It appears in Armenian with the usual plural marker -k' in *mek'*, in Lithuanian *me-s*, and in Old Church Slavic *my*, all meaning 'we' (nominative).

First-person singular -m also occurs in the nominative singular of the independent pronoun, usually reconstructed as **eĝ(h)om* in Proto-Indo-European. For discussion of this form see Nos. 7 and 8 below.

In Uralic **-m* is reconstructed as the first-person singular verb subject. In the independent pronouns the -n extension noted above for Indo-European appears throughout the case inflection, including the nominative in most Uralic languages, e.g. Finnish *minä* 'I.' However, some Baltic Finnic languages have a distinction between the nominative without n and the other cases with n, e.g. Votic *miä* (nominative), *minū* (genitive), or as a variant, e.g. Livonian *mina* ~ *ma* (nominative), *min* (genitive), and Finnish itself has a variant *mä* in the nominative. The Vach dialect of Ostyak also has *mä* and Rédei (1988: 294) simply reconstructs **m* followed by an unspecified front vowel for the stem of the first-person singular pronoun.

This pronoun also occurs in Uralic as a suffix indicating the first-person singular possessor in nouns. It survives in its original form -mi most clearly in dialectal Finnish and Yurak Samoyed. For the first-person plural independent pronoun *me is reconstructed for Uralic and in combination with the dual/plural marker k (see No. 14) we find *-mek as the suffix of the first-person plural subject in the verb.

In Yukaghir the independent first-person pronouns are met 'I' and mit 'we.' That the true indicator of the first person is m is shown by the parallel contrast in the second-person pronouns tet 'thou' and tit 'you.' A suffixed -m is found as a first-person singular subject of the verb in its interrogative form. Elsewhere in the verbal system the first-person singular subject is indicated by zero. All the forms cited thus far are from the two surviving dialects of Yukaghir, Kolyma and Tundra, both of which are relatively well documented. These dialects do not have possessive suffixes, but -m 'my' is attested in the extinct Omok dialect (Tailleur 1959a). In addition, Collinder (1940: 11) discovered an undoubted example of -m 'my' in Jochelson's texts of the Kolyma dialect, and single examples of -t (second-person possessive) in the Kolyma and Tundra dialects.

For Altaic as a whole Ramstedt (1952–57, II: 68) reconstructs *min as the first-person singular independent pronoun in the nominative case. However, there are indications, as will be seen in the following discussion, that -n was originally confined to the genitive and oblique cases (as in Indo-European). In Turkic the stem of the first-person singular nominative has been reconstructed as *ben ~ *bin, with a vowel that varies across languages. As we saw in Chapter 2, we encounter this e ~ i alternation elsewhere in Eurasiatic languages. It is generally assumed that earlier initial *m became *b in Proto-Turkic. However, in spite of the *b- reconstruction, m- occurs in many Turkic languages, e.g. Uzbek men and even in Old Turkish there is dialect variation between b- and m- in this form. The usual explanation of m- is that it results from the assimilation of *b to m before the following nasal consonant. However, variation of m and b is also found in the plural, e.g. Turkish biz 'we,' but -miz 'our' without a following nasal consonant.

The foregoing Turkic reconstructions are based on the non-Chuvash Turkic languages and it is clear that Chuvash is genetically the most divergent Turkic language. In Chuvash we find nominative e-pě (for the initial deictic e-, see No. 8), but in the non-nominative case the stem is *man-*. This difference is echoed in Mongolian *bi* (nominative), *mini* 'genitive,' and in Tungus as well, e.g. Manchu *bi* (nominative), *mini* (genitive), *mimbe* (< **minbe* [accusative]), with *min-* as stem in all cases except the nominative.

In Turkic -*m* also occurs as the marker of the first-person singular subject in the verb and as possessive in the noun, and the plural forms exhibit additional number affixes. In the Mongolian languages there are no suffixes marking the subject in verbs except, as a result of fairly recent developments, in Kalmyk and Buriat. In Tungus, except for Manchu, such suffixes do exist and take the form -*mi* or -*m*. Examples are Solon *wā-mi* 'I kill' and Evenki *wā-m* with the same meaning. In addition, Benzing (1955: 108) reconstructs both *b* and *m* forms for the plural independent pronoun **büä* 'we (exclusive),' **mün-ti* 'we (inclusive).' I believe these are unrealistic reconstructions. All Tungus languages have *u*, never *ü*. The *ü* is reconstructed on the basis of the correspondence Tungusic *u* ~ Mongolian *ü*, with the implicit assumption that the Mongolian system is earlier. Proto-Tungus surely had *u* in these forms. More realistic reconstructions are **bu* (exclusive) and **mi-ti*, or perhaps **bi-ti*, (inclusive). The final vowel in Benzing's *büä* reflects only a special politeness marker in Gold and Ulch. The *u* vowel of some languages in the inclusive (e.g. Orok *mun*) can be explained as the result of the influence of the exclusive pronoun **bu*, oblique stem **mun-*. The inclusive forms in *b-*, like Oroch *bi-ti*, are to be attributed to the influence of the nominative singular **bi*. The most probable reconstruction, **mi-ti*, is simply a sequence of first- and second-person singular forms, a common typological source of inclusive pronouns. (For -*ti*, see No. 4.) This reconstruction is accepted by Menges (1968: 72) and the general notion of the inclusive plural as first person plus second person is found in still earlier sources.

In Korean, Ramstedt was the first to hypothesize that the first person plural pronoun **u-li* developed from **wu-li*, and ultimately from **bu-li*. The plural -*li* in this form clearly corresponds to the Turkic first-person plural pronouns with **-r₂* (< **-ri*) mentioned above. Ramsey (1978: 110) cites several modern Korean dialect forms *wuli*.

The first-person singular *m* may also survive in the Korean verbal suffix -*ma*, called Intentionalis by Lewin (1970: 129), which expresses an emphatic wish or promise on the part of the speaker. Andre Eckardt (1965) translates -ma as 'ich möchte' ('I should like to . . . ') and all his examples are in the first-person singular. Honsol Lee (1989: 103) explicitly indicates that -ma can only have a first-person subject and cannot be followed by any tense suffixes except zero. Lewin derives this suffix from the verbal noun in -m (see No. 39) followed by the -a vocative (see No. 35), but this seems implausible. We should also note the survival of m in the first-person imperative of the Chukchi-Koryak verb. Survival of active m, in opposition to stative k, seems particularly plausible in these cases because an exhortation or wish usually refers to an inceptive action rather than a state.

Lewin describes -ma as appropriate to his first and second social levels, i.e. speech addressed to inferiors. It would thus contrast with the survival of honorific -si, interpreted in Nos. 5 and 16 as an original second-person plural.

For Japanese, Miller (1971: 158) notes that Old Japanese mi occurs as a first-person singular in a wide variety of texts from the entire history of the language. In addition, wa and ware (for -re see No. 13), which may be compared with the Altaic (Mongolian) plural ba, are common. Miller (1967: 163) quotes a poem from the Manyoshu, the earliest Japanese literary work, of which several portions are in a non-standard dialect (not specified as to locality), containing wan(u) 'me.' In Ryukyuan one finds nominative baa and oblique banu as first-person pronouns (Martin 1966: 188). These forms point back to earlier ban(u) (cf. Turkish ben 'I'). The resemblance of these forms to Altaic was recognized by both Martin and Miller. Gerard Groot (1940: 310) noted in Okinawa the redundant form wa-mi.

In the Amur dialect of Gilyak, m- is found in the first-person dual pronoun me-gi (< *men-gin; see No. 14) and the plural me-r. The Amur Gilyak verb ma-d' 'to be near' (Panfilov 1962–65, II: 186) possibly involves the first-person deictic root ma (cf. Eskimo).

In the Chukotian group, Chukchi has the first-person independent pronoun ɣəm and, in predication, -iɣəm ~ -eɣəm (for i ~ e see No. 8 and for ɣə see No. 7), with corresponding forms in the other Chukotian languages. In these forms -m is shown to be the first-person singular by comparison with the second-person singular

γət and -*iγət* ~ -*eγət*. An accusative *ma* from the extinct Southern Kamchadal dialect is found in Radliński's material (1891–94) in
place of the usual Chukotian non-nominative case forms based on
the nominative *γəm*. In the eighteenth century data presented by
Krashenninikov (1972) we find the first-person plural verbal ending -*mk* (for *k* see No. 14). This ending is not found in modern
(Western) Kamchadal, but is attested in both Chukchi and Koryak.
The Chukchi first-person plural is *muri* (with corresponding forms in
Koryak). In all the Chukotian languages *m*- is also found as the verb
subject of the imperative, e.g. Chukchi *m*- (singular), *mən*- (plural).

For Eskimo, as noted by Menovshchikov (1962, I: 53) "it is entirely acceptable to posit -*ma* as first person." In Sirenik, a Siberian
form of Eskimo that seems to have a special genetic position within
the Eskimo family, we find *məŋa* as first-person singular independent pronoun, whereas other dialects have such forms as Greenlandic *uvaŋa*. One is reminded of the *m* ~ *b* variation in Altaic and
Japanese. Note also Greenlandic *ma*, described by Kleinschmidt
(1851: 21) as a deictic root glossed 'here, where I am.' It is also
found in the Yupik branch of Eskimo (Jacobson 1984: 221), where
it occurs, as in Inuit, with the various locative affixes that differ
from the usual nominal ones throughout Eskimo, e.g. Yupik *maa-ni*
'here,' *maa-ken* 'from here' (for -*ken* [< **kət*], see No. 33.). I believe
first-person *m* survives in the bipersonal forms of the verb suffix -*m-
kən* 'I . . . thee' and -*mta-kən* 'we . . . thee' (Menovshchikov 1964:
82). Similar forms are found generally in the Yupik and Inuit forms
of Eskimo. This *m* might, however, be the marker of the relative
case, which is also *m*.

In Aleut first-person *m* survives in the affixed plural forms -*mas*
(Central dialect), -*man* (Eastern and Western dialects), and in the
corresponding independent possessive pronouns built by suffixation
on the base *ti*- or *txi*-, e.g. *ti-man* in Unalaska, an Eastern dialect.
Just as in Eskimo, there is a demonstrative **ma* meaning 'here,
where I am.' Marsh and Swadesh (1951), in etymology No. 123,
compare Aleut **wa*, Western Aleut *ma*, with Proto-Eskimo **ma*
'this here.'

As can be seen from the foregoing review of the evidence, -*m* is
found in every branch of the Eurasiatic family except Ainu. Practically without exception all previous comparisons between two or

more branches of Eurasiatic (except, of course, Ainu) have noted first-person *m*. Some of the examples given here are, however, new.

2. First-Person K

Less widely distributed than *m* for the first-person singular is *k*. Wherever they both appear, the general contrast is *m* as ergative versus absolutive *k*, *m* as active versus middle or passive *k*, and *m* as active versus stative *k*. I am inclined to believe that this last contrast is the basic one from which the others developed. A contrast of this kind between *m* and *k* seems to be attested only in the first-person singular.

In Chapter 2 I suggested, as a working hypothesis, that Indo-European **H* ultimately derives from one or more velar stops in many, though perhaps not all, instances. Furthermore, I have not committed myself to a specific number of laryngeals in Proto-Indo-European. In Hittite **H* frequently appears as *x*. Hittite contrasts a -*x-i* conjugation (so-called because of the first-person present active singular ending) with a conjugation in -*m-i*. Luwian, another Anatolian language, has the first-person singular active preterite in -*x-a*, which, according to Annalies Kammenhuber (1969: 320), is the predecessor of -*x-i* and corresponds exactly to the first-person perfect reconstructed for Indo-European as **-Ha*. The perfect is originally stative and cannot take an object. An example is the widespread form of the root for 'see' in the perfect, e.g. Greek *oîda* 'I know,' i.e. 'I have seen and am now in the state of knowing.' The identification of the Hittite -*x-i* conjugation and the Indo-European perfect first became current as a result of Kuryłowicz's treatment (1932) and is now generally accepted. The stative *k*- possibly survives in the hitherto enigmatic perfects: Tocharian A (preterite active) *tākā* 'I was,' Latin *fēcī* 'I made,' Greek *éthēka* 'I put.'

In Uralic, Hungarian also has two conjugational classes, called the subjective and the objective. The first has -*k* in the first-person singular present and its membership is exclusively intransitive. Verbs in the objective conjugational class have both -*k* and -*m* in the first-person singular, the former with an indefinite object and the latter with a definite object. In the third-person singular the subjective conjugation has zero, whereas the objective has an overt ending. This is a typological characteristic found in many languages; statives have zero third-person subjects, while actives have an overt third-person marker.

The Hungarian distinction between a subjective conjugation in -k and an objective conjugation in -m is found elsewhere in Uralic, namely, in Selkup Samoyed, which also has zero for the third-person singular in the subjective and an overt third-person singular -t (see No. 11) in the objective conjugation. In Selkup the subjective conjugation is not only characteristic of intransitive verbs, but may also be used to predicate adjectives and nouns, e.g. *kum-ak* 'I am a man.' It is therefore a true stative. The -k first-person singular also possibly survives in the Permian languages of the Finnic subgroup of Finno-Ugric in the negative verb, e.g. Komi-Zyrian *o-g* 'I am not,' *e-g* 'I was not, and Udmurt *u-g* 'I am not.' The relation of these forms to Hungarian -k was already noted by Budenz (1879: 32–34). The reconstruction for Uralic proposed here coincides exactly with the conclusions of Khelimskij (1982: 81), which was based on a comparison of Hungarian and Samoyed. See also Kerns (1967: 40). As usual there are attempts to explain the -k internally and, as is so often the case, by an implausible semantic hypothesis. Thus, the -k of the first-person subject in Hungarian is connected with the -k plural of that language. This is rejected as improbable by Samu Imré (1988). The identification of the Hittite -xi and -mi conjugations with the subjective and objective conjugations of Hungarian was made by Bernhard Rosenkranz (1950), who also mentions the Selkup forms.

The only evidence for -ku in Altaic occurs in Tungus, where we find -ku in a special "destinative" case found only in the possessed noun declension. In the Ulch dialect of Lamut the form is -ya-ku, as in, for example, æ-ya-ku 'this-for-me' (Novikova 1960: 61).

For Chukotian, Bogoras (1922: 736) reconstructs a set of suffixes for the intransitive verb with -k as first-person singular and zero as third-person singular. These languages have, in addition, prefixes in some of the forms, used simultaneously with members of the set of suffixes reconstructed by Bogoras. These forms in k are found in all the Chukotian languages.

In Eskimo, the contrast between an ergative -m versus an absolutive -k as first-person singular is shown most obviously by the first-person singular possessive -ma suffixed to nouns that are the subject of transitive verbs as against -ka suffixed to nouns that are the object of transitive or the subject of intransitive verbs.

There are many points of contact between the nominal posses-sive suffixes and the verb subject suffixes in Eskimo. In the first person singular of intransitive verbs the subject is marked by -ŋa (< *ka). There is, as has been noted in Chapter 2, constant al-ternation between non-nasal and the corresponding nasal stops in Eskimo and elsewhere in Eurasiatic. That in this instance -ŋ really does originate in -k is shown by the first-person dual and plural in-transitive subject affixes -kuk and -kut, respectively. In these forms the final consonants are dual/plural -k (see No. 14) and plural -t (see No. 15).

In addition, Sirenik, which deviates in many ways from the rest of Eskimo, displays additional evidence for -k as first-person intran-sitive in -k-i, which is used to indicate the first-person plural subject of intransitive verbs and the object of transitive verbs. The -i here is a very common plural indicator in Eurasiatic (see No. 16). Uhlen-beck (1907: 18) concludes that the original form of the first-person singular possessor is -ka.

The first-person singular independent pronoun appears in the nominative-accusative as wa-ŋa, where -ŋa is the usual first-person singular possessive affix (cf. second-person singular possessive -t in the Greenlandic second-person singular independent pronoun ilvit, with cognate forms in the rest of Eskimo.). However, this wa- may well derive from kwa. In his dictionary of Alaskan Yupik, Jacobson (1984: 635) cites the vocabulary of Orlov-Pinart, published in 1871, as having kwiinga 'I' instead of wii or wiinga and says that the form in initial kw- still survives in Nunivak (Fortescue et al. 1994: 383). In Ekogmiut, a southwestern Alaska dialect reported in Dall (1897: 539) we find hwik 'I' and Chugach kū-ih. According to Shimkin (1960) the first-person pronoun on Kodiak is xvi. In addition, in Siberian Yupik the Chaplino dialect has xwaŋa 'I.' The original form may well have been *kwa-ŋa. The interpretation of -ŋa as merely the suffixed first-person singular possessive is strengthened by the Yupik form without -ŋa just cited. Note also that the root in the first-person dual and plural in Alaskan Yupik is wa- (not wi), e.g. waŋkuk 'we two,' thus agreeing with the vowel elsewhere in Eskimo.

In Aleut the first person singular suffixed verb subject is -ŋ, to be identified with the Eskimo -ŋa mentioned earlier. In Aleut the verb does not mark the person of the object in transitive verbs as part of the verbal pronominal complex, but rather by a separate preposition. Hence the intransitive -ŋa (< *ka) has been generalized to all verbs. We also find first-person -ŋ in the independent possessive pronoun ti-ŋ, in which the base is ti-. In Aleut, as noted in No. 1, m as first person survives only in the first-person plurals -mas or -man, which are dialect variants. Marsh and Swadesh (1951) reconstruct Proto-Eskimo-Aleut *-ŋa, leading to Eskimo -ŋa and Aleut -ŋ. It is possible that Ainu ku 'I' belongs here.

Of the comparisons made here we have already observed that between Indo-European and Uralic in Rosenkranz (1950). Knut Bergsland (1959: 14) notes that Uhlenbeck and Sauvageot, in seeking to demonstrate the relationship between Uralic and Eskimo, stressed especially the similarity between the intransitive and transitive conjugation of the Eskimo verb and the subjective and objective conjugations of Hungarian and Samoyed.

The Eskimo evidence for -u as the final vowel (*ku) strongly suggests the ultimate identity of this first-person marker with the near demonstrative ku (see No. 10).

3. First-Person N

A much rarer first-person pronoun than either of the foregoing is -n. Ainu en, a first-person singular object pronoun, may perhaps be compared with the Korean first-person singular pronoun na. Gilyak has a first-person dual imperative ni-te, plural ni-kta, and an independent first-person singular pronoun ńi. A first-person n also occurs in Turkic *-(a)yin, a verbal hortatory form. Kissling notes that Turkish had an earlier first-person singular aorist -maz-in ~ mez-in and a positive aorist -ir-in (Kissling 1960: 82, 101). We may perhaps also compare the Indo-European first-person dual and plural pronouns in n, e.g. Latin nōs 'we,' Greek nố 'we two.' It has been suggested, however, that the Indo-European forms in n- are secondary, arising from *ns-mes < mes-mes with ns-mes subsequently reanalyzed as *n + *-sme (a common emphatic pronominal particle) + s (plural); see Szemerényi (1978: 281) for discussion and further references.

4. Second-Person T

The most widely found second-person marker in Eurasiatic is *t*, only rivalled by *s* (see No. 5). Pokorny (1959: 1097) reconstructs the following as stems of the second-person singular pronoun in Proto-Indo-European: *tŭ-, teu̯o-, teu̯e-, tu̯o, tu̯e, te*. The only parallel to the *-u* and *-u̯* of the Indo-European stem is found in Chukotian, as discussed below.

In the verb, *-te* is the second-person plural ending in the active of the present and aorist system and the usual reconstruction for the second-person singular is **-tHa*. Corresponding to this Hittite has *-ti* in the present active of the *-xi* conjugation and *-ta* in the preterite. Tokharian has generalized *-t* as second-person singular active throughout the verbal system.

The frequent Eurasiatic combination of second-person *t* and dual *k* (see No. 14) in the form *tVk*, paralleling *mVk* in the first-person dual (also frequently plural), perhaps survives within Indo-European in the Armenian second-person plural independent pronoun *duk'* and in the verbal suffix *-ajk'* < **-atk'*. Pisani (1976) identifies the Armenian forms with comparable ones in Uralic.

In Uralic the basic second-person marker is also *t*. The second-person singular independent pronoun in Finnish is *sinä* (< **tina*; cf. *minä* 'I') and in Hungarian we find *të* 'thou,' *ti* 'you.' Evidence for the second-person *t* can be found in virtually every Uralic language. In the verb the second-person subject suffix is reconstructed as **-t* in the singular and as **-tek* in the plural, with parallel forms for the nominal possessive. For second-person *n*, which is particularly common in Ob-Ugric as a possible variant of *t*, see No. 6 and the discussion in Chapter 2.

In Yukaghir the second-person independent pronouns are *tet* 'thou' and *tit* 'you' (cf. *met* 'I,' *mit* 'we'). A possessive suffix paradigm probably once existed in Yukaghir. It was noted in No. 1 that *-m* 'my' is attested in the extinct Omok dialect. In addition, Collinder (1940: 11) noted in Jochelson's texts the Kolyma form *numo-ge-t* 'house-in-thy' and, as its equivalent, *nima-ɣa-t* in the Tundra version of the same text. The context makes clear that *-get/-ɣat* cannot be the ablative, but rather locative *-ge-/-ɣa-* followed by second-person *-t*.

In Altaic the most common second-person marker is *s* (see No. 5). However, the Mongolian branch has *t*, as seen in Classical Mongolian *či* (< **ti*) 'thou' and *ta* 'you.' The second-person *t* is quite probably found in the Tungus forms for the first-person plural inclusive, which may be posited as Proto-Tungus **mi-ti*, that is, first-person *mi* and second-person *ti* (see the discussion in Chapter 1). Among the forms to be reckoned as belonging here are Literary Evenki *mi-ti*, Solon *mi-ti*, Xunke Orochon *mi-tii*, and Negidal *bit* (Li 1996: 15–16). Typologically the usual situation is one in which the exclusive first-person plural is the plural of 'I' or a separate form, whereas the inclusive form is frequently a compound of the first-person singular and second-person singular or plural (cf. Melanesian Pidgin *yu-mi* 'we inclusive')

The same combination as in Tungus is seen in the Mongolian first-person plural inclusive pronoun *bi-da*, except that -*da* probably derives from the second-person plural pronoun *ta*, rather than from the singular. The interpretation presented here of the first-person plural pronouns as containing first-person *m*- and second-person *t*- was earlier proposed by Menges (1952: 99). (See also Ramstedt 1904).

The Gilyak second-person singular pronoun *či* probably belongs with No. 5 rather than here for reasons set forth in that section. However, a form *ti* is reported in Grube (1892: 125) as having been recorded by Seeland at Nikolayevsk, near the mouth of the Amur. Perhaps both *ti* and *si* existed in Gilyak.

In Chukotian, *t* is the basic second-person exponent found in the Chukchi second-person singular independent pronoun *ɣət* and its predicative form -*iɣət* ∼ -*eɣət*, with which we may compare the first-person singular forms listed in No. 1. The same *t* is found in the Chukchi plural form *tu-ri* 'you' (cf. *mu-ri* 'we'). In addition the second-person plural of verbs has -*tək* as subject marker with the originally dual -*k*. This form is obviously cognate with Uralic -*tek* in the same function.

Chukotian is the only subfamily of Eurasiatic, except for Indo-European, to have *tu* as the second-person pronoun. This is seen clearly in Ukä, the extinct Northeastern dialect of Kamchadal that is reported in Klaproth (1823) to have *tu* as the second-person singular pronoun. In Radliński's (1891-94) vocabulary of the extinct Eastern dialect, *tue* is cited as the equivalent of Polish *ty* and Latin *tu*. A third occurrence is found in Dall (1897: 552), who published for the first time a vocabulary collected by William Stimpson on the Reingold and Rodgers North Pacific Exploring Expedition (1852–1863). Here we find *tūa* 'thou.' There are thus three independent instances of *tu* as the second-person singular pronoun in Chukotian. It is moreover presupposed by the Chukchi second-person plural (nominative) *tu-ri*. This *u* vowel also appears in the plurals *buze* 'we' and *suze* 'you' of Eastern Kamchadal. Contemporary (Western) Kamchadal has *kəzza* 'thou' (cf. *kəmma* 'I'). However, *u* is found in the plurals *muza(ʔn)* 'we,' *tuza(ʔn)* 'you,' which show an optional affixation of the nominal plural *-ʔn*. These forms may be compared to Chukchi *mu-ri* 'we,' *tu-ri* 'you,' the latter of which was cited above. It would appear that in view of the appearance of *u* in Eastern and Northeastern Kamchadal and Chukchi only in second-person singular forms, it must have originated there and spread to Chukchi *tu-ri* 'you (plural),' and later to *mu-ri* 'we' with corresponding forms in Koryak. It thus presents a striking agreement between Chukotian and Indo-European.

In Eskimo, *-t* (in western dialects *-n* < *-t*) is the second-person singular possessive, with dual possessive *-tik* and plural *-tit* (western *-tin* < *tit*). Similar forms are found as subject markers in the indicative of intransitive verbs, second-person singular *-tit* (final *-t* is of uncertain origin) and dual *-tik*. For *-t* in the Eskimo second-person singular object form *-kit* in the combination *-am-kət* (first person acts on second-person singular), probably cognate with Chukchi *yət* (see No. 7). The interrogative shows the expected second-person singular *-t*.

Aleut second-person singular *-n* as a possessive and intransitive subject corresponds regularly to Eskimo *t*. Aleut also has *-ðix* (< *tik* ?) as second-person dual possessor and as intransitive verb subject. Marsh and Swadesh (1951) equate Aleut *n* and Eskimo *t* and reconstruct *t*.

There is thus a five-way agreement between Armenian, Uralic, Chukchi, Eskimo, and Aleut in a form *-tik* indicating second-person dual or plural. The interrelations of the dual and plural meanings of *-k* are discussed in No. 14.

As with No. 1 (first-person *m*), it is unnecessary to cite previous observations in the literature since second-person *t* has figured in all previous comparisons of branches of Eurasiatic in which it is present.

5. Second-Person S

The second most widely distributed second-person singular pronoun is *s*. In Indo-European it occurs as subject in the present-aorist system both in thematic and athematic verbs. Examples from Sanskrit are *bhar-a-si* 'you (singular) carry' (thematic) and *at-si* 'you (singular) eat' (athematic). Since second-person singular *t* appears in the perfect and is basically stative, and since the contrast appears clearly in Hittite with present -*ti* in the -*xi* conjugation as against -*si* in the -*mi* conjugation, it might be hypothesized that we have here a contrast like that of the first-person singular active *m* versus stative *k*, i.e. $m : k = s : t$. However, I have found no support for this outside of Indo-European.

In two of the three branches of Altaic, Turkic and Tungus, the basic second-person marker is *s*, contrasting with the *t* of Mongolian. For non-Chuvash Turkic the second-person singular pronoun in the nominative may be reconstructed as **sen* ~ **sin* with so-called pronominal -*n* (see Nos. 1 and 25). The variation here is not vowel harmonic since in Turkic vowel harmony alternants are based on back versus front articulation. Rather there is variation across languages in the *e* ~ *i* alternation that we discussed in Chapter 2. The non-Chuvash Turkic plural is **siz* ($< *sir_2 < *siri$; cf. the first-person Turkic plurals discussed in No. 1). In Chuvash, *n* is only found in the oblique cases, the nominative singular being *e-sĕ* (cf. first-person singular *e-pĕ* in No. 1).

For Proto-Tungus Benzing (1955) reconstructs the second-person singular nominative as **si*. It is probable that the Manchu first-person plural inclusive, *mu-se*, is to be analyzed as first-person *mu* + second-person *se*. In this regard we should recall the discussion of Proto-Tungus first-person inclusive **mi-ti* in No. 4.

The Korean verb has a polite honorific -*si*- used when referring to an honored person including the addressee (Ramstedt 1939: 31; Pultr 1960: 46). It was already equated by Heinrich Koppelman (1928: 214) in his comparison of Indo-European and Korean with

Indo-European -s. However, further analysis indicates that si was perhaps originally second-person plural (s + i [plural]; see No. 16). The same combination -si for the second-person plural occurs in Eskimo and Aleut (and possibly in Southern Kamchadal), where it is clearly to be analyzed in this way. Thus an original second-person plural would, in Korean, have assumed honorific functions, whereas, as will be seen in the following section, an original second-person singular would be the source of the present Korean non-honorific second-person pronoun. Such an evolutionary path is, of course, in agreement with what we know about the development of politeness forms in other languages (e.g. French).

There is an Old Japanese second-person pronoun si (Miller 1971: 159) limited in its use to conditional or contingent sentences. Miller posits the proportion mi : wanu 'first person' = si : söne 'second person.' However, even in the earliest texts söne has assumed a demonstrative function and the variant sono 'that' has become the basis for the modern second-person pronoun. See No. 12 for further discussion of the relationship between person deixis and personal pronouns.

In addition, Old Japanese had a respectful honorific in -s(u) in a large number of verbs, e.g. ki-r(u) 'wear,' ke-s(u) 'wear' (honorific). In its conjugation it is distinct from the causative -s(u) (Komai 1979: 33; see No. 50) and is a point of resemblance between Japanese and Korean.

The Gilyak second-person singular pronoun či probably belongs here since in the consonant alternation series č is related to s and not to t. However, Grube (1892: 125) reports the dialect variant ti recorded by Seeland at Nikolayevsk, near the mouth of the Amur. Whether Gilyak či derives from *ti or *si requires further investigation. As discussed in Chapter 2, these two series show considerable interdialectal alternation in Gilyak and may ultimately have a common origin.

A second-person s is found in Kamchadal, the most divergent member of the Chukotian group, in the second-person plural verb inflection and in the vocative plural -sx, which is obviously the same item. The -x is possibly to be analyzed as a reflex of the dual/plural k (see No. 14).

In the extinct Eastern dialect of Kamchadal (Radliński 1891–94) the independent second-person plural pronoun, nominative-accusative, is given as *suze* (compared to modern Western *tuza*) and in the Southern dialect (also extinct) *si* is glossed as Polish *ciebie,* Latin *te* 'thee' as compared with *kiz* for the nominative singular *ty/tu.* Since, however, in this area second-person plurals are often used as politeness forms, Southern Kamchadal *si* 'thee' may very well be a second-person plural to be analyzed as *s-* (second person) + *-i* (plural). If this is so, then we would have an agreement in this form among Southern Kamchadal, Korean, and Eskimo. Eastern Kamchadal *su-ze* 'you' (cited above) contrasts with *tue* 'thou' in the same dialect and the base *su-* reminds us once more of the Eskimo and Korean second-person plural pronouns in *s-.* For plural *-ze,* see No. 17.

In Eskimo the second-person plural subject affix of intransitive verbs is *-si,* also used as a possessive on nouns. As noted above in the discussion of the corresponding form in Korean, this is to be analyzed as second-person *s* + plural *i.* A cognate form in Aleut is written by Veniaminov as *-ci.* This *c* is described by Jochelson (1912) as a medial (i.e. mid-palatal) unvoiced affricate (probably *č*). The correspondence of this Aleut sound before *i* to Eskimo *s* was pointed out by Bergsland (1956).

6. Second-Person N

There is a second-person *n* common to Japanese and Korean, as was first pointed out by William Aston (1879: 329). He compared Japanese *na* with Korean *nə.* Japanese *na* occurs in the earliest Japanese document, the Kojiki (early eighth century), and, in his dictionary of classical Japanese, Ivan Morris (1966) glosses *na* as 'thou, you.' Martin, Lee, and Chang (1967: 329) report that the Korean form is used with children and inferiors. Compare this with the Korean honorific *si* (No. 5), which, on comparative grounds, is probably a plural.

A second-person *n-* also occurs in Uralic—mainly, but not exclusively, in Ob-Ugric—and has been extensively discussed. The question is whether, alongside the widespread second-person **t-* (see No. 4), a Uralic form in **n-* also existed and whether, if it did, it was merely a variant of **t-* under conditions that have so far resisted specification. The basic facts concerning Uralic second-person *n* are given in Chapter 2 in the context of a widespread Eurasiatic alternation between nasal and non-nasal consonants. Whatever the explanation of Uralic second-person *n*, I do not believe that it is historically connected with the Japanese and Korean pronouns.

7. Pronoun Base GE

In this section we will consider a morpheme of the general form *ge ~ ga*, which always appears in bound form in association with pronouns, particularly the first- and/or second-person singular. Its original meaning, which we may as an initial hypothesis characterize as a copula, will become clearer in the course of the discussion.

Consider first the nominative case of the first-person singular pronoun in Indo-European, usually reconstructed as **eĝ(h)om*. (The reason for the parentheses around the *h* is that Sanskrit irregularly shows an aspirate that is not reflected in the other Indo-European languages.) It is in suppletive alternation with *m-* in the other cases. There are also forms without final *-m*, e.g. Latin *egō* (an early form, later shortened to *ego* by the iambic shortening law), Greek *egó*, alongside of *egón*, whose final *-n* derives from **-m*. The forms without the final *-m* were early explained as analogical with the *-ō* of the first-person present active of the thematic verb conjugation (Schmidt 1899: 405) and this explanation has been fairly generally accepted (e.g. Brugmann and Delbrück 1897–1916, II: 71, Pokorny 1959: 159). However, **eĝ(h)om* itself was usually analyzed as containing an initial deictic *e-* and the final *-om* was interpreted, for example by Brugmann, as a neuter ending with abstract meaning. Thus Brugmann translates the form as a whole as "Meine Hierheit," literally 'my hereness,' but he also talks of the problem as leading us into the abysses of Proto-Indo-European, where we can only find our way by groping. Brugmann also says that the identification of the initial *e-* with the deictic element found, for example, in Greek *e-keînos* 'that,' alongside of *keînos*, is well worth considering.

More recently Savchenko's suggestion (1960) that the final *-m* of **eĝ(h)om* is to be identified with the common first-person singular pronoun *m* (No. 1), which is found also in the oblique cases of 'I,' has received support from Myrkin (1964) and is accepted in the standard comparative work of Szemerényi (1996: 216). However, these more recent interpretations, though they identify -*m* as the first-person singular marker, consider the form as a whole to be a late formation within Indo-European. They suppose that the mark of the first person is -*ĝ(h)*- or *eĝ(h)*- and that -*m* has been added redundantly.

The most important Eurasiatic evidence on this question comes from the Chukotian group. In Chukchi itself the first-person form is -*iyəm* ~ -*eyəm*, in which *i* ~ *e* is a vowel harmonic alternation. The corresponding second-person singular is -*iyət* ~ -*eyət*. This pattern is only found in the first- and second-person singular.

The existence of these Chukotian forms obviously strengthens the case of Indo-European -*m* being the first-person singular pronominal form. However, they also suggest, contrary to Savchenko and others, that the form itself is very old since it has correspondences in Chukchi and, as we shall see, elsewhere in Eurasiatic.

Thus far I have cited only Chukchi forms which contain an initial *i* ~ *e*. These are treated in Chukchi grammars as basically markers of person on the noun (i.e. 'I being a man'), but they also have important predicative uses, as, for example, in *ənpənačy-iyəm* 'I am an old man' (literally, 'An old man-I'). The same form also occurs, as would be expected, in stative forms of the verb, e.g. *ye-čejv-iyəm* 'I am gone.' In this construction the prefix *ye*- expresses perfectivity (see No. 34). The second main use of the "predicative" form is as an object suffix following a first-person subject suffix in the verb complex.

In addition to -*iyəm* ~ -*eyəm* there are shorter forms, *yəm* 'I' and *yət* 'thou,' which are independent pronouns. The contrast in Chukotian of forms with and without the initial vowel obviously supports Brugmann's conjecture that the initial vowel is a separate element and its function as a predicator in Chukotian is a plausible one for a deictic. For a typological parallel compare the Coptic enclitic demonstrative *pe* (masculine singular), *te* (feminine singular), *ne* (plural), which is also employed as a copula. However, in accordance with the widespread Eurasiatic alternation of final nasals and stops, as discussed in Chapter 2, modern (Western) Kamchadal may have been an *N* language. Compare also the plural -*ʔn* of Western Kamchadal (No. 15) with the non-nasal stop plurals in the same form in the extinct Eastern and Southern dialects and even in the northern subdialect of Western Kamchadal spoken at Sedanka.

Specialists in Chukotian always reconstruct the first- and second-person singular pronouns of Chukotian as *gəm and *gət and consider the dependent form as having a connecting vowel or deriving from the copula. However, this vowel does not appear in the plural, which never have -i-muri or -i-turi. This restriction to the first- and second-person singular (which probably started with the first-person singular, to which it is confined in Indo-European) is thus in agreement with the other Eurasiatic evidence. Furthermore, that igəm was not always bound is strongly suggested by the form ichem in Dall (1897), based on material from the Reingold and Roger's expedition in the 1850's, since it was elicited in isolation and could therefore not have been preceded by anything.

A further use of the short form in all the Chuckchi-Koryak languages (the major subgroup of Chukotian, from which Kamchadal stands somewhat apart) is as the bipersonal object pronominal markers of the transitive verb. Here -gət is suffixed to denote second-person singular object with first- or third-person singular or plural subjects. Examples from Chukchi are tə-l'u-gət 'I saw thee'; ne-l'u-gət 'they saw thee.' First-person -gəm as object only occurs with a third-person plural pronoun, e.g. Chukchi ne-l'u-gəm 'they see me.' In Kamchadal -gən- is employed as a second-person singular object in a manner parallel to that of Chukchi-Koryak, e.g. ańči-yən 'he teaches thee.' Whether the final -n of Kamchadal corresponds to -t of Chukchi-Koryak is uncertain, but it may be the n variant of the t ~ n alternation discussed in Chapter 2. The form cited is from Western Kamchadal, the only surviving dialect. This dialect has an independent first-person pronoun kəmma, corresponding to Chukchi yəm. Here, as almost everywhere in Chukotian, the oblique case forms of the first- (and second-) person pronouns are built on nominatives such as yəm, kəmma (e.g. Western Kamchadal locative kəmma-nk). However, in the extinct Southern Kamchadal dialect, the Indo-European suppletion between eĝ(h)om and m- forms recurs. This evidence is found in Radliński's publication of Dybowski's material on Southern Kamchadal (1891–94, Part III), in which kim (cf. Western Kamchadal kəmma) is glossed as ja and ego in Polish and Latin, whereas ma is translated as mnię and me, the latter form the same as English 'me.' This is the only known non-Indo-European instance of this irregular suppletion.

The Chukchi use of -yət as a second-person singular object has a striking parallel in Eskimo. The bipersonal form of transitive verbs ("I . . . thee"), which is found in all Eskimo dialects, can probably be reconstructed as *-m-kət. This form was described as irregular by Uhlenbeck (1907) in his survey of Eskimo morphology. Almost all dialects have extended this form analogically with additional markers to designate action by first-person dual and first-person plural on a second-person singular object. What is irregular about Eskimo—and cannot be explained internally—is the medial -k-. Hence m- indicates first-person singular and t-, second-person singular. The -k- of *-m-kət corresponds exactly to Chukotian -g- in -gət. In some forms of Eskimo, *-m-kət has been extended to the first-person dual and even to the first-person plural acting on second-person singular. It is possible here that m is rather Eskimo subjective m rather than first person, but even the deviant Sirenik dialect has these forms, i.e. -mkən < *-mkət 'I . . . thee' and -mtəkən < *-mtəkət 'we . . . thee.'

The remaining evidence is from Uralic. In Hungarian there is an independent accusative pronoun that, in the first-person singular, has the variants engem and engemet. Similarly in the second-person singular we find téged and tégedet. The same structure has been posited for the first- and second-person plural pronouns because, between vowels, Proto-Uralic *k > y > zero in Hungarian. Thus the second-person plural ti-tek-et would arise from ti-ti(ki)tek-et (Khelimskij 1982: 94).

The analysis of the first- and second-person singular is clear. The facultative final -et is simply the nominal accusative singular that has been added analogically and is not yet established. The initial morphemes en- and té- are the independent pronouns én and te. This leaves us with -gem- and -get-, which correspond exactly with the Chukchi independent pronouns yəm and yət. As in Chukchi the forms without initial vowel are used independently.

The Hungarian pronouns we have been discussing are related to the emphatic pronouns of Vogul, a member of the Ob-Ugric branch of Finno-Ugric. An example is am-kkem 'I alone' from the Middle Sosvin dialect. The analysis is once again clear, with the initial element am- identical to the first-person singular independent pronoun and the remainder, -kkem, cognate with Hungarian -gem-. The geminate *k* in the Vogul form is historically secondary. Edith Vértes (1967: 214) connects the Vogul and Hungarian forms.

A similar structure occurs in Samoyed languages such as Kamassian, Enets, and Yurak, thus assuring us that this formation is Proto-Uralic. Once again we have independent accusative pronouns formed in the same manner, e.g. Selkup (Tāz) *šim* (or *mašim*) 'I,' where *š* is the regular reflex of Proto-Uralic **k* before front vowels (Khelimskij 1982: 91). A final bit of evidence comes from Kamassian, in which there is a suppletive stem of the verb 'to be' that only occurs in the present, e.g. *i-gä-m* 'I am.' The stem is conjugated for all persons and numbers. If the Kamassian form belongs here, it provides further evidence that the initial vowel is characteristic of the predicative.

On the basis of the foregoing evidence, the most probable conclusion is that the formation we have been discussing was original in the first- and second-person singular, as in Hungarian and possibly Chukotian. Indo-European, nevertheless, raises the possibility that it was original only in the first-person singular. However, if Khelimski is right in his reconstructions of the first- and second-person plurals in Hungarian, Ob-Ugric, and Samoyed, then the original formation was found in all non-third person forms and was only later restricted to the singular.

The entire form, with the initial vowel found in Indo-European and Chukotian, may then be interpreted as *e-ĝhe/a-m*, an emphatic focusing *e-* 'that' (No. 9), + *ĝhe* ~ *ĝha* 'am,' + *-m* 'I' (No. 1). However, the interpretation of initial *e-* as an instance of the near demonstrative *i* ~ *e* (No. 8) rather than the far demonstrative (No. 9) accords better with the Chukotian vowel variation *i* ~ *e*. Moreover, the identification with the closer demonstrative of No. 8 is semantically more plausible for a first-person pronoun. The identification with No. 9 rests on the widespread use of the latter as a deictic prefix on demonstratives and pronouns otherwise unattested for No. 8.

8. Third-Person I ~ E

A common Eurasiatic third-person singular pronoun is *i* ~ *e*. It evidently originates from a near demonstrative, but its anaphoric function is so widespread that it perhaps already was both demonstrative and anaphoric in Proto-Eurasiatic. The alternation *i ~ e* is one we have already encountered in Nos. 1, 5, and 7 and which we will find elsewhere.

A further development occurs in some languages where, when affixed to a verb, it transitivizes it. This is a typological development similar to what occurs in many English-based pidgins in which, for example, 'hit 'em' (< 'hit him') means simply 'hit' and the *m* is employed quite generally as a marker of transitivity. Verbal transitivizers are also frequently used as denominatives, forming verbs from nouns without the resulting verb necessarily being transitive. The transitivizing and nominalizing uses are treated separately in section 8.2, whereas *i ~ e* as a demonstrative and/or anaphoric pronoun is discussed in section 8.1.

8.1. Pronoun/Demonstrative.   In Indo-European there is a demonstrative that has first-person deixis, e.g. Sanskrit *iy(ám)* 'this,' or is a demonstrative unmarked for person deixis that also functions as an anaphoric pronoun, e.g. Latin *i(-s)*, or finally may function purely anaphorically, e.g. Gothic *i(-s)*. It is reconstructed for Proto-Indo-European as having two stem alternants, *i* and *e* (Szemerényi 1978: 209). For example, whereas the neuter nominative and accusative singular is reconstructed as **i(-d)*, the genitive masculine and neuter is reconstructed as **e(-syo)*. The demonstrative use survives also in many Indo-European languages in adverbs, e.g. Latin *i-bī* 'there,' Sanskrit *i-ha* 'here.' The Lydian enclitic personal pronoun *-i(-s)* perhaps belongs here also, although Gusmani believes it derives secondarily from *-a-* (Gusmani 1964: 40, 129).

Uralic has a near demonstrative that likewise shows variant forms in *e* and *i*. This can be illustrated by Hungarian *e-(z)* 'this' (cf. *a-z* 'that'), but *i-(tt)* means 'here' and there is a variant dialect form of the latter: *e-(tt)*. Collinder (1965a: 56–57) not only connects the Indo-European forms with the Uralic forms, but also cites the similar vowel alternations as supporting evidence.

All three branches of Altaic concur in **i* as the third-person singular pronoun. In Turkic it only survives in the form *-i ~ i* (vowel harmony variants) suffixed as a third-person singular possessive to nouns that end in a consonant. It alternates with *-si ~ si* after a vowel (see No. 12.). In Turkic, as in Indo-European, it often sur-

vives in adverbs with near deixis, e.g. Sagai *i-dä* 'here,' which may
be directly comparable to Sanskrit *i-ha* 'here' (< **i-dha*; for *da* see
No. 32). That both *i* and *si* in Turkic were originally independent
pronouns, whose bound possessive status is recent, is shown by the
fact that in Old Turkish they are not subject to vowel harmony
(Tekin 1968: 172) and in Chuvash *ĕ* (< **i*) and *šĕ* (< **si*) likewise do not harmonize (Levitskaja 1976: 15). According to Menges
(1968: 114), *si* is a pleonasm of *s* + *i* (see No. 12). As noted by
Serebrennikov and Gazhdieva (1986: 101), the original demonstrative meaning of the third-person possessive alternants appears in the
use of *-i* and *-si* as a definite article in Turkic languages, especially
Chuvash.

In Mongolian it occurs in the independent third-person singular
pronoun, but only in the oblique cases, e.g. Classical Mongolian *i-*
mada 'to him/her.' On this basis Mongolicists reconstruct **i* and
assume that it formerly existed in the nominative. Mongolian also
furnishes evidence for the variant in *e-* in the verb 'to do this,' Classical Mongolian *e-ji* (Poppe 1964: 66), with which we may compare
in the same language *te-ji* 'to act in that manner' and *je-ji* 'to do
what?' For the initial elements of these formations see Nos. 11 and
61. Mongolian provides further evidence for *e* in *e-ne* 'this' (plural
e-de).

The situation in Tungus is similar to that in Mongolian in that
i does not usually survive in the nominative. However, Manchu is
an exception and maintains *i* as the nominative form of the third-
person pronoun. The form with the vowel alternant *e* rather than
i is found in the demonstrative **e(-ri)* (Benzing 1955: 1061). For
-ri see No. 13. Although oblique inflections are usually added to
the stem *eri*, such forms as Evenki *e-duk* (dative) and *e-lī* (locative)
show that the true stem is *e-* (Menges 1968). Similarly *e-* functions
as a base in adverbs of place, e.g. Evenki *e-le* 'here,' Negidal *e-lē*
'hither.'

In Ainu *i* appears before nouns as the third-person singular possessive, and before verbs as the third-person singular object. Hattori
(1964: 310) cites Ainu *e-ne* 'thus, in this way,' in which *ne* means
'manner, form' and the proposed *e-* produces the meaning 'in *this*
manner.' The use of *i-* as a transitivizer, along with the variant *e-*,
will be discussed in 8.2. Ainu *i-ne* 'which?' can probably be analyzed

as demonstrative *i* followed by interrogative *-ne.* For a similar analysis see Shibatani (1990: 46–47). The form *i-ne* 'where?,' discussed in No. 30, is probably a homonym.

In Korean the near demonstrative 'this' is *i* and it precedes the noun it modifies. It also survives in the adverb *i-mi* 'now' (for *-mi* see No. 27). The case marker *-i* of the nominative, which occurs after consonants and alternates with *-ka* after vowels, has been considered by some to come from the same demonstrative source. Ramstedt (1939: 36–37, following Kanazawa 1910) asserts that though it is called a nominative in grammars, it is really the near demonstrative *i.* Thus *čip-i* may be translated as 'the house' (Ramstedt 1939: 39). Moreover, there are instances, also noted by Ramstedt, in which there are variant forms of the same word with and without *-i*, e.g. *palgu, palgui* 'sledge.' As pointed out in Greenberg (1978), this phenomenon is characteristic of articles in a late stage of their development.

The development of the demonstrative *i* in Korean into a nominative case marker, which seems to be generally accepted, strengthens the case for a similar development of the *i* demonstrative into a nominative singular common gender in Indo-European interrogatives, relatives, and demonstratives. It occurs in the Latin relative pronoun *quī* ($<$ **quo-i*) (masculine singular), *quae* ($<$ **qua-i*) (feminine singular), and in other languages of the Italic branch, e.g. Oscan *pui, pai.* It also occurs in Celtic (e.g. Welsh *pwy* 'who?'), Germanic, Old Prussian in the Baltic branch, and in Avestan. Brugmann and Delbrück (1897–1916, II: 356) considered it to be Proto-Indo-European in the q^u- stem. This resemblance of Indo-European to Korean was noted by Koppelmann (1933: 67).

In early Japanese there were also frequent final vowel alternations in nouns, particularly between *e* and *a*, but also between *u* and *i* and, far more rarely, between *o* and *i.* The first of the two alternants characteristically appears in a non-compounded form, e.g. Old Japanese *ame* 'heaven, sky' as contrasted with *ama-hire* 'sky shawl,' i.e. 'cloud.' Yoshitake (1930) plausibly derives the alternants in the non-compounded form from that in the compounded form with a suffixed *-i.* Thus in the foregoing example *ame* is derived from *ama + i.* However, his explanation of *-i* as a genitive seems to me unlikely. It is rather the first member of the compound, not the uncompounded form, that should have the -*i*, if indeed it were a genitive. However, Miller (1971: 29) believes it to be a Korean gloss.

A more plausible account would treat the first member as generic and therefore lacking a definiteness marker, whereas the -*i* of the second member would mark the definite that, in its final stages, no longer has a definite interpretation, thus leading to the apparently functionless variation found in Japanese outside of the indefinite form as the initial member of compounds. In this respect also the development of Japanese *i* would be parallel to that of Korean. Numerous examples of these variant forms are found in Chamberlain (1889).

Finally *i* actually survives in its original near demonstrative force in the Japanese adverb *i-ma* 'now.' The second part is also found in Japanese as an independent noun meaning 'a space, an interval of time' (see No. 27).

All dialects of Gilyak have a prefixed *i* ~ *e* (vowel harmony variants) that marks a third-person singular possessor in nouns and a pronominal object in the verb. In the Western Sakhalin dialect (which belongs genetically with those of the Amur), *i*- is used in the absolute case. In the remaining dialects of the Amur group *i*-occurs as the stem in the allative and instrumental cases, as well as with postpositions and adverbs (Panfilov 1962–65, I: 159). For its transitivizing function with verbs and its vowel harmonic variation see the discussion below.

8.2. Transitivizer/Nominalizer. Yukaghir has a causative in -*i*, one example of which, in the Tundra dialect, is *law*- 'drink,' *law-i*- 'cause to drink' (Krejnovich 1958: 118). In Gilyak the prefixed object pronoun of the verb (*i* ~ *e*) has come to have a transitivizing function, a development that has its parallel in Ainu, Korean, and perhaps Japanese, as we shall see later. Gilyak is instructive in two regards. Phonologically, the earlier (presumably general) vowel harmonic system based on vowel height survives in this construction as well as in the numeral classifier system, as has been generally recognized. Thus, with the third-person singular object prefix, the alternant *i*-occurs before stems whose vowels are *i*, *u*, or *ɨ*, and *e*- before stems in *a*, *o*, or *e*. From a diachronic perspective we find a transitional phase between the normal anaphoric use of an object pronoun and its compulsory use in which it has become simply a marker of transitivity. In this phase the prefixed pronoun is not used when the object is overtly expressed. It retains its anaphoric use when the object has been mentioned in the previous sentence. However, it is also used when an unmentioned indefinite object is involved, as in 'After hunting, X ate and then left again.' In Gilyak the verb 'to eat' would have the object prefix $i \sim e$, which might be paraphrased as 'something.' As is well known (cf. the Romance languages) a demonstrative can develop into an article or into a pronoun. The further stages by which, in the former case, it becomes an indefinite specific article (a stage II article), and finally, in stage III, a meaningless marker on a large number of nouns with either sporadic survival, or preference for certain categories, are discussed in Greenberg (1978). In the Gilyak case we have the equivalent of a stage II article. In Ainu, and less clearly in Japanese, we find evidence that an original demonstrative has developed into a stage III article.

In Korean, *-i* suffixed to a verb has the force of a causative (Koppelmann 1933: 91), e.g. *me-ta* 'to be full,' *mei-ta* 'to fill.' In Gilyak a suffixed *-i* occurs as a denominative in the form *ju* or *ji* (Panfilov 1962–65, II: 14.) Thus, from *la* 'wind' is derived a verb *laju(-d')* 'to blow.'

In Ainu both *e-* and *i-* occur prefixed to verb stems. The former has become a regular and productive derivational morpheme for transitivity. As noted in Batchelor's dictionary of Ainu, "when prefixed to an intransitive verb *e* has the power of changing it to a transitive" (Batchelor 1905). As for *i*, as we saw above, it still functions as an object pronoun. In addition, however, we have instances of variant forms of the verb with and without *i-*. Some of these involve no change in meaning, e.g. *ikem, kem* 'to lick.' In a few cases the form with prefixed *i-* seems to have an intensive meaning, e.g. *komui* 'pick out lice from the head,' *i-komui* 'search for lice.' George Simeon (1968: 55) also reports the use of *i-* as an intensifier, e.g. *nu* 'hear,' *i-nu* 'listen.'

There is, however, one clear example of *i-* as transitivizer: *kusa* 'to ferry across a river' (intransitive), *i-kusa* 'to ferry across a river' (transitive). There is also one instance of suffixed *-i* as a transitivizer in *as* 'to stand' (intransitive), *as-i* 'to set up, cause to stand.' The examples just cited are from Batchelor's dictionary. The more recent grammar of Refsing (1986: 31) notes, regarding *i-*, that "it functions to make intransitives out of transitive ones (sci. verbs) by providing them with an inbuilt object meaning 'somebody or something.'" In the Hokkaido dialect studied by Simeon (1968) -*e* is suffixed to the verb as a transitivizer.

In early Japanese there is a hitherto unexplained variation in a considerable number of verbs between forms with and without a prefixed *i-*. One example is the common verb 'to be' *i-masu, masu*. What we have here is an example parallel to the sporadic survival in Ainu of *i-* without transitivizing force (except for the example of *i-kusa*). An examination of the relevant texts might show, however, some distinction between the two forms parallel to those of Ainu, i.e. *i-* with an intensive or transitivizing function.

There are a few instances of denominative -*i* in the Korean verb (Ramstedt 1952–57, II: 202), for example, *ča* 'a measure,' *čä* < *ča-i* 'to measure.' The numerous Indo-European denominative verbal formations involving suffixed -*j* (e.g. **-j, *-eje-*) remind one of the Gilyak and Ainu forms already mentioned. Noteworthy also is the common Turkic -*aj*, which forms verbs from nouns.

9. Demonstrative A ∼ E

There is a far demonstrative **a-* that alternates with **e-*. In addition to its independent use it is frequently prefixed to other demonstratives to indicate greater distances, and also to both demonstratives and non-demonstratives (e.g. personal pronouns) as a marker of emphasis. Since **e* participates in an alternation with **a*, but also occurs as an alternant in third-person *i ∼ e* (No. 8), this ambiguous situation can lead historically to reinterpretation of *e*, as well as to occasional problems with the *e* variant regarding whether it belongs with the third-person pronoun, or with the demonstrative discussed in this section. Nonetheless, I believe it is generally possible to distinguish them.

In Indo-European, Brugmann (1904: 115) makes a distinction between the *i-* demonstrative of Latin *i-s*, etc. (No. 8) and its **e* variant in the oblique cases that derives from an **e* which typically occurs as a deictic prefixed to other forms, e.g. Sanskrit *a-sau* 'that' (*a* < **e*), Oscan *e-tanto* 'that much,' Latin *e-quidem* 'indeed,' Russian *e-tot* 'this,' Greek *e-keî* 'there,' *e-keînos* 'that, he,' alongside *keînos* with the same meaning, etc.

As we saw in the discussion of Indo-European *e-ĝ(h)om* 'I,' Brugmann also conjectured that it was the same 'deictic *e-*' that we are discussing here. It has also been identified with the 'temporal augment' *e-* that is prefixed to past tenses; this would harmonize well with its presumed fundamental meaning of far deixis.

The second member of the Eurasiatic alternation *e* ~ *a* would be expected to appear as *o* in Indo-European. Both members of the alternation seem to occur in Hittite. On the one hand we have the enclitic third-person pronoun *-a-* and, on the other hand, there is a defective independent pronoun *e-* that only occurs in certain oblique cases. Johannes Friedrich (1960: 68) considers these two forms connected, exhibiting the common Indo-European ablaut alternation **e* ~ **o*, which appears as Hittite *e* ~ *a* since Hittite had no *o*. Kronasser (1956: 144), though apparently not connecting enclitic *-a-* with the independent stem *e-*, does identify the latter with the deictic *e-* seen in Greek *e-keî* 'there.' A combination of Kronasser's and Friedrich's hypotheses would make Indo-European **e* ~ **o*, as attested in Hittite and the other Anatolian languages, a third-person anaphoric pronoun. The most common source for such pronouns is a distance deictic.

In Sanskrit there is a far demonstrative stem *an-* which has the peculiarity that it only occurs in certain oblique cases (Pokorny 1959: 319), for example, *an-éna, an-áyā* (instrumental singular, masculine and feminine) and *an-áyos* (genitive locative dual). Although only a few occurrences are Vedic, its antiquity is assured by its occurrence in Avestan *an-ayå̄* (genitive dual), *an-a* (instrumental singular), *an-āiš* (instrumental plural). Pokorny connects these Indo-Iranian forms with Lithuanian *an-às* 'that,' Old Church Slavic *onŭ* 'he,' and (apparently with reservations) Hittite *ann-iš* 'that,' from which forms he reconstructs Proto-Indo-European **eno* ~ **ono* 'that.' It appears likely that these forms are derived from the *e* ~ *a* distance demonstrative discussed in this section extended by the oblique *n* of ultimate genitive origin. This would explain why in Indo-Iranian it only occurs in oblique cases. In fact, in Vedic forms without the *n-* extension occur (e.g. *a-yā* [feminine instrumental singular], instead of *a-na-yā*). The instrumental masculine singular a-nā, instead of an-enā, has become fossilized as an adverb 'thereby' (Wackernagel and Debrunner 1930, III: 526). In Slavic and elsewhere the oblique n has been analogically extended to the nominative. The original nominative was probably the distance demonstrative exemplified by Latin *ille* (preclassical *olus*; Pokorny 1959: 24), so that we had here an *l/n* stem (see No. 67) with a counterpart in Turkic, discussed below. This helps to reduce the apparently excessive number of demonstratives reconstructed for Proto-Indo-European and, furthermore, the generalization of each member of a suppletive paradigm is a well known phenomenon. The Hittite pronominal forms discussed in the preceding paragraphs are simply the same *e* ~ *a* distance demonstrative without the oblique marker -*n*.

Evidence for *e* ~ *a* as a distance demonstrative is marginal, or perhaps non-existent, in Uralic. As possible support we can cite Hungarian *az* 'that' contrasting with *ez* 'this' (No. 8) and the Komi-Zyrian demonstrative *e-sy*, *e-syja* 'this, that,' which corresponds to Moksha Mordvin *e-sa*. In Komi-Zyrian it contrasts with *sy*, glossed as 'he, this, that.' Although, as we can see, it is unmarked for distance, the *e-* component of *e-sy* does contrast with *sy* and such prefixation to other demonstrative or pronominal markers is characteristic, not only of Indo-European, but of other branches of Eurasiatic. The reason for the rarity, or perhaps non-appearance, of this demonstrative in Uralic is that it has been largely replaced by the unmarked *t* demonstrative (No. 11) and the *s* demonstrative (No. 12).

In Yukaghir, *a-* occurs as a far demonstrative, e.g. Tundra Yukaghir *a-n* 'that,' contrasting with *te-n* 'this' (No. 11), as well as in a whole series of other demonstratives involving the same contrast, such as Kolyma *a-da* 'thither, there' (Angere 1957; for -*da* see No. 32). The final -*n* of these forms may be interpreted as the former -*n* genitive-oblique (No. 25), which has spread to the nominative just as in Hittite *ann-iš*, Old Church Slavic *onŭ*, etc., discussed above.

In Altaic the distance demonstrative is found in Turkic. In the Turkic of the Orkhon inscriptions (Tekin 1968: 118) there is *a-n-taɣ* 'like that' and the oblique base of the distance demonstrative and anaphoric pronoun is *a-n-* (the *n* here is a genitive and oblique case marker discussed in No. 25). Virtually everywhere in non-Chuvash Turkic is a form *a-rï*, with the most common meaning 'on the other side of, thither,' and analyzed by Räsänen (1969: 256) as consisting of a- 'that' and -ri (directive) (see No. 29). Note also such phrases as Kirghiz arɨ beri 'in that and in this direction, back and forth,' in which beri is most probably related to be(-n) 'I' and bu 'this.' In Chuvash we find e- prefixed to the nominative forms of the first- and second-person pronouns e-pĕ 'I,' e-sĕ 'thou,' e-pir 'we,' e-sir 'you.' Menges (1968: 119) equates this e- with the Indo-European deictic e- included in this section.

The third-person singular pronoun, both in Chuvash and non-Chuvash Turkic, shows an alternation between the nominative and the remaining cases in which, in most languages, -l occurs in the nominative and -n elsewhere (except in the dative, as illustrated below). There is usually an irregular vowel alternation seen, for example, in Khakas ol 'he/she,' a-n-ɨ 'him/her,' but the oblique vowel is often analogically changed to o (e.g. Kazakh ol/onɨ) and the whole pattern extended to other demonstratives, as in Kazakh bu-l/bu-nɨ 'this,' so-l/so-nɨ 'that.' The dative, however, appears to be reconstructible as *a-ga (see No. 26). The first- and second-person pronouns in Turkic, in which (except in Chuvash) the oblique -n has spread to the nominative, also lack -n forms in the dative. For the l ~ n alternation, see No. 67.

In Ainu, Batchelor (1905, s.v. a) describes a as "sometimes used for the third-person pronoun 'he, she, it' and even the relative 'who.'" He also cites a-ri 'that,' with a substantivizing suffix -ri that is evidently related to the -re of Mongolian te-re 'that' and to the -ri of Tungus e-ri. This latter form was mentioned in No. 8. (For -re, -ri as a substantivizer see No. 13.) Ainu a-ri is the exact equivalent of Japanese to 'that' in the Ainu calque sik ari a-ye-p 'the thing called the eye' ('eye thus say') on Japanese me to iu 'the thing called the eye' ('eye that say'). In addition a-ri is common as a relativizer, e.g. pirika ari 'that it is good.' In Ainu I have also encountered a form a-ne in Dobrotvorskij (1875) with the Russian glosses 'that' and 'he.' In the Sakhalin dialect of Ainu a-n 'that' occurs in the far demonstrative tara an 'that there.' (For -n see No. 25.) Compare tara 'there' in the same dialect. Batchelor (1905: s.v. e) mentions the use of e- as a prefix accompanied by the suffix -keta (see Nos. 26 and 32) with adverbs of time to express definiteness or exactness, e.g. nei toho-ta 'on that day,' but e-toho-keta 'on that very day.'

In contemporary standard Japanese a-re 'that' is substantival and *a-no* is the corresponding demonstrative adjective. In addition it is prefixed to the demonstrative *-so-*, which has second-person deixis, in the form *a-soko* 'there (distant).' The usual distance demonstrative in literary Japanese is *ka-re, ka-no*. However, both *a* 'that place, yonder' and *are* 'there, that, he, you' occur in the classical language (Morris 1966: 3, 5–6) and there is the modern expression *a-ti ko-ti* 'there and here' and the contemporary use of *a* or *ā* in the phrase *a iu* 'that kind of' parallel to *so iu* or *sō iu*. Its antiquity is further guaranteed by Ryukyuan *a-ri* and *a-nu*, which, with the usual vowel changes, correspond exactly to Japanese *a-re* and *a-no*. It also occurs in the Ryukyuan adverb *a-ma* 'there,' with the locative suffix *-ma* that we also saw in the Japanese adverb *i-ma* 'now' (for *i-* see No. 8; for *-ma* see No. 27). Ryukyuan *a-ma* is unlikely to be a borrowing from Japanese because it is a historically independent compound of two morphemes in a combination not found in Japanese.

Gilyak too has a distance demonstrative *a* 'that, far but visible.' Once again we find that *a*, in addition to its separate use as a demonstrative base, is prefixed to another demonstrative to give it a meaning 'still more distant.' The forms include *a-hɨ* 'that (very distant)' and *a-hur* 'there (far away).' The second member occurs independently in Gilyak as *hɨ* 'this,' *hur* 'here.' We also find it in Gilyak *a-ŋg, a-g* (< *aŋg*) 'there it is' (Russian *von tam*), which corresponds exactly to Chukchi *enk ~ ank* 'there, then.' In both the Gilyak and Chukchi forms the suffix is a complex consisting of the *n* genitive (see No. 25) and the dative-locative in *-k* (see No. 26). These forms may be compared with the Kamchadal substantival case inflections *-enk* (locative) and *-anke* (dative).

10. Demonstrative KU

A contrast between *e ~ a* as a distance demonstrative and *ku ~ ko* as a near demonstrative appeared several times in the preceding section, e.g. Japanese *ko-no, ko-re* 'this' and Ryukyuan *ku-ni, ku-ri* 'this,' both with first-person deixis. In Japanese there are also adverbs of time and place, e.g. *kotosi* 'this year'; *ko-ko, ko-ti, ko-ti-ra* 'here.' According to Bruno Lewin (1959: 55), in both the literary and colloquial language the local adverbs can also indicate persons. There are similar adverbs of place in Ryukyuan, e.g. *ku-ma* 'here' (cf. *a-ma* 'there,' cited in No. 9.). It is possible that Ainu *ku* 'I' also belongs here. As noted in No. 2, Ainu *ku* might be the first-person marker. This is not necessarily contradictory since first-person *ku* may ultimately be the same element as the near demonstrative *ku*. (For the relation between personal deictics and the corresponding pronouns, see the discussion of Japanese *so-no* and similar forms in No. 5 and the previously mentioned examples of Japanese adverbs in *ko-* with personal reference.)

Gilyak *ku* 'that (absent, just mentioned)' probably exhibits the same root. The equation of the Japanese and Ryukyuan near demonstrative with Turkic Chuvash *ku* and Southern Uighur *ko* 'this' in Altaic is straightforward.

Panfilov (1973: 9) notes the resemblance between the Gilyak form *ku* cited earlier and the Turkic demonstratives, to which he adds the Mongolian emphatic suffix *-ku*. Ramstedt (1939: 4) connects the Korean distance demonstrative *kɨ* (which also has a variant *ko*) with the Turkic forms mentioned in the preceding paragraph. Martin, Lee, and Chang (1967) give two meanings for *ko*. The first is a derogatory form of *kɨ*; the second has the meaning 'that' and introduces a quotation.

There is a widespread Altaic suffix *-ki*, with a demonstrative and relativizing function, which may belong here. In Turkic there are two basic uses, which may be illustrated from Turkish. Here *ki*, which is unchangeable (i.e. not subject to vowel harmony when added to the genitive of a pronoun), forms a possessive pronoun (e.g. *benim* 'my,' *benim-ki* 'mine'). It also occurs after the locative of a noun (e.g. *ev-de-ki*, 'that which is in the house, the one in the house'; literally, 'house-in-that'). Both uses are found in Mongolian. Poppe (1964: 41) describes a suffix *-da-ki/-ta-ki* whose function is "to form nouns designating the fact of being in or belonging to something' (e.g. *usun-da-ki* 'aquatic,' literally, 'water-in-that which is'). It also occurs with the possessive (e.g. Baoan *čene-ge* 'thine'). For another Mongolian language of China, Dagur, Martin (1961: 151) reports similar forms (e.g. *šini-he* 'thine'), but also wider use, for example, *haa-ni-he* 'the thing from what place?,' literally, 'what-locative-he.'

This same formation is found in South Tungusic, where it is suffixed to possessives to substantivize them (e.g. Ulch *mini* 'my,' *miŋ-gi* 'mine'), or to nouns (e.g. Orok *kolxoz-ŋi* 'belonging to the collective farm, the collective farm's'). It is also found in North Tungusic (e.g. Even *min-ŋi* 'mine'), but the locative construction is apparently absent from Tungusic. According to Kotwicz (1962: 117–26), who gives a detailed account of this construction, occasional forms in *ku* occur in all branches of Altaic, strengthening the case for the origin of *-ki* from demonstative *ku*.

Even if it derives from general Eurasiatic *ku*, the syntactic uses of *ki* constitute an Altaic innovation which—unless it it a case of language contact—strengthens the case for the validity of a separate Altaic node in Eurasiatic.

Another probable cognate form is the Eskimo third-person marker *-yu* ∼ *-yi* in the "participial mode," which is actually a verbal participle in *lu-*: *-lu-yu* (singular), *-lu-yi-k* (dual), *-lu-yi-t* (plural).

Indo-European had a near demonstrative that is seen in Hittite *kā-*, Palaic *ka-*, Lithuanian *ši-s*, all meaning 'this.' It is also found in Latin adverbs such as *ci-s* 'on this side.' The meaning agrees with that of other Eurasiatic branches, but the vowel does not. Pokorny (1959: 609) reconstructs Proto-Indo-European $*\hat{k}e$-, $*\hat{k}o$-, $*\hat{k}(e)i$, and $*\hat{k}(i)i̯o$-. This suggests original *ki* ∼ *ke* rather than *ku* ∼ *ko*. Pokorny glosses it as 'this,' but notes that it shifts in meaning to distance deixis in some languages, e.g. Greek. We saw the same shift of meaning in Gilyak. The vowel of the Hittite accusative singular, common gender, *kūn* and the nominative-accusative plural, common gender, *kūs* disagree in quality with the other branches of Eurasiatic. In all probability this is an archaism. The non-Anatolian Indo-European vowel variants of this demonstrative are easily explained as analogical with a whole series of other demonstratives (Nos. 8 and 11).

Sommer and Falkenstein (1938: 167) sought to explain the ending of Hittite *kūs* by analogy with the *-us* accusative plural of nouns, an explanation accepted by Friedrich (1960: 67). However, this fails to account for the accusative singular *kūn*. In Hittite the far demonstrative *apās* follows *kās* exactly in its inflection. That the *-ū* forms are analogical with *kās* can be shown from the adverb *apidda* 'thither.' The former existence of demonstrative stems in *-i*, which could serve as a model, as in the rest of Indo-European, is also attested in other Anatolian languages, e.g. Hieroglyphic Hittite *ī-* 'this' (generally thought to derive from **ki-*), Lycian *ebe*, a demonstrative unmarked for distance, and above all Lydian *bi-s,* unmarked and anaphoric. These latter forms are undisputed cognates of Hittite *apā-s* 'that.'

In summary, the above data suggest that demonstratives in *e ~ i* existed in Anatolian, as elsewhere in Indo-European. They provided a model for the change of vowel in original **ku-*, with the *-u* vowel only surviving in the Hittite forms *kūn* and *kūs*. These forms, in turn, affected the vowels of the corresponding inflections of *apās* 'that' in Hittite, but not in other Anatolian languages.

11. Demonstrative T

The most common Eurasiatic demonstrative is **tV*. As we shall see, the vowel varies from group to group. The *t-* demonstrative appears in every branch of Indo-European except Anatolian; it may be either unmarked for distance, or a marker of near or far deixis, depending on the language. It is also a source of anaphoric pronouns. As reconstructed for Proto-Indo-European, it has a suppletive alternation with *s-* (No. 12). Of the two alternants, *s-* occurs in the nominative masculine or feminine and *t-* elsewhere in the paradigm (Szemerényi 1978: 265). That a broader suppletion or competition of *s-* and *t-* forms existed is suggested by the fact that in Vedic Sanskrit, in the locative singular masculine and neuter, *sasmin* occurs in about one third of the text occurrences, *tasmin* in the remainder (Whitney 1879: 190). Another noteworthy feature of the *t-* demonstrative is the stem vowel. Although the ablaut alternation *e ~ o* is fundamental in Indo-European, we find only **to*, never **te*. In addition a stem *tjo-* is found in Vedic Sanskrit and is supported by evidence from Old Persian, Lithuanian, Albanian, and Germanic (Pokorny 1959: 1087). This suggests an earlier stem **ti-*, to which a vowel has been added to bring it into conformity with the prevailing ablaut system of Indo-European. The same situation holds for the *s-* demonstrative (No. 12), where we also find forms with *-j-* after the initial consonant.

In Hittite there is a conjoining particle *ta* 'and, then' that is usually derived from Proto-Indo-European **to-*. The development of *t-* into a coordinating particle is also illustrated below in Tungus, Korean, Japanese, and Koryak.

The third-person *-t*, subject of the verb in the present-aorist system of the Indo-European verb (e.g. Sanskrit *abhara-t* 'he, she was carrying,' *a-dā-t* 'he, she gave' [aorist]), has often been identified with the demonstrative *t-* (cf. Brugmann and Delbrück 1897–1916, II.3.2: 594). This *-t* does not occur in Greek or Baltic. Furthermore, in Vedic Sanskrit there are zero forms in the third-person singular of the imperfect middle of the verb 'to milk,' *aduha*, alongside forms with an analogically added *-t*. There are also *t*-less forms in the third-person present middle indicative. According to William Dwight Whitney (1879: 233), forms without *-t* are more common in the present middle indicative than those containing it. Moreover, Tokharian has *-s* rather than *-t*, and *-s* also appears in Hittite in the third-person singular preterite of the *-mi* conjugation. On the other hand, *t* is found for the second-person singular in the Indo-European perfect and the second-person plural in the present-aorist system (see Nos. 4 and 5), as well as in Tokharian throughout the verbal system.

The foregoing evidence suggests a fluid situation in Proto-Indo-European in which the *s* and *t* demonstratives were in the process of becoming markers of the second and third person in the verb, and in which the assignment of each to a particular person was not complete. Watkins (1969: 49) claimed that the third person was fundamentally zero, whereas Bomhard (1988: 4) surmised that the athematic third-person *t-* might originally have marked the second person, while the third-person marker was *s*.

In Uralic there are two forms of demonstrative *t-*, *tu/to* 'that' contrasting with *ti/te* 'this,' e.g. Udmurt *tu* 'that,' Mordvin *to* 'that,' but Cheremis *ti* 'this,' Mordvin *te* 'this.' In his comparison of Indo-European and Uralic, Collinder (1965a) only considers the form **to* for Indo-European, connecting it with Uralic **to*. The front vowel forms are reconstructed by him as *tä* and are related to various Altaic demonstratives such as Mongolian *te(-re)* 'this, that, he, she.'

Majtinskaja (1974: 385) has proposed that the Hungarian accusative *-t* derives from the *t* demonstrative and was formerly confined to the definite object. A survival of this is its optional use with nouns that have first- or second-person possessive suffixes, e.g. *ház-am* ~ *ház-am-at* 'my house' (accusative). There is a general typological tendency for definiteness to be marked in the accusative case, which often involves first mention and is therefore usually indefinite and hence requires a definiteness marker, in contrast with the subject/topic, which is usually or, in some languages, compulsorily definite (Moravcsik 1974). For a typologically parallel development of demonstrative -s in the Permian branch of Finno-Ugric, see No. 12. In one Permian language, Komi-Zyrian -id (< *-it) has become a rival definite article to -is, e.g. mort-is, mort-id 'the man.'

The t- demonstrative is basic in Yukaghir. Jochelson (1905) gives t- forms with vowel differentiation very similar to Uralic. For 'this' he cites Tundra tiŋ and Kolyma tuŋ; for 'that,' taŋ in both dialects. We have already seen (No. 9) that Krejnovich reports Tundra te-n 'this' versus a-n 'that.' In the extinct Chuvan dialect we find ti-ne 'this,' where -ne is a locative marker (see No. 30). In Yukaghir t- also occurs in a number of adverbs, e.g. Tundra tā 'there' and tī 'here' (Krejnovich 1958).

The evidence presented up to this point, together with that in No. 9, suggests that in Eurasiatic the far demonstrative was indicated by *e ~ *a, but demonstrative *t- (at least in Indo-European, Uralic, Yukaghir, and Ainu) had two variant forms tu ~ to for far or intermediate location and ti ~ te for near location.

In Turkic a t- demonstrative (ta ~ ti) occurs in Yakut as a third-person possessor suffixed to nouns ending in vowels; other Turkic languages have -si. Yakut is genetically divergent within non-Chuvash Turkic and is therefore likely to furnish important independent historical evidence. Menges (1968: 114) identifies Yakut -ti (along with iti 'this, that' in the same language) with the demonstrative t- of Indo-European and Uralic, whereas other Altaicists derive it from -si (irregularly). Whatever the derivation of -ti in Yakut, one can cite a fair number of examples from Turkic languages of an unbound t- demonstrative, e.g. Tatar tege 'that,' Altai tu, tuol 'that (exclamatory, Russian von tot),' Karagas te 'that' (Castrén 1957: 22).

In Mongolian the near demonstrative is te(-re) (plural te-de). It may also be unmarked for distance and employed anaphorically. As we saw in No. 9, this contrasts with e(-ne) (plural e-de) 'that.' Mongolian also has a verb te-ji 'to do in that manner' that contrasts with e-ji 'to do in this manner.' For Tungus, Benzing (1955: 1060) reconstructs *ta(-ri) 'that' (for -ri see No. 13).

In Tungus languages adverbs and conjunctions are often formed from a *t* demonstrative followed by a locative element, e.g. Evenki *ta-ri* 'therefore,' *tē-li* 'then,' *ta-duq* 'and' (= 'so that'); Even *ta-duq* 'then, after, and'; Negidal *tē-tā* 'there,' *tā-dū* 'there.' All these examples are from Northern Tungus.

The *t*- demonstrative is well represented in Ainu, again with vowel differentiation: *to* 'there, yonder, *te* 'here,' *ta-p* 'this.' Note in particular *taata toata* 'here and there' (for -*da* see No. 32). These forms are from Batchelor's account of Hokkaido Ainu. In the Sakhalin dialect we find *ta-n* 'this,' *ta-ra* 'there' (for -*ra* see No. 29). In Chiri's grammar (cited in Dettmer 1989: 318), *te* is said to indicate something in the near vicinity, e.g. *te-ta ante* 'put it here' ('this-at put') (for -*ta* see No. 32). The usual word for 'now' in Ainu varies dialectally as *ta-ne* ~ *ta-ni* (see No. 30). Tamura cites *te-ta* 'here' for Sara Ainu (Dettmer 1989).

The Korean middle-distance demonstrative is *čə* and has been connected by Martin (1966) with Japanese *so-re, so-no,* demonstratives with second-person deixis (No. 12), rather than with the *t*- demonstratives. However, the North Korean form of the same demonstrative, *tjə,* is strikingly like Sanskrit *tja-* and other Indo-European forms. Ramsey (1978: 7) reconstructs Middle Korean *tye* 'that one, over there, he.' It is also possible that the enclitic *to* 'also, too,' likewise used as a coordinator (*to . . . to . . . to . . .* 'both . . . and . . . and . . . '), belongs here. Compare the Russian use of repeated *to* in such expressions as *on živjot to v gorode to v derevne* 'sometimes he lives in town, sometimes in the country' (i.e. 'He lives *to* in town *to* in country.'). For a detailed account of *to* and its uses in Korean, see Martin, Lee, and Chang (1967: 459).

In Japanese *t*- occurs marginally. In comparing Japanese with Uralic, Wilhelm Pröhle (1916: 177) cites the Japanese phrase *to mo kaku mo* 'this and that, so and so' and *to,* the quotative particle that, as would be expected in an SOV language, follows rather than precedes the quotation. If Pröhle is correct, then the English use of 'that' to introduce reported speech is both a typological and genetic parallel. Aston (1904: 139) says that *to* was originally a demonstrative and still has this meaning in a number of instances, e.g. *to kaku* 'in that way or in this.' According to the same writer, in many instances it is best construed as equivalent to 'this' or 'thus.' It appears then, as elsewhere, to have been unmarked for distance. In

Japanese *to* is also used as a coordinator in a way very similar to that in Korean. Morris (1966: 121–23) considers that both the quotative and coordinating *to* are the same particle, which also has a concessive use.

In Gilyak the *t* demonstrative indicates an object that is near the speaker. The basic one is Amur *ty* 'this' and Eastern Sakhalin *tu* 'this,' substantivized as *ty-d′* and *tu-d′*, respectively. There are also adverbs, such as *tu-g* (< *tu-ŋ-k*) 'here,' *tu-ŋs* 'this many' (cf. *rša-ŋs* 'how many?'). All of the foregoing forms are found in Saval'eva (1970). In addition, Panfilov (1962–65, I: 247) mentions *tu-ŋ-ge* 'here, hence' and *tu-r*, *tu-s*, *tu-in* 'here.' For analyses of the postinitial element of these forms, see Nos. 25 and 26. In *tu-in*, *-in* is the locative case ending of substantives.

In the Chukotian group Kamchadal has the demonstrative *tiʔ-n* (for *-n* see No. 21), with the variant *te-* in the adverb *te-ank* 'here' (*-ank* is a locative marker in Kamchadal) and *t-* in *t-ke* 'hither.' In Chukchi further evidence for the *t-* demonstrative is provided by the third-person independent pronoun, nominative singular *ət-lon* and nominative plural *ət-ri*. In Koryak (Zhukova 1972: 290) *to* means 'and.' With regard to a coordinator arising from a demonstrative, recall the Korean example discussed above.

In Eskimo the basic demonstrative *ta* occurs prefixed to any of the other demonstratives in Greenlandic except *tass-*, in which it is already present. Kleinschmidt (1851: 21) says that the root of *tass* is *ta-* and indeed it occurs in just this form in Siberian Yupik *ta-na* 'this,' *ta-kuk* 'these,' and elsewhere in Eskimo. Fortescue (1984: 261) describes the function of prefixed *ta-* in West Greenlandic as an anaphoric prefix "in the sense previously mentioned/understood as a present topic." Uhlenbeck (1935: 16) compares Eskimo *ta-* with Indo-European **to-*. Since Eskimo has a three-vowel system (*a*, *i*, *u*), beside a reduced vowel (*ə*), it may be hypothesized that earlier **e* and **o* have merged with a. Thus Eskimo *ta-* would correspond exactly to Indo-European **to-*. Hinz (1944) lists *toi*, *tua* 'so' and *toi-ka* 'Is it so?' for the Kuskokwim dialect of Alaskan Yupik. For *-ka*, see No. 60.

In Aleut *-ta* is suffixed to the interrogative *kin* 'who?' as an enclitic and gives it the indefinite meaning 'someone.' This function of the demonstrative is an exact typological parallel to Russian *kto-*

to 'someone,' *čto-to* 'something' and evidently involves the same demonstrative *t*. Similarly *-ta* is suffixed to *alkuχ* 'what' to form the indefinite *alkuχ-ta* 'something.'

The distance distinction *tu* ∼ *to* (far) versus *ti* ∼ *te* (near) is found in a considerable number of Eurasiatic languages. As we have seen, *t-* is probably the most widespread and unmarked of the Eurasiatic demonstratives. Considering the well-known sound symbolic value of the vowels involved, it is difficult to tell whether the vowel differentiation is primary or secondary. The secondary differentiation of an unmarked demonstrative that has replaced the others is of course well known, for example, in French *celui-çi* 'this,' *celui-là* 'that.' Brugmann and Delbrück (1897–1916, II, 3.2: 594) connect demonstrative and third-person *t* in Indo-European. Uhlenbeck (1942–45) equates Eskimo *ta* with Indo-European *to*.

12. Demonstrative S

The Proto-Indo-European suppletion of *s-* in the masculine and feminine nominative singular with *t-* in the remainder of the paradigm was mentioned in the preceding section. Indications of its wider use, however, are not lacking. In Vedic it occurs in the masculine and neuter locative singular *sasmin*, alongside *tasmin*. Moreover, the stem **so-* appears elsewhere, without being suppletive to **t-*, e.g. in the Avestan masculine dative singular pronoun *hoi* (< **soi*).

Like *t-*, it has variants with a following *-j-* in Vedic, e.g. *sj-as* (masculine nominative singular) and *sj-ā* (feminine nominative singular). In the discussion of *tj-* (No. 11) it was suggested that the basic stem was *ti-*, which was subsequently incorporated into the prevailing ablaut system by the addition of *-o*. However, for *s-* the hypothesized original form **si* is well attested. Friedrich (1960: 64) discusses an independent third-person pronoun *si-* in Hittite, without gender distinction in the oblique cases. There is also a third-person singular possessive suffix *-si-* in the same language, followed by case markers that agree with the modified noun. Other instances of Indo-European *si-* are mentioned in Pokorny (1959: 979), e.g. the Old Persian accusative *sī-m* 'her' and the Old Norse enclitic *si*, prefixed, or more commonly suffixed, to other demonstratives, e.g. *su-si* (feminine nominative singular), *θat-si* (neuter nominative and accusative singular).

The old theory of Bopp that the Indo-European common gender nominative singular *s* derives from the *s* demonstrative has received support from later Indo-Europeanists such as Hirt (1921–37,
III: 140), Thumb (1958–59, II: 136), Schmalstieg (1980: 49–52), and
Shields (1982: 54–60). It appears to me to be strengthened by the
fact that the Indo-European demonstrative, formed by the suppletion of *s-* and *t-* stems, is to be reconstructed in the nominative
singular masculine as **so* rather than the expected *so-s*. The second *-s* would have been redundant if in fact the nominative singular
masculine *-s* derived from **so-*.

Uralic examples of the *s-* demonstrative include Finnish *hän* 'he,
she' (< **sä-n*), Saami *son* 'he, she,' and Udmurt *so* 'that.' These
forms were related to the Indo-European demonstrative **so-* by
Collinder (1934: 55). The third-person singular possessive suffix is
reconstructed for Proto-Finno-Ugric as *-s*, a shortened form of the
full pronoun (Majtinskaja 1974, I: 273), e.g. Saami *oabba-s* 'his, her
sister.' The demonstrative has developed into a postposed article in
the Volga Finnic, Permian, and Ob-Ugric languages, e.g. Mordvin
či-ze 'the sun.'

In Udmurt, a Permian language, *-əz* (< **əs*) has become an
accusative by a process parallel to that by which the demonstrative
t (No. 11) became the mark of the accusative in Hungarian. In
the case of Permian the earlier stage is recoverable since in Komi-
Zyrian, a language closely related to Udmurt, *-s* functions only as
the definite accusative, e.g. *mort-əs* 'the man' (accusative; cf. *mort*
'man' (nominative or indefinite accusative).

In Altaic, *s* apparently occurs in Turkic, most obviously in non-
Chuvash Turkic in the *-sï ~ -si* third-person possessive that is suffixed to vowel stems in suppletive alternation with *-ï ~ i* after consonant stems (No. 9). Like *i*, *si* in Old Turkish does not vary in the
vowel harmony system. Chuvash uses *-šə*, *-š* with kinship terms as a
third-person possessive and Menges (1968: 114) identifies this with
non-Chuvash *-sï ~ -si*, as does Levitskaja (1976) in her discussion of
Chuvash historical morphology.

There appears to be a lone survival of demonstrative *s* in Ainu
sa-ta 'here' (for *ta-* see No. 32.). In Old Japanese there is a form *si*
(Sansom 1928: 74) that appears to be used as a personal pronoun
and is said by Sansom to derive from the same root as *sö-*. According

to the same source, *si* and *sö* have the same meaning, except that *si* may be used as a personal pronoun, whereas *sö* in Old Japanese is a demonstrative that can also function as a third-person pronoun.

Räsänen (1965: 163) related the Uralic and Altaic forms and Pröhle (1916: 159) connected the Japanese forms in *so-* with those of Altaic. If Austerlitz's conjecture (1990: 19) that Gilyak *h* derives from an earlier *s* is correct, then Gilyak *hi* 'this' may belong here as well.

13. Substantivizer RE

At several points in the discussion of demonstratives in the preceding sections we found a substantivizing morpheme *-ri* ~ *-re*, which is especially characteristic of the singular. Its distribution may be summarized as follows. In Mongolian it occurs in *te-re* 'this' (plural *te-de*) and is used as both an adjective and a substantive. In Tungus (Benzing 1955: 1060) all the substantivized forms of the demonstrative are reconstructed as ending in *-ri*. In Manchu it is only found in the singular, but in other Tungus languages it is found in both numbers. In Tungus also, as compared to Mongolian, *-r-* has been extended to the rest of the case paradigm. That *-ri-* is a later extension from the nominative can be seen from variant forms in the oblique cases with and without *-ri* (e.g. Evenki *e-reduk* ~ *e-duk* 'to this one'). It is also found in Ainu *a-ri* 'that, that which' (for the first part see No. 9) and Japanese *ko-re, so-re, a-re*, all substantivized forms of demonstratives. Related forms are found in Ryukyuan, with the usual vowel changes **o > u* and **e > i*, e.g. *ku-ri* 'this.' Sansom (1928: 74–75) noted the further extension of *-re* in Old Japanese, as compared with the other languages, to *na-re* 'thou' (for *na* see No. 6) and to *itu-re* 'which?' (cf. *itu* 'when?'). It also occurs in the interrogative pronoun *ta-re* (modern *da-re*) 'who?' (for *ta-* see No. 63) and in the first-person singular personal pronoun *wa, wa-re* 'I' (for *wa-* see No. 1). A further extension of *-re* is *ono* ~ *onore* 'oneself' (Old Japanese *ön*).

14. Dual KI(N)

The coincidence of the pattern *k* 'dual,' *t* 'plural' between Samoyed (Uralic) and Eskimo was already noticed by Rasmus Rask in the early nineteenth century. However, k often appears as a plural. For example, in Finno-Ugric *t is reconstructed as a nominal plural, whereas *k is reconstructed in the first-person plural *-mek and second-person plural *-tek of the nominal possessive and the verb. Similar phenomena are encountered elsewhere. A possible historical explanation would be that k was originally a plural that was being displaced already in Proto-Eurasiatic by another plural marker (invariably the t plural, No. 15). Where the process was complete, the k might survive as a dual.

I believe, however, that the hypothesis that best accounts for the facts is that k was originally a dual and was in fact followed by a vowel i that was often lost. There is scattered evidence that there was also a final nasal consonant, probably n, so that the complete form was kin. This ki(n) expanded its function in some instances to become a plural. Both processes are well attested, a dual displacing a plural and a plural absorbing a dual.

In the Baltic Finnic branch of Finno-Ugric, although -t occurs as a nominal plural, we saw above that -mek and -tek are used as first- and second-person plural possessives and as verb subject markers. The -t plural occurs elsewhere in the Finnic group and is also found in the more distantly related Samoyed group. It therefore seems that a *-t nominal plural can be reconstructed for Uralic and this is generally accepted.

However, k occurs as a plural of nouns in Hungarian as well as in the verbal and possessive forms -mek and -tek. Saami also has a nominal plural in -k. On this basis many Uralicists have accepted -k as another plural formation in Proto-Uralic. Ravila (1941: 67) argues against this position, deriving the Hungarian -k plural from a Finno-Ugric collective suffix -kko. It would subsequently have spread analogically to the Hungarian first- and second-person plural possessives and verb subject. Were this accepted, then of course the agreement between Hungarian -mek, -tek and the corresponding forms in Finnic would be accidental. I find this hard to believe.

Thus far we have only considered Uralic languages that lack a dual. But there are also Uralic languages in which a dual k contrasts with a plural t. In the Ugric branch of Finno-Ugric, Ostyak has a dual in k, x, or g, depending on the phonetic environment, to which -an is added. In Samoyed, duals have a basic k, to which may be added either -aj (Tavgy) or -an (Enets). Collinder (1960: 302) tries to reconcile these forms by reconstructing a final -ń. Southern Samoyed (Selkup) has basic -qi, -qɨ as a dual marker in both nouns and verbs.

Even Ravila (1941: 7), who argues against a -k plural in Hungarian and elsewhere, does not deny the existence of a Uralic dual -k, based on the evidence from Ob-Ugric and Samoyed. In the nineteenth century Yukaghir material of Maydell (edited by Schiefner) a number of -k plurals occur, for example, kadi-k 'which?' (plural), noludak 'poplar trees' (cf. singular noludd).

In the Amur dialect of Gilyak the first-person dual pronoun is me-gi, which contrasts with the first-person plural inclusive me-r. The fact that 'we two' is megi rather than *meyi, with the expected form of *k between vowels, shows that a nasal has been lost from an earlier form such as *men-gi(n) or *meŋ-gi(n). The analysis is thus clearly *men 'I' (cf. Turkic ben ~ men and similar forms elsewhere) followed by dual *ki(n). Moreover, the fact that megi(n) changes the initial consonant of the next word to the expected post-nasal variant in the system of Gilyak consonant alternations adds to the evidence for a former final nasal in this form, which we have already found in Uralic. (See also the discussion of Eskimo below.)

Gilyak also shows evidence of the form kin 'two' in the Amur coordinator ke(n), Sakhalin -kin, which is normally used only to coordinate two members and may be omitted with the first. There is an areal-typological resemblance here to the Mongolian use of hojor 'two' after the second member as a coordinator with the meaning 'and.' Panfilov (1962–65, I: 205–7, 238–39) proposed that *men contains the numeral 'two.' The reasons for which this hypothesis is inadequate are set forth in Greenberg (1997: 192).

In Chukotian, Chukchi agrees fully with Finno-Ugric in having a nominal plural -t, whereas the verb has first- and second-person plurals -mǝk and -tǝk, respectively. Chukchi and Koryak -q in the numeral expressions for two, three, and four may involve the survival of k in its use as a dual. That -q is a formative is clearly shown both by its occurrence only on these three numerals and by contrasts such as Chukchi ŋiroq kupr-et 'three whales,' alternatively expressed as ŋɨro-n kopra-ta in which -ta is the marker of the instrumental. This use of -ta is probably a survival of its original partitive-ablative meaning (see No. 33).

The posited spread of an original dual to expressions for 'three' and 'four' has an obvious typological parallel in modern Slavic languages such as Russian in which -a, originally the masculine dual, has been reinterpreted as genitive singular and extended to the constructions with 'three' and 'four.' Another closely similar developement, perhaps even involving the same suffix -k, is Armenian erku-(k') 'two,' ere-k' 'three,' and č'or-k' 'four' (see Schmidt 1981: 111). Here, however, the -k' of erku-k' is probably a later extension. This is in accord with the basic function of -k' in Armenian as a plural rather than dual marker.

Kamchadal, the most divergent member of Chukotian, shows plural -x in the second-person plural suffix -sx (< *sk) found in the indicative and imperative of the verb and in the vocative plural of the noun (see No. 5). In Krasheninnikov's eighteenth century material we find for the first person plural rendering of 'we stand' Southern Kamchadal buzhe ushisha-mk, in agreement with Chukchi, along with similar evidence from Northern and Western Kamchadal, but not with modern Western Kamchadal, in which -mk is lacking.

The Eskimo noun, outside of Sirenik with its -i plural, has a -k dual and a -t plural. Sirenik, which does not have the dual as an inflectional plural, preserves the -k dual in the numeral 'two,' malɣu-ɣ, from which it has spread to 'three,' piŋaju-ɣ. Numerals greater than 'three' have the -i plural, just as the noun. The spread of the dual inflection to immediately higher numerals is similar to what was noted above with regard to Chukchi and Armenian. In the Eskimo intransitive verb the second-person dual is *-tik. It should be noted that in a whole series of both nominal and verbal categories in those forms of Eskimo which have retained a dual, the dual and plural are both expressed by -k. For example, the West Greenlandic reflexive possessive -tik in the absolutive case is suffixed to a singular possessum to indicate possession by either dual or plural possessors, and, similarly, reflexive -mik is also suffixed to a noun in the relative case, with similar meaning. In these instances the -k thus signifies a plural meaning 'two or more.' In those forms of Eskimo which have lost the dual category, the -k then, without change of meaning, becomes the plural indicator in a system without a dual. We have already encountered instances of -k as a plural, for example, in the verb in Uralic and Chukotian, and in the verb and noun in Armenian. All of this suggests, of course, that *k* was originally a plural in a system without a dual. However, as we have seen, *k* or rather *k(-in)*, has specific ties with the numeral 'two.' One possible solution is that *k* was indeed originally a dual, with perhaps the now somewhat marginal *i* as plural. It then expanded its meaning to a two-or-more plural and was finally restricted in many instances by the more recent *t* plural so that it once more became a dual. All this is, of course, rather precarious and speculative, but seems to best account for the facts.

A number of duals in *-ki* are attested in Sakhalin Ainu in Dobrotvorskij (1875). One of these is the word for 'eyes,' which is generally *sik* in present-day Ainu. Here Dobrotvorskij has *sis* 'a single eye,' *sik* 'eyes.' The validity of *sis* is shown in Hattori (1964: 20, 23) by the forms from the Sakhalin dialect of Ainu for 'eyelashes,' *sis-rah*, as against *sik-rap* in Hokkaido dialects, and by Sakhalin *sis-num* 'eyeballs,' as against Hokkaido *sik-num*. In their glottochronological study Hattori and Chiri (1960) found *sis* 'eye' in three Sakhalin dialects, Ochiho, Shiraura, and Raichishka. That *sik* is a dual is also confirmed by Voznesenskij's hitherto unpublished vocabulary of Kurile Ainu in Vovin (1993). Here we find *ar-sik* 'a single eye,' in which *ar* = *ara* 'one of a pair' (cf. Proto-Indo-European **al-i* 'other,' Greek *allos*, Latin *alius*). Thus *ar-sik* means 'one of a pair of eyes.' Dobrotvorskij also explicitly distinguishes *ima* 'tooth' and *ima-ki* 'teeth,' the latter presumably a dual meaning 'upper and lower teeth.' In addition, Friedrich Müller (1876–88, II: 143) cites the plural (really dual) form *kema-ki* 'feet.'

We saw above that in Gilyak *-ki* (Amur) and *-kin* (Eastern Sakhalin) mean 'and,' with this use of the numeral 'two' for 'and' finding a typological parallel in Mongolian. This suggests that the *-k* dual, which, as we have seen, takes the form *-ki* in a number of languages, is to be identified with Turkish *iki* 'two' and Yukaghir *ki* 'two.' The latter is a variant of *kijo* that appears immediately before a modifier, whereas *kijo* is used independently. Perhaps Hungarian *két* 'two' and other related forms in Uralic also belong here. In a discussion of Uralic morphology, Majtinskaja (1974: 230) endorses Ravila's opinion that the *k* dual of Uralic is historically connected with the word for 'two' in that family (e.g. Hungarian *két*).

Following the proposal in Chapter 2, final dual *-k* may be reflected in Proto-Indo-European as a laryngeal that, in accordance with the usual theory of Indo-Europeanists, was lost, resulting in a long vowel. In fact, long vowels are characteristic of the nominative-accusative of *o*-stems, namely *-ō, and of *i*- and *u*-stems, *ī and *ū, respectively (Szemerényi 1996: 184–86). In the oblique cases the ablative, dative, and instrumental of thematic stems is reconstructed as *-bhyō(m), *-mō in the same source.

Finally we may note the Armenian plural *-k'* that occurs in nouns, pronouns, numerals, and verbs. The first-person plural *-mk'* and second-person plural *-jk'* (< *tk'*) agree closely with the plural pronominal forms of Finno-Ugric and Chukchi and with the dual forms of Eskimo. This Armenian *-k'* has never really found a satisfactory solution within Indo-European. Pisani (1976) identifies Armenian *-k'* with the *-k* plural of Hungarian and other Uralic languages, noting in particular the agreement between Armenian *-mk'*, *-jk'* and the first-person plural and second-person plural possessives and verb subject affixes of Finno-Ugric.

15. Plural T

As we saw in the previous section, dual *k* (or *ki*) often contrasts with a plural *t*. In Uralic, *t* is the most widespread exponent of the nominal plural and is unanimously reconstructed for Proto-Uralic. The *-t* plural also occurs as the third-person plural of the verb, e.g. Mordvin *kundyt* 'they catch,' and in the Cheremis third-person plural possessive *-š-t*, in which *-š-* indicates the third-person singular possessor.

In Yukaghir the usual nominal plural is *-pe*. However, in the pronouns of the two surviving dialects we have *met* 'I,' *tet* 'thou,' *mit* 'we,' and *tit* 'you.' The extinct Omok dialect has *ti-p* 'you,' whose *-p* is obviously to be identified with the nominal plural. This suggests that the *-t* of *mi-t* and *ti-t* is really a plural and that the *-t* of the singular has a different origin. The *-t* plural is probably also found in Kolyma Yukaghir *čumu* ~ *čumu-t* 'all.'

It occurs in all three branches of Altaic, as documented in Sinor (1952), a study of Uralic and Altaic plurals. Although *-t* does not occur in modern Turkic languages it is found in Old Turkish, for example in the Orkhon inscriptions (Tekin 1968: 122) and in the medieval dictionary of Ali el-Kashgari (pointed out in Menges 1968: 111). In Mongolian, -d is the most common nominal plural marker and has as its source an earlier *-t (Poppe 1953: 27). In Tungus we find Manchu -ta and -te as the plural of certain kinship terms. The Manchu suffixes are clearly cognate with the first portion of the irregular plurals of kin terms in other Tungus languages, where they are followed by -l, the most common Tungus plural marker (e.g. Negidal am-tɪl 'fathers'). Benzing (1955) reconstructs Proto-Tungus *ti 'they' and *-ti 'their.' This may be a hypercharacterized form containing the i- plural (No. 16).

An Ainu -ti plural probably survives in the second-person plural independent pronoun e-či. The corresponding singular form is e and in Ainu či derives from *ti. In fact, the sequence ti does not occur in contemporary Ainu. This may also be, as in Tungus, a hypercharacterized form. In Ainu some verbs have a special plural stem. Examples include o 'to be,' plural o-t, and ki 'to do,' plural ki-či (< *ki-ti). There are also a few nouns with a -t plural, e.g. pe 'water,' plural peči (< *peti), and ka 'thread,' plural kaat, kaot. All these are Hokkaido forms from Batchelor. In his grammar (1905: 38) he says in summary that "cha, chi and t are all plural endings." In the Sakhalin dialect -či (< *ti) or -ači (< *ati) may be suffixed to verbs to indicate the third-person plural subject. In addition, či survives as a nominal plural in the word for 'arm' in Sakhalin Ainu in Dobrotvorskij (1875): mompe 'arm,' mompiči ~ mumpiče (see mon ~ mun 'arm' in the Appendix). This plural is further confirmed by the Sakhalin form for 'finger' in Hattori (1964, II: 93) monpeh, with the 'belonging form' monpeh-čihi. Here the final -h in monpeh comes from *t and the -či (< *ti) survives in the plural, followed by the usual 'belonging form' suffix -hi.

In Gilyak the verb has a suffixed -t to indicate all three persons of the plural in the participle indicating action simultaneous with that of the main verb. In Chukchi -t is the noun plural in the nominative case after vowels, alternating with -ti after consonants. It also occurs commonly as a third-person plural in verbal forms, for example, nəčejvəqin 'he/she goes' and nəčejvəqinet 'they go' (Skorik 1968: 263). In Koryak the plural has become a dual and has the same alternants. The -i of -ti may be the i plural (see No. 16). In Kamchadal, the most divergent member of the Chukotian group, Bogoras (1922: 695) noted that in the material collected by Dybowsky in southern Kamchatka -*t* and -*d* occur as noun plurals. The *t* plural may also occur in Kamchadal *t-lwin* 'they themselves' (cf. *kmi-lwin* 'I myself'). In the Sedanka dialect of Western Kamchadal, Bogoras (1922: 696) has pointed out the existence of the -*t* plural, as in *sünkil* 'the one who flew' and *sünkil-at* 'those who fly.'

Finally, Eskimo has a -*t* plural, except in the divergent Sirenik dialect of Siberia. The *t* plural does, however, survive there in a few instances, for example in the nominal plural prolative case ending -*t-kən* and in the plural noun with second-person singular possessor -*t-ən*. This -*t* has become -*n* in western Eskimo dialects or is in sandhi alternation with -*n*, the latter occurring before an initial vowel in the following word. In Western and Eastern Aleut we have -*n*, as expected, in place of **-t*. For Central Aleut plural -*s*, see No. 19.

16. Plural I

Indo-European has an -*i* plural in demonstratives that has sometimes spread to nominal inflections. It was equated with the Uralic -*i* plural by Nikolai Anderson (1879) in the first systematic comparison of Indo-European with Uralic. Collinder (1934: 132) also mentions the -*i*- of the first-person plural independent pronoun in Sanskrit *va-y-ám* and Gothic *weis* (Gothic *ei* was phonetically *ī*). Perhaps the nominal neuter plural attested in Hittite and Palaic also belongs here, as well as the Luwian plural -*inzi* used in all genders.

In Latin both demonstratives and relatives have -*i* in the nominative of all three genders, e.g. *hī*, *hae*, *hae* 'these,' *quī*, *quae*, *quae* 'who, which.' The Sanskrit neuter plural in -*i* is commonly said to derive from Proto-Indo-European **ə*, but Thumb (1958-59: 14), who compares it to Hittite -*i*, derives it from **i* (see also Burrow 1965: 236). The Sanskrit neuter plural -*i*, frequently equated with Greek -*a*, e.g. Sanskrit *bharanti* = Greek *pheronta* 'those which carry (neuter),' and which would thus derive from Proto-Indo-European **ə*, is compared by other Indo-Europeanists to Hittite neuter plural -*i* and thus results from Proto-Indo-European **-i* (see Burrow 1965: 236, Thumb 1958–59, II: 14, Kortlandt 1987).

In Uralic, the Finnic languages have -*i*- in all the plural oblique cases, contrasting with -*t* in the nominative. The same pattern is found in Saami and Kamassian Samoyed. Another function in Uralic is to indicate the plural of the thing possessed with pronominal possessive suffixes, e.g. Hungarian *ház-am* 'my house,' *háza-i-m* 'my houses.' A similar construction occurs in Northern Samoyed. In Yurak Samoyed *-i-* occurs in the objective verb conjugation to indicate plurality of objects, e.g. *mada-i-n* 'I cut them.' We also find *-i* as an indicator of the plural in independent pronouns, e.g. Hungarian *mi* 'we,' *ti* 'you.' The same phenomenon occurs in Mordvin and in the Permian languages of the Finnic branch of Finno-Ugric, e.g. Udmurt *mi* 'we,' *ti* 'you.' It is possible that the vowel in Yukaghir *mit* 'we,' *tit* 'you,' as compared with the singular forms *met* 'I,' *tet* 'thou,' is to be identified with the *-i* plural.

In Gilyak it occurs in the variant *bej* of the plural imperative, alongside of *be*. The possible existence of the *-i* plural in hypercharacterized forms preceded by *-t-* (No. 15) was mentioned in that section in regard to Tungus, Ainu, Chukotian, and Eskimo.

For the Chukotian languages Muravjova (1979, p. 159 of the supplement) reconstructs **-i* as the Chukchi plural and the Koryak and Aliutor dual (which derives from the plural) of pronouns, as seen in Chukchi *mu-r-i* 'we,' *tu-r-i* 'you.' This coincides exactly with Indo-European, in which the pronominal plural is clearly *-i*. These Chukotian forms have a redundant plural marking in which *-i* is preceded by *-r* (see No. 17). As mentioned in No. 5, Southern Kamchadal *si* 'thee' might well be a polite plural and therefore contain the *-i* plural that we see in Eskimo *-si* and similar forms in other languages discussed there.

Outside of Indo-European and Uralic, the most certain indication of the *-i* plural is found in Eskimo. In the genetically divergent Sirenik dialect of Siberia, the general noun plural is *-j*. In the third-person plural subject of the intransitive verb it is *-uj*, corresponding to *-ut* in other forms of Eskimo. In the Sirenik dialect it also appears in *-k-i* (for *k* see No. 2), which functions as first-person plural for intransitive subjects and transitive objects. It is general in Eskimo for *-i* to indicate the plural of the possessed object in the third-person, e.g. *iɣlu-i* 'his, her houses' (cf. *iɣlu-a* 'his, her house'). A similar contrast of singular *a* versus plural *i* is found in the possessed form of nouns used in the absolutive, e.g. Greenlandic *-i-sa* (< **i-ta*) 'plural' as against *-a-ta* 'singular.' The change of **-t* to

-s after Proto-Eskimo *i is regular in this and some other dialects.
I believe that the nominal -i plural survives in non-Sirenik Eskimo
in a considerable number of nouns in which the more widely used
-t plural (No. 15) has been added analogically (cf. Sauvageot 1924:
285). These examples were discussed in regard to Greenlandic Eskimo by Kleinschmidt (1851: 130). Besides nouns in -aluaq, which
have a plural -alu-i-t (-q is the singular absolutive, the citation form),
there are stems in -tsiaq 'too much of,' plural tsiait, and some other
isolated instances in stems in singular absolutive -q, e.g. suʁqa-q
'fishbone,' plural suʁqa-i-t. There are examples in other dialects of
the -i-t plural in stems without singular absolutive -q. For example,
in Central Arctic Eskimo Spalding (1960) gives as plural of tunu
'back,' a word with zero absolutive singular, tunu-i-t. In his discussion of Eskimo plurals, Uhlenbeck (1907: 13) states that alongside of
the t plural there is also an -i plural in the third-person possessive,
as noted above. He also notes that in Labrador and the Mackenzie
regions we find forms of the -t suffix with or without preceding -i.
Thalbitzer (1911: 1015) talks of the plural inflection as -t, or -it.
Uhlenbeck believed, in view of the agreement of Greenlandic and
Alaskan Eskimo, that the -i plural existed in Proto-Eskimo.

Finally, the second-person plural -si in the Eskimo verbal intransitive subject and noun possessive consists of second-person -s
(No. 5) followed by the -i plural suffix. As we saw in No. 5, the
same combination (-c-i < *-si) is also found in Aleut, in Southern
Kamchadal si 'thee' (if this is indeed a polite second-person plural),
and in Korean in the honorific second-person form si. If the interpretation advanced here is correct, then the -i plural would also have
existed in Korean at an earlier period.

17. Plural R(I)

In Indo-European there is a passive/deponent -r in some branches
of the family. This was at first considered to be an Italo-Celtic
isogloss, strengthening the case for a special relationship between
the two. However, it was later discovered in Tocharian, Phrygian,
Venetic, and the Anatolian languages.

It was equated by Zimmer (1888) with the third-person plural verb ending -r of Italic and Indic that was later also found in

Tocharian and Hittite. To demonstrate the connection between the third-person plural and the passive, Zimmer pointed especially to the impersonal -r of Italic (e.g. Umbrian i-er 'they go, one goes'), Old Irish berar 'one carries,' and Brythonic Celtic (e.g. Breton am gwel-er 'one sees me, I am seen'). Zimmer's view has been widely accepted (Kammenhuber 1969: 317, Georgiev 1985: 226, Kuryłowicz 1932). Haim Rosén (1978: 144) interprets the -t- of Latin ama-t-ur 'he/she is loved' as the third-person t (No. 11), functioning as object, so that he paraphrases it "loves-him-one." However, some Indo-Europeanists see the third-person plural or impersonal as distinct from mediopassive r.

Diachronic parallels for the development of a passive from the reinterpretation of a third-person plural subject are easily found. Maasai, a language belonging to the Eastern Sudanic branch of Nilo-Saharan, has a verb form that is usually treated as a passive in descriptive grammars. Both internal reconstruction and comparative evidence indicate that it involved a suffixed -i that is identical with the third-person plural in other languages of the group (Greenberg 1959). Another instance is found in the Chamorro language of Guam. Shibatani (1985: 829) cites approvingly Topping's suggestion in his Chamorro grammar that the third-person plural ma is related to the passive prefix in the same language.

In the case of Indo-European there are complications due to the existence of a middle voice that has sometimes affected the passive forms in -r. We shall see that there is widespread evidence in other branches of Eurasiatic for r as a third-person plural pronominal form and, more generally, as a personal plural. It is also an exponent of the passive and semantically related forms of the verb such as the middle voice.

Before proceeding, however, to the evidence outside Indo-European let us examine the specific phonological form it takes in Indo-European. It is relevant, considering the widespread e ~ i alternation already found in a whole series of cases in Eurasiatic, to note the third-person plural perfects in -re of Latin and Tocharian B. In fact, the Latin forms could derive from -ri since word-final -e has final -i as one of its sources (cf. mare 'sea' [nominative/accusative singular] < *mari). However, Indo-Europeanists generally derive medio-passive -r from Proto-Indo-European *ro. Further evidence for -re as a variant is provided by the Vedic third-person plural imperfect active aduh-ra 'they milked,' in which ra derives from *re. This verb preserves a number of archaic forms.

As can be seen, there is much uncertainty about the precise form of the Indo-European passive and third-person plural (indefinite) *r. Andrew Sihler (1995: 474) notes that it has recently been suggested that the Proto-Indo-European marker of the present tense in the middle endings was *-ri and not *-r, and that this has certain advantages. The Chukotian reflexes discussed below are relevant here. If the -ri of Chukchi mu-ri 'we,' tu-ri 'you (plural),' is a single element, then *-ri is preferable. However, as will be seen, it is possibly complex and the final -i may correspond to the common pronominal plural -i found elsewhere (see No. 16). Hence it has been symbolized here as r(i). A further, and perhaps more decisive piece of evidence is from Tungus, in which the basic nominal plural is ri (Doerfer 1970: 247). In the following discussion r(i) as a plural is considered separately from its developments into a marker of the passive and related forms such as the middle and intransitive.

It is a common typological development for a nominal plural to become attached to a verb to express third-person plural subject. A well known example is the Turkish nominal plural lar ~ ler, which also secondarily expresses third-person subject when suffixed to the verb, e.g. Turkish el-ler 'hands,' gel-di-ler 'they came.' Note also what might be called the floating plural of Moru, a language of the Central Sudanic branch of Nilo-Saharan, which may be attached either to the subject noun or the verb to express plurality of action. In some non-Chuvash Turkic languages an original nominal plural has spread (redundantly) to the first- and second-person plural pronouns biz and siz, which are no longer transparent when compared with the singular forms ben and sen. We thus have an authenticated route of typological change by which an original nominal plural can become the indicator of third-person plurality and from there spread to the first and second persons as well.

Turning now to Chukchi we find the first- and second-person plural pronouns mu-ri and tu-ri. These are to be analyzed as containing the first-person indicator m (No. 1) and the second-person marker t (No. 4) followed by the plural -r + i, possibly deduced from the Indo-European evidence. These forms are in fact the plurals in the same paradigm as singular *iɣəm* ~ *eɣəm* and *iɣət* ~ *eɣət* (see No. 7). In Chukchi the third-person plural independent pronoun in the nominative case is *ət-ri*, consisting of third-person *t* (No. 11) followed by *-ri*. In addition *-r-* functions in Chukchi as a plural marker in the oblique cases of personal plural nouns. It is only personal nouns that have plurals in these cases. The order of the elements in this case is noun stem + *r* + oblique case marker. The extinct Northern and Southern dialects of Kamchadal, described in Krasheninnikov's material, show forms of the first-person plural pronoun which are clearly related to Chukchi *muri*, for example, Northern *buzhe* 'we,' Southern *mush*, the final sibilant being a natural change of the palatalized r_2 (cf. Turkic *-miz*). In the Lord's prayer in the Southern dialect 'our father' is *apač bur-in*, in which *bur-in* 'our' has as its second component the genitive *-in* (see No. 25). Similar forms for these dialects are also given by Radliński.

In Altaic also there is evidence for the personal plural *r* in the Tungus and Turkic languages. In Tungus, Manchu has a plural *-ri* that is confined to certain kinship terms, e.g. *mufa-ri* 'grandfathers.' This *-ri* plural occurs outside of Manchu, for example, in Gold *mama-ri-sa-l* 'old women,' in which the common, but historically complex, plural *-sa-l* has been added to the *-ri* plural. Benzing (1955) reconstructs **-ri* for the plural of Tungus reflexive pronouns. He also posits for the Proto-Tungus aorist an *-r-* in the plural subject suffixes *-r-bün* (first-person plural exclusive), *-r-pu* (first-person plural inclusive), *-r-sün* (second-person plural) A plural in *-ri* also occurs widely with the verbal participle in *-mi* (see No. 39), the conditional in *-pi* (e.g. Gold *-pi* [singular], *pa-ri* [plural]), and the Orok verbal participle indicating an event occurring at a different time from that of the main verb (e.g. *-ɣamči* [singular], *-ɣamčeri* [plural]).

In Turkic, whose primary genetic division, as we have seen, is between Chuvash and the remainder of the family, Chuvash *r* sometimes corresponds to non-Chuvash *r*. This is reconstructed as $*r_1$ and is presumed to have been phonetically *r*. In other cases, however, we find non-Chuvash *z* corresponding to Chuvash *r* and this proto-phoneme is generally symbolized as $*r_2$. This sound is considered by many to have been a palatalized *r*, for which $*ri$ would be a natural source.

For the first- and second-person plural pronouns of Turkic the accepted reconstructions are mi-r_2 and si-r_2. The reconstructions with r_2 are based on non-Chuvash Turkish *biz*, *siz* and Chuvash *epir*, *esir*. The initial *e* of Chuvash may perhaps be identified with the deictic *e-* of Proto-Indo-European **e-ĝhom* 'I' and other forms (see No. 9), as proposed by Menges (1968: 19).

In Korean the first-person plural is *u-li*. Since Korean has only a single liquid, here transcribed as l, it frequently corresponds to r elsewhere. Ramstedt (1939: 46) proposed that *u-li* derived from **wu-li*, with the initial *w-* corresponding to Turkic *b* (see No. 1). Whether this is accepted or not, the personal pronominal plural *-li* is exactly what we would expect as the correspondent of Turkic and Chukotian *-ri*.

A further example of this formation occurs in the Amur dialect of Gilyak, where we find *me-r* 'we inclusive' (cf. *me-gi* 'we two'). It is also possible that the *-r* suffixed to numeral stems 2–5 as a classifier for persons and animals belongs here. Finally, the r plural survives in a single Yukaghir plural *uo-r-pe* 'children,' a hypercharacterized formation in which the general and productive plural *-pe* has been added to the older plural in *-r*.

A development parallel to that of Indo-European, by which a personal plural has given rise to a passive or passive-like construction (middle, intransitive, stative), has taken place in Altaic and Japanese. This is a productive method of verb derivation in Mongolian. Examples from Classical Mongolian include *asqa-* 'to spill' (transitive), *asqa-ra* 'to be spilled'; *ebede-* 'to break' (transitive), *ebede-re* 'to go to pieces.' In Turkic it is only found in the most archaic form of non-Chuvash Turkic, the language of the Orkhon inscriptions, in which there is an *-r-* middle verb derivational morpheme.

Finally, in the language of the Ryukyu Islands (which is close to Japanese) there is a verbal suffix *-ri-* that is characterized by Chamberlain (1895) as "passive, potential." This same formation is productive in standard Japanese, in which it has developed a number of variants. Examples include *kake-ru* 'hang' (transitive), *kak-ar-u* 'hang' (intransitive); *oku-* 'put,' *ok-are-ru* 'be put'; *i-ru* 'shoot,' *i-rar-eru* 'be shot.'

18. Plural KU

A plural of limited distribution within Eurasiatic is -*ku*. It seems to have been originally confined to demonstratives and interrogatives from which, in a few instances, it has spread to independent pronouns, and probably in one case to nouns. It consistently shows -*u* as the final vowel and is, I believe, to be distinguished from the dual/plural *k(i)(n)* (No. 14).

The clearest indication of its existence and function is to be found in Eskimo and Aleut. In the Greenlandic dialect of Eskimo described by Kleinschmidt, the demonstratives and the interrogative 'who?' (but not 'what?') have -*ku* throughout the plural, replacing an absolutive singular in -*na* (No. 22) and a singular suffix -*šuma* in the other singular cases. These demonstratives and the interrogative 'who?,' unlike nouns and verbs in Eskimo, have no dual. Furthermore, they also differ, at least in Greenlandic, in that in the plural there is a nominative-accusative rather than an ergative-absolutive system that is otherwise dominant in the language. An example is *iv-na* 'that' (absolutive singular), *iv-ku* 'those' (accusative plural, cf. the nominative plural *iv-kua*). In the Kuskokwim dialect of Yupik we find, not surprisingly, that the common Eskimo -*t* plural (No. 15) has been added analogically, e.g. *ki-na* (singular), *ki-ku-t* (plural), both meaning 'who?' In Siberian Yupik, Eskimo -*ku*- also occurs in the first-person pronoun *xwaŋa* 'I,' *xwaŋ-ku-tuŋ* 'we two,' *xwaŋ-ku-ta* 'we.' In Sirenik Eskimo the first person plural pronoun is *mə-kə-ta*.

The Eskimo pattern for demonstratives of -*n* (singular), -*ku* (plural) also occurs in Aleut, but with the analogical addition of the ordinary dual and plural inflections. An example is found in the Bering Island dialect of Central Aleut, in which 'this' is *wa-n/wa-ku-x/wa-ku-s*, with the same pattern in the other demonstratives and in the interrogative (where the singular marker *n* has spread to the dual and plural), e.g. *ki-n/ki-n-ku-x/ki-n-ku-s*. In this dialect of Aleut -*ku*- also occurs in the word for 'what?,' which, however, otherwise follows more closely the usual nominal pattern, *al-ku-χ/al-ku-x/al-ku-t*.

This same morpheme may be present in general Eskimo *(n-)ku-t* 'X and his companions, X and his family,' which is used almost exclusively in the plural with proper names. Kleinschmidt (1851) gives the basic form in West Greenlandic as -*kut* and for Alaskan Yupik Jacobsen (1984) also mentions a dual form, e.g. X-*nkuk* 'X and his companion.' The -*n*- here may well be the personal -*n* (No. 21). It appears that -*kut* is basically Inuit and -*nkut* is Yupik.

This -*ku* may have existed in Proto-Chukotian, but, if so, it apparently only survives in the Kerek language of the Koryak group where -*kku* is the plural of demonstratives, interrogatives, pronouns, and nouns in the absolutive case of an ergative or inverse system.

The strongest case for plural -*ku* outside of Eskimo-Aleut is found in Gilyak, in which the nominative plural in the Amur dialect is -*ku*. It also occurs as the mark of the third-person plural subject in the otherwise uninflected form of the verb, an indication of possible pronominal origin. The Sakhalin dialect of Gilyak has -*kun*, with a final nasal of unknown origin, in many forms where it is not present in the Amur dialect. This -*n* may well be the reflex of the common Eurasiatic plural -*n* in accordance with the final $n \sim t$ alternation discussed in No. 4. The Amur form -*ku* implies a final nasal since it is followed by the voiced stop alternant that occurs after original nasal grade in the Gilyak consonant alternation system, e.g. -*ku-dox* (dative plural).

Panfilov (1973) compares the Gilyak plural with the Mongol collective in -*xin* and with the -*xan* or -*xon* of some Mongolian and Turkic languages. The Orkhon inscriptions (Tekin 1968: 121) have a plural for some kinship terms in -*kun* $\sim$ -*kün*, which is closer both semantically and formally to the Sakhalin Gilyak plural.

19. Plural S

There is another plural marker, in -*s*, which is of rather limited distribution. It is, of course, the usual nominal plural in Indo-European for non-neuter nouns; in consonant stems the nominative form is *-*es*. That *-*s* was conceived quite generally as a mark of nominal plurality can also be seen from the Sanskrit instrumental plural in *bhi-s, which is clearly a plural -*s* added to the general locative/instrumental in -*bhi* (No. 28). It also occurs in the verb in Indo-European, e.g. Doric Greek -*mes* (first-person plural subject).

The surest examples outside of Indo-European occur in Altaic.

In Mongolian -s is the usual plural of consonant stems. In Baoan, a Mongolian language of China (Yellow Uighur), -s plurals are found on demonstratives, e.g. ene-s 'these,' tere-s 'those' (Todaeva 1964: 57). In Old Turkish -s is a plural in the names of ranks and nationalities (Tekin 1968: 122). There is also a Tungus collective in -sa that, according to Poppe (1953), is related to Mongolian -s; Sinor (1952) believes that the Manchu form is borrowed from Mongolian. However, the Tungus forms in -sa are widespread outside of Manchu and are unlikely to have been borrowed from Mongol since they must be old in Tungus because they enter into a variety of complex forms, especially with the common plural -l in the plural suffix -sa-l in Evenki, Negidal, Ulch, and Orok.

Outside of Altaic and Indo-European the most likely candidate is Aleut, in which the Central dialects have -s as the basic indicator of plurality throughout the inflectional system, whereas the Eastern and Western dialects have -n < *-t. The question is whether or not this -s derives from *-t by phonological change. The only relevant example is the second-person singular -t (No. 4) and here the Central dialect has the expected -n (< *-t) rather than -s. Moreover, the second-person singular possessive suffix in Atka (a Central dialect) is -mit, consisting of the relative suffix m- and the second-person singular marker -t. It thus seems likely that Central Aleut constitutes a valid third instance of plural -s, in addition to Indo-European and Altaic. However, Bergsland (1951: 168) derives it from *-t so that, in his view, all Aleut nominal plurals derive from *-t.

Other apparent instances can be dismissed, e.g. Udmurt -as, Komi-Zyrian -jas, which are completely isolated in Uralic, and Yakut -s in Turkic, which derives regularly from non-Chuvash -z and is therefore an example of the *-r plural (No. 17).

20. Collective L

In a comparison of Uralic and Altaic plural suffixes Sinor (1952: 214–15) discusses a formant -l, or -la, which has a basically collective meaning, but has sometimes become a plural. In Uralic it is found in Estonian, Cheremis, and Selkup. In the first two it is clearly collective, as in Cheremis koš 'fir tree,' kož-la 'fir grove'; it is found with similar meaning in Estonian -la, whereas in Selkup -la is a plural.

Räsänen (1957: 85) posits a Turkic collective suffix *-ala* ~ *-la* that is used with numerals, for example, Altai *eki-le* 'the two together' (Russian *vdvojem*; Baskakov 1966: 511). In Tungus, Nanai and Ulch have an *-l* plural alongside of *-sa-l*. The combination *sal* is found elsewhere in Tungus. It is clearly a compound of *sa-* (cf. Manchu plural *-sa*, No. 19) and *-l* and is so analyzed by Tungus specialists.

The Japanese plural *-ra*, as in *kodomo-ra* 'the children' may belong here (Miller 1971: 28). According to Lewin (1959: 44) this and other Japanese "plural" markers are basically collectives, and Martin (1987: 805) translates *-ra* as 'quantity, group.'

In Chukotian, Kamchadal has a collective *-al* (Volodin 1976: 288). An example very similar to the Cheremis example cited above is *ič'* 'birch,' *ič'al* 'birch forest.' With these we may compare the ordinary plural *iče?n* 'birches.' This suffix also exists in the Chukchi-Koryak branch, for example, Palana Koryak *-l?aj* 'place where something abounds, especially plants or trees, a grove' (Zhukova 1980: 39).

Eurasiatic collective *-l* perhaps also survives in some forms of Hittite numerals, written ideographically *+li* (possibly phonetically *-alli*), e.g. 5-*li* 'containing 5 size or weight units' (Friedrich 1960: 72). I am indebted to V. V. Ivanov for this suggestion. One might also compare here the similar Turkic use with numerals.

21. Personal N

There is some evidence for an element *n* that appears in a variety of circumstances distinguishing human or animal from non-human and non-animal. In Tungus it appears in two main functions, as a numeral classifier and as a plural confined to certain kin-terms and therefore to humans. Kotwicz (1962: 138) reports that Vasilevich discovered in Northern Tungus languages a system of numeral classifiers, which in its Evenki form suffixes *-ni* to numerals modifying persons, *-na* to numerals modifying wild animals, and *-nu* to numerals modifying domestic animals. In some Northern and Southern Tungus languages, plurals of certain kin terms are formed with *-na* ~ *-ne* alone, as in Ulch *aga-na* 'elder brothers,' *ege-ne* 'elder sisters,' *ama-na* 'fathers' (Sunik 1968a: 154) and Udihe *aga-na-nɪ* 'his older brothers' (literally, 'older brother-na-his'; Sunik 1968b: 215), or followed by the common and productive plurals -l and -sa-l, as in Negidal ax-nɪ-l 'older brothers' (Kolesnikova and Konstantinova 1968: 112) and Evenki -na-sal (Ramstedt 1949: 158). In addition there is a widespread Eurasiatic lexical item for 'person, man,' which occurs in Tungus in such forms as Gold nai, Oroch nä, Udihe nī and which may represent the lexical source for the grammatical items being discussed. Outside Tungus, the only likely occurrence in Altaic is the Old Turkish plural oylan 'sons, children.'

Similar to the Tungus use as a personal numeral classifier is Ainu tu-n 'two, applied to people' (cf. tu-p 'two things' < tu-pe 'two-thing'). The Ainu -n here is no doubt a shortened form of niu 'person.' Patrie (1982: 124) reports that -n occurs after open syllables and -niu after closed syllables. This same -n occurs in ne-n 'who?' (cf. ne-p 'what?'). For interrogative ne see No. 64. It is possible that Ainu niu is to be equated with the stem niv- of the Gilyak word niv-kʻ 'people,' which is also used as the ethnic name Nivkh (= Gilyak).

Old Korean had a plural nai (modern ne) used only for persons, but now obsolescent (Kim Boo-Kyom 1959: 35). The same -ne occurs as a personal singular (e.g. anak-ne 'women,' elun-ne 'honored person, my father'). Korean also has the lexical item nä (< naj) 'person.'

In Old Japanese, in the Kojiki, there is a word for 'person,' na, explained there as a term used politely for a man or woman. As pointed out in Kazár (1980: 257), the contrast of Old Japanese o-mi-na 'old woman' and o-ki-na 'old man,' found in the standard lexicographical source for Old Japanese (Ōno et al. 1974), shows that -na meant 'person.' Initial o- is an honorific.

In Gilyak we find this same -n in the numeral classifier system suffixed to numerals when persons are being enumerated. In addition, we find -n in derivational formations indicating persons, for example, vo 'village,' vo-n 'villager' in the Amur dialect, ta-f 'house,' ta-n 'household' in the East Sakhalin dialect. The final -f in 'house' is probably a locative (see No. 28).

In the Chukchi-Koryak subgroup of Chukotian there are two declensions of nouns. The first (I) includes all animate and inanimate generics. The second declension (II) contains proper names and some kin terms when used with definite reference (i.e. not grand-mother in general, but as applied to a specific person). In Chukchi, declension I distinguishes number (singular vs. plural) only in the absolutive; elsewhere number is neutralized. The plural of I nouns is -t after vowels and -ti ~ -te after consonants (see No. 15). Declension II distinguishes singular from plural in all cases. In the absolutive we find the plural -n-ti ~ -n-te, so here once more an -n- is found in the declension that exclusively indicates specific persons. In Koryak the situation is similar, but more complex in that the -t plural has been confined to the dual and a new plural formed. Otherwise the situation is parallel to that in Chukchi. The dual ending is -n-ti ~ -n-te in II, but -ti ~ -te in I. In the Koryak singular declension, II has a suffix -na- ~ -ne-, preceding the inflectional ending, that is absent in I. For example, we have in declension I dative kajŋa-ŋ 'to a bear,' but in declension II kajŋǝ-na-ŋ 'to Bear' (i.e. a person called 'Bear'). This -na- does not appear in the dual or plural of II. In Aliutor, however, in II, in place of the -n- of Chukchi -n-ti (plural), we have nominative dual -na-t and plural -na-wwi (Mel'chuk and Savvina 1978: 7). This is good evidence that the -n- personal plural of Chukchi and Koryak is identical with -na- in the singular oblique, and that the basic form is na with the meaning 'personal.'

Personal -n- may appear in the Eskimo (Yupik) plural *-n-kut, which is generally used with proper names, 'X and his family, or companions' (see No. 18). It is possible that the -n of the Turkic third-person singular cohortative su-n ~ sü-n (restricted to persons) may belong here. For the initial su-, see No. 52.

Finally, in the Hittite suffixed first-person possessive there is a hitherto unexplained -n in -ma-n that only occurs when an animate being is the possessed. It consists of first-person -m (No. 1) and the formative discussed here.

22. Absolutive NA

There is a suffix -na, or -n, that appears originally to have indi-cated either the nominative singular or the absolutive singular in ergative systems. Its chief peculiarity is that it seems everywhere to be confined to a small set of stems, namely, the demonstratives and the interrogatives, especially the k- interrogative (No. 60). It perhaps only occurred originally with the k- interrogative and has in certain languages spread analogically to demonstratives. Another quite natural line of development is for the -n, given its restricted distribution, to be reinterpreted as part of the stem and then to take number and/or case affixes.

The distribution of -n or -na with the interrogative ki- ~ ke- is particularly striking, e.g. Finnish ke-n 'who?' (the archaic nominative singular, the current form being ku-ka). The stem ken- is still found in the singulars ken-en (genitive), ken-et (accusative), ken-essä (inessive), etc. That the stem is really ke- can be seen from the plural stem ke-i- (for the i plural see No. 16). Similarly, in the Finnic language Veps, the interrogative pronoun has a stem ken in the nominative, kenen in the genitive, but in most other cases ke-, as in the nominative plural ke-d (Zajtseva 1981: 240–42). Forms such as kin for 'who?' are found in other Finnic languages, e.g. in the Permian group, Votyak kin and Komi-Zyrian kin, and in the Samoyed group, Kamassian šǝn-di, in which -di is an added demonstrative element (Rédei 1988: 140).

In Yukaghir we find kin 'who?,' in Mongolian, ken, in Eskimo, kina, and in Aleut kin. All of these forms are, of course, remarkably similar, but the way in which -n or -na is treated in the inflectional system, with varying degrees of analogical spread to demonstratives, differs from language to language.

In Uralic, in addition to the interrogative, there is the third-person pronoun *se-n (> Finnish hän), plural *se-k. The absence of -n in the plural se-k shows that it is not part of the stem. In addition, there are some Uralic languages that retain the -n, and others that do not, in either the interrogative or the third-person pronoun, the distribution varying from language to language, e.g. Mordvin ki 'who?,' Udmurt, Komi-Zyrian kin; Estonian sen 'he, she,' Komi-Zyrian si (for further details see Collinder 1955: 24 and Szinnyei 1910: 112–13).

In Yukaghir kin is 'who?' in the Tundra dialect and the -n is treated as part of the stem in inflection. A plural apparently does not occur. In the Kolyma dialect 'who?' is kinek or kintek.

As in Finnish, the -n of Mongolian ke-n is treated as part of the stem in the singular. However, the plural ke-d shows that -n is a historically distinct element.

In Eskimo the word for 'who?' is *ki-na*. The separate status of the *-na* is clearly shown in that it does not appear in the oblique cases of the singular nor in any dual or plural forms. In Eskimo this pattern is found not only in *ki-na* 'who?,' but in *su-na* 'what?' and in the large class of place demonstratives, e.g. *iv-na* 'this' (distant but visible). These are Greenlandic forms from Kleinschmidt, but similar forms are found in all Eskimo dialects.

In Aleut *kin* 'who?' the *-n* is treated as part of the stem, e.g. Bering Island *kin* (singular), *kin-ku-x* (dual), *kin-ku-s* (plural). (For *ku-* see No. 18). However, as in Eskimo, this pattern extends to the demonstratives, where the *-n* is not treated as part of the stem, e.g. *wa-n/wa-ku-x/wa-ku-s* in the same dialect.

The same *-n* is probably found in Chukchi, in which, as noted by Bogoras (1922: 724), most of the numerous demonstratives end in *-n* (which is retained in inflection, with three exceptions). The interrogative in *k* occurs in Kamchadal, but is absent from the Chukchi-Koryak branch. It takes the form *k'e* without final *-n ~ -na*.

It is highly likely that this absolutive/nominative formative survives as enclitic *-ne* in Proto-Indo-European **kwe-ne* (Pokorny 1959: 641), where it occurs in Indic and Germanic with an indefinite or generalizing meaning, a common development for interrogatives (e.g. Sanskrit *kaś-cana* 'anyone' and Avestan *-cina* with similar meaning). In Germanic it is found in Anglo-Saxon, Old Saxon, and Old High German in *hwer-gin* 'somewhere,' and from the frequent use of the indefinite with the negative it takes on a negative meaning in Old Norse *hvergi* 'nowhere,' a variant without *-n*. In Kola Saami, through a development similar to that of Indo-European, we find the generalizing pronoun *ke-ne*, plural *ke-ɢ-ne* (Kert 1966: 162).

A similar development has occurred in Gilyak in which an enclitic *-ha-gin* is suffixed to interrogatives with an indefinite or generalizing force, e.g. *aŋ-ha-gin* 'each one, anyone.' The analysis of *-ha-gin* as a compound of *ha* 'to be' followed by *-gin* is transparent. In Koryak, a member of the Chukotian family, *-kin* as a generalizing particle is probably found in *meki-ŋən* 'whoever' (Korsakov 1939). Alternation of *k* and *ŋ* is frequent in Chukotian (cf. *meki* 'who?,' *meŋin* 'which?,' and *meŋko* 'whence?'

The independent development of *-kin ~ -ken* as an indefinite and generalizing enclitic in distant areas is strong evidence that *-ne ~ -na* originally occurred with the interrogative *k-* and that its generalization to all interrogatives and demonstratives in Eskimo-Aleut is a later development.

23. Absolutive K

Proto-Eurasiatic appears to have had a suffixed -*k* that was probably somewhere between a Stage II and Stage III article. In Greenberg (1978, 1981) such developments are discussed in detail; examples include Nilo-Saharan *k-* and Penutian -*s*. A stage II article is one that in addition to the meaning of definiteness has acquired a meaning of indefinite specific, 'a certain.' Its very frequent use leads to a final stage (Stage III) in which there is no longer a general contrast between unarticulated and articulated nouns and either the unarticulated or articulated form (usually the latter) spreads analogically to a large number or virtually all nouns. In this final stage it acquires new functions. Since it has been reduced to a marker of mere nominality it frequently becomes a way of deriving nouns from verbs. In the remainder of this section examples of these and other related phenomena of Eurasiatic -*k* are discussed. All of these developments have attested parallels in other historically independent instances. Where necessary, reference is made to the discussion of particular points in Greenberg (1978, 1981) and/or examples are given from other language families.

Actual survival in Eskimo of the variant -*q* as a kind of article (presumably Stage II) is attested only twice, but in the genetically and geographically most distant of Eskimo dialects. One example comes from Kleinschmidt (1851: 36), who describes West Greenlandic final -*q* (usually one of the four chief ways of expressing the singular absolutive: -*k*, -*q*, -*t*, zero) as a kind of article. Unfortunately no further details concerning its function are given. For the Siberian dialect of Sirenik, Menovshchikov (1964: 29) gives a similarly vague statement about final χ (the normal reflex of *q*) as characterizing the singular number and a certain definiteness of the object talked about. It is true of Eskimo in general that nouns in -*k*, -*q* in the singular absolutive retain it in certain derivational formations, but not in others. The -*q* of the third-person singular intransitive (found only in the indicative) is clearly identical with this. The third-person intransitive is simply a participle (often the *t* participle, No. 43) in the absolutive case (cf. Jacobson 1984: 610). The ultimate common origin of *k* and *q*, which arose as allophones in the vicinity of different vowels that had merged even in Proto-Eskimo-Aleut, is shown most strikingly in the pair *ki-na* 'who?,' *qa-ŋa* 'when?' This problem was discussed in Chapter 2. In regard to other phenomena associated with advanced stages of the article, -*k* and -*q* behave similarly. One such phenomenon is the sporadic survival or loss among different dialects. An example is Greenlandic *qauk* 'dawn,' Labrador *qau*, compared by Sauvageot (1924) with Finnish *koi* and other Uralic forms. In Thibert (1970), a dictionary of Eastern Canadian Eskimo, there are examples such as *kiluk* and *kilu* 'seam' in the Eskimo-English and English-Eskimo parts, respectively. Here we do not know whether these are regional differences or variant forms from the same dialect. In Spalding (1960), probably a more reliable source, we find "Central Arctic" *aiviq* 'walrus,' but "Eastern Arctic" *aivik*. Rasmussen gives *tikik* 'index finger' for the language of Norton Sound and the St. Lawrence Island, but *tikiq* 'thimble' (clearly the same root) for Greenland, Labrador, and Northwestern Alaska. In Chaplino, a Siberian Yupik dialect, *nuna* is 'earth, as generally in Eskimo, but *nuna-q* is 'settlement,' a more definite meaning. In Labrador Eskimo, as described in Smith (1977), the sole singular absolutive is -*k*. I am not aware of any form of Eskimo in which -*k* or -*q* simply forms verbal nouns, but we find many examples of nominal derivational formations in which -*k* or -*q* is part of a more complex suffix and indicates nominality, e.g. **-vi-k* 'place of or where' with initial -*vi-*, a widespread Eurasiatic locative (No. 28). Note also Kleinschmidt's observation (1851: 24) that especially nominal vowel stems tend to have -*q*.

The situation in Aleut is similar to that of Eskimo insofar as χ (< **q*) forms absolutive singulars in the noun and indicates the third-person singular in the verb. Aleut does not have bipersonal (transitive) inflective forms so all verbs exhibit the intransitive inflection. Also, unlike Eskimo, *q* is the only singular absolutive morpheme in the noun. The -*q* of the absolutive is, in the words of Geoghegan (1944: 80) "almost invariably apocopated when preceded by the genitive" (i.e. the so-called "relative -*m*" of Eskimo and Aleut), thus Aleut *aguyum tunu* 'God's word' rather than *aguyum tunuq*. This is

also a widespread property of possessive constructions in languages
with Stage III articles since the possessed form usually definitizes
the whole phrase, rendering the article superfluous.

In Chukotian there is a whole series of singular absolutive suffixes
and identical forms are used for stative predication of the noun in
the third-person singular. Some of these may contain k, but I am not
certain of them. The most noteworthy is what on the surface appears
to be a partial reduplication in which the first part contains $k \sim q$
$\sim y$, which is not found in the second part. Examples are Chukchi
tirkətir 'sun,' *qelyiqel* 'a chaining or connection.' In all probability
the root does not contain the velar. For example, *qel-vən* 'palate'
probably contains the root of *qelyiqel*. This suggests that the velar
in this case represents the item under discussion. The -k would
indicate subject or topic and the second occurrence of the stem, a
predication. In Kamchadal, absolutives like *pilyəpil* 'hunger,' with
stem *pil-*, clearly represent the same formation as that just cited
from Chukchi. In Chukchi, absolutive -q apparently is also found in
the numerals 'two,' 'three,' and 'four.' That this -q is a formative is
shown by its omission in the so-called collective numerals, e.g. *ŋəra-
q* 'four,' *ŋəra-more* 'the four of us.' In Kamchadal, -*uq* forms verbal
nouns, e.g. *č'ir-* $\sim$ *č'er-* 'to steal,' *č'iruq* 'thief.' The Kamchadal word
for 'father,' *is-x*, compared to forms without a final velar in other
languages, in all probability shows a fossilized form of -k (see the
discussion of Gilyak kin terms below).

In Gilyak, there are clear examples of -k forming deverbative
nouns, e.g. *asqa-* 'be younger,' *asqa-k* 'younger brother,' *heu-* 'be
crooked,' *heu-k* 'a cross-eyed person.' Grube (1892: 5) gives other
examples of substantivization, e.g. *kalxal* 'white,' *kalxal-x* 'goose.'
Here -x is the normal reflex of -k in the Gilyak system of consonant
alternation. An example of interdialectal variation is Amur *qaur*
'brain,' East Sakhalin *ŋaur̯k*. There is also comparative evidence.
Thus Gilyak *pax* 'stone' ($<$ *pak) is cognate with Yurak Samoyed
pae, pə and Selkup *pö, pu*.

One of the commonest survivals of the non-articulated form is in
vocatives (Greenberg 1978: 73) because vocatives are automatically
definite and therefore do not acquire an article in earlier stages. In
the Amur dialect of Gilyak there are a number of kinship terms with
zero vocative contrasting with a -k stem in all the other forms, e.g. in

the word for 'father-in-law,' which is *apa* in the vocative but *apak* everywhere else. There is also a non-kin term for 'master,' with *izi* in the vocative and *izik* elsewhere in the paradigm.

In Korean there exist variant forms of the same noun with and without -*k*, e.g *thər*, *thərək* 'hair,' as well as nouns derived from verbs by the suffixation of -*k*, e.g. *sa-(ta)* 'to buy,' *sa-k* 'price' (Ramstedt 1939: 174). For Japanese, Lewin (1959: 8) describes a "special nominalizing form -*ku*" that appears only in the Nara period, the earliest from which we have linguistic evidence. The Japanese writing system does not permit the writing of syllable-final consonants (except *n*) so this may have been -*k*. In the Tungus family Even demonstratives and interrogatives have -*q* or -*k* (depending on the preceding vowel) confined to the nominative singular, much as in Eskimo, e.g. *ere-k* 'this' (nominative), *er-ɪl* 'these.'

Evidence for -*k* is particularly abundant in Turkic languages, where it derives nouns from verbs, e.g. Altai *tara-* 'to comb,' *tara-k* 'a comb.' There are also interdialectal variants as in Tatar *čakma* 'flint,' Turkmen *čakmak*, and even intradialectal variants as in Chuvash *pülme*, *pülmek* 'corn bin.' A number of suffixes have forms with and without -*k*. For example, Krejnovich (1976) notes that Turkic -*lɪ* and -*lɪk*, meaning 'possessing something, having a certain property,' are "connected." Turkic languages form verbal nouns in -*ma* and -*mak*, and these are often used as infinitives. According to Menges (1968: 133), "these two suffixes evidently are intimately related to each other . . . . Their semantic shades cannot be delimited." The common Turkic infinitive, as we have seen, ends in *ma-* or *ma-k* (for *ma*, see No. 39). The -*k* of the latter form has been interpreted as the dative (Serebrennikov and Gazhdijeva 1986: 80) and of course infinitives are frequently datives of verbal nouns (cf. English 'to go'). (For the -*k* dative of Eurasiatic, see No. 26.) However, I believe it to be more probable that the -*k* here is the third-stage article functioning as a nominalizer. In medieval Khwarezm Turkish (Eckmann 1959: 125), *mak* itself takes the dative suffix to form an infinitive. What is even more decisive, in Armenian Qipchak (Pritsak 1959: 83)—and also in modern Karaim, its probable descendant—there is a distinction between a 'real infinitive' in *ma* and a verbal noun in *ma-x*, e.g. *kor-ma* 'to see,' *buyur-ma-x* 'a command,' the latter form deriving from *buyur-* 'to command.' Chuvash, moreover, has only *ma* ~ *me* as an infinitive. In Mongolian there is a verbal noun in *-sa-γ* ~ *-se-g* containing the desiderative *-sa-* ~ *-se-* (see No. 52), whose function is to "form nouns indicating penchant for or fondness for something" (Poppe 1964: 43).

In Krejnovich's grammar of Yukaghir (1958: 24–25), he discusses a final *-ŋ* that has many of the properties of a stage II or stage III article. For example, there are interdialectal variants such as Tundra *nimeŋ* 'dwelling,' Kolyma *numo*, but the Kurilew subdialect of Tundra Yukaghir lacks the final *-ŋ* in such words. The Kolyma dialect lacks this *-ŋ*, but it is very frequent in the Tundra dialect, with the exception just noted. Furthermore, when it is present, it is lost before all inflections except the nominative singular, e.g. *nimeγa* 'in the house.' It also does not occur with determiners, e.g. *met nime* 'my house.' This is again a characteristic of stage II articles in that the possessor automatically makes the phrase determined so that no article is needed. Furthermore, the locative singular *-γane* of the Tundra dialect has a variant *-γaneŋ* which is characterized by a "nuance of assertion" (Krejnovich 1958: 54). This *-ŋ* derives from **-k* and corresponds to final *-k* in the Kolyma dialect, where this phenomenon is not found.

Yukaghir has a system of focus constructions that provides morphological expression of the so-called logical accent whereby sentences with the same truth value are distinguished, for example in transitive constructions, by whether they are answers to questions in which the subject, verb, or object has been queried. In this system the suffixation of *-k* or *-le-k* (in which *-le-* is clearly the Yukaghir form of a widespread Eurasiatic verb 'to be') plays a prominant role as a marker of focus. For *le*, see No. 58. In English, focus is commonly shown by stress, but one can also use a focusing construction of the type "It was *John* who came." This has a parallel in the suffixing of *-le-k* (Kolyma), *-le-ŋ* (Tundra) to the focused noun, whereas the equivalent of the relative clause "who came" is a participle in Yukaghir. If the noun is modified, or the focussed nominal is a pronoun, only *k* appears. An example of the latter is Kolyma *met lodoje* 'I played' vs. *met-ek lodo-l* 'I played' (Jochelson 1905: 125). Here the *-l* of *lodo-l* is a participle (see No. 45). In the extinct Chuvan dialect of Yukaghir, Tailleur (1962: 85) notes the existence of a final "gutturale" with emphatic meaning in the nominative/accusative case. It also appears in the extinct Omok dialect.

Krejnovich's (1958: 24–25) enumeration of the cases in which the second stage article *ŋ* derives from **k* in the Tundra dialect of Yukaghir is a model example. Thus we have *nime-ŋ* 'house' with the stage II article except in the following cases, in which we have *nime*: 1. Whenever there is a case suffix, e.g. *nime-ɣa* 'in the house'; 2. When the noun is preceded by a determining expression, e.g. *met-nime* 'my house'; 3. When the noun has the logical accent as the subject of a transitive verb; it may also lose it if it is the subject of an intransitive verb, e.g. *ile-ŋ* 'reindeer,' *ile law* 'the reindeer drank.'

Uralicists such as Szinnyei (1910: 93–94), Collinder (1960: 264–66), and Majtinskaja (1979: 42) posit a Uralic deverbative suffix **-k* ~ **-ɣe* which in Finnic forms nouns of action. Examples include Finnish *sade'* (< *sadek* 'rain,' cf. *sata-* 'to rain'), Cheremis *šerge* 'comb' (cf. *šerä-* 'to comb'), and Kamassian *t'eemdəge* 'a warmed up thing' (cf. *t'eemdə-* 'to warm up'). In Selkup the word for 'dog' is *kanak* in the nominative singular, with a *-k* that is lost elsewhere in the inflection, for example, *kanan* 'of the dog' (cf. Gilyak *qan* and Proto-Indo-European **kwon-*).

There are several puzzling phenomena in Indo-European that I believe belong here. These all involve a *-k* that is clearly suffixal in the noun and confined to the nominative singular or to the singular as distinct from the plural. Fuller discussion of this property of stage III articles may be found in Greenberg (1981: 109). In Indo-European one of the common *r/n* stems (i.e. stems with *-r* in the neuter nominative and accusative singular and *-n* elsewhere) is the word for 'blood.' In Sanskrit the nominative and accusative singular is *as-r̥-k* with an additional *-k* that has never been satisfactorily explained. In Latin, *senex* 'old man' has a *-k* in the nominative singular followed by an analogical *-s*, the common nominative singular ending of the third declension. In the rest of the declension this *-k* is absent, e.g. *sen-is* (genitive singular; cf. also *senior* 'older'). In Lithuanian the word for 'man' is *žmuo* in the nominative singular, but there is also a stem in *-g*, *žmogus* (nominative singular), that is replaced by a stem *žmon-* in the plural. All these various occurrences, and others, have been connected by Indo-Europeanists (for further details see Vaillant 1950–66, II, 1: 194 and Martinet 1955), but, as noted in Walde-Pokorny's (1928–32, II: 509) discussion of Latin *senex*, "why the -*k* is confined to the nominative singular is not clear."

24. Accusative M

For Indo-European *-*m* is reconstructed as accusative singular for masculine and feminine nouns, and in neuter thematic stems for both the nominative and accusative singular. In Uralic, *-*m* is reconstructed for the accusative and is found in all three branches, Finnic, Ugric, and Samoyed. It is generally singular, but in Cheremis, Vogul, Selkup, and Kamassian it also occurs in the plural and in the dual, where those categories exist. The relationship of Indo-European and Uralic *-*m* has figured in all comparisons of the two families, beginning at least with Anderson (1879), the first systematic attempt to relate Indo-European to Uralic. The possibility that accusative -*m* derives from locative -*m* is discussed in No. 27.

Evidence for an -*m* accusative is found in two branches of Altaic, Mongolian and Tungus. In classical Mongolian there is a defective third-person singular pronoun that only occurs in the genitive *i-nu* (for *i-* see No. 8). The first- and second-person singular pronouns have -*ma* suffixed to their base in all cases except the genitive (e.g. *či* 'thou,' *či-nu* 'thy,' but *či-ma-yi* 'thee,' *či-ma-dur* 'to thee'). This -*ma* is not found in nouns. Poppe (1924: 672) found in pre-classical documents the accusative *i-ma*, *i-ma-yi* 'him/her' and the dative *i-ma-dur* 'to him/her.' From this it becomes clear that the pronominal accusative was -*ma* in singular pronouns and that -*yi* was added from the nominal declension, thus producing a new base *ima*, *čima-*, etc., for the remaining cases. In Tungus we have, as both a nominal and pronominal accusative marker, -*wa* ~ -*we*, -*ba* ~ -*be*, or *ma* ~ *me*, depending on the phonological environment. These are parallel to the variants found in the first-person singular Tungus marker *w* ~ *b* ~ *m* (see No. 1).

The cognacy of the Tungus accusative with Japanese *wo*, also an accusative marker, is discussed by Miller (1971: 27) and Menges (1975: 11). This connection was apparently first pointed out by Murayama (1957). A century earlier Boller (1857) had compared Japanese *wo* with the Uralic -*m* accusative.

25. Genitive N

There is an -*n* genitive in Eurasiatic that frequently serves as a marker of the oblique case along with more specific indicators of location, instrument, etc. When this occurs it invariably precedes the more specific indicator. In certain cases it has also spread to the nominative. One of its manifestations in this form is what Uralicists and Altaicists have called pronominal -*n*, e.g. the -*n* of Turkish *ben* 'I,' an -*n* also found in other cases but which contrasts with its absence in the plural, *biz* 'we.' The absence of this -*n* in the nominative of such Altaic languages as Chuvash, Mongol, and Tungus indicates that its spread to the nominative is relatively recent.

Specialists in Mongolian also talk of variable *n*- stems in the noun. In Classical Mongolian there are "true" -*n* stems that occur in all forms, and "variable" -*n* stems in which the -*n* is required in certain cases, but may be present or absent in others, e.g. the nominative. The resemblance to Indo-European -*n* stems is obvious.

Hannes Sköld (1927) first suggested that the Uralic -*n* genitive was connected with the -*n* of the oblique cases in Indo-European "heteroclites," the -*n* of the *r/n* stems such as Latin *femur* 'thigh,' whose genitive is *feminis*. This neuter type turned out to be prominent in Hittite. The scholars who have linked pronominal *n* of Uralic and Altaic with the Indo-European -*n* stems of *r/n* heteroclites (and still other phenomena) in their fullest generality are the Nostraticists (Illich-Svitych 1976: 78–81).

Connected in some way with the -*n* genitive is a suffix -*in* that typically forms possessive adjectives which agree with the head noun in languages that have gender or number agreement. In Kamchadal -*in* and -*n* both occur and form possessive adjectives with the same meaning but arbitrary distribution. An example is *kəmma-n* 'my,' but *knin* (< **k-t-in*) 'thine,' completely parallel formations with -*n* and -*in*.

The use of the genitive as an accompaniment of oblique case markers is well known typologically (cf. English 'back of'). The modern Indic languages have renewed their case system by an oblique form to which postpositions are suffixed and which has a different stem from the nominative. The source of the oblique is Old Indic and Prakrit genitive case markers.

In the following exposition each branch of Eurasiatic that mani-
fests genitive -*n* is considered in turn in the following order: *n* as an
actual genitive, -*in* as a genitive or possessive adjective, and -*n* as a
marker of oblique cases.

For Proto-Indo-European an *-*n* genitive for the noun is not usually reconstructed; however, it is reconstructed for the first-person
singular pronoun in the form **me-ne.* In Slavic and Baltic the -*n*
is found in all the oblique cases, e.g. Old Church Slavic *mŭnojǫ,*
Lithuanian *man-imi,* both instrumental singulars. I believe that the
-*n* genitive also occurs in Tocharian with nouns denoting humans,
where it also forms the base for oblique cases. It is written with
the nasalization sign (*anuṣvara*) in an Indian-derived alphabet and
is interpreted as the *m* accusative by Windekens (1944). However,
the meaning of the case is actually close to the genitive (see Krause
and Thomas 1960: 80). Furthermore, it appears as *n* in oblique cases
and, according to Ivanov (1959), *anuṣvaraṁ* is the normal way of indicating final *n*. The interpretation suggested here was also adopted
by Illich-Svitych (1976: 79).

The possessive adjective in *-*in* is most conspicuous in Slavic.
In Old Church Slavic, when the possessor is personal the -*in* possessive adjective must be used rather than the genitive of the personal
pronoun. Meillet (1934: 366) relates it to formations in Lithuanian,
Sanskrit, Greek, and Latin. In all these cases derivations indicating
persons are included.

With regard to the use of -*n* in oblique cases in Indo-European,
the discussion usually centers on the *r/n* stems. It is clear that *r* and
n have different histories and have moved into a suppletive relationship. One indication is that oblique -*n* also occurs with stems that
have inflections other than -*r* in the nominative-accusative singular,
even those with zero inflection. For example, in Sanskrit there are
a number of roots with non-oblique cases (i.e. nominative and accusative) in -*i*, e.g. *ásthi* 'bone,' *asthnás* (genitive). There are also
a few Sanskrit nouns with zero nominative singular and an oblique
base in -*an*-, for example, *ás* 'mouth' (nominative singular), *āsán-as*
(genitive singular). The nominative-accusative -*r* of the -*u* declension in Armenian (e.g. *as-r* 'fleece,' genitive *as-u*) may be the *r*- of
the *r/n* stems (Schmidt 1981: 80).

In Hittite, in addition to the *r/n* stems, there is a so-called "mixed declension" that has thematic forms in the nominative and accusative singular and *n* forms in the oblique cases. This indicates that -*n* is being employed as a suffix of oblique cases. These nouns are of common gender, not neuter. An example is the word for 'eagle,' *ḫar-as* in the nominative singular and *ḫar-an-as* in the genitive. Palaic (Carruba 1970: 42) even has zero in the nominative of the word for 'blood,' an *r/n* stem in Hittite. The Palaic nominative is *ešḫa* and the oblique base is *ešḫan-*. In addition to the *i*, *r*, and zero nominatives already mentioned, there is one instance— the Indo-European root for 'sun,' *sṵel/sṵen*—which Pokorny (1959: 881) called an old *l/n* stem. In most languages either the *l* or *n* has been generalized; Avestan, however, still shows a nominative *r* (< **l*), oblique *n* opposition. Sihler (1995: 302) also includes H_2el/H_2en 'other' (i.e. *al* ∼ *an*) as a second example of this alternation. For further information on *l/n* stems, see No. 67.

This brings us to the large and important class of Indo-European "*n* stems." These show unusual behavior in that in some languages there is no ending in the nominative (or nominative-accusative for neuters), e.g. Latin *homo* 'person,' *hominis* (genitive singular). On the other hand, Greek always has *n*. This has lead most Indo-Europeanists to set up both *n* and *n*-less nominative forms for Proto-Indo-European and often to posit phonetic word sandhi conditions for alternation of the two forms. Others have posited the loss of *n* as Proto-Indo-European, with later introduction of -*n* by analogy with oblique case forms. There are also other peculiarities such as ablaut alternations between the nominative and the oblique, and a lengthening of the final stem vowel in the nominative singular.

In light of the evidence presented here (see also Illich-Svitych 1976), it is clear that these are not really "*n*-stems," but stems in which oblique -*n* has spread to the nominative, whether as a variant in Proto-Indo-European or by independent analogical change later. The situation is very similar to that in Mongolian, as we shall see presently.

It seems probable that in the Indo-European middle participle and verbal noun in **-men* (e.g. the Homeric infinitive -*menai* [dative singular] exactly corresponding to Vedic -*mane*) we have a combination of the oblique stem of the verbal noun and the infinitive in -*m* (No. 39).

In Uralic the nominal genitive is reconstructed as *n. It has been suggested that this n is identical with that of possessive adjectives (Lytkin 1974: 23). Some Uralicists consider the -n- with possessive suffixes an analogical extension of a plural n. For discussion see Majtinskaja (1974: 225–27). In the first- and second-person singular independent pronouns the -n has been extended to the nominative from the non-nominative cases. The nominatives are reconstructed as *minä 'I,' *tinä 'thou.' However, as noted in No. 1, some Baltic Finnic languages have no n in the nominative of the first- and second-person singular pronouns.

In Yukaghir both d and n appear as genitives or more general markers of attribution, for example, mārka-d-ile 'one reindeer' ('one-d-reindeer'), but mārka-n-gile 'one person.' Contrary to the pattern of alternation discussed in Chapter 2 it is the non-nasal variant that occurs before a vowel and the nasal before a consonant. Whether this is really a genitive in n in Yukaghir, which would then be cognate with the Uralic genitive, has been much discussed in the literature. Krejnovich (1982: 23–24) makes an important contribution in pointing out other examples of an n ∼ d alternation in Yukaghir. The matter is really cleared up by the early material on the extinct Chuvan dialect (Tailleur 1962), which shows that the form was -nt- and regularly gives n before consonants and d before vowels in the later language. Whether the n of nt, evidently a complex form, is the genitive n is not certain, but other forms in Chuvan show the undoubtable existence of oblique n in locative cases, e.g. Chuvan ablative numa-n-ga-t 'from the house,' where the Kolyma dialect of modern Yukaghir has numoget (Nikolaieva 1988: 144).

Evidence for the -n genitive appears in all three branches of Altaic. In Turkic the genitive of nouns is *-n. In non-Chuvash Turkic (except Yakut, which has lost the -n genitive) the oblique n appears in the locative and ablative inflections, e.g. Turkish -nda, -ndan (cf. Chuvash -ta, -tan). In Yakut the -n genitive survives in the personal possessive pronouns, e.g. miene (< *mine) 'my.' On the other hand, there is important evidence in Old Turkish of the existence of a stem without -n in the adverbs, e.g. be-ru 'hither' (i.e. 'to me,' see Nos. 1 and 29). In the first- and second-person singular pronouns, non-Chuvash Turkic has generalized the oblique stem by extending it to the nominative, as in Uralic, e.g. Turkish *ben, sen.* This did not happen in Chuvash, in which the nominatives *epĕ, esĕ* contrast with the oblique stems *man-, san-.* In the genitives *manăn, sanăn,* the *-n* genitive has been added once more to the oblique stem. Non-Chuvash Turkic retains the contrast between oblique *-n* and a nominative without *n* in demonstratives and third-person pronouns, e.g. Turkish *ol* 'he, she,' *a-n-in* 'his, her'; Old Turkish *bu* 'this,' *bu-n-uŋ* (genitive). Some Turkic languages have *-ŋ* rather than *-n* in the genitive. Ramstedt (1952, II: 25) derives *-ŋ* from **-n.*

The Mongolian noun shows a state of affairs, with regard to nominal "*-n*" stems, similar in a number of ways to Indo-European. In the Classical language there are "true *n*-stems" that have *-n* through all their inflections. There is also a much larger class of nouns that is called by Mongolicists "variable *n*-stems." In Classical Mongolian *n-* is found in all oblique cases except the comitative in *-tai* (which appears to be a recent postposition) and the instrumental. In the nominative, accusative, and instrumental, forms with and without *-n* appear in free variation. This is naturally enough an unstable situation. In the Moghol of Afghanistan the *-n* has been generalized throughout the whole declension, whereas in Dagur, a South Mongolian language, it has been lost everywhere. Buck (1955) quotes instances in which forms with and without *-n* have developed different functions, e.g. Buriat *mod-oor* 'by means of the wood,' *modnoor* 'together with the wood,' or idiomatic differences of meaning in the same stem, e.g. Ordos *goto-n-du* 'in the enclosure,' *goto-du* 'in the town.'

The actual genitive in Classical Mongolian is *-un* in consonant stems, *-jin* in vowel stems, and in variable *-n* stems, *-u,* in which possibly a second *-n* for the genitive has been lost by dissimilation. The form in *-jin* after vowel stems may reflect the variant form *-in* mentioned earlier. The original *-n* genitive survives also in its use with attributives, e.g. Kalmyk *mod-n ger* 'wooden house,' Classical *modon* 'wooden.'

In the Mongolian pronouns the *-n* oblique has not been extended to the nominative. In this regard it resembles Chuvash, but in this case the same pattern also holds in the first- and second-person plural pronouns. We have for the nominative and genitive *bi/minu* 'I, my,' *či/činu* 'thou, thy,' *ba/manu* 'we, our,' and *ta/tanu* 'you, your.' Outside the genitive the oblique stem shows an innovation in the singular in the form of a suffix -ma- derived from the accusative (see No. 24), for example, či-ma-dur 'to thee,' but in the plural the oblique stems are man- and tan-.

In South Tungusic there is a large class of nouns in which -n occurs in the oblique cases, but not in the nominative or accusative. In North Tungusic the -n has apparently been extended through the whole paradigm, the class of -n stems being a large one with many forms cognate with South Tungusic variable -n stems.

Another point of resemblance between Tungusic and Indo-European, showing that in n-stems n is not part of the stem, appears in the formation of compounds. Thus, Even murin 'horse' is synchronically an n-stem, but in compounds the earlier form without -n appears in such formations as muri-ksa 'horse hide' and muri-kān 'possessing a horse.' Similarly, in classical Mongolian we have orun 'place,' but oru-si- 'to take one's place, enter.' With these formations we may compare Sanskrit rāja-putra 'king's son, prince' in which, instead of the theoretical stem rājan 'king,' we find rāja. Vedic also has -i instead of -in in compounds, e.g. śaci-gu 'having strong cattle' from śacin 'strong.' In fact, in Sanskrit there is a general rule that final n of a derivative suffix is regularly dropped before a consonant in inflection and composition (Whitney 1879: 64).

Although there is no genitive inflection in the noun, in pronouns we find in North Tungusic a genitive in -n, e.g. Negidal min, minŋi 'my' contrasting with nominative bi. In South Tungusic the oblique -n has been extended to the accusative of the first- and second-person pronouns in both the singular and plural, e.g. Udihe mineve 'me.' It does not appear in the noun.

In Ainu the n- genitive may survive as an oblique marker that has become part of the stem in Hokkaido taan, Sakhalin tan 'this' (cf. Yukaghir ten 'this,' which presumably arose by a similar process). For the t demonstrative, see No. 11. In Korean the usual genitive is -ii or -i (generally personal), but a genitive -n survives in present-day Korean in the word hai, genitive hai-n 'sun, day' (Ramstedt 1952: 27).

In Japanese the genitive particle no (Ryukyuan nu < no) may be an example of the genitival n. Miller (1971: 172) derives it from na, which still survives in Japanese to form attributive adjectives.

Sansom (1928: 234) also finds *na* in fossilized form in the earliest forms of Japanese, e.g. *ma-na-kö* 'eye-of-ball.' Miller (1971: 160) has noted in early Japanese texts variations between the nominative and oblique forms of the first- and second-person pronouns, *mi/wanu* and *si/sõne*, which are obviously similar to the alternations in Altaic.

Gilyak, like many of the languages of the northeastern part of Asia, has no nominal genitive inflection. The independent pronouns form genitives by suffixing *-ni*, e.g. *ni-ni* 'my.' In the Amur dialect (Panfilov 1962–65, I: 236) there is simply suffixed *-n* before nominal postpositions, e.g. *tʰxi* 'upon,' *ni-n tʰxi* 'upon me.' The *-n* genitive is also found with the interrogative *aŋ-ni*, *ay-ni* 'whose?' In the third person, in addition to forms with postpositions like those just cited, after *i-* (a bound prefixed possessive) the noun takes a voiced stop in the initial consonant alternation. This is normally the indication of a lost nasal, hence **in-*. For this interpretation of the consonant gradation system, see Krejnovich (1937: 44) who, however, does not apply it to this case. The typological parallel to the Old Irish initial consonantal alternation is striking. A similar analysis holds for the Gilyak demonstrative locative adverb *ag* 'there.' We should reconstruct **-ank*, thus making these adverbs identical to the Kamchadal locative case in *-ank*.

Chukotian has an *-n* genitive, seen most obviously in Kamchadal *k'e* 'who,' *k'e-n* 'whose?' In Chukchi-Koryak, which has no inflected genitive, possession by a person is indicated by an inflected possessive derivative in *-in* (cf. Indo-European, especially Slavic). In Chukchi several "pronominal" adjectives insert *-ne* ~ *-na* in the oblique cases, e.g. *qutə-na-jpə* 'from the other.' Kamchadal forms genitives both from pronouns and nouns (in the latter instances called derivatives), for example, *mineʔin* 'whose?,' *k'elču-ʔin* 'pertaining to a mosquito.' Both *-n* and *-in* occur, depending on the specific word, but Volodin (1976: 168) notes that it is hard to find any difference between them. In addition, oblique *-n* is found in the nominal and pronominal locative *-n-k* and dative *-n-ke* in the pronoun; in the pronoun it is extended to additional cases, *-nxʔal* (instrumental, prolative), *-ne-kit* (causal). Volodin (1976: 191, f.n.) analyzes these as containing the *-n* possessive.

In addition, Chukchi and Koryak have an attributive form in *-n* in the oblique cases of the numerals 2–4, which in their isolated form end in -q (see No. 14), for example, Chukchi ŋəre-q 'three,' ŋəro-n pojya 'with three spears.' For this construction with the attributive form of numerals, compare Yukaghir above.

26. Dative KA

A suffix that most frequently takes the form -ka seems originally, and still in many languages, to have had the general meaning of dative-allative, i.e. motion to or transaction with a person or thing. In some instances it is a general locative, exhibiting a very common semantic shift. The transition is clearly observable in Yakut, the most divergent language within non-Chuvash Turkic. Although the rest of non-Chuvash Turkic has *-ka as dative-allative, Yakut has -ya (< *ka), both as dative-allative and locative. Once its meaning has shifted to general location it often occurs with coaffixes that provide further specification as to the type of locative meaning. Its occurrence in Indo-European is marginal and will be left for later discussion.

For Finno-Ugric, Décsy (1965: 157) reconstructs a case ending -k that he calls lative I; it is sometimes called prolative. It also survives in adverbs, in which the meaning 'motion towards' is clear, e.g. Finnish kotia' (< *kotia-k) 'homewards.' In the Samoyed languages it occurs as a coaffix followed by other markers of location, which, in two cases, can be reconstructed as *-ka-na (locative, see No. 30) and *-ka-ta (ablative, see No. 33). The Selkup infinitive in -qo probably belongs here inasmuch as infinitives are frequently dative in origin (e.g. English).

In the Kolyma dialect of Yukaghir there is a case ending, -ge ~ -go (vowel harmony variants), that frequently means 'motion towards.' Similar forms are found in other dialects of Yukaghir. It also appears before the coaffixes -n (No. 30) (e.g. Tundra prolative -ya-n) and ablative -t (No. 33) -ya-t, -ya-te. Collinder (1940) relates the Uralic and Yukaghir forms.

In Altaic, a *-ka dative-allative occurs as a case inflection everywhere in Turkic. In Mongolian it occurs in adverbs as a coaffix in -ya-na 'in' (No. 30), -ya-ru 'towards' (No. 29), and ya-du (No. 32). The first two of these combinations also occur in Kirghiz and in the Old Turkish of the Orkhon inscriptions. In Tungusic, -k- occurs as a case marker only with coaffixes, e.g. Evenki -k-la (lative), -k-it (ablative) (No. 33). However, it survives without coaffixes in adverbs, e.g. Even āk 'to whom?,' which derives from *kak according to Benzing (1955: 1062). In other branches of Tungusic there are further examples of adverbial use. In Altaic there are also instances of adverbial use. An example is Mongol qa-mi-ɣa 'where?, whither?' Its analysis is clear. It consists of an interrogative element (No. 60) + locative -mi- (No. 27) + -ɣa (< *ka), which presumably contributes the nuance of 'motion towards.'

Korean has a dative, -ɨike, that is only used with persons. In Japanese, adverbs of place are formed with -ko, e.g. so-ko 'there,' do-ko 'where?' In Ainu -k appears in the adverb na-k 'where?,' in which the first part is an interrogative (No. 64). There is also a noun ke meaning 'locality.' Ainu also has a common prefix ko- affixed to the verbal stem and frequently translatable as 'to,' e.g. ko-kira 'flee to' (cf. kira 'to flee'). However, its fundamental meaning appears to be comitative (see No. 34).

In Gilyak there is a dative-accusative in -ax. The Amur dialect has a series of adverbials of place derived from demonstratives and interrogatives by suffixing -g, with variant forms in -ŋg as well as -ŋge. These must derive from *-nk, *nke. An example is a-ŋg 'there,' hu-ŋge 'here' (Panfilov 1962–65, I: 247). They are, of course, remarkably similar to the Kamchadal locative and dative case endings and to the Chukchi form əŋkə 'there, then,' cited below. Note also the Gilyak suffix -ak in kʻe-qr-ak 'place and direction upstream' (cf. kʻe-qr 'territory upstream'), and similar formations.

In Chukotian, Chukchi and Koryak have locatives in -k, -ki. In Kamchadal -k combines with the oblique case marker -n-, originally a genitive (No. 25), in the forms -an-ke 'toward' and -an-k 'in.' These case forms are similar to the Chukchi adverb ənkə 'there, then' (Moll 1957: 167). In the Chukotian group there are also historically complex inflections in which k figures as a coaffix. These combinations are very similar to those in Samoyed, Yukaghir, Tungus, and Ainu. In the Chukchi-Koryak group there is a case form in -kjit that in Chukchi indicates 'direction of,' but in Koryak is called causative and is semantically similar to an ablative, a meaning derived from its final component (see Nos. 31 and 33). Kamchadal -k-it is likewise a causative marker. In Aliutor, of the Koryak group, -ka still survives with its original meaning of 'direction toward' in such pronominal forms as *yəmə-ka* 'toward me.' The Chukchi-Koryak group has an infinitive in *-k* (cf. Selkup). There are also survivals in adverbs such as Chukchi *mi-k* 'where?' (see No. 62) and Kamchadal *zal-k* 'behind,' *č'is-k* 'inside,' etc. These are directional adverbs that contrast with *zal* 'the area behind,' *č'is* 'the inside.' The extinct eastern dialect of Kamchadal has a locative in *-k* and a dative in *-ko* (e.g. *atno-k* 'at home,' *atno-ko* 'homewards,' *atoda-ko* 'to the companions,' cf. *atod* 'companions').

The *-k* under discussion survives in Eskimo only in adverbs with coaffixes. An example is Labrador *na-k-it* 'whence?,' formed from *na-* (interrogative; see No. 64) + *-k-* (locative) + *it* (ablative; see No. 33). In Siberian Yupik *-k* also appears with clear dative-allative meaning in Chaplino *na-və-k* 'whither?,' *sama-və-k* 'thither downwards,' and other locative adverbs. The *-və-* here is probably the *bh* locative (see No. 28).

I believe that in Indo-European the *k* in question survives in the irregular dative of the first-person singular pronoun, e.g. Latin *mihī* (< *mehei*), Umbrian *mehe*, Sanskrit *mahy-am*. This is an anomalous form. An attempt has been made to explain it with *gh* (< **bh*, Proto-Indo-European **mebhi*), as in the second-person singular pronoun, e.g. Latin *tibī*. This change is attributed to dissimilation because of the initial nasal consonant in the first-person pronoun. This ad hoc solution, originally proposed by Loewe, was rejected by Hermann (1934), but has been accepted by Szemerényi (1978: 198). The resemblance of this isolated form to the Turkic dative (e.g. Nogai *maga*, Altai *mege*) is striking.

27. Locative M

In a number of Indo-European oblique nominal cases largely parallel forms with both **m* and **bh* occur. In this section **m* will be considered along with the problem of the interrelations of the two forms. Szemerényi (1978: 208) reconstructs **-bhi/-mi* for the instrumental singular, **-bhyō/-mō* for the dual ablative, dative, and instrumental, and **-bh(y)os/-mos* for the dative and ablative plural. As nominal inflections **-m* is characteristic of Germanic, Slavic, and Baltic, whereas **-bh* is found in Italic, Celtic, Armenian, and Indic.

However, *m* forms occur in languages that otherwise have *bh*. For example, Burrow (1965: 19) equates Sanskrit -*āyām*, locative singular of -*ā* stems, with Old Church Slavic -*ojǫ*, instrumental singular in the same stem class. Others have considered the -*b* of the Balto-Slavic second-person singular and reflexive pronouns (e.g. Old Church Slavic *tebĕ*, *sebĕ*, Old Prussian *tebbei*, *sebbei*) as representatives of *bh* in a branch of Indo-European usually characterized by *m* inflections.

Naturally enough there have been attempts to derive one from the other, usually the *m* from the *bh*. However, Hirt, Meillet, Szemerényi, and others believe that both must be reconstructed for Proto-Indo-European. Moreover, as Meillet (1964: 298) states, the forms are not completely parallel. In an important discussion Hirt (1895) not only maintains that one cannot derive one from the other by sound change, but also points out that they have different phonological characteristics, namely, *bh* is generally followed by -*i*, whereas *m* tends to be followed by -*o*. In fact the forms in -*bhy-as*, etc., found in Sanskrit, show original *bhi-* followed by a thematic vowel that is characteristic of the basic Indo-European ablaut alternation.

In addition to the phonological difference pointed out by Hirt, a consideration of the **m* and **bh* forms in other branches of Eurasiatic shows a fairly consistent semantic difference. The **m* is more concrete in nature and is often found as an independent lexical item meaning 'earth, ground.' In contrast, *bh* is more abstract with meanings such as 'location in time and space.' This difference is shown in Gilyak *mi-f* 'earth,' in which the stem is *mi-* 'earth,' with a concrete meaning, and -*f* is a locative suffix indicating place or time that is extremely productive in the language. The difference is also seen in Japanese *hiro-ma* 'hall, salon' vs. *hiro-ba* 'an open space, a square' (Takahashi 1952). As can be seen from these examples, both **m* and **bh* are old, going back at least to Proto-Eurasiatic.

In Indo-European, in addition to the occurrence of *m* in the nominal inflection, there is a root *me-* (Pokorny 1959: 702–3) that occurs as the basis of a number of prepositions indicating position within, e.g. Greek *me-tá* 'in,' Gothic *miθ* 'with.' Locative -*m* survives in adverbial use in Tocharian A *āläm* 'elsewhere' (cf. Yupik Eskimo *allami* 'elsewhere').

In Uralic it occurs as a lexical item, e.g. Finnish *maa*, Tavgy

Samoyed *mou* 'earth.' However, the Proto-Uralic form is usually re-constructed with an additional syllable as **maye* 'land, earth' (Rédei 1988, I: 282) and this would remain unexplained. Additional Uralic forms may be found in Collinder (1955: 33). In Vogul it has been grammaticized to form nouns from verbs with the meaning 'place of action,' e.g. *xujne* 'lie down,' *xujne-ma* 'bed.' To my knowledge this is the only instance of such a derivation in Uralic.

In Yukaghir there is a suffix *-me* ∼ *-mo* (Kolyma), *-meŋ* (Tun-dra), *-ma* ∼ *-mu* (Chuvan), *-m* (Omok), all meaning 'time when,' e.g. Kolyma *pojerxo-mo* 'in the daytime.' In Omok it occurs with the names of seasons, e.g. *nałło-m* 'in autumn.'

In Altaic locative *m* is marginal. It occurs in Tungus as a locative-instrumental adverbial suffix, as in, for example, Orok *gitu-mi* 'on foot, by foot' (Petrova 1968: 80). Elsewhere in Tungus (Ben-zing 1955: 1038) it indicates spatial extension as an adjective for-mant in *xorü-mi* 'extending over a small space.' It probably is also found in the Mongolian derivational suffix for nouns of instrument, e.g. Classical Mongolian *uqa-* 'to dig,' *uqa-mi* 'a chisel.'

In Ainu it occurs once more as a noun *ma* 'earth, peninsula, is-land, dry.' It also functions as a locative suffix in spatial adverbs, e.g. *asa-m(a)* 'underneath' (cf. Sirenik Eskimo *asi* 'earth'); *ka* 'top of anything,' *ka-m* 'over, above,' and *be-ma* (i.e. *pe-ma*) 'in the water' (Dobrotvorsky 1875). Vovin (1993) considers Proto-Ainu **ma-k* 'in-side' as having a *-k* suffix. This would presumably be absolutive *-k* (see No. 23); compare also Proto-Uralic **maye* 'earth' above.

Contemporary Japanese has a lexical item *ma* 'place, room, time,' which goes back to Old Japanese. There is also in Old Japanese a suffix *-mi* 'neighborhood' (Yoshitake 1934) that occurs as a variant alongside of *-pe*, *-be*, *-pi* (Chamberlain 1889). Old Japanese also had a suffix *-mo*, found in *si-mo* 'underneath' (cf. Ainu *asa-m*, Sirenik *as-i*, mentioned above). Its identity as a locational suffix is clear from the existence of a synonymous form *si-ta* that still exists in Japanese (for *-ta* see No. 32). Note also Japanese *i-ma* 'now,' literally 'this time,' in which *-ma* is suffixed to the near demonstrative *i-* (No. 8). The Japanese suffix *-mi*, which forms ab-stracts, e.g. *taka-mi* 'height' (< *taka-i* 'high'), also often has a con-crete spatial meaning in the classical language and may belong here (Aston 1904: 42), e.g. *taka-mi* 'hill,' *fuka-mi* 'a deep place, depth.'

However, this meaning could be secondary and the formative may belong with No. 39.

In Ryukyuan there is a series of adverbs of which the first component is a demonstrative and the second, -ma, a locative: ku-ma 'here' (see No. 10), a-ma 'there' (see No. 9). It also probably occurs in the Ryukyuan interrogative mā 'where?' (cf. Kamchadal below).

In Gilyak, in addition to the word mi-f 'earth,' which contains bh (No. 28) as a suffix, there is a postposition -mi 'inside.' The same item occurs occasionally in nominal derivation, e.g. il 'mouth,' il-mi 'palate' (literally 'that which is in the mouth'). The suffix -m, added to certain locational roots as well as interrogative and demonstrative pronouns, forms verbs, for example, kʻi-m- 'to be located above,' with which we may compare kʻi-r 'a place located above something' (for -r see No. 29). Other examples are řa-m- 'to be where?' and tu-m- 'to be here' (cf. řa-in 'where?,' which contains the nominal locative inflection -in), and tu-r 'place near the speaker, here' (Panfilov 1962–65, II: 18). From basically the same locative, interrogative, and demonstrative roots, verbs are likewise formed by suffixing -mi- (Panfilov 1962–65: II: 21–22). In contrast however to the formation in -m-, that in -mi- is suffixed to locational roots in the fricative grade in the system of initial consonant alternations, which indicates a lost vowel that cannot be reconstructed. Thus, corresponding to kʻi-m- 'to be located above,' there is xi-mi- 'to be oriented in an upward direction.' In addition to these uses there is a noun mi- 'the inside,' as in ńyŋ pry mi-uin qo-nɨ-dʹ-ra (Saval'eva 1970, s. v. mi) 'we will sleep in the tent' (literally, 'we tent inside-locative sleep-future-indicative-assertion'). In addition, -mi forms adverbs of place, e.g. xi-mi 'above.'

Within Chukotian locative -m only seems to occur in Kamchadal (Volodin 1976: 93), in which -no-m indicates place of action, e.g. axt 'to divide up fish,' axt-no-m 'place of division of fish.' That -m is distinct from -no- is shown by the fact that it only appears in the absolutive singular. That -m- here means 'place' is shown further in Stebnickij (1934: 91), where we find a contrast between atə-no-m 'village' and atə-no-lan 'inhabitant of a village.' It may also occur in Kamchadal ma 'where?, somewhere' unless this is simply the m interrogative (No. 62). There is the same alternative explanation for Ryukyuan mā 'where?,' cited above, but the occurence of mi as a separate interrogative in that language, as well as other locatives in *ma* in Ryukyuan and probably in Chukotian, favors the locative explanation. The locative -*ma* also probably occurs in the Chukchi and Koryak comitative case, which is marked by the circumfix *ɣa* . . . *ma* (for *ɣa* see No. 34), and in the corresponding *k* . . . *m* found in the western dialects of Kamchadal (Volodin 1976: 139).

Its chief occurrence in Eskimo is the plural suffix -*mi-u-t*, in which -*t* is the plural marker (see No. 15). It means 'those who live in place X' and is not confined to proper names. Jacobson (1984: 499), in discussing -*mi-u-*, says that it is from the locative case ending -*mi*. The -*u-* is doubtless the common verb 'to be' so that -*mi-u-* means 'those who are in or at.' Indeed -*u-* can be omitted in Chaplino, a form of Siberian Yupik (Menovshchikov 1962–67, I: 90), where it takes the form -*mi-t*. Chaplino *ma-ku-mi-t* 'those from here' shows that it is not confined to proper names (for *ma-*, see No. 1 and for -*ku-*, see No. 18). It also occurs in incorporated form in a number of demonstrative pronouns derived from place adverbs, both in Yupik and Inuit, e.g. Alaskan Yupik *a-m-na* 'the one over there,' *i-m-na* 'the aforementioned one,' *pa-m-na* 'the one back there, away from the river' (Jacobson 1984: 658–62).

In Aleut it occurs in adverbs of place, similar in structure to those of Ryukyuan, e.g. *ka-ma* 'where' (for *ka-* see No. 60). It is also probably preceded by locative *i* (No. 31) in the formative -*ja-m*, e.g. *qa-na-ja-m* 'where?' (for -*na-* see No. 30) and *wa-ja-m* 'today,' the initial element of which is the demonstrative *wa*. There is also a suffix -*mi-* (Geoghegan 1944: 69) whose meaning is given as 'indeed, truly, just this.' In spite of the remoteness of these meanings from that of a locative several of the examples suggest this meaning. Thus, from *kitaq* 'foot' we have *kita-mi-xtakuqiŋ* 'I kick, I push with the foot' and from *qwixi-kuqiŋ* 'to spit' we derive *qwixi-mi-ɣikuqiŋ* 'I spit on, I spit at.' It has a temporal meaning in *qila-m* 'morning.'

It was noted under No. 24, the -*m* accusative, that the Indo-European and Uralic accusative might have originated from locative -*m*. In languages like Latin the accusative is used for time periods or for spatial extent. In Walde (1938–54, II: 645) *tam* 'for such a distance, to such an extent' (correlative with *quam* 'for what distance, to what extent') is derived from **tām*, the feminine accusative singular of the Indo-European demonstrative -*t-* (No. 11). Compare also, with an emphasizing -c, Latin *tunc* 'then.' These have been related to Gothic *hwan* 'when?' and similar forms in other branches of Indo-European. In Old Church Slavic the accusative may indicate 'time when,' as in *prebystŭ dĭnŭ tŭ* 'he arrived on that day,' literally, 'arrived-he day (accusative) that (accusative).' In Vedic, *uṣrā́m* 'in the morning' is interpreted by Brugmann as a locative, whereas others consider it to be an accusative.

In his description of the accusative in his grammar of Sanskrit, Whitney (1879: 92) notes that it is "often used in more adverbial constructions (a) occasionally for measures of spaces (b) much more often for measures of time." Beke (1928), comparing Indo-European and Finno-Ugric, notes similar usages in both families and concludes that at an earlier period the Indo-European and Uralic case in -*m* had two central semantic components: location in time and space and direct object. For a typological parallel see the discussion of the Tungusic accusative in the next section.

28. Locative BH

As was noted in the preceding section, Indo-European has a series of oblique case inflections with parallel forms in *m* and *bh*. In regard to *bh*, Hirt (1895) started with a -*bhi* suffix (indifferent to number) that actually occurs in Homeric Greek and is found sporadically in later Greek. When the meaning is not further specified by prepositions, the signification is locative, e.g. *naû-pʰi* 'at the ships,' or instrumental, e.g. *î-pʰi* 'by force.' When Mycenean was deciphered it was discovered that the form in -*pi*, corresponding to classical *pʰi*, was quite frequent. The suffix -*bhi* has generally been connected etymologically with the Germanic preposition seen in Gothic *bi* and English 'by' (Pokorny 1959: 34). Brugmann, and others, also related it to the Greek *amphi*, Latin *ambi*, etc. 'in the vicinity of, on both sides of.' In his discussion (1897–1916, II.2: 795), Brugmann declares that there is no proof that the initial element was *am*- or *m̥*-; it could as well have been **an*- or *n̥*-. The reason for this suggestion is the initial element of Sanskrit *an-yas* 'other' and similar forms in other Indo-European languages. Since then the form *anpi* 'both' has been discovered in Tocharian B. We shall see that close correspondents of the forms with initial *n* are found in Yukaghir and Chukotian.

In Yukaghir, -nube, -nubo, and -be all occur in the Kolyma dialect to form expressions of place, and similar forms are found in other dialects. An example is ammal- 'to spend the night' and ammal-be 'sleeping place for the night.' The suffixes -nube, -nubo are of course close to the forms postulated by Brugmann.

Within the Turkic branch of Altaic, Chuvash has an instrumental in -pa concerning which John Krueger (1961: 109) notes that it can also be used for the place in which an action occurs. In non-Chuvash Turkic, instrumental -ba occurs in Shor and in Karaim.

Tungus forms adverbs of time with -ba, e.g. *dol-ba 'at night' (Benzing 1955: 95). There is also an accusative in -ba ~ -wa, Manchu -be. In Tsintsius' comparative Tungus dictionary (1975–77, I: 78), a lexical item bē 'place' occurs with citations from a variety of Tungus languages. Benzing discusses the connection between the accusative and the adverbial place and time uses. He is uncertain whether there is a direct connection between the accusative and the adverbial uses but adds: "However, in any case, one must keep in mind the extended use of the accusative in time expressions (especially Northern Tungus) and the by no means rare spatial applications, especially in Southern Tungus" (Benzing 1955: 1048).

In addition to the word ba 'place,' Manchu has substantival expressions like u-ba-iŋge 'found here' and ai-ba-de 'found in what place' (for -de see No. 32). It also occurs in the adverbs tan-pa 'this year' and oya-pa 'next year' (Pfizmaier 1851: 36) and in local demonstratives such as taa-pa 'here, there.' This latter expression contains the unmarked demonstrative t (No. 11).

In Ainu there is a word pa 'season, year,' which is optionally suffixed to the names of seasons, e.g. mata, mata-pa 'winter.' It also occurs in adverbs of place like taa-pa 'here, there.' This last expression contains the unmarked demonstrative t (No. 11). In Dobrotvorskij's Sakhalin material (1875) we find teva 'here' and in Bronisław Piłsudski's (1912) recordings from the same general area we have tava 'thereupon, then.'

In Korean there is a word pa 'way, means, thing, that which.' This may be related to the common Ainu word pe 'thing, circumstance.' Their meaning is not incompatible with the general local reference in related languages.

In contemporary Japanese there is a word ba 'place' that already existed in the classical period (Lewin 1959: 48), to which Ryukyuan *bā* 'occasion, when?' is related. In Old Japanese there was a postposition *-be, -bi* 'neighborhood, direction, quarter' that was also used in time expressions, e.g. *yupu-be* 'evening.' The Japanese form here shows *nigori*, i.e. intervocalic voicing. It also exists in Old Japanese without voicing, e.g. *sita-pe* 'the underworld,' literally 'under-place' (Syromiatnikov 1972: 90). The variant without *nigori* may occur in modern Japanese *-e* 'towards' (< Old Japanese *he* < *pe* [Komai 1979: 34]). The *-be* suffix still exists in contemporary Japanese, for example, in *hama, hamabe* 'the beach,' *umi-be* 'seaside,' and *kawa-be* 'riverside.' A variant *-ba* occurs, for example, in *hiro-ba* 'wide place' (cf. *hiroi* 'wide') and *asobiba* 'playground' (cf. *asobu* 'to play'). Since *nigori* is usually a reflex of an earlier nasal plus stop, the Japanese forms with it may perhaps be compared with Chukotian *-nv-* and Indo-European *-mbh(-i)*.

Gilyak suffixes *-f* to form names of place that are not inflected for case and number, e.g. *urla-* 'be good,' *urla-f* 'a good place.' There is also a verb *fi-(d')* 'to be in a place' and a suffix $p^h i$-*ŋ* 'inhabitants of . . . .' In Gilyak there is the time expression *na-f* 'now,' with which we may compare Kamchadal *nu-f* 'now.' In Amur and other dialects, which are the basis of most descriptions of Gilyak, the base form would be $*p^h(i)$ in a system with two sets of basic stops, aspirated and unaspirated. However, in the southeastern Sakhalin dialect described by Hattori (1962) there are morphophonemically two forms of *f* which go back to p^h elsewhere. In one, f_1, *f* remains as a member of a compound with a following morpheme. In f_2, we have rather a voiced fricative *v*. This would then go back to a voiced aspirate $*b^h$. It occurs in locatives such as *mi-f_2* 'earth' and thus corresponds to the Indo-European voiced aspirate.

In Chukchi and Koryak there is a suffix *-nv ~ -n*; Aliutor has *-nv ~ -na*. The rules for this alternation vary. In Chukchi (Skorik 1961–77, I: 330) *-n* is found in the absolutive, although a few nouns have *-nəv*, and *-nv-ən* is a general alternative form. In other nominal cases the alternant is *-nv-*. As elsewhere there is also an independent noun, for example, Koryak *va-nv* 'place' (Korsakov 1939), in this instance followed by the suffixal form just discussed. In Chukchi it derives nouns from verbs and means 'place of habitual activity.' (With *nv*, compare Yukaghir and Indo-European.) In Kamchadal the locative suffix in question may occur with temporal meaning in *nu-f* 'now,' as compared with *nu* 'this' (Worth 1969).

In Eskimo the most common derivational forms for nouns of place is *-vi-k* (for *-k* see No. 23). In some forms of Eskimo a verb may be derived from such nouns, with the meaning 'it is a place for . . . ing.' In Yupik an element *-və-* occurs with the meaning 'place' in interrogative and demonstrative adverbs, for example, Chaplino (Siberia) *na-və-k* 'whither' (see No. 64 for *na-* and No. 26 for *-k*), and Alaskan Yupik *qava-ve-t* 'to the inside, inland, upriver' (Jacobson 1984: 661–62).

29. Locative RU

In Indo-European there is a locative *-r* that never occurs as a regular inflection, but survives in adverbs and in certain verbal compounds. It is found with interrogative *k* in Sanskrit *kar-hi* 'when?,' Lithuanian *kur̃* 'where?, whither?,' Albanian *kur* 'therefore, when?,' Latin *cūr* (< **qʷor*) 'why?,' Gothic *hwar* 'where?,' Greek *nuktōr* 'at night,' Sanskrit *uṣar* 'at dawn,' and Armenian *ur* 'where?' (< **kʷur*). There are parallel forms with the *t-* demonstrative that are reconstructed by Pokorny (1959: 1087) as **tor, *tēr* with the meaning 'there,' e.g. Latvian *tur*. Further instances include Lithuanian *visur* 'everywhere' and Gothic *aljar* 'somewhere else.'

Bartholemae (1889) pointed to additional examples of adverbs in *-r* in Indic, including several instances in which it is embedded in composite verb forms, e.g. Sanskrit *ratha-r-yāmi* 'I go in a chariot' ('chariot-in-go I') and Avestan *zəma-r-gūz-* 'hidden in the earth' (see Benveniste 1935: 87–88, which contains a list of such formations).

Can anything more definite be said regarding either the form or function of this element? The Greek *deûro* (Aeolic *deûru*) has in Homer two uses. One means 'hither' with verbs of motion. The other, which is used as a particle meaning 'come, let's' before the imperative, has a plural *deûte*. That the first part is a deictic *de*, comparable to the latter part of *hó-de* 'this (near me),' is generally agreed. In his etymological dictionary of Greek (s.v. *deûro*) Hjalmar Frisk (1960–70) suggests that the latter portion is to be compared not only with Lithuanian *kur̃*, which means both 'where?' and 'whither?,' but also with Umbrian *uru* 'to him.' These data suggest that the basic meaning might be 'motion towards' and that the associated vocalism is $u \sim o$. As we shall see, there is some support for this in other branches of Eurasiatic.

In Uralic there is only the Hungarian dative -ra ~ -re and along with it the forms with the possessive suffix rá-m (from earlier Hungarian re-ám 'onto me'; see Szinnyei 1910: 83). There is also Komi-Zyrian kor 'when?' In Yukaghir the only example I have found is Tundra tigi-ra 'there' (cf. tigi-n 'there it is!' [Krejnovich 1958: 209]).

In Altaic, however, the -r suffix is common. There are adverbs in -ra such as Old Turkish as-ra 'downward.' More commonly, however, -ra in Turkic connotes just place, for example, Turkish bu-ra 'this place,' bu-ra-da 'in this place, here' (for da, see No. 32), ne-re 'what place?,' ne-re-de 'in what place?, where?' There is also a variant form in ru ~ rü in Old Turkish that even functions as a nominal inflection (e.g. äb-im-rü 'to my house' ['house-my-to']). In Old Turkish we also find be-rü 'hither' (actually 'to me' with the first-person singular pronominal base without the oblique n) and ina-ru 'thither' (actually 'to him, to her'). The form -ru is found, especially in pronouns, following the coaffix -ka (see No. 26) where it forms a directive, for example, Old Turkish -yaru (Gabain 1959: 28). In later forms of Turkic it is often -gar, -ŋar, and is called a directive case by Brockelmann (1954: 72) in his grammar of medieval Turkic literary languages (e.g. a-ŋar 'to that,' ma-ŋar 'to me'). It is also found in modern languages, for example, Khakas xaj-da-r 'whither?' alongside of xaj-da 'where?' (Karpov 1966: 436). In addition there is a variant in -ri found in Turkish dialects, for example, a-rï 'on that side, in that direction' (Lewicki 1930: 20).

Mongol forms numerous adverbs in -ra parallel to those in -na (No. 30) without any difference of meaning, e.g. dotu-na, dotu-ra 'inside' (Kotwicz 1936: 65). Although not found in the literary language, other forms of Mongolian have a case suffix ru ~ rü with the meaning 'motion toward,' for which Ramstedt (1952–57, II: 38) posits *-uru after consonants and *-ru after vowels. In Classical Mongolian the dative -dur is analyzed by Poppe (1955: 199) as consisting of an earlier dative du plus r directive.

In Tungus I have only found -r in adverbs, e.g. Even ər 'there, the one there,' tar 'yonder, the one yonder.' The variant -ri is found in Manchu *e-de-ri* 'hither' and *te-de-ri* 'thither.' Lewicki (1930) is a monograph devoted to locational affixes in *-rV*.

In Ainu locative *-r* occurs in the interrogative adverb *nakoro* 'whither?' (cf. *na-k* 'where?'), in which *na* is interrogative (No. 64), *k(o)* is dative or locative (No. 26), and *-(o)ro* evidently indicates motion towards. There is also a verb *oro* 'to be in, at, by' that is also used as a postposition (e.g. *chisei oro* 'in the house,' literally, 'house in'). In the Sakhalin dialect there is an adverb *ta-ra* 'there.'

In Korean there is a case suffix *-lo* (South Korean), *-lu* (North Korean) that is usually called instrumental in grammars of the contemporary language. Its meanings include 'by means of, through, towards.' The meaning 'direction towards' is clear in a number of adverbs, e.g. North Korean *čibulu* 'homewards,' South Korean *al-lo* 'downwards.' Ramstedt (1952–57: 38–40) considers the relation of the Korean forms to those of Altaic "obvious."

In Japanese Miller (1971: 181) calls the *-ra* of *doti-ra* 'where?, which?' "an important modern survival of an old Altaic locative suffix *-ra* . . ." There is also in Old Japanese the interrogative adverb *izu-ra* 'where?, whereabouts?' (Morris 1966) and other locatives based on demonstratives, e.g. *kotira* 'here.'

In Gilyak there are two sets of occurrences to be considered. The first is the dative *-toxo* ~ *-doxo* ~ *-roxo*. These alternants are instances of the Gilyak system of consonant gradation that depend on the preceding sound. The voiceless stop is normally the historically basic alternant, but **r* can also be a source. If so, the basic form is **-rokʻ* and we probably have a combination of *ro* with the *k* dative (No. 26). The other instance to be considered is the use of *-r* in the Amur dialect to form adverbs of place (Panfilov 1962–65, II: 187), e.g. *tu-r* 'here,' *hu-r* 'there,' *tʻa-r* 'on water near the shore,' *kʻe-r* 'upstream,' *kʻi-r* 'a higher place' (cf. *kʻi-m-dʹ* 'be in a higher place'). The first of these is identical with Latvian *tur* 'here' in sound and meaning. In Chukchi we find the pairs *ənkə* 'there, then,' *ənkə-ri* 'thither,' and *miŋkə* 'where?,' *miŋkəri* 'whither?' (Moll 1957).

I believe that a fairly strong case can be made that the basic form is *ru* ~ *ro* and the basic meaning is 'direction towards.' When *re* ~ *ra* occurs it is often under the probable influence of the rival locative in *n* (No. 30) that never occurs with a back vowel. This is clear in Turkish in which *ru* is archaic and non-productive, unlike

-na, and in which -ra evidently arose under the influence of na. We
have also noted in Mongolian the free variation of adverbs in -na
and -ra. In Japanese, -na is found fairly frequently, whereas -ra only
occurs in dotira and izura. It is also noteworthy that forms with
a final vowel usually indicate direction towards and those without
more frequently denote rest in a place. This may have been the
original state of affairs.

30. Locative N

There are a variety of n locatives in Indo-European whose extent
and internal connections have been a subject of dispute. First, it is
generally agreed that there is an independent form en that appears
mainly as a preposition, e.g. Greek en(i), Latin in. Pokorny (1959:
311–14) includes some postpositional uses that are particularly clear
in Oscan, which suffixes -en in locational cases. He is inclined to
interpret Greek i in en-i as the Indo-European locative i (No. 31).

Brugmann (1897–1916, II: 178) interpreted the Vedic kṣǽm-an
'on earth' as consisting of the stem kṣ̌ám 'earth,' with zero locative,
to which -an (< *en) has been suffixed. As Hirt (1913: 294) noted,
"the situation becomes clear and simple once one not only accepts
the postposition -en in kṣ̌ám-an but also all locatives in -en." He does
not, however, specify which these are. Karl Johansson (1890: 146ff)
had included here not only Indic examples, but the Latin -ne of
super-ne 'upwards, from above,' infer-ne 'below,' etc.; and in Germanic, Old High German ūfa-na 'above,' Gothic inna-na 'within,'
etc.

In addition to these, Brugmann also considered the -n of Vedic
pronominal locatives asmi-n 'in that,' tasmi-n 'in this,' kasmi-n 'in
whom?' (cf. the Iranian forms without -n) and compared these with
Greek pronominal datives like ammi(n) 'to us' (Aeolic). The -n of
asmi-n and tasmi-n is accepted as a locative by Rob Beekes (1982–
83) and the identification with the Greek datives is recognized by
Frisk (1960: 135).

When Hittite was discovered it was found that in the Old Hittite period spatial adverbs in -an (along with forms in -a) were very
common (Kammenhuber 1980). Examples are antan 'inside,' ap-
pan 'behind,' piran 'in front.' The first of these has generally been
identified with Greek endon 'within.'

In Uralic, the Baltic Finnic languages have a case in *-na that
is usually called the essive. Its most common meaning is locative
and it also occurs in adverbs such as Finnish koto-na 'at home,'
Komi-Zyrian tu-n 'there' (see No. 11), and dialectal Hungarian hu-n
'where?' (see No. 60). An inessive case in -ssa (< *-s-na with a coaffix -s-), which occurs in other locational cases, is also reconstructed
for Baltic Finnic (Majtinskaja 1966). A locative in -na also occurs in
Samoyed, both in adverbs, e.g. Yurak hu-na 'where?,' and following
the coaffix *ka- (No. 26) in Northern Samoyed, e.g. Yurak -ka-na,
which is described as locative-instrumental. In fact the Baltic Finnic
essive shows instrumental and modal meanings, e.g. Finnish alan
'by foot.' The essive is described as indicating temporary state,
which easily shades into manner, e.g. Finnish poika-na 'as a boy,
when I was a boy.' A related nuance of meaning is also displayed
in other Finno-Ugric languages in numeral adverbs, e.g. Hungarian
kett-en, Komi-Zyrian kik-en 'by twos.' We will encounter similar
meanings in Altaic. Serebrennikov (1964: 12) notes that traces of
the old locative with suffix -na are found in all Uralic languages. In
Uralic, in striking resemblance to Eskimo (see below), there is also
a noun that Rédei (1988: 592) reconstructs as ǐnɜ 'place.' Here the
first syllable has an unspecified front vowel and the last syllable a
completely unspecified vowel. A locative -n is found in Yukaghir adverbs, e.g. pure-n (Kolyma), pude-n (Tundra) 'above,' hon (Kolyma)
(< *kon) 'where?, whither?,' ty-ne ~ ti-ne 'here' (Chuvan).

Similar adverbs of place are found in Turkic, e.g. Turkish, Kirghiz
ka-na 'where?' (for ka- see No. 60) and there are also instrumental-
modal uses reminiscent of Uralic, e.g. Old Turkish jadayïn 'on foot.'
Old Turkish also had the phonetic variants -an and -un. This is
most striking in Chuvash, in which -ĕn is the regular manner of deriving adverbs, e.g. xull-ĕn 'slowly.' In Mongolian we once more find
-na in locative adverbs, e.g. ka-na 'where?,' či-na (< *ti-na) 'there,'
and numerous locative adverbs of the type dotu-na 'inside,' ɣada-na
'outside.'

For Tungus, Benzing (1955) mentions adverbs of time in -ni,
-na, and adverbs of place in -nu. Examples include *tima-na 'tomorrow,' *tima-ni 'morning,' and *dō-nu 'inside.' There is also a
Tungus word *nā 'earth, place,' found in Negidal, Oroch, Udihe,
Ulch, Orok, Nanai, and Manchu (Tsintsius 1975–77). Thus it is

found in Southern and Northern Tungus as well as in Manchu. A similar word is found in Old Japanese, as we will see below.

A variety of formations in -n form adverbs of place in Ainu, e.g. na-k-an 'whither?' (cf. na-k 'where?'; see Nos. 26 and 64), rik-un 'above' (cf. riki 'height'), mak-un 'behind, in the rear' (cf. mak-ta 'behind, away with'; for -ta see No. 32). With this common -un formation we may compare Old Turkish -un. In pok(e) 'underside,' pok-na 'under, beneath,' we see the same -na that also occurs in Germanic, Uralic, Mongolian, and Japanese. In addition there are a number of adverbs of location in Ainu, e.g. ma-na 'where?' (No. 62), i-ne 'where?' (No. 61), and tane 'now.' In Hattori's Ainu dialect dictionary, dialects 1–8 have tane for 'now,' and dialects 9 and 10 have tani.

A noun anh 'inside' occurs in Korean. Ramstedt derives Korean -h from an earlier -s, but Martin considers it cognate with Japanese k. If Ramstedt is correct anh may be compared with Greek eis (< *en-s) 'into,' which shows the same -s that appears in Greek ek-s 'out of,' alongside of ek.

In Japanese -na forms adverbs of time, e.g. asa-na 'in the morning,' yū-na 'in the evening.' Perhaps the postposition -ni 'in,' which is also found in Ryukyuan, belongs here. Old Japanese likewise has a noun na 'earth' (Syromiatnikov 1972: 27), which may be compared to Tungus *nā with the same meaning.

Taxtin and some of the Lower Amur dialects of Gilyak have a locative in -n (Panfilov 1962–65, I: 133). Elsewhere it is syncretized with the ablative. This locative-ablative has the form -uin after a consonant, -in or -un after a vowel (except that after -i it is simply -n). Sometimes -uine is found without any difference of meaning. These dative-locatives may well contain locative -n.

In a reconstruction of Proto-Eskimo-Aleut, Marsh and Swadesh (1951: 216) posit (No. 132) Proto-Eskimo *-nə or *-ni, Aleut -n, and Proto-Eskimo-Aleut *-nə (locative case). One should also mention the widespread Eskimo etymon *ənə, with reflexes such as Sigluit (Inuit) ini 'inside, house,' Imaklik (Inuit) ənə 'building,' and Kuskokwim (Yupik) ina, na 'house.'

31. Locative I

There is general consensus among Indo-Europeanists that the locative singular is to be reconstructed as *-i (see Szemerényi 1978: 208). It also occurs in adpositions. Kronasser (1956: 160) notes the proportion en : eni = ser : hri, in which the first pair are Greek variant forms for 'in' and the second consists of the Hittite and Lycian words for 'above' (Lycian h < *s). Besides its rise as a case marker, Proto-Indo-European *-i also survives in adverbs, e.g. Greek ekeî 'there.'

Koppelman (1928) compared Indo-European -i with similar forms in Korean and Ainu. We shall see that Eskimo and Aleut (and possibly Chukotian) should be drawn into the comparison. The locative of present-day Korean is -e. However, this sound is written in the Hangul syllabary by a sign that clearly denotes a diphthong ai. Ramstedt (1939: 42) says that earlier, during the period when Korean had vowel harmony, it was ai or ąi after low vowels and əi or ïi after high vowels. The sound transcribed ą by Ramstedt no longer exists in Korean. He conjectures that its phonetic value was ʌ. Others transcribe it as æ.

In Ainu there is a noun i 'time, place' that is often affixed to place names (Batchelor 1905: 161), e.g. e-kurok-i, literally, 'the-black-place.' It also occurs in adverbs, e.g. toan 'that,' toan-i 'there,' ne-i-ta 'where?' (for ne see No. 64; for ta see No. 32), etc. For the Sakhalin dialect, Alfred and Elżbieta Majewicz (1983–85: 35) list an -i locational among the grammatical markers (e.g. niste 'hard,' niste-i 'a hard place'). Dettmer (1989: 304) cites ne-i and ne-i-ta 'who?' from Kindaichi (see No. 64).

Eskimo has a verb i 'to be in a place' (Spalding 1960: 3) that is always used with a noun in the locative case. The locative case in Eskimo is -mi in the singular and -ni in the plural. Except for the prosecutive in -kut, all the oblique cases are formed from singular m, which is probably to be identified with the singular subjective case m. The plural n is probably derived from an original t, the plural subjective with the common alternation between nasal and non-nasal. This would leave -i as the locative marker. In Sirenik Eskimo -i occurs in adverbs such as as-i 'on the ground' (cf. Ainu asa-m 'on the ground' with m locative [No. 27]). In Hinz's grammar of Kuskokwim (Alaskan Yupik) there are a number of locatives such as *aka-i* 'there, on that side,' *paka-i* 'up there,' and *kakma-i* 'outside (said when one is inside).' These have parallel forms with the -*ni* locative (e.g. *kakma-ni* 'inside'). Jacobson (1984: 661–62) calls these *i*- locatives interjectional forms used to point out an object or event, as distinct from the locatives in -*ni*, which lack this nuance of meaning. In *uvlumi* 'in the morning' it has a temporal meaning.

In Bering Aleut -*i*- is used to derive verbs (from nouns) that indicate location in the place specified by the noun. An example is *ulaχ* 'house,' *ulaʁ-i-ku-χ* 'he, she is in the house.' Here -*ku*- marks the present tense and -*χ* indicates third-person singular.

In Chukchi, locatives such as *k-j-it* contain an "extra" -*j*- in addition to other locative markers (No. 26 dative and No. 32 locative). This -*j*- is also found in the ablative -*j-peŋ*. Scott Krause (1980: 43–44), in a generative analysis, talks of a "deep *i*-locative." In Aliutor, a language of the Koryak group, personal pronouns have a locative in -*ki*, contrasting with -*k* in the noun. In Kerek (of the same group) all nouns in -*ŋ* have a locative in -*ki* instead of -*k* found in other nominal and pronominal paradigms. These are probably hypercharacterized forms in which -*i* has been suffixed to *k*- (No. 26). The only evidence for an -*i* locative in Altaic appears to be Manchu -*i*, an instrumental-locative suffix seen in *tu-ba-i tacin* 'the custom of that place' ('that-place-in custom'; Sinor 1968: 265).

I have not equated the Ainu noun *i* 'place' and the Eskimo verbal derivative -*i*- with Turkic -*i* 'to be,' or Korean *i* 'to be,' because both these latter forms are predicative, not locational. However, the locative -*i* is found in Sakhalin Ainu *ne-y* ~ *ne-y-ta* 'where?' (Dettmer 1989: 305, see Nos. 32 and 64). It is possible that Finno-Ugric -*j* (lative), rejected by some (e.g. Hajdú), but considered even to be Uralic by others (e.g. Serebrennikov) belongs here (see Majtinskaja 1974: 263–64). Its basic sense is motion towards, rather than location in a place, but a semantic shift in this direction is common (cf. modern English 'where?,' which replaced 'whither?' and acquired a directional meaning in addition to its earlier purely locative sense). Finno-Ugric examples include Estonian *edaja* 'forewards,' Komi-Zyrian *il-i* 'far away,' and Ostyak *joɣ-i* 'homewards, back.'

32. Locative TA

A locative in *ta* (with variants in other dental-alveolar stops, as will be discussed shortly) is to be distinguished from an ablative-instrumental in -*t*, which will be treated in the next section. Given their similarity in both form and function, it will sometimes be difficult to distinguish them, but there are good reasons for considering them to be different.

Indo-Europeanists have reconstructed an ablative singular in *-t* (or more probably *-d* on the basis of the Latin evidence) that is never identified with the *-dhe* or *-dha* which is reconstructed on the basis of adverbs like Sanskrit *i-ha* 'here,' Avestan *i-ða* 'here,' Greek *itha-genḗs* 'native, born here,' and Umbrian *i-fe* 'there' (with *f* < *dh*).

Similarly, all Uralicists distinguish between a locative -*t* and a partitive or separative -*ta*. The latter has always been identified with the Indo-European ablative in comparisons between Uralic and Indo-European. Moreover, there are a few instances in which both occur in the same formation and the separate functions of each are clear. Examples are Avestan *ya-ðā̆-t* 'whence' (relative), with locative -*ða* (cf. *i-ða* 'here') followed by ablative -*t*, and Tundra Yukaghir *qa-da-t* 'whence?,' with a parallel analysis.

In Indo-European we have already noted a suffixed *-dhe*, *-dha*, found in adverbs of place (Pokorny 1959: 285), but there are also adverbs of time like Sanskrit *ta-dā* 'then' and Lithuanian *kadà* 'when' (Pokorny 1959: 183), which are reconstructed as having -*d*- rather than -*dh*-, although the Baltic and Slavic forms could come from an original *dh* since both *dh* and *d* give *d* in these groups. In regard to some other Slavic examples, without the guide of semantic identity, Pokorny gives both *d* and *dh* as possible sources, e.g. Old Church Slavic *tǫdě* 'thence,' Russian *kudá* 'whither?' There are also cases in Celtic in which Indo-Europeanists have hesitated between *dh* and *d* as sources. This would presumably also hold for Hittite *dame-da* 'elsewhere' (either rest or motion towards) and *appe-da* 'thither' since Hittite makes no distinction between aspirated and unaspirated stops. Sturtevant (1932: 6) identifies it with the Sanskrit *da* of *kadā* 'when,' etc., thus deriving it from Proto-Indo-European *d*.

A locative in *-t/-tt* is posited for Finno-Ugric, but is especially characteristic of the Ugric subgroup (Majtinskaja 1974: 250–51). In Vogul it forms a locative case (e.g. *paŋk-ət* 'on the head') and in the Permian group there is likewise a locative in *-ti* (e.g. Udmurt *östü* 'at the door, through the door'). Elsewhere it survives either as a coaffix (e.g. Ostyak *law-na-t* 'on the horse'; see No. 30) or in adverbs (e.g. Mordvin *ve-t'* 'at night,' with palatalization of *t* after the front vowel, Ostyak *ko-t* 'where?,' *to-t* 'there' [see Nos. 60 and 11], Finnish *ny-t* 'now,' Estonian *nüü-d* 'now' [cf. Finnish *ny-ky* 'contemporary']).

The variants *-da* (Tundra), *-de* (Kolyma) are well attested in Yukaghir adverbs. Examples include Tundra *ta-da* 'there' and *qa-da* 'where?, whither?' and Kolyma *tiŋi-de* 'this way,' *xon-de* 'every-where,' and *migi-de* 'whither.' In non-Chuvash Turkic the regular nominal locative case is *da* ~ *de* (vowel harmony variants) and in Chuvash it is *-ta*. In addition *-t* forms derived nominals such as *al-t-* 'front side' and adverbial free forms, e.g. Baraba *art* 'back of,' *alt* 'in front' (cf. Bashkir *al* 'in front').

Mongolian languages have similar forms in both nominal cases and adverbs, e.g. Khalka *en-de* 'here,' *uuliin xadžuu-da* 'at the side of the mountain' (Buck 1955: 30). The locative in *da* ~ *de* is char-acteristic of non-literary Mongolian, but *du* ~ *dü* is also found. It seems probable that the vowel here has been influenced by the dative-allative *ru* (No. 29). In general, *-da* ~ *-de* is characteristic of adverbs and *du* ~ *dü*, of nouns. This suggests that *da* is earlier. A perhaps stronger indication is that Mongolian shares with Turkic a suffix *-da-ki* meaning 'that which is in a specified place'; in this complex formative *da* would not have been influenced by *-ru*. The literary language has *-dur* ~ *-dür*, whose final *-r* is of unknown origin (Ramstedt 1952–57, II: 36). Crossing with the dative *-ru* seems to me a possible source.

The Tungus languages, except for Manchu, have a locative *-du*. In Manchu it is *-de* with an inflection that is not subject to vowel harmony.

In Hokkaido Ainu, as described by Batchelor (1905), *ta* is the ordinary locative postposition. It also occurs in *i-ta* 'where' (relative; for interrogative *i-* see No. 61), *sa-ta* 'here' (see No. 12), and in *te-ta* 'here' (see No. 11). Patrie (1982: 80) gives *-ta* and *-te* as variant

forms. He asserts the relationship of these to Korean *te* 'place that
. . . , situation where . . . .' It is also reported for Sakhalin Ainu in
ta-ta 'hither' (Dobrotvorskij 1875, Piłsudski 1912). Dettmer (1989:
304) cites *ne-y* and *ney-ta* 'where?' The analysis here is transparent:
ne- (interrogative) + *i-* (locative) + *-ta* (locative).

The Korean adverb *itte* 'now' may be analyzed as consisting
of the near demonstrative *i-* (No. 8) and a locative element that
would be the same as the word *te* 'place' cited by Patrie. Korean
has another word *thə* 'site, place, building land' (Martin, Lee, and
Chang 1967: 1699). Since Korean retains a distinction between aspirated and unaspirated consonants that seems to correspond to that
of Indo-European, the first of the two words mentioned might be
related to the Indo-European *d*-locative and the second to *dh-*.

Japanese retains a locative *-ta* only in a few adverbs. In Old
Japanese, *si-ta* and *si-mo* both mean 'under.' In contemporary
Japanese *sita* means 'bottom.' We may also note *asita* 'tomorrow,'
which has a variant *asu* in Old Japanese and is related to *asa* 'morning.'

The only trace of this locative that I have found in Gilyak
is Northern Sakhalin *sid'a-ta* and *nud'a-ta*, both meaning 'what's
there?' (Russian *čto tam*). In Chukotian the only indication of a
locative *-t* is in the Koryak group. Koryak has an interrogative *tite*, and Aliutor has *ti-ta*, both meaning 'when?' The interrogative
base is *ti* (see No. 63). Aliutor has lost the vowel harmony system by
mergers that include *e > a*. In addition there is the adverb *nəki-ta*
'at night' in Aliutor.

33. Ablative T

In Indo-European the ablative singular of thematic vowel stems is
reconstructed as *-ōd* ~ *ēd*. It also occurs in adverbs, e.g. in Sanskrit *paścāt* 'from behind,' Delphic Greek *woíkō(-d)* 'from the house,'
Gothic *aftarō(d)* 'from behind.' In Baltic and Slavic it is the source
of the genitive singular in *-a* of thematic stems. The long vowel is
generally believed to be a contraction of the thematic vowel with a
short vowel inflection, e.g. *-o + ed > ōd*. In the Sanskrit first- and
second-person singular pronouns the ablative is *mat* and *tvat*, with
a short vowel that supports the foregoing analysis.

In Avestan, alongside of -āt we find -āδa. Since a voiced final stop is otherwise unattested in Indo-European, it is tempting to assume that there was a final vowel. The usual interpretation of the final -a in Avestan is that it is the postposition ā 'towards, at' that is also used in Sanskrit with the ablative. This is not disputed here, but it is noteworthy that there is other evidence in Indo-European (and elsewhere) for a final vowel, as seen in Lycian -adi, which will figure in the following discussion.

Hittite has a much discussed ablative in -ts that is generally believed not to belong here. It also has an instrumental in -et, -it and in certain archaic consonantal stems, an instrumental in -ta. Thus in Hittite one has both weten-it and weden-da 'with, by means of water.' Furthermore, in Hittite the ablative and instrumental often exchange functions, and nouns in the ablative frequently have a possessive suffix in the instrumental. Kammenhuber (1969: 303) considers the Hittite instrumental to be related to the Luwian ablative-instrumental in -ati and to Lycian -adi. This is the generally received view.

The basic meaning is evidently 'source,' from which genitive (e.g. Balto-Slavic), instrumental, and ablative uses are easily derived. Phonetically we may, on the basis of the foregoing evidence, posit an original form *e/adV.

The connection of the Indo-European ablative in -t with the Uralic partitive -ta has figured in every comparison of Uralic and Indo-European. The Uralic form is variously called partitive, separative, or ablative (see Szinnyei 1910: 65 for the last). In Finnish, adverbs in -ta indicate motion from, e.g. al-ta 'from below.' This phenomenon is general in Finno-Ugric, e.g. Hungarian alol with the same meaning (in Hungarian -l derives regularly from original *-t).

In Baltic Finnic languages, -ta occurs as a coaffix in two cases, the elative -as-ta 'from the interior of' and the ablative -al-ta 'from the surface of.' There is no dissent from the view that the Baltic Finnic partitive case in -ta has the same origin. This indicates that the subject, or more often the object, is only partially affected (cf. French de).

In addition to these uses, Ob-Ugric has developed an instrumental in a manner parallel to that of the Anatolian languages, e.g. Ostyak -at, Vogul -l (< *t), whose origin in the partitive -ta was first asserted by Patkanow and Fuchs (1910: 64) and has been accepted by others (Vértes 1967). In Northern Samoyed an ablative is formed by combination with the coaffix -k (No. 26), e.g. Yurak -ka-d, Tavgy -ki-tə.

The ablative also is found in the two surviving dialects of Yukaghir, both in simple form in adverbs, e.g. Kolyma xot 'whence?' (see No. 60) and Tundra ta-t 'thence' (see No. 11), and as a nominal case with a -k coaffix, e.g. Tundra Yukaghir -get. The ablative significance of -t in Yukaghir is particularly clear in the contrast in the Kolyma dialect between juko 'far' and juko-t 'from afar.' The ablative in -t also appears clearly in Maydell's nineteenth-century material, published by Schiefner, for example, milaŋidat 'from the right' and tolugdat 'from the left' in describing the confluence of two rivers (Schiefner 1871: 607).

In Altaic the ablative-instrumental t is only found in Yakut, the non-Chuvash Turkic language that is genetically the most divergent. Here we find an instrumental -tɨ ~ -ti and an indefinite accusative -ta. The former is said by Menges (1968: 115) to be cognate with the Yakut instrumental -tɨ; the latter is, as Menges notes, strongly reminiscent of the Baltic Finnic partitive -ta in its uses. In Northern Tungus, Evenki has an ablative in -kit that is parallel in its formation to forms we have already noted in Yukaghir and Northern Samoyed and which is found in Ainu as -ke-ta, e.g. tumu-ke-ta 'in the middle' and numerous other instances.

In Northern and Southern Tungus (but not in Manchu), there is an instrumental -ti. In Evenki we find -t after vowels, -di after n, l, or r, and -ti in other environments. In other languages we find simply -di (Nanai) or forms easily derivable from -di. In Southern Tungus an ablative is formed not by -kit, as in the Northern dialects, but by adding -adi to the instrumental (e.g. Nanai di-adi) or just -di (e.g. Oroch ji-ji < *di-di, Ulch dᶻi-dᶻi < *didi). All this is, of course, very reminiscent of Anatolian.

Pröhle (1916: 160) considers tu in the archaic Japanese formula ama-tu kumi 'the god of heaven' ('heaven-tu god') to be cognate with the Uralic ablative-partitive -ta. In Gilyak the -t ablative seems only to survive in ho-ɣa-t 'then, thereafter' (Panfilov 1962–65, I: 46, 123).

In the Chukchi-Koryak branch of Chukotian, nouns form an instrumental (which is also used as subject) by adding the suffix -a ~ -ta. The former occurs after consonants, the latter, after vowels. The partitive use probably survives in the construction after the numbers 2–4. In addition, a case form called "causative" (with the basic meaning 'on account of') is found both in Chukchi-Koryak and in Kamchadal. In the former it is -kjit and in the latter, -kit. In both instances we have the combination with k (No. 26) that we have already encountered in several instances. In Chukchi-Koryak there appears to be in addition a locative -i in the form -j, discussed under No. 31. Karl Bouda (1952) asserts the relationship of the Chukchi instrumental-ergative -a ~ -ta with the Uralic partitive -ta and the Yakut instrumental tɨ ~ ti.

In the Inuit dialects of Eskimo the ablative case is formed by suffixing -it to the absolutive, resulting in -m-it in the singular and -ni-t in the plural. In Labrador (and probably elsewhere in Inuit outside of Greenlandic) a -t is suffixed in the ablative of demonstratives. Thus we find Greenlandic maŋŋa, but Labrador maŋŋa-t 'hence' (Kleinschmidt 1851: 21). In both Yupik and Inuit the combination -kit, which we have already encountered a number of times, forms ablative adverbial forms, e.g. Greenlandic na-ki-t 'whence?' (for na see No. 64), Siberian Yupik nakən 'whence?' (< *nakət), taxkən 'thence,' makən 'hence.' The probable equivalence of Siberian ma-kən with Labrador maŋŋat suggests that the latter also contains -k, which has become a nasal in intervocalic position. Eskimo also derives nouns of instruments in -ut, which may be compared to the similar formation in Gilyak. In Naukan, a Yupik dialect of Siberia, Menovshchikov (1975: 47) reports a derivative suffix -ta(-q), which forms nouns of instruments.

There is also evidence for ablative -t in Aleut. Thus, alongside of qanayam 'where?' (for -m see No. 27), we find qanayan 'whence,' with the usual Aleut shift of final *-t to -n. In addition, there is evidence for the combination of the t ablative with a preceding coaffix k- that we have already encountered in Eskimo and elsewhere (e.g. Atka qana-ɣan 'whence?,' wa-ɣan 'hence'). Bergsland (1951: No. 292) reconstructs this complex ending as "perhaps -ɣən ~ -kən." Subsequent work on Aleut showed that the suffix here was not -ɣan, but -ɣaan, which Bergsland conjectures to have derived from *ɣaɣən, hence the cautionary "perhaps."

34. Comitative KO(-N) ∼ KO(-M)

The Latin preposition *cum* 'with' is also employed as a verbal prefix *com-* (usually *cŏ-* before stems beginning with a vowel or *v*). Related forms with similar meanings occur in other Italic languages and in Celtic. It is also generally assumed that the Greek adjective *koinós* 'common' derives from *kom-i̯o-s* 'coming together.' The variant without -*m* is found outside of Latin in Albanian *kë* 'with.' Pokorny (1959: 613) believes that Germanic *ga-* belongs here also, as do many other Indo-Europeanists. One would expect *ha-* and the voiced form *ga-* is attributed to the fact that it occurs only as an unstressed prefix.

The meaning 'with, together' is traceable in such substantival forms as Gothic *ga-juka* 'companion' (literally, 'together-yoked') and *ga-mains* 'common' (cf. Latin *commūnīs*). However, even in Gothic it had already acquired an important additional function in that it often denotes perfectivity in verb compounds. According to Otto Behagel (1923-32, II: 100–1) this development started from instances in which there is movement that results in a new unity from originally distinct parts, e.g. German *gefrieren* 'to freeze.'

In Proto-West Germanic this development had proceeded further in that *ge-* was regularly prefixed to the past participle of almost all verbs, except those that already had a prepositional prefix. In Old High German *ge-* is not always present in the past passive participle and it is regularly not used with verbs that are by their meaning already perfect, e.g. *cuman* 'arrived.' In the eastern branch of West Germanic, *ge-* has spread so that all verbs require it (except those already having inseparable prefixes and those with polysyllabic stems). There are two main uses with auxiliaries in modern German, as perfective active with *sein* 'to be' or *haben* 'to have,' and as a passive with *werden* 'to become.' In Anglo-Frisian the course of events has been the opposite. Although Anglo-Saxon was much like Old High German in this respect, it is not found in modern English, except for archaic forms such as 'y-clept,' and it disappeared early in Frisian.

The basic parallel here is with Chukotian. Unlike Germanic, however, the prepositional use exists in all the languages of the group and in every instance the preposition is supplemented by one of two suffixes, called comitative I and comitative II. In all the languages comitative I involves the locative -*ma* (see No. 27) as a suffix and indicates more intimate connection, e.g. 'the pot with its handle.' Comitative II, in the Chukchi-Koryak group, suffixes the instrumental and indicates accompaniment, e.g. Chukchi *ɣa-pojɣ-əta* 'with a spear.' Since the genetically most isolated language in the group, Kamchadal, shares to a lesser degree in the development to be discussed (but does show the prepositional use), it is reasonable to assume for Proto-Chukotian the existence of a comitative with *ɣe-* ~ *ɣa-* (< **ka-*; Kamchadal *k-*) since all the languages agree in this use.

Koryak has gone farthest in developments that are to some extent parallel with Germanic. In No. 7 there was discussion of the Chukchi-Koryak predication of a noun by means of first- and second-person pronouns, e.g. Chukchi *ənpənačɣ-eɣəm* 'I am an old man.' In the third person we have simply the absolutive form of the noun in the appropriate number.

This construction does not involve *ɣe-*. There is, however, a paradigm using *ɣe-* with the meaning 'have, having,' e.g. *ɣe-kupre-jɣəm* 'with-a whale-I,' (i.e. 'I have a whale,' or 'I, having a whale'). In the third-person singular, in place of the personal pronoun, we have a suffix -*lin* and in the plural, -*lin-et*, e.g. *ɣe-kupre-lin* 'he has a whale' (or 'he, having a whale'). The suffix -*li-n* can be analyzed as containing a verb 'to be' (cf. Kamchadal -*le* 'become,' Yukaghir *le* 'be') and -*n*, a common marker of the third person in the Chukchi verb. We may call this the *ɣe-lin* construction and it exists in virtually identical form in Koryak.

In Chukchi, the *ɣe-lin* construction also occurs in intransitive verbs to form what Menovshchikov (1968, II: 73) calls the Past II. Thus, in the third singular we have *ɣe-čejvə-li-n* 'he has gone,' which might be paraphrased in German as *ge-gangen ist er* 'gone is he.' We thus see that *ɣe-* has developed a perfect meaning, as in Germanic. In the transitive verb, which marks the person and number of both the subject and object, we also have a tense formed with *ɣe-* that is called Past II by Menovshchikov. However, it is not semantically homogeneous. If the object is first person and the subject is second person of any number or third-person singular, it is basically similar to the German perfect active, e.g. *ɣ-ina-lu-lin* 'he has seen me.' Here *ina* is the first-person object, or more accurately an inverse marker (see Comrie 1980), and together with *ɣe-lin* (in which *ɣe-* automatically loses its vowel before the following vowel) it becomes literally 'with-me-seen-he is' or 'me-seen-he has.' When, however, the object is second or third person, or is the first person with third-person plural subject, only the object is expressed and the construction is distinctly passive. An example is *ɣe-lu-lin*, translated by Menovshchikov as 'I, thou, he, we, you, they saw him,' which is obviously 'he is seen.' Similarly *ɣe-lu-jɣət* means 'thou art seen.'

Koryak has gone even further than Chukchi in that the passive based on *ɣe-lin* has been extended to all persons and numbers. It is interesting that Zhukova, our main authority on Koryak, in seeking to explain how a comitative can evolve into a perfective, arrives at virtually the same theory as that of Behagel cited earlier and, no doubt, quite independently (see Zhukova 1980: 63).

Kamchadal has also, in all probability independently of Chukchi-Koryak, expanded the construction with the comitative. Volodin (1976: 24) considers these to be later developments. One is the so-called Infinitive III, which takes two forms, *k . . . ʔin* (III.A) and *k . . . knen* (III.B). Both of these are confined to the third-person singular, the former being used with transitive and the latter with intransitive verbs, e.g. *k'-an'čp-ʔan* 'he taught him' and *k-sč'el-knen* 'he went away.' It is clear that the final element of III.A is the possessive *ʔin ~ ʔan* (see No. 25), whereas *-k-nen* consists of *k-*, the marker of intransitivity, and *-nen*, another variant of the possessive. In fact, as Volodin (1976: 298) points out, there are adjectival uses of what is clearly the same construction, e.g. *k-xplal-ʔan urwaq* 'a shirt full of holes,' and also predicative uses as in *t'in uʔw lɣi k-sŋak-ʔan* 'this tree (is) very gnarled.'

Forms cognate to those of Indo-European and Chukotian are possibly found in Ainu and Gilyak. In Ainu, *ko-* prefixed to a verb has a variety of meanings, 'to, from, with.' Dettmer (1989: 545) believes that from Batchelor's examples it is clear that the comitative meaning is primary and he agrees with Pierre Naert (1958: 198) in this respect. An example is *niki* 'to fold,' *ko-niki* 'to fold together.'

The Gilyak suffix *-ko(n)* occurs as a nominal coordinator, particularly of plural items. In the Amur dialect the final *-n* may appear overtly (Panfilov 1962–65, I: 115). An example showing an overt -*n* meaning 'with'—which in many languages is expressed in the same way as 'and' (e.g. Hausa *da*)—is Amur *hoyat hy umgu-gon vi-d'-yu* 'then they went away with this woman' ('then this woman-with go-non-future-plural' (Panfilov 1962–65, I: 169).

35. Vocative E

The Indo-European thematic noun stems have a vocative singular in *-e*. According to Brugmann (1897–1916, II, 3: 7), this does not appear to be distinct from the second-person singular imperative *-e*, a view that has often been repeated. However, the imperative in *-e* is only characteristic of the thematic conjugation, the athematic simply having zero. Hence the occurrence of *-e* in the imperative is inextricably bound up with the problem of the origin of the thematic conjugation and may have a different origin from the *-e* vocative of nouns. In fact this argument also applies to nouns. The vocative in -*e* may simply be the thematic vowel so that the vocative is really zero.

However that may be, forms corresponding to the -*e* vocative are found in several branches of Eurasiatic. Old Turkish has a suffixed a ∼ e that may also be used in the plural, e.g. *beglerim-e* 'my lords' (Tekin 1968: 174). A vocative -*a* is found in Korean and was related to Indo-European -*e* by Eckhardt (1965: 217). Gilyak likewise has a vocative *a*. Kamchadal, of the Chukotian group, has a singular vocative in *e* ∼ *a*, and Aleut also has an *a* vocative (Geoghegan 1944: 26).

36. Diminutive K

In Indo-European there is widespread use of -*k* as a general nominal and adjectival derivational suffix. Brugmann (1897–1916, II, 1: 490) evidently considers the original form to be *ik-e/-o* and its common diminutive uses to be historically secondary. Even in Sanskrit we find derivative formations with diminutive meanings, e.g. *paśu* 'domestic animal,' *paśu-k-a* 'small domestic animal.' Various diminutive formations in -*k* are found elsewhere in Indo-European. In a cross-linguistic study of the semantics of diminutives, with special emphasis on Indo-European, Daniel Jurafsky (1996: 565) arrives at the conclusion that the fundamental meaning of Indo-European *-ko- is 'child' and not 'pertaining to' (Brugmann). It would thus be essentially identical with Japanese ko 'child,' which is the source of the diminutive in Japanese, with particular female connotations.

Such diminutives are found in other branches of Eurasiatic, often associated with feminine meanings both synchronically and diachronically. After reviewing the broader Eurasiatic context, we will consider its possible bearing on the origin of the Indo-European feminine gender.

Szinnyei (1910: 97) reconstructs Finno-Ugric diminutives in -k and ka ~ kä. In Northern Samoyed there are diminutives in -ku that are connected by Collinder (1965b: 106) with those of Finno-Ugric.

In Old Turkish there was a diminutive in -k, usually -ak (Gabain 1950). In modern Turkic languages we find suffixes -ka and -ke, both of which are exempt from vowel harmony. The two variants -ka and -ke both contain low vowels—back and front, respectively—which are in regular alternation in the Turkic vowel harmony system. Examples include Karaim kułka 'female peasant' (cf. kuł 'peasant') and Gagauz qomšuika '(female) neighbor' (cf. qomšu 'neighbor'). In Chuvash there is also a -k that is connected by Ramstedt (1952–57, II: 212) with the non-Chuvash diminutive and is assumed by Levitskaja (1976: 143) to have originally had a diminutive signification. According to Poppe (1964: 42), the Mongolian noun has a suffix -ka(n) ~ -ke(n) that is used "to form nouns designating diminutives, sometimes female beings." The -(n) here is "variable n," which is not part of the stem (see No. 25). An example of feminine use is noya(n) 'prince,' noy-ika(n) 'princess.'

Dobrotvorskij (1875) gives a pair of examples from the Moshiogusa in which Ainu ko- prefixed to a verb appears to have a diminutive force, anukaru 'to look at for a long time,' koanukaru 'to look at (for some time).' As a verbal prefix, ko- is frequent in Ainu, but fundamentally employed to indicate a comitative relation.

Korean has a -k diminutive, especially in archaic and dialect words (Martin, Lee, and Chang 1967: 1). In Old Japanese the word ko 'child' is sometimes prefixed as a diminutive, e.g. ko-jima 'small island.' In more recent times -ko has become a common suffix to form female names, e.g. Masa-ko. Gilyak regularly forms feminine proper names by suffixing -k. Possibly kanak 'rabbit,' cited in Grube (1892), is a diminutive of kan 'dog.'

In Kamchadal there is a diminutive suffix -k'e-čχ (Volodin 1976: 123), in which -čχ is one of the common absolutive formations that have all been extended throughout the singular, but are absent in the plural. Volodin cites an example without -čχ-, ẉits-k'e 'young of akiba seal' (cf. ẉit 'akiba seal').

Eskimo has a common nominal diminutive suffix that in Greenlandic has the form -aʁ-aq (Kleinschmidt 1851: 127); in Asiatic Yupik (Menovshchikov 1962–67, II: 106) the form -xa-q or χa-q; and in the Kuskokwim (Yupik) dialect of Alaska, -γγa-q 'a little bit of.'

If we accept as a tentative working hypothesis that in some instances Indo-European laryngeals derive from k, and given the generally accepted view that a lost laryngeal lengthens a preceding vowel, then a theory of the origin of the Indo-European feminine, particularly the -ī stems, presents itself. Both the -ā and -ī stems are agreed to be the original feminine forms and to be derivational formations. Moreover, they are asigmatic, that is, they do not have -s in the nominative singular. Brugmann (1897–1916, II, 1: 490) considers it remarkable that in Indic feminine diminutives end in -ikā, whereas masculine diminutives end in -aka, and in Lithuanian diminutives (in -ike) are restricted to feminine nouns. It is noticeable that in a number of instances the form appears to be -ik rather than -k- (e.g. Turkic, Mongolian).

This strengthens the case for Indo-European feminine ī to have been derived from *-iH (< *-ik). It is not excluded that feminine derivatives in -ā may have been derived in a similar way through an a-colored laryngeal. In fact, -ā is generally believed to derive from original *-eH₂. In general, all long vowel stems in Indo-European are feminine, e.g. -ū stems in Sanskrit such as vadhū 'woman' and -ō stems in Greek, which indicate feminine names and feminine beings (Schwyzer 1939–50, I: 178).

If we accept this hypothesis, whose speculative character I am well aware of, it may help explain the deviant stem of Greek guna-ik- 'woman,' as against forms in related languages that lack the -(i)k- (see Pokorny 1959: 473).

37. Instrumental S

A derivational suffix -s(i) forms nouns of instrument (and others with related meanings) in some of the eastern Eurasiatic languages. Korean suffixes -ssə to nouns with the instrumental case marker -lo (formerly a dative, see No. 29). Ramstedt (1939: 411) derives it from a verb stem ssɨ 'to use.'

In Gilyak, -s (Eastern Sakhalin -ř) is suffixed to verb stems mainly to form nouns of instrument or agent, but also nouns of action, or result of action, e.g. qor-s 'a scoop, basket,' which is derived from the verb qor 'to scoop out.' In addition Gilyak derives verbs from nouns by suffixing -z, e.g. kʻe 'a net,' kʻɨj-z 'to set up a net.' Panfilov (1962–65, II) considers these two usages as involving the same suffix.

A similar dual usage is found in Eskimo. A suffix in -si- is common in Eskimo for deriving nouns of instrument from verbs, e.g. Greenlandic -usi-q, Chaplino (Siberian Yupik) -si-q. In Sirenik, verbs meaning 'make use of' are derived from nouns by suffixing -si and nouns of instrument are derived from verbs by suffixing -si-ʁ-aχ. Here -aχ is the absolutive singular ending and is not part of the stem; -ʁ- is a general nominalizer (see No. 23).

Aleut also exhibits this dual usage of deriving verbs from nouns and nouns from verbs. For example, in the Bering Island dialect nouns of instrument are formed from verbs by suffixing -si-χ, and verbs are formed from nouns by suffixing -si, e.g. ulaχ 'house,' ulaχ-si- 'to construct a house.' In an interesting discussion of this usage in Aleut, Jochelson (1934: 134) asserts that "the element of instrument . . . is an infix in the transitive verb and not in the noun which is an instrument."

38. Nominalizer I

A number of branches of Eurasiatic show an -i suffixed to a verbal stem to form what is fundamentally a noun of action. Brugmann (1897–1916, II, 1: 167) describes it as Proto-Indo-European. Among the examples he cites are Proto-Germanic *luʒʒi and Old Church Slavic lĭžĭ, both meaning 'lie' (noun) and derived from verbs meaning 'to lie.' In Sanskrit, dr̥śi-š 'seeing' (noun) is derived from the verb stem *darš-* 'to see' and in Vedic the dative with *-i* stem inflection forms an infinitive, e.g. *yudhaye* 'to fight.' From the simple meaning of verbal noun, it is but a short step to the designation of that which carries out the action, e.g. Latin *fluv-i-us* 'river' (i.e. 'the one that carries out the action of flowing,' cf. *flu-ere* 'to flow).

In the first systematic comparison of Indo-European and Uralic, Anderson (1879: 59) equates the Indo-European forms with Finnish *-ja* and Mordvin *-i*, both of which form agent nouns from verbs. In fact, Baltic Finnic languages also suffix *-i* to form nouns of action, e.g. Finnish *oppi* 'teaching.' Lauri Hakulinen (1957) describes *-i* as denoting action, the result of action, and the ability to do; it is also found in agent nouns. The agentive meaning occurs in both Finnic and Samoyed (see Collinder 1965b: 264) and Szinnyei (1910: 94) reconstructs **-i* for Proto-Finno-Ugric.

As a formative for verbal nouns *i* is also found in all branches of Altaic, although it is no longer productive in Mongolian (Ramstedt 1952, II: 100–2). Examples are Azerbaijani (Turkic) *jaz-i* 'writing' (cf. *jaz-* 'to write') and Even (Tungus) *tät-i* 'clothing' (cf. *tät* 'to clothe oneself').

In his comparison of Ainu, Korean, and Japanese, Patrie (1982: 108) observes that *-i* is found in all three languages and is in fact common and productive in all of them. Ramstedt (1945), in an article devoted specifically to the Altaic deverbal noun in *-i*, notes its existence in all branches of Altaic and connects it genetically with Korean *-i*. Street (1978: 173) similarly, after discussing *-i* in Japanese as a frequent and productive formative of verbal nouns at all stages of its history, connects these with similar formations in Altaic languages (see also Kazár 1980: 259 regarding Japanese-Altaic). With regard to Ainu, Batchelor (1905) notes that "when suffixed to adjectives or verbs, *i* has the power of changing them into nouns." Examples are *pirika* 'good,' *pirika-i* 'goodness'; *akara* 'to be done,' *akara-i* 'a thing to be done.'

I would suggest that the Sanskrit intensive form of the verb, a form that also occurs in Avestan (see Whitney 1879: 362–72 for a detailed discussion) and Hittite, involves the verbal noun in *-i* in its formation. In Sanskrit it is one of a number of reduplicative formations, but it is unusual in two respects. In the reduplication, which always precedes, the final consonant of the stem is included. Furthermore, in many instances a vowel *-i* or *-ī* appears after the reduplicated syllable. The rule is that -*ī* appears before a single consonant and -*i* before a double consonant. However, there is one exception, *davidhāv-*, which is derived from the root *dhāv-* 'to run.' Brugmann (1897–1916, II, 3: 23) considered the long vowel form to be secondary and believed the form to be Proto-Indo-European. The Vedic accentuation on the first syllable (e.g. *bhárībharti* 'he carries') strengthens the case for the first part being a verbal noun since the Vedic verb was enclitic in main clauses except when sentence or verse initial, and this state of affairs is generally assumed for Proto-Indo-European. No doubt synchronically in Vedic it was considered a single word so that it is unaccented as a whole in main clauses, as are other verbs, but the old accentuation appears in other sentence positions. An additional irregularity—the occasional retention of aspiration in the reduplicating syllable—also strengthens the case for the initial portion being a verbal noun in *i*.

This same formation has been found to occur in Hittite in forms such as *wariwarant-* 'burning' and *paripara-i* 'he blows a musical instrument.' The genetic connection between the Indic forms and those of Hittite was apparently first noted by Sommer (1947: 63). I believe the Indo-European intensive is the verbal noun in -*i* preceding the stem of the same verb (*figura etymologica*). Thus Hittite *pari-parai* is literally 'a blowing he blows.' Since Brugmann's time it has also been found to occur in Greek (Winter 1950).

There is a quite exact typological parallel in the so-called infinitive absolute of Hebrew of the verbal measure *qǝṭol*, which is used both as a verbal noun and in construction with a verb of the same root, usually immediately preceding it and with an emphatic meaning. An example occurs in *Genesis* 2: 17; the Hebrew text has *mōt tǝmūt* 'a dying thou shalt die,' which is translated in the King James version as 'thou shalt surely die.' In Hebrew the verbal noun occasionally follows the root if the verb is imperative (see Cowley 1910: 339). A similar construction occurs in Korean with *m*, the other common Eurasiatic verbal formant (see No. 39).

39. Nominalizer M

The second important verbal noun formant in Eurasiatic is -*m*. In comparison with the -*i* discussed in the preceding section, -*m* involves a greater variety of meanings and syntactic functions, all of which, however, have parallels in the English gerund in '-ing,' e.g. as a noun of action, infinitive, nominal or adverbial participle, and even as a passive, e.g. 'a singing telegram,' 'the lady is not for burning.'

Besides the variety of syntactic usage in Indo-European, there is, alongside of the suffix -m, the occurrence of forms such as the Greek middle and passive participle in -men-os, the Sanskrit passive participle of the thematic verb -mān-as, etc. Brugmann (1897–1916, II, 1: 230–32) believed that the forms with and without -n were related. He derived the latter from *-mn-o and thought it probable that the variant in *-m-o arose from this by contraction. He has been generally followed in assuming the ultimate common origin of forms with and without -n. I would explain the forms in -n as having arisen from m- and the oblique marker -n (No. 25). Particularly striking in this respect is the agreement of the Vedic infinitive in -mane (e.g. damane 'to give') with the Greek infinitive dómenai, both datives of verbal nouns used as infinitives. By the analogical spread of oblique -n to the nominative, and of forms without -n to the oblique, there would arise the doublets that we find in Indo-European. Brugmann also posited the existence of -mo- as a "primary formant" in the Indo-European word *gʷherm- 'hot,' derived from the verb *gʷher- 'to burn.'

Benveniste (1959) noted that this use as a verbal adjective is the only specific one that is common to a number of branches of Indo-European and proposed that this function is the original one. He pointed also to the frequent occurrence of such adjectives in Indic, e.g. Sanskrit tij- 'to be sharp,' tig-m-as 'sharp,' and the survival of this use in other branches of Indo-European. Thus in Balto-Slavic we find an instance of this earlier use in Lithuanian tiñkam-as 'pleasant, convenient' and in Old Church Slavic vědomŭ 'knowing.' The close connection between active and passive means is shown in English 'fearful,' which from meaning 'full of fear' also comes to mean 'causing fear in others, feared.' Benveniste's thesis of the original meaning of -m as a verbal adjective was adopted and further elaborated by Eric Hamp (1982), who also points out that such adjectives can easily be syntactically nominalized to produce nouns of action.

Outside of the middle and passive participles and the infinitives in -men in Greek, and the Sanskrit infinitive in -mane, the most

conspicuous Indo-European development is the passive participle in
-m of Baltic, Slavic, Anatolian, and possibly Armenian. In the Anatolian group this passive participle occurs in Luwian, Hieroglyphic
Hittite, and Lycian, but is not found in Hittite or Palaic. However,
-ma does survive in Hittite in fossilized forms such as la-lukki-ma
'brightness' (V. V. Ivanov, personal communication). An example
of the passive participle is Luwian piyama- 'given.' Kammenhuber (1969) notes the occurrence in Luwian of such participles in
-(m)ma, -mmi, and because of the great analogic spread in Luwian
of -i stems she considers -(m)ma to be the original form. She also
believes the identification with the Baltic and Slavic passive participles to be obvious. The forms -mma and -mmi presumably derive from *-mna and would constitute yet another example of the
widespread variant with -n. The argument that -n is the oblique
marker in -me-n is strengthened by the evidence from Tocharian, as
pointed out by Ivanov (1959: 23), where the present participles in
-mer, with medio-passive meaning, would represent the nominative
-r in the well-known Proto-Indo-European alternation in r/n stems.

    Scholars who compared Indo-European with Uralic noted from
the outset the resemblance of Uralic -ma ~ -mä to the Indo-European
suffix just discussed. It is found in all branches of Uralic and shows
a similar range of semantic and syntactic variation. In addition
to forming infinitives, and nouns and adjectives indicating actions
or qualities, it can also form passive participles, as in Saami ahče
čallem kirje 'the letter written by father,' literally 'the by-father
written letter' (Collinder 1965b: 112). With regard to its widespread
infinitival use, see particularly Pauli Saukkonen's (1964) discussion
of Mordvin. Another example is the so-called fourth infinitive of the
Finnish verb, which suffixes -ma and has the meaning of a participial
relative.

    In comparing Uralic and Yukaghir, Collinder (1940: 50) showed
that the transitive verb conjugation of Yukaghir was based on a suffix
-m that is directly comparable to the Uralic verbal noun and adjective in -ma ~ -mä, e.g. Yukaghir met čomoǰelŋin punda-me 'by-me
to-my-teacher told' or 'I told my teacher' is parallel in its construction to Finnish isän anta-ma kirja 'by-my-father given book.' In
the nineteenth-century Yukaghir material edited by Schiefner (1871:
619), we find -ma as a passive participle in Kolyma moi-ma 'held,

brought.' The verb *moi* 'hold, have' is well attested in the Kolyma dialect of Yukaghir, as can be seen in the wordlist accompanying Krejnovich's grammar (1958).

Ramstedt (1950: 225) is devoted to a comparison of the verbal noun in -*m* in the Altaic languages, among which he includes Korean. As he notes, "one can find in all Altaic languages numerous instances of primitive Altaic verbal nouns in -*m* which, judging from the further developments it gave rise to, must be very old." Examples of verbal nouns in Turkic, which are extremely common, are Turkish *öl-* 'to die,' *ölüm* 'death, disease'; Nogai *öl-* 'to die,' *ölim* 'death'; Uighur *käð-* 'to dress,' *käðim* 'garment.' Included in these are passive uses such as Turkish *jazma* 'written' and the common Turkic infinitives in -*ma* or -*mak* (for *k* see No. 23). Chuvash forms infinitives in *ma-* ∼ *me-*. The form in *mak* is also found in Mongolian and Korean.

In Tungus there is a simultaneous verbal participle in -*mi* that is found in virtually all Northern and Southern Tungus languages, including Manchu, for example Orok (Petrova 1968: 184), as well as a verbal noun in -*ma* in Oroch (Avrorin and Lebedeva 1968: 199). In Manchu there is a verbal suffix -*me*, indicating that the action is simultaneous with the main verb, which belongs here also.

Ainu has a small number of adjectives in -*ma* (Dettmer 1989: 812). Examples are *tuy-ma* 'far' (with which compare the adverbial form *tuy-no*), *ram-ma* 'constant,' and *mos-ma* 'outside of, near.' In Korean, in addition to the extremely common verbal noun in -*m*, there is a verbal suffix -*mej* ∼ -*maj* meaning 'because,' which is found mainly in epistolary style (Pultr 1960: 135).

In Chukchi and languages of the Koryak group there is a verbal suffix -*ma*, whose construction is very similar to Manchu -*me*. An example is Kerek *kaliwaŋi-ma . . . nəkumŋillaŋi* 'they embroidered-*ma*, they sang,' i.e. 'they sang as they embroidered.'

We may compare here the suffix -*(ɣ)ma-* of Greenlandic and Labrador Eskimo, which is also found in Eastern Canada. It is called the subjunctive by Kleinschmidt. The use of -*ma-* in this construction is confined to third-person subject and it must be different from the subject of the main verb. A Greenlandic example is *nukaa tikiŋ-ma-t, tuquvuq* 'When his younger brother arrived, he (i.e. the older brother) died.' More directly comparable to examples elsewhere is the Sirenik participle in *-mi-*, for example, *an-mi-χ* 'one who has just gone out' ('go out-participle-absolutive'; Menovshchikov 1964: 96).

40. Possessive L

In Turkic there is a common suffix *-li* that derives adjectives or nouns from nouns, with the resulting meaning 'possessing the thing or quality expressed in the noun.' Related forms are found in Eskimo and probably in Indo-European. Examples from Turkish are *ev* 'house,' *ev-li* 'possessing a house'; *el* 'hand,' *el-li* 'having a hand, or handle' (Kissling 1960: 225). Connected with this is the common noun suffix *-li-k* (see No. 23). In Turkish the meaning is sometimes passive, e.g. *yazï-lï* 'registered' (cf. *yaz-ï* 'writing,' which is itself derived from the verb *yaz-* 'to write' by means of the verbal noun suffix discussed in No. 38. In Old Turkish there is also a suffix *-lä* with essentially the same meaning, e.g. *körk-lä* 'beautiful,' *körk-* 'form' (Gabain 1950: 65). Chuvash has a similar adjectival suffix *-lă*, e.g. *čap-lă* 'famous,' *čap-* 'fame' (Krueger 1961: 130–31).

It is general in Eskimo to suffix *-li* to nouns with the meaning 'possessor,' e.g. Eastern Canadian (Inuit of Southhampton Island) *umi-li-q* 'bearded,' from *umi-q* 'beard' (Thibert 1970). In this example *-q* is the absolutive ending (see No. 23). In some forms of Eskimo a noun suffix with *-l* becomes a participle meaning 'possessing X,' or 'since one possesses X,' as for example in the Siberian Yupik dialect of Chaplino (Menovshchikov 1962–67, I: 104), where, from the noun stem *kamǝ-* 'shoe,' one can form *kamǝ-lǝ-ŋa* 'shoe-possessing-first person singular' (i.e. 'I possessing a shoe . . .' or 'since I have a shoe . . .'). Menovshchikov also notes the resemblance between the Eskimo form and the common Turkic *-li-g*, but concludes that it must be accidental because Eskimo and Turkic are not related. In Aleut there is a formative *-li*, which when added to nouns indicates instrument (Geoghegan 1944: 67). Whether this formative is cognate with the other forms discussed here I am uncertain.

In Mongolian there is a suffix *-lig* ~ *-liγ* that forms nouns of abundance, e.g. *ǰimis-lig* 'orchard' (literally, 'having fruit'), *miqa-liγ* 'fat' (adjective) (literally, 'having fat,' cf. *miqa-n* 'flesh') (Poppe 1964: 42). Similar forms are found in Tungus, for example, Orok *-lʊ* ~ *-lu* 'having' and *-la* ~ *-le* 'having' (with negatives), as in *asi-la ana nari* (wife-possessing not man) 'a bachelor.'

As noted below in regard to Yukaghir, *l'i* 'possessing' is in all probability one of a pair of verbs, **l'e* 'to be,' **l'i* 'to have.' Of these *le* appears clearly in Kamchadal *le-ke-s* 'to become' (Volodin 1976: 25), in which *-ke-* is a marker of intransitivity and *-s* indicates the infinitive. A variant is *ɬ'* 'to be,' which derives verbs from nouns or adjectives (Volodin 1976: 94), e.g. *k'isx* 'dry,' *k'isx-ɬ'-ke-s* 'to dry out' (intransitive). In Kamchadal the difference between the unvoiced and voiced lateral is probably not phonemic. A likely cognate formation appears in Chukchi forms like *jara-lʔ-ən* 'having a house,' in which *-ən* is the absolutive (Menovshchikov 1968: 258; cf. *jara-ŋa* 'house').

These forms may have Indo-European cognates. When Lydian was deciphered it was found to have a "genitive" in *-li-* (actually a possessive adjective), e.g. *mane-li-d* 'pertaining to or belonging to Mane.' Here *-d* is the neuter nominative-accusative in agreement with the modified noun. Lydian *-li* is obviously related to the Hittite adjectives and adverbs in *-li* and *-ili,* and pronominal genitives such as *ammel* 'my,' which represent a development of a common Indo-European derivational affix that is particularly prominent in Latin, e.g. *currū-li-s* 'pertaining to a chariot,' from *curru-s* 'chariot.'

It should be noted that there is, however, an important difference in meaning between the Indo-European and extra-Indo-European forms. In Indo-European the general meaning is 'pertaining to, or belonging to,' whereas elsewhere it means 'possessing.' The process of semantic transition is illustrated by Chuvash *čul-lă pĕve* 'rocky dam,' which is quite close in meaning to such English turns of phrase as 'dam of rock.'

Finally, it seems plausible to see a connection between the affix discussed here and the Yukaghir verb *l'i* 'to have.' Jochelson distinguishes between *l'i* 'to have' and *l'e* 'to be,' the latter of which has cognates in other branches of Eurasiatic. However, in many languages 'have' and 'be' are not distinguished so the differentiation in Yukaghir may be secondary. At any rate, the Yukaghir verb *l'i* 'to have' represents a plausible verbal source for the construction discussed in this section. Jochelson, in fact, connects these verbs with the *-le-(k)* of focussing constructions in Yukaghir (1905: 106). If, however, *-l'i* is really participial this difficulty disappears. It seems likely that participles in general in Eurasiatic could be construed actively or passively, hence -*l'i* 'possessing' could also be 'possessed of' or 'possessed by.'

Krejnovich (1976) connected the Turkic and Eskimo formatives discussed here. He also included Gilyak -*la* and Kamchadal -*la-χ*, which derive adjectives from qualitative verbs. For reasons discussed below (see No. 45) I consider these Gilyak and Kamchadal forms, whose similarity is obvious, under the gerundive-participial -*l* treated in that section.

41. Adverbial Participle P

There is in Eurasiatic a widely distributed element **pa* (more rarely **pi*) that is usually suffixed to verbs. Its probable original meaning is well illustrated in Turkic, where Menges (1968: 135–36) describes it as an "expression of successive actions whose time levels are not essentially different or distant from each other." In Turkic its syntax and meaning are much like the Russian adverbial participle (*de-jeprichastije*) in -*ja*, e.g. 'weeping, he came.' Since Turkic languages do not mark adjectives for number, gender, person, or case, there are no participles in the proper sense. Moreover, as with the Russian adverbial participle, the subjects of the subordinate and main verbal form are the same. With such a form as the probable starting point a number of developments, syntactic and semantic, can take place. The adverbial participle can become an ordinary participle ('weeping he came' becomes 'he the weeping one came'). Moreover, simultaneous or nearly simultaneous action easily takes on a causal or conditional nuance.

In all branches of Uralic there is a participle in **-p* or **-pa* (-*va*- intervocalically in the consonant gradation system, see Collinder 1965b: 114). In Finnish, in addition to forming adjectives like *elä-vä* 'living,' it forms the third-person singular and plural of the verb, e.g. *tule-vä-t* 'they come.' It is, of course, a common development for participles to be the source of finite verb forms, the usual entry point being the third person. An example is the Slavic -*lŭ* past participle, which in Old Church Slavic was accompanied by a copular verb in all persons and numbers that was sometimes omitted in the third-person singular. In Czech it is obligatorily omitted in the third person, but is required in the first and second person, e.g. *viděl jsem* 'I saw' (masculine subject), *viděl* 'he saw.' The final stage is that of modern Russian, in which the participle has become the imperfect tense in all persons and numbers. Setälä (1887: 166) noted that the "formal similarity of the suffix in question [sci. the present in -*p*] . . . with the Finno-Ugric '*nomen agentis*' (participle) makes us assume that there is an original connection between them." In a discussion of Yurak Samoyed, Irene Sebestyén (1970) reports a gerund in *b* and says it can be identified with the verbal noun in **pa*, which in turn occurs with possessive suffixes in Old Hungarian. Both in Yurak and Old Hungarian such pronominal suffixes indicate the subject of the action expressed in the verbal noun.

Menges (1995: 135–36) connects Turkic -*p*/-V*p* (also *pan, ban* in the Uighur inscriptions) with Tungus -*pi, -fi,* as well as (following Räsänen) the Uralic present participle in *pa* ~ *pä*. In Mongolian there is a past converb (i.e. adverbial participle) in -*ba*- found in the conditional *ba-su* (< *ba-asu*), in which *a-su* means 'would be.' Ramstedt (1952) considers this to be related to the Turkic forms in -*p*-. In Sunik's (1968c: 63) summary of common Tungus, we find in tabular form the following examples of an adverbial participle expressing actions earlier in time than the main verb: Manchu -*fi*, Ju-chen *fēi*, Nanai *pa*, and Ulch *pa*.

In Ainu, the Majewiczes (1983–85: 32, note 47) list a participial in -*va* or -*ua* for the Sakhalin dialect. Batchelor gives *wa* in his dictionary of the Hokkaido dialect and translates it as '. . . ing' or 'and.' He cites as an example *oman wa ye* 'take it and come' ('take *wa* come').

I believe the Japanese conditional form of the verb in -*ba* belongs here. In Gilyak, -*pa* is suffixed to the verb with the meaning 'after or when doing X,' e.g. 'he to-the-house come-*pa*, something does,' i.e. 'he does something as soon as he comes to the house' (Panfilov 1962–65, II: 145). The use here is virtually identical to that of Turkic.

The most common Eskimo present tense in -*p*-—for example, West Greenlandic *tikippuq* < *tikit-pu-q* 'he/she arrives'—is probably the *p*- participial which has here assumed the role of predicate in an independent clause, typologically a frequent development. In Labrador and Greenlandic Eskimo, the verb has a conditional form in which -*pa*- functions as the suffix only in the third-person, i.e. *pa-t* (singular), *pa-nik* (dual), *pa-ta* (plural). (For the *-t* in *pa-t*, see No. 11.)

In the Anatolian subgroup of Indo-European both Luwian and the almost identical Hieroglyphic Hittite show a suffix *-pa-* that sometimes occurs in initial position. Laroche (1958: 167) describes it as having the general function, when an affix, of introducing a coordination. The connection between the two members is often an opposition, sometimes an alternative. In other cases it involves an addition. It may be clause initial, sometimes introducing the apodosis. In this case its meaning would presumably be 'then, therefore.' Cuneiform Hittite also has a suffix *-pa, -ap(a)*, whose meaning is not clear and whose connection with Luwian *-pa* is considered doubtful by Laroche and by Friedrich (1952: 24). Friedrich gives the meaning as 'because, therefore' with a query.

The Luwian, Hieroglyphic Hittite, and possibly the cuneiform Hittite forms would seem reasonably to belong with those cited by Pokorny (1959: 113) under *bhě, bhŏ*. Note especially the Gothic conditional particle *ba* and Old Church Slavic *bo* 'because, since, therefore.'

It is possible that the Korean suffix *-pa* (already included as a locative in No. 28) may be homonymous with the morpheme discussed here. Martin, Lee, and Chang (1967: 701) give two distinct meanings. The first is 'way, means, a thing, that which' (according to Ramstedt originally 'place'). The second meaning is 'and/but.' In the example given, "We few people have sponsored the society and it has prospered beyond our expectations," *-pa* is suffixed to "sponsored" and the sentence is easily paraphrased as 'since we few people have sponsored the society, . . .' Derivability from the first meaning seems semantically difficult.

42. Participle N

In Indo-European there are two common ways of forming past (basically passive) participles, with *-n* and with *-t*. Some branches have generalized one at the expense of the other, which often survives only in isolated forms. For example, in Latin the normal past participle marker is *-t-*, but *-n-* survived in words like *plē-n-us* 'full.' Where both *-n-* and *-t-* are parts of the verbal inflectional system, the rules governing the choice between them differ in individual branches, e.g. Indic and Slavic.

Although the meaning is passive with transitive verbs, the participle has active meaning with intransitives, e.g. German *gekommen* 'arrived.' In addition to its use as a noun qualifier, it is often substantivized, as in German *Gesandte* 'envoy' (literally, 'a sent person'). In all of these uses there is no essential distinction between the two formatives (see Szemerényi 1978: 408). We shall consider *-n* first. Unlike *-t*, it is very widely distributed in the Eurasiatic family.

In Finno-Ugric, Szinnyei (1910: 95) considers *-n* among the formatives that derive nouns and adjectives from verbs. In addition to forming verbal nouns, there are uses very similar to the *-n* participle of Indo-European. Examples include Cheremis *tolǝn*, glossed in German as *gekommen*, from a verb *tol-* 'to come,' and Mordvin *kadoń* 'abandoned' from *kad-* 'to abandon.' Unlike Cheremis and Mordvin, it is not a productive formation in Samoyed. Collinder (1960b: 262) cites a few examples from Northern Samoyed languages, Tavgy *d'ienea* 'mossy,' from *d'ie* 'moss,' and Enets *fionoo* 'exterior' (adjective), from *fio* 'the exterior.' These are of course derived from nouns, not from verbs, but similar instances are found in Indo-European languages.

A participle in *-n* in Altaic is discussed by Ramstedt (1952, II: 94–100). In non-Chuvash Turkic and Mongolian it only survives in scattered nouns and adjectives. However, Chuvash has a productive participle in *-nă*, as seen in *kur-nă sin* 'the man who was seen' ('see-nă man'; Krueger 1961: 155). Another productive use is in the Tungus present tense in the first- and second-person singular of some languages where, however, it has an active meaning, for example, Evenki *wā-n-ni* < **wā-n-si* 'thou killest.' A use closer to that of Indo-European, Korean, and Ainu is Evenki *-na* ~ *-ne* ~ *-no*, which, when suffixed to a verb stem, indicates the result of an act, as in, for example, *dukū-na-w* 'what I have written' ('thing-written-my'; Menges 1968: 82).

In Ainu *-na* is suffixed to verbs to express state or condition, e.g. *mak* 'to open,' *mak-na* 'opened up.' Naert (1958: 102) compares this suffix to the similar form in Indo-European. There is also a variant *-ne* that is seen, for example, in *taku-ne* 'agglomerated' with the same stem as the verb *taku-kara* (*kara* 'to do, to make'). The same variant is probably to be seen in *pe-ne* 'watery' (cf. *pe* 'water'). Here, as noted below with respect to Japanese and probably Gilyak, an ultimate connection with genitive *n* seems possible. In Korean the regular inflection for the past participle is *-n*, e.g. *po-n* 'seen,' from *po* 'to see,' and the resemblance to Indo-European was pointed out by Koppelmann (1933).

In Old Japanese *-nu* is added to verb stems to form verbal nouns, e.g. *ki-nu* 'garment,' related to *ki-ru* 'to dress.' Perhaps the Japanese genitive particle *no* (originally 'that which'; it still forms relative clauses) belongs here rather than with No. 25. Lewin (1959: 139) mentions adjectives in *-na-*, for example, *abu-na-si* 'dangerous,' *okka-na-si* 'fearful,' and *osa-na-si* 'young.' Here the *-si* is an inflection that marks the word as adjectival. Martin (1991: 285) equates Amami (Ryukyuan) *-n* (e.g. *a-n* 'done,' *wu-n* 'been') with Korean *-n*.

In Grube (1892: 19), which is based on Gilyak material collected by Glehn and Schrenk, a formative *-n-*, described as a participle (Grube 1892: 33), appears to be cognate with the forms just discussed. The following examples are given: *xob-en tamak* 'cigar' (= 'wrapped up tobacco'; cf. *xov* 'to wrap up' in Saval'eva 1970); *taiɣon-an tif* 'Milky way' (= 'unknown road'; cf. *taiɣ-o-č* 'to not know'). Substantivized forms also occur in forms such as *iń-nɨ-dʹ* 'food' (< *iń* 'to eat'; Saval'eva 1970: 524). The *dʹ* is the same substantivizer as that found in the Gilyak infinitive (see No. 44).

Aleut has a participle in *-na* with perfective meaning, e.g. *kikaɣ-na-χ* 'bedraggled,' *umla-na-χ* 'one who has overslept,' *saku-na-χ* 'one who is weak, has wasted away.' When predicated it forms a past perfective tense (Menovshchikov 1968: 400–1).

43. Passive Participle T

Unlike the *-n* passive participle, the *-t* participle is not widely distributed in Eurasiatic. In Indo-European, however, it occurs in all branches except Tocharian and Anatolian. Like the *-n* participle, it can have both an active and passive meaning. Thus in Sanskrit we have *gatás* 'gone' from an intransitive stem. In Latin deponent verbs the meaning is active, e.g. *secū-t-us* 'having followed,' but *fac-t-us* 'having been made.' Szemerényi (1978: 408) considers that it was originally not specified for voice, but in the later history of

Indo-European languages there was a tendency to restrict it to the passive use.

Wiklund (1906) connected the Indo-European *t* participle with Finno-Ugric *t* found in infinitives and participles, e.g. Mordvin *panža-do* 'opened' (past participle), Veps *ištu-d* 'sitting.' Collinder (1960: 271–72, 1964: 48) endorses Wicklund's views. According to Collinder this formative is found in Finnic, Saami, Ob-Ugric, and Samoyed languages so it is in fact Uralic, not merely Finno-Ugric.

In Piłsudski's texts of Sakhalin Ainu, there occurs a suffix *-te* listed as a 'participial' by the Majewiczes in their concordance (1983–85: 5), for example, *an-ki-te* 'I making' ('I-make–*te*'; Piłsudski, 1912: 12). It also occurs as *-tex*, in which Sakhalin Ainu *-x* could derive from *p*, *t*, or *k*.

In Yukaghir, there is a verbal suffix *-t* that expresses an action taking place simultaneously with that indicated by the predicate. An example is *mi anil legu-t šorile* 'I while eating fish was writing' ('I fish eat-*t* write-I'). Jochelson (1905: 134–35) considers this *-t* to be the ablative (see No. 33), but I believe it is preferable to consider the *-t* here to be a participle, 'I fish eating write' in the foregoing example.

The situation within Eskimo is complex and a fully detailed study would require an extended article or small monograph. In short, I believe that a *-t* medio-passive participle can be reconstructed for Proto-Eskimo. Although it is a participle in Eastern Inuit (Greenland and Labrador), there is a tendency to predicate it so that it becomes a main verb, a tendency which grows stronger as one goes westward. It becomes the intransitive indicative in Alaskan Inuit and Yupik and even the general marker of the indicative (both transitive and intransitive) in Siberian Sirenik.

In Labrador and Greenland there are three *-t* forms, which (as Kleinschmidt 1851: 112 indicates) have an obvious common origin. The first variant, *-tuq*, indicates only the actor, normally with intransitive verbs; with transitive verbs an additional preceding suffix is usually required. A Greenlandic example is *ajur-t-uq* 'he who is bad' (cf. *ajur-p-uq* 'he is bad,' in which the *-p-* suffix is confined to the indicative). This participle is inflected for person and number with inflections identical to those of the intransitive (unipersonal) verb, e.g. *ajur-tuŋa* 'I who am bad.' A second suffix is *-taq* (usually, but not always, replaced by -ɣaq in Greenlandic). Since Klein-schmidt gives no examples of this participle, I cite one from the Hudson Bay area that has the same construction, *puiɣuq-tait* 'your forgotten thing, what you forgot' (Spalding 1960: 117). Unlike the *-tuq* particle it is a noun and can take possessive suffixes, as in the preceding example. The third type in Greenlandic Eskimo consists of *-t-* followed by the bipersonal suffixes of the transitive verb. Thus, paralleling *urniʁpai* 'he comes to them,' with third-person singular subject and third-person plural object, is *urniʁtai* 'he who comes to them.' These, as Kleinschmidt maintained, are all based on the same *-t*. The vowel difference, as in the *u* of *-tu-ŋa* versus the *a* of *-ta-it*, is incidental to the verbal and nominal forms. The transitive form does not seem to occur elsewhere, but see the discussion below.

In Eastern Canada, the area of the Central Eskimo (who might be more appropriately called the Central Inuit), one finds a strong tendency to use the first form as a main declarative instead of the p- form. In Spalding's grammar forms like *pisuɣpuq* 'he comes' and *pisuɣtuq* 'he or she who comes' seem to be used indifferently as main verbs or as participles, whereas with transitive verbs the forms in p- are used, as in Labrador and Greenland. In the only detailed grammar of the Central Inuit area available to me, though no rule is given, it is clear from a number of examples in Spalding (1960: 64) that the participle is used essentially in focused constructions that are answers to questions, i.e. "They are the ones who do X." This construction has, however, become a virtual equivalent of the usual indicative in p-. The nominalized participle in *-tuq* is also used in this area.

In the Western Inuit dialects of Northern Alaska (see Rasmussen 1941), intransitive verbs are invariably cited in their *-t-* form. For transitives there is no marker for the indicative beyond the person-number indicator that is added directly to the stem. An example in Kangianermiut (near the mouth of the Yukon river) is *iməɣ-tuq* 'he drinks' (cf. Greenlandic *imiɣ-puq*) and *akilaɣ-aa* 'he pays it.' This same situation holds in Alaskan Yupik, so this characteristic cuts across the generally accepted main dialectal division of Eskimo. In his grammar of Kuskokwim (Yupik) Hinz expressly notes the difference between *atuɣ-tuq* 'it is used' and *atuɣ-aa* 'he uses it.'

In Siberian Yupik the intransitive indicative has *-t-* as in Alaskan

Yupik, but -ta- is used in transitives, e.g. kajux-tuŋa 'I drink,' but tuku-ta-mkin 'I kill thee.' In the latter, -mkin has the meaning 'first-person singular acts on second-person singular.' I believe that this -ta- is causative in origin (see No. 49).

The process by which the t- participle finally becomes the general mark of the indicative reaches its climax in Sirenik, a genetically distinctive Siberian dialect, in which -tə- is used for both transitives and intransitives, the difference being shown simply by the employment of unipersonal and bipersonal suffixes. The contrast between the use of t in eastern and western areas of Eskimo described here was noted in general terms by Uhlenbeck (1907: 36), who pointed out that this participle "is used particularly in the west as a finite verb."

Aleut also has a participle in -ta- that can be used substantivally both with transitive and intransitive verbs, e.g. max-ta-χ 'wet,' from a verb meaning 'to become wet,' saʁakuχ-ta-χ 'having fallen asleep' (Menovshchikov 1968: 400–1). In both of these forms -χ is the marker of the absolutive case.

In addition to verbal and substantival uses (e.g. 'the one who comes'), this participle also forms adjectives in Eskimo, for example, Naukan (Siberian Yupik) napaxtux-ta-q 'wooded, foresty,' derived from napaxtux- 'tree' (Menovshchikov 1975: 127).

44. Participle NT

The common active participle of Indo-European is -nt-, with preceding thematic vowel or weak grade of n (i.e. -ṇt-), e.g. Sanskrit bhárant- 'carrying,' which is associated with a thematic verb stem bhara- (cf. Latin ferent- 'carrying'). As pointed out by Brugmann (1897–1916, II: 454ff), and others before him, such a participle easily functions as an ordinary adjective, without a corresponding verb stem, and can in turn be substantivized, e.g. Gothic frijond-s 'friend.' The Indo-European root for 'tooth,' *dent-, has long been recognized as a zero-grade participle of the verb *ed- 'to eat.' Another use occurs in Uralic languages, in which the -nt participle is used much as the periphrastic present of English ('is going'). An example from the Ob-Ugric branch is Vogul (Tavdy dialect) šäur-änt-em 'I am going' ('go-ing-I'; Collinder 1965b: 119).

When the Anatolian languages were discovered, there was, in this matter as in so many others, a surprise for Indo-Europeanists. Hittite had a participle in -ant that, in addition to its active meaning, also formed passive participles from transitive verbs, e.g. kunant- 'killed' (cf. kuen-tsi 'he, she kills'). The same passive use with transitive verbs, and active use with intransitive verbs, was found in Hieroglyphic Hittite and Palaic, but in Luwian it is exclusively passive. Laroche (1962) proposed that -ant- expresses the actor function in neuters (inanimates), which normally designate non-actors. Thus, when water purifies it takes the form wetenant-, but when it is poured, it is watar. Laroche reports that this distinction also occurs in Luwian.

In addition to its use as a participle, -ant- was found to be frequent in Hittite not only in forming adjectives (as it does elsewhere in Indo-European), e.g. perun-ant 'rocky,' from peruna- 'rock', but also as a quite common collective and noun formant, alongside of corresponding forms without -ant, e.g. antuḫsant- 'mankind,' from antuḫsa- 'man' (Friedrich 1960: 40). In many cases no difference in meaning is really discernible, e.g. sankunni- and sankunniant- 'priest.'

Since it is an easy semantic shift from collective to plural, it has been proposed that the Hittite -ant- collective is related to the Luwian common gender plural markers, -inzi (nominative) and -anza (accusative), and to the Tocharian B neuter plural in -ant, e.g. el 'gift,' elant 'gifts' (Kronasser (1956: 125).

However, both Benveniste (1935: 126) and Wolfgang Krause (1956) reject this and consider the collective in -ant to have nothing to do with the participle. Actually the transition in meaning is quite natural, e.g. 'Housing in Palo Alto is very expensive.' Whether we accept the participle and collective as having the same historical origin or not is immaterial to the following argument.

Brugmann (1892–1900, II: 886) long ago suggested another connection, namely, with the -nt- third-person plural marker of the present-aorist system of the verb. In the second edition of his work (1897–1916, II: 455) he repeats this and makes it more precise by saying that it "is a credible hypothesis that the third-person plural of the verb is simply a predicative use of the participle." In fact, this usage has been found, since Brugmann's time, to occur in

Hittite, for example, *garg-ant-es* 'they are hung up' ('hung up-ones-plural'; Rosenkranz 1978: 78). More recently Pulleyblank (1993: 82) asserted, regarding the *-nt* third-person plural, that it "is clearly related to the present participle in *-ent/-ont*." This is a matter to which we will return in connection with the Gilyak verbal form in *-nd, -nč* (Amur *d'*).

In Finno-Ugric there is a nominal derivational suffix *-nt-* (Szinnyei 1910: 100). In a comparison of Indo-European and Uralic, Collinder (1934: 44) notes two distinct functions: a denominative that is Uralic in scope and a deverbative found in Baltic Finnic, Saami, Udmurt, and Komi-Zyrian. He believes that these two formatives are probably identical and are related to the Indo-European participle in *-nt*. Examples are Cheremis *kukšənde* 'lean, meager' (cf. *kukšə* 'dry'), Selkup *eddedde* 'joyous' (cf. *edde* 'joy'), Finnish *etsintä* 'seeking' (German gloss '*das Suchen*'; cf. *etsi-* 'to seek'). In Vogul *-nt* forms the basis of a present tense, where, in the Tavgy dialect, we find *miń-änt-em* 'I am going.'

In Gilyak there is a verb suffix that in the standard dialect of the Amur region takes the form *-d'* and in Northeastern Sakhalin, *-nd*. Grube (1892: 30) notes that in the collection of Gilyak data of Glehn and Schrenk it includes as variants *-nt, -nč*, and *-č*. The first is characteristic of the Tym dialect of Sakhalin, whereas the latter are found on the west coast of the same island.

This form of the verb is overwhelmingly frequent in texts and is variously called the indicative and the infinitive, but it also has substantival uses. According to Panfilov (1962–65, II: 153ff), it can be used as an infinitive in construction with verbs such as 'finish,' 'fear,' 'learn,' etc. It also occurs as an indicative (but never imperative) main verb, usually past or present. The future is formed by suffixing it to *-ni*. Furthermore, it is used productively to form verbal nouns, a use close to the infinitival one, e.g. *juru-d'* 'to read, reading.' With qualitative verbs in *-la* we find examples such as *per-la-d'* 'to be heavy' and 'weight.' When substantivized it can take the plural suffix, e.g. *mat'ka-d'-yu* 'the small ones.' It is often quite like a participle, e.g. *itik aqr p'i-d' amaja* 'look at the one who is sitting below your father' (literally, 'father underneath be-in-a-place-*d'* look at'; Panfilov 1962–65, II: 182). Another example is *if mu-d' ni vo-d'* 'he took the things of the dying one' (literally, 'he die-*d'* of take-*d'*'). Here the -*d'* of *vo-d'* illustrates the common indicative use. In addition Gilyak -*d'* forms abstracts reminiscent of Hittite, e.g. *umla-d'* 'wickedness.' Hattori (1962: 81) gives an example from the southeastern dialect of a true collective, *haqtunt* 'cooking utensils on which one cuts up vegetables, fish, etc.' This also is reminiscent of Hittite. These examples show uses virtually identical with that of the Indo-European active participle.

It is reasonable to assume that the participial use is earlier and it then came to be predicated (see the discussion of the Eskimo *t* participle in No. 43). The substantival uses are quite like those of Indo-European, e.g. Gothic *frijond-s* 'friend' (literally, 'the one who loves'), to which we may compare Gilyak *mu-d'* 'the dead one.' If the indicative use arose from the predication of a participle, then the development would be parallel to that posited for Indo-European by Brugmann.

I conjecture that the Indo-European third-person plural -*nti* of the present tense is simply the neuter plural of the participle. In Sanskrit they are identical even in details of vowel alternation and accent, e.g. *bháranti* 'they carry, the carrying ones (neuter),' *adánti* 'they eat, the eating ones (neuter),' and *júhvati* 'they sacrifice, the sacrificing ones (neuter).' There are, however, a few Vedic neuter plurals with *ā* instead of *a*, e.g. *íyānti* 'going ones,' *sānti* 'being ones' (see Schmidt 1889: 164). Can these be analogical after *mahā* 'large,' which has similar forms?

The Sanskrit final -*i* of the neuter plural participle is usually equated with the Greek neuter *a* plural, *bháranti* (= *phéronta*), and the final vowels are held to derive from Proto-Indo-European *schwa primum*. This idea was first attacked by Schmidt (1889) and more recently the well-known Indologist T. Burrow (1979) devoted an entire volume to refuting the existence of Indo-European *schwa primum*, which is based on the correspondence of Indic *i* with *a* in other branches of Indo-European.

I consider it probable, since the other branches of Eurasiatic do not have grammatical gender, that it is an Indo-European innovation and that the first step was the distinction of common from neuter gender. In many instances the neuter is the "relict" gender that continues earlier forms undifferentiated for gender.

Since we now have a well attested -*i* neuter plural in Hittite, it is not necessary to reject the whole doctrine of Indo-European schwa to identify the third-person plural -*nti* with the neuter plural of the participle. Moreover, it would provide a concrete starting point for the interpretation of -*i* as the marker of the present active instead of the vague doctrine of a deictic -*i*. The contrast of -*nti*/-*ti* (third-person singular), with -*i* by contamination from the plural, leads in Sanskrit to the interpretation of an infixed nasal as the mark of the neuter plural, e.g. in -*s* stems in which a nominative-accusative plural with an inserted nasal contrasts with common gender without it, e.g. *sumanas-as, sumanāṁsi,* the nominative and accusative plural of the common gender and neuter, respectively, of an adjective meaning 'favorably minded.'

45. Gerundive-Participle L

Until the discovery of Tocharian, Slavic and Armenian alone among the branches of Indo-European had a substantive (participial or infinitive) morpheme -*l* as a part of the verbal inflectional system. However, as was pointed out by Brugmann (1892–1900, II.1: 199), similar formations exist in other Indo-European languages that form substantival derivatives from verb roots. The variety of meanings and uses within Indo-European of these forms in -*l* is considerable but their unity has never, to my knowledge, been seriously questioned.

In Armenian there are no less than five such forms, one of which is, however, not part of the verbal inflectional system since it cannot be formed freely from verb stems. In the following exposition it should be borne in mind that the Armenian verbal system is based on two stems, a present and an aorist. From the present stem an infinitive can be formed, e.g. *bere-m* 'I carry,' *bere-l* 'to carry, to be carried.' It can take -*o* stem inflection, which corresponds to the thematic inflection of Indo-European; hence the suffix is *-*le* ~ *-*lo*. Note that it may be either active or passive and this indifference to voice is characteristic of the -*l* formative here as elsewhere in Indo-European. From the infinitive we get a substantival derivative in -*li* (again indifferent to voice) that is inflected for case and number. Thus, *sire-li* is either 'loveable, one who can be loved' or 'one who loves, loving.' From the present stem infinitive one can also form a future participle, e.g. *bere-l-oç* 'one who is to carry or be carried.' Here, as is often the case, the future meaning takes on a nuance of necessity, e.g. Luke 9, 44, "The son of man must be betrayed" (*matneloç*).

In addition to these three forms derived from the present stem is one based on the aorist stem, e.g. *gorç-ea-l* 'having done, having been done' (cf. *gorç-ea-ç* 'he/she did'). With the verb 'to be' it forms a compound tense that is normally intransitive, e.g. *cneal em* 'I am born,' but it can also be used with transitive verbs by means of a construction in which the agent is in the genitive, i.e. 'they who saw him' becomes 'those of whom he was seen.'

The *-l* formation we are discussing is not only basically indifferent to voice, but to tense as well. Its meaning as present, past, or future is determined by the tense stem from which it is derived or by a tense marker, as in the future *bere-l-oç*.

In addition to these inflectional forms there is in Armenian a relatively infrequent and unproductive form in *-oł*, e.g. *ber-oł* 'carrying,' which was compared by Meillet (1932) to the type found in Greek *mainólēs* 'a raving, frenzied person' (cf. *maínomai* 'I rage, am furious') and *skōptólēs* 'jester' (cf. *skṓptō* 'I joke'). In his discussion of *-oł*, Meillet follows Mariès (1930), who equates this form with the *-el-* of the Umbrian future perfect *apel-us-t* 'shall have expended,' in which *-us* is future and *-l* forms the perfect stem. The perfect itself does not occur in Umbrian texts.

In Old Church Slavic a participle in *-lŭ*, derived from the infinitive-aorist stem of the verb, forms compound tenses with various forms of the verb 'to be,' e.g. *neslŭ jesmĭ* 'I have carried,' (literally, 'having carried,' or 'a carrier I am). Meillet considers this Slavic form to correspond to the Armenian compound tense based on the *-l* participle of the aorist stem, e.g. *bereal em* 'I have carried.'

Like Armenian, Slavic has derivational forms in *l* that, though based on the verb, are not part of the verbal inflectional system. Vaillant (1950–66, III: 83) cites such examples as *obilŭ* 'abundant' and *teplŭ* 'hot,' the latter related to *top-iti* 'to heat' (transitive). The meaning 'having a disposition or quality,' in some instances a lasting disposition, is also found in many of the examples cited by Brugmann, e.g. Lithuanian *akylas* 'observant,' Latin *crēdulus* 'credulous,' Old High German *essal* 'a glutton.' When substantivized these become agent nouns, e.g. Latin *figulus* 'potter.'

Tocharian was discovered to have a variety of -*l* participles and verbal nouns that rivalled those of Armenian. In Tocharian B verbal adjectives in -*l* are derived from both the present stem and the subjunctive, which is almost always the same as the preterite. Werner Thomas (1952) showed that the form derived from the present stem indicated necessity and those from the subjunctive, possibility. These are often called Gerundive I and Gerundive II in the literature on Tocharian. They may be either attributive or predicative, in the latter case usually without a copula. The meaning seems to be generally intransitive or passive. An example of attributive use is Tocharian B *kärsanälyem wäntarwane* 'in things which one must know.' Here a noun in the locative is preceded by Gerundive I, agreeing with it in case. A predicative example is Tocharian A *sāmam mā ñomā kcnal* 'he is not to be called a monk.' It may be substantivized, e.g. Tocharian B *akalsälle* 'a student, one who should be taught.' Windekens (1944: 102) notes also abstract and concrete substantives derived from verb roots, e.g. Tocharian (A and B) *cmol* 'birth,' Tocharian B *wsäl* 'clothing,' and compares them with Hittite abstracts in -*ul*, e.g. *išḫiul* 'bond, agreement' (cf. *išḫiyāmi* 'I tie, bind'). Lydian has a suffix -*ol* (Gusmani 1964: 42) that has been interpreted as either a participle or an infinitive.

Indo-European has been treated here at some length in order to show the great semantic and syntactic variety of these forms in -*l*, whose historical unity apparently no one doubts. A similar variety is found outside of Indo-European; there is, I believe, only a single type that does not have a parallel within Indo-European.

In Uralic the form in -*l* appears to be confined to Samoyed. In Kamassian the aorist, which is used to indicate both past and present tense, is formed by a participle in -*la*, -*le*, or -*l*, for example, *nere-le-m* 'I fear' ('fear-le-I'). This participle occurs also in Selkup (e.g. *ity-lä* 'taking'), where it is used as a verbal participle just like Russian *berja* (Serebrennikov 1964: 89).

The *l*- morpheme we have been discussing is prominent in Yukaghir. What is sometimes described as the infinitive is formed by an -*l* suffix, e.g. Kolyma *kelu-l* 'arrival, to arrive' (Krejnovich 1979b: 355). It may also qualify a noun, e.g. *lodo-l adilek* 'a playing youth.'

The verbal noun in *-l* also forms an optative, e.g. *ā-l-uol* 'wish to do' (Kolyma dialect, literally, 'do-*l*-wish'). In addition, if it is intransitive it may be predicated, in what is called the definite conjugation, that is, when the verb is unfocused and the statement supplies definite information about the subject (if the verb is intransitive), i.e. is an answer to such questions as 'who played?' An appropriate answer is *met-ek lodo-l,* which might be paraphrased as 'I-am-the-one who-played' (for *-ek,* see No. 23). The *-l* participle is also found in the extinct Omok dialect of Yukaghir (Tailleur 1959a: 94).

In Orkhon Turkish *-l* forms nouns and adjectives from verbs, e.g. *ine-l* 'trustworthy' (a name) (cf. *ine-* 'to trust'), *qïsï-l* 'mountain-cliff, canyon' (cf. *qïs* 'make narrow'). The first of these is strikingly similar to Latin examples such as *crēdulus* cited earlier. In Mongolian, *-l* forms nouns of action "not taken in any particular way" (Groenbech and Kruger 1955: 41), e.g. *ab-ul* 'a taking,' *ay-ul* 'fright.' After a consonant stem the suffix is *-ul ~ -ül*; after a vowel, *-l*.

What is usually called the future participle in Korean is formed by suffixing *-l* to the verb, e.g. *po-l saram* 'a man who will see.' Its meaning is, however, broader and is described as "future action or action as such without any determination of time" (Ramstedt 1939: 125). In Old Japanese there was a distinction between the attributive and final forms of the verb, e.g. *hito ku* 'the man comes,' but *kuru hito* 'the man who comes.' In present-day Japanese only *kuru* is used, but in other instances it is the final form that triumphed. Miller (1967: 324) concludes, using techniques of internal reconstruction, that although even in Old Japanese not all attributive verb forms contained *r*, "all the historical developments were the result of adding *-r-* followed by the same *-u* as in the case of the present indicative just mentioned." The conditional, which uses the same base as the attributive in Old Japanese (e.g. *kur-e-ba* 'if he should come'), derives from *-r-* + *-e-* (< *ai*). The origin of *-a + i* is discussed by Miller, but is not considered here (for *-ba,* see No. 41). The Old Japanese attribute had a broader use than that of qualifying nouns. Thus *taburu,* the attributive of the verb 'to eat,' meant not only 'eating' as an adjective, but also 'a person who eats' or a 'non-person which eats.' John Whitman (1990: 539) reconstructs the Old Japanese verb attributive suffix as **-ru* and notes that it is generally compared to Middle and Old Korean *-(l)ul/-(l)ol*.

Gilyak adjectives are productively derived from qualitative verbs by the suffix -la, e.g. veu-d' 'to be deep,' veu-la 'deep.' However, adjectives in -la, by far the most common type in Gilyak, are not confined to derivation from qualitative verbs, but also may be formed from active and processual ones (Panfilov 1962–65, II: 85). Moreover, in striking resemblance to Indo-European, especially Latin forms like bibulus 'drunkard,' -la indicates a lasting disposition in contrast to forms without -la, which indicate transient properties, e.g. čomsomu nivx 'a silent man' (i.e. 'silent at the moment') vs. čomsomu-la nivx 'a taciturn man.'

In Chukchi the suffix -lʔ- forms participles that are inflected for case and person, as are Chukchi nouns and adjectives in general, e.g. tipʔejŋe-lʔ-ən 'singing, having sung (cf. tipejŋe-k 'to sing'). Here -ən is the absolutive singular. An example of a noun formed in this way is ərətku-lʔ-ən 'archer,' from ərətku-k 'to shoot.' In the Koryak group the corresponding forms of the standard Chavchuven dialect of Koryak is -lh-ən, and that of Kerek, -lhan, in which the absolutive has become incorporated in the stem, a common historical process.

These Chukchi and Koryak forms obviously fit semantically and syntactically the pattern of the -l morpheme encountered in other languages. There is, however, a phonological problem, the source of Chukchi ʔ, Koryak h. I suspect it is an old absolutive that has become incorporated in the stem.

Kamchadal forms adjectives from qualitative verbs, in a manner strikingly similar to Gilyak, by suffixing -la-χ, e.g. om- 'to be hot,' om-la-χ 'hot.' Here -χ represents the absolutive *-k (No. 23). Its status as a formative is shown by the existence of a suffix -la-n in the same language that derives agentive nouns from verbs, wet-la-n 'a worker' (cf. weta-tek 'to work'). The relation of -la-χ to -la-n is obvious (cf. Volodin 1976: 94, where the two are identified).

There is a general Eskimo verb inflectional category in -l- that is everywhere very frequent in texts and is variously called 'infinitive' (Kleinschmidt), 'subject participial' (Swadesh), or 'gerund' (Menovshchikov). It is in fact an adverbial participial of the same general type as Turkish -ip or Russian -ja. It is formed from both intransitive and transitive verbs and in the latter case it is in most dialects inflected only for number and third-person object regardless of the actual person of the object. In most forms of Eskimo it takes the form -lu- (but in Sirenik it is -lə-) and can indicate action either simultaneous or previous to that of the main verb. In narrative there is often a shift of reference so that it becomes semantically like the Latin ablative absolute. Spalding (1960: 55) offers the following example of its use in narrative: "The deer meat *being on the ground* [third singular intransitive], the dogs *being very hungry* [third plural intransitive], it was eaten."

A similar form and usage occurs in Aleut. Menovshchikov (1968) gives the following example: *gaðna-l aðaŋ gazitaχ hilakuχ* 'smoking-l the-father paper reads.' The adverbial participial use found in Eskimo and Aleut is the only usage in non-Indo-European languages of Eurasiatic for which I do not find an exact Indo-European parallel.

46. Verbal Noun S

Uralicists reconstruct a verbal noun in *-ś and a past tense formed from it by suffixing person-number subject markers (except in the third-person singular, which is therefore identical with the verbal noun; see Szinnyei 1910: 143). Collinder (1934: 47) proposed that this Uralic formation was related to the s- aorist of Indo-European.

Rosenkranz (1950) interpreted the third-person -s of the preterite of the Hittite -ḫi conjugation (e.g. *dās* 'he, she put') as the starting point for second-person singular *dāsta* (probably to be interpreted as a cuneiform rendition of *dās-t* since this form of writing cannot express consonant clusters in final and certain other positions) and second-person plural forms like *memisten* 'you remembered.' Moreover, he asserted that "the Hittite forms are most easily explained as a verbal noun incorporated into the verbal system." Rosenkranz then observed that, if this is so, the parallel with Uralic is complete.

Burrow (1954), apparently independently of Rosenkranz (whom he does not cite), arrived at the same analysis of the Hittite ḫi-preterite and did so without any reference to Uralic. His starting point was the Vedic Sanskrit precative, e.g. *bhū-yā-s* 'may he, she be,' from which there developed a full inflection with *bhūyās-* reinterpreted as the base. He compared this not only with Hittite, but also with Tocharian and with Phrygian, e.g. *edaes* 'he gave,' and concluded that "we may regard the preterite conjugation of the -ḫi verbs as representing the basis from which the -s aorist developed."

This theory of the origin of the Indo-European -s aorist was further elaborated in Watkins (1962), a monograph devoted to this subject that includes data from still other branches of Indo-European (e.g. Latin, Celtic).

It is possible that the Chuvash remote past in -sa-ttă- belongs here, e.g. pir-sa-ttă-m 'I went.' Levitskaja (1976: 72) derives this tense from a participle in -sa ~ -se and the past tense of the verb 'to be,' e or i. In this case the participle in -sa ~ -se corresponds closely to the Indo-European thematized -s forms included by Brugmann, many of which have adjectival meaning, e.g. Sanskrit ruk-ša- 'shining.' The chief objection to connecting the Chuvash remote past with the Indo-European and Uralic examples just discussed is that it appears to be isolated within Altaic.

The probable origin of -s as a verbal noun was noted at the beginning of this section. A connection with Gilyak -s, the usual formative in that language for abstract nouns, is therefore possible. Most commonly these are formed from adjective-verbs, e.g. ver 'be broad,' ver-s 'breadth,' but examples with transitive verbs also occur, e.g. ugu-d' 'to kindle a light,' ugu-s 'a lighter.' It is possible that Japanese -sa, which forms abstracts from adjective-verbs, belongs here, e.g. aka-sa 'redness,' atu-sa 'thickness,' etc.

In the Chukotian group, Kamchadal has an unproductive suffix -s that derives nouns from verbs, e.g. sonḷ'e-s 'life' (< sonḷ' ~ sunḷ' 'to live'), ḷma-s 'spoils, catch (of fish)' (< ḷ'm- 'kill'; Volodin 1976: 121). There is also the common productive suffix -s of the infinitive, which is very possibly the same element. There are a few instances in which they differ, for example, ḷ'me-s 'to kill' compared to the verbal noun ḷ'mas cited above, but in most cases they are identical.

If this is the case, the parallel to Indo-European is striking since alongside the common abstract noun in -es ~ -os (Indic, Greek, Latin, Slavic), there is the Vedic infinitive in -as-e (e.g. jay-as-e 'to conquer'), in which -e is the dative singular. Wackernagel and Debrunner (1896–1930, III: 280) consider the connection with the verbal nouns in -es ~ -os to be probable, and Szemerényi (1978: 409) accepts it unconditionally.

It is possible that in this section we are dealing with two historically distinct formations, one a past verbal noun, the other, a morpheme that derives abstract nouns from verbs. It is also possible that the -s of Hittite *das* etc. is simply the demonstrative -s (No. 12) functioning as third person.

47. Imperative KA

For Proto-Indo-European the imperative is usually reconstructed as being identical to the verb stem itself, -e in thematic verbs (e.g. Greek *phér-e* 'carry!') and zero in athematic verbs. In the latter case a suffix *-dhi is also reconstructed, e.g. Greek *í-thi*, Avestan *i-ði* 'go!' However, the Baltic languages have a suffix -k, -ki, e.g. Lithuanian *duo-k* 'give.' This was extended in Old Lithuanian into a fuller paradigm: -kiva (first-person dual), -kita (second-person dual), -kime (first-person plural), -kite (second-person plural). Christian Stang (1966), and others before him, compare the Baltic forms, which he reconstructs as *-ké for the second-person singular, with a set of particles found in all the Slavic languages, though not in Old Church Slavic (Vaillant 1950–66, II: 697). Examples are Russian *ka, ko*, which are sometimes put after the imperative to make a request more pressing. Other examples are Serbo-Croatian *ka* and Ukrainian *ko*. Both in Russian and South Slavic these particles may also occur after pronouns, e.g. Russian *tebě ka jexat'* 'you must go' (literally, 'to-you ka to-go'). The comparison of the Baltic and Slavic forms was first made by Martin Solmsen (1899), who also compared them to the Greek particle *ke, ka* that is used with the optative. Particularly close to the Slavic usage is Elean *ka*, which converts an optative into an imperative. This *ka* either immediately precedes the verb in the optative or follows some other word earlier in the sentence. Brugmann (1892–1900, II: 1317) considered the comparison with Latin *ce-do* 'give!' "attractive" and this suggestion has been accepted by others (e.g. Walde-Pokorny 1928: 193, who qualify it, however, as "probable").

I believe that the same *k is found in the Hittite middle imperative -ḫut(i). Pedersen (1938) explains the final part, -ti, as a reflex of *-dhi, which, as we have already seen, occurs with the imperative of athematic verb stems. Moreover, e-ḫu 'come!' is found without the -ti affix. Pedersen goes on to compare -u- with the -u found in the Hittite third-person imperative forms, e.g. third-person plural -andu. This same -u is found in Sanskrit -antu. He notes, however, that -ḫ- is unexplained. We have already seen instances in which Hittite ḫ corresponds to k in other Indo-European languages. Hence, -ḫ-u-(ti) might be analyzed as deriving from *-k-u-(ti). A similar analysis of the Hittite form, together with a comparison to Uralic, was proposed by Rosenkranz (1966).

An imperative in -k, usually suffixed, is found in a number of other branches of Eurasiatic. Szinnyei (1910: 145) reconstructs a Finno-Ugric imperative exponent as *-k, as does Majtinskaja (1979: 13). This occurs widely alongside of a zero imperative. Collinder (1965a) related the Uralic imperative, which he reconstructed as *ka ~ *kä, to the Yukaghir imperative and also (1965b) to Altaic, though without citing the Altaic evidence.

Most Uralicists explain this imperative as a specialization of the present tense marker *-k, which in turn derives from the verbal noun in *-k (see Majtinskaja 1979: 42). It would thus be identical with No. 23. This is a highly speculative line of reasoning based exclusively on internal Uralic evidence. Hajdú (1981: 155) objects to it on the ground that the basis of supporting evidence is extremely narrow in regard to the number and distribution of languages. Collinder (1960: 303–4) accepts the identification of Uralic -k imperative and -k present, and derives the former from the latter, but he also says that this must have occurred very early because Proto-Uralic already had a -k imperative. Clearly this internal explanation also fails to explain the widespread occurrence of -k outside Uralic. In the Kolyma, Tundra, and the extinct Chuvan dialect of Yukaghir— the language most closely related to Uralic—the singular imperative is -k.

In Altaic, Chuvash (the most divergent Turkic language) has a suffix -ax ~ -ex to strengthen and make polite a request; this suffix may be added to any person of the imperative. This is very similar to the Slavic uses. In non-Chuvash Turkic we also find the -k imperative, for example, Old Turkish, Nogai, and Shor -ok, Karalkapak -ak, Tatar and Bashkir -uk (Levitskaja 1976: 124). In Old Turkish it is a general particle of emphasis that may follow words other than verbs. In Tungus, Benzing (1955: 1092) compares imperative forms in various languages and concludes that they are built from a suffix *-ki, or *-gi, which appears by itself in the second-person singular and, with various additional markers, in other persons and numbers.

There is actually vowel variation and South Tungus second-person singular imperative -ka (e.g. Gold) is identical to the imperative reconstructed for Finno-Ugric.

In Korean there is an adverbial enclitic key (Martin, Lee, and Chang 1967: 106–7) whose first meaning is given as 'so that, in a manner such that.' It is also used in familiar commands, often followed by -na which is said to soften imperatives, e.g. o-key(-na) 'come!'

In Sakhalin Ainu the imperative is -ka (Tittel 1922: 84). There are also variant forms in ne suffixed to -ka (e.g. -kāne, -kanne) to which no specific functions are ascribed. An imperative -ka is not found in Hokkaido Ainu. However, Batchelor (1905) gives a "softening" particle ka that is always followed by the verb (though not necessarily in the imperative) and which thus resembles in both its function and syntactic use the Slavic particles ka and ko.

Grube (1892: 33), summarizing Schrenk's material on Gilyak, notes a number of suffixes marking the imperative, including -ke and -kaje. These are Sakhalin forms, only -ja being found in the Amur dialect. Possibly -kaje is a conflation of -ke and -ja. Gilyak also has a third-person imperative that is used both in the singular and plural, -qazo on the Amur and -qajra in eastern Sakhalin (Saval'eva 1970: 523).

In Chukchi-Koryak a prefixed q- is the mark of the second-person singular imperative. Second-person dual and plural are indicated by suffixing the usual pronominal indicators of these categories. In Kamchadal, k- is prefixed with the same function and type of number marking and is likewise confined to the second person.

In Eskimo, the Yupik (but not the Inuit) group of dialects has an imperative -ka for the second-person singular, e.g. Kuskokwim pi-ka 'do!' In Siberian Yupik (e.g. Naukan) it is called by Menovshchikov (1975: 248) desiderative-hortatory and has become the basis of an inflected category for all persons and numbers, e.g. -ka-ɬta 'let us . . . !' It is interesting to note that the -ka forms of Naukan are translated by the ka forms of Russian, e.g. tē-kā 'come!' is translated as prixodi ka. In the eastern Inuit dialects there is an imperative -k that occurs in conjunction with negative na-, for example, Labrador, Greenlandic qia-na-k 'don't cry!' (Hammerich 1936: 173), and similarly in Alaskan Yupik kannuqpirk-na-k 'don't talk so much!' (Barnum 1901: 484ff). Aleut also has an imperative-hortative involving a suffix -ka- or -kuδa-, to which person and number exponents are suffixed.

My general conclusion is that in addition to the widespread use of bare verb stems for the second-person imperative in Eurasiatic, there was a particle ke ~ ka that might precede or follow the verb, usually the latter. Its basic meaning seems to have been both politeness and insistence. These two nuances are closely connected semantically (cf. English 'please,' German doch).

48. Hortatory L

In Indo-European languages generally there is no special form of the first-person hortative; it is expressed typically by an optative or subjunctive. In Hittite, however, there is a first-person singular -allu that is used in this function. In this suffix -u is probably the non-second-person imperative mentioned in No. 47. Benveniste (1962: 18) proposed a genetic connection with forms of the Baltic optative and imperative. Old Prussian has an optative-conditional in -lai, e.g. bou-lai 'that it be, let it be.' The vowels -ai in this form are, according to Benveniste, adopted from the imperative -ai. It has been expanded into a partial paradigm: -lai-si (second-person singular) and -lai-ti (second-person plural). There is also Lithuanian es-le 'let it be' and a Latvian dialect form î-tu-l'u 'I would go' in which -l' has been added to the -tu- of the optative. According to Benveniste this form in -l is a morphological survival of great antiquity.

With these -l forms of Indo-European we may compare Turkish -alïm (first-person singular hortatory), in which -m is clearly the indicator of the first-person singular (No. 1). For Turkic in general, Menges (1968: 139) reconstructs the basic form *-alï, to which -m may be added for first-person singular and -k for first-person plural.

Patrie (1982: 104) relates Ainu -ro (first-person plural hortatory) to Korean -ra and Old Japanese -ro, both imperatives. Hyogmyon Kwon (1962) had already compared the Korean and Japanese forms. Batchelor (1905) indicates an imperative use of ro in Ainu that is broader than the first-person plural use described by Patrie (1982) and Dobrotvorsky (1875). Batchelor characterizes it as a general imperative or potential and gives variants with other vowels, -ra,

-re, and -ru. Since Ainu, Korean, and Japanese all have a single liquid the equation of r with Indo-European and Turkic l is normal. I use l in Korean transcription (following Martin, Lee, and Chang 1967), but this choice is an arbitrary one.

All dialects of Eskimo use a verb suffix -li to express an optative or imperative of the first and third person. The unmarked form is -li for the third-person singular intransitive. Kleinschmidt (1851), and others, combine it with a second-person singular intransitive marker -i that does not contain l. In Naukan, a Siberian Yupik dialect, the -l hortatory (called by Menovshchikov 1975 "optative") is also confined to the first and third persons, with -lē (first-person singular intransitive) and -li (third-person singular intransitive). The second-person singular marker is zero. The contrast between optative-hortatory -li and imperative -ka (No. 47) is clear here, and elsewhere in Yupik, e.g. tē-li 'let him come, may he come,' tē-kā 'come!' (singular). Sirenik has -l'aŋ as first-person singular imperative (cf. Greenlandic -laŋa), third-person singular -l'a, but imperative -a. It seems likely that the vowels of the third-person singular and imperative have been reshaped analogically as a result of the influence of the first-person singular.

Since hortatory and optative markers easily acquire the meaning of interrogative alternatives or general indefinites, it is possible that the following two instances belong here. Gilyak has a suffix -lu whose use is illustrated in the following sentence: ni vinyd'-lu, č'i vinyd'-lu, ŋalad'ra 'Whether I come, or you come, doesn't matter' (Saval'eva 1970: 164). This could easily be paraphrased as 'Let me come, let you come, it doesn't matter.' According to Bogoras (1937), in Chukchi there is a prefix l'ə- used with interrogatives to give a generalized meaning, e.g. xli l'-meŋko 'from wherever you wish' (cf. meŋko 'from'). Perhaps the Kamchadal desiderative suffix -al ~ -a- belongs here.

49. Denominative T

There is evidence in every branch of Eurasiatic for a dental stop that functions as a denominative and/or transitivizer. In what is still the basic exposition of the topic in Indo-European, Brugmann (1897–1916, II.3.1: 372–79) does not attempt to separate denominative from deverbative constructions. Although a denominative need not be transitive, it frequently is, e.g. 'to name.' The Hebrew *hiph'il*, which is usually defined as a causative derivational form of the simple verb, is frequently denominative. The same holds for the analogous fourth form *'af'ala* of the Arabic verb.

There is a further complication in Indo-European, involving **-dh* and **-d*. Since in a large number of languages, namely, Iranian, Italic, Celtic, and Balto-Slavic, original **dh* has become *d*, thus merging with Proto-Indo-European **d*, it becomes impossible in many instances, duly noted by Brugmann, to distinguish the reflexes of the two. In some cases it is likely, or even certain, that compounding with the Indo-European verb roots **dhē* 'to place,' or **dō-* 'to give,' is involved. A clear example is Latin *crēd-ere*, Old Irish *cret(-id)*, compared to Sanskrit *śrad (da-)dhā(-ti)* 'to believe.' The root **dō-* has cognates elsewhere in Eurasiatic. In almost all branches of Eurasiatic we find a phonetic merger similar to that of most branches of Indo-European, namely, **dh > *d*. However, the two appear to be distinct in Korean, which thus gives additional evidence for **dh*. In the following discussion I shall, wherever possible, distinguish between denominative and deverbal affixes.

In Uralic, **-t* is found both as a denominative and as a causative in the verb. Uralicists generally treat them as distinct (Collinder 1965b: 117, 120; Szinnyei 1910: 129, 133). Examples are Ostyak *nämə-t* 'to name' (denominative) and Vogul *ui-t* 'to sink' (transitive) (cf. *ui* 'to sink' [intransitive]).

Yukaghir has a *-te-* denominative. In the Kolyma dialect Jochelson (1905: 119) distinguishes *-te*, which forms transitive verbs, from *-de*, which produces intransitives. With the usual vowel harmonic variation *e ∼ o* of Yukaghir we find, for example, Kolyma *juhor* 'a wound,' *juhor-to-* 'to wound.'

In Altaic we find evidence in all three branches. In Turkic there is a *-t* causative that is found in the Orkhon inscriptions and which occurs in both Chuvash and non-Chuvash languages. Examples include Turkish *parla-t-* 'to cause to shine' (from *parla-* 'to shine') and Chuvash *tipe-t* 'to dry' (transitive). What appears to be the same morpheme derives verbs from nouns (e.g. Altai *iš* 'work,' *iš-te-* 'to work') and adjectives (e.g. Chuvash *xura-t* 'to blacken'). In regard to Mongolian, Ramstedt (1912) equates *-či* (< **ti*), a verb transitivizer, with Turkic -t. He also compares a Mongolian denominative in -da, -ta with Turkish -ta ~ -te, da ~ de.

These same derivative elements appear in Tungus, e.g. the Manchu denominative in -ta, as in al-ta 'to deceive' (cf. al 'craftiness') and the Even causative -t, e.g. hoŋi-t 'cause to cry' (cf. hoŋi 'to cry'). It does appear that in Altaic -t, or -ti, is consistently causative and -ta ~ -te, denominative. Poppe (1960) considers a causative t- to be one of the grammatical markers common to Uralic and Altaic.

The Ainu causative in -te, e.g. uk-te 'cause to take' (cf. uk 'to take') was compared by Naert (1958: 101) with the Indo-European forms mentioned above. There is likewise a causative $-t^{h}i$ in North Korean that was compared by Ramstedt (1939: 136) with the Altaic causatives. In Japanese a causative in -t is less common than that in -s, which has become the productive form. An example is hana-t-u 'to let go, to free' compared with hana-re- 'be freed' (for re, see No. 17). In Gilyak I have found a single example of the denominative use in Schrenk's material (see Grube 1892: 16), namely, ja-d-ent 'to measure,' derived from ja 'fathom, span.'

Denominatives in -t are found throughout Chukotian, e.g. Chukchi miɣsir-et- 'to work,' miɣsir 'work' (noun); Koryak ajkol-at- 'to make a bed,' ajkol 'bed'; Kamchadal aano-t-kəs 'to spend the spring,' aano-k 'spring.' In Chukchi and Koryak the same -at ~ -et, when added to an intransitive verb (which has a prefixed r- in Chukchi, j- in Koryak), forms a transitive, e.g. Chukchi rə-qit-et 'to freeze' (transitive), qit- 'to freeze' (intransitive). Chukchi r often corresponds to Koryak j, cognate with Proto-Altaic r_2 (palatalized r). I have no theory regarding the r/j prefix in this instance. Aliutor, a member of the Koryak subgroup, has a simultaneous prefixed and suffixed t which forms causatives. For a probable -t- denominative in Aliutor and Kerek in combination with ku, see No. 51. In Kamchadal, in addition to the -t denominative, there is a prefixed t- causative that is confined to four common verbs, e.g. t-ews 'to raise,' ews 'to rise' (see Volodin 1976: 202, where this t- prefix is called an old formation). In addition, there is a causative auxiliary verb it. Kamchadal also has a suffixed -t denominative. An indication of the general Chukotian character of the denominative -t is found in Mudrak's (1989a: 109) reconstructions *wji-wji 'breath,' *wjə-t 'to breathe.'

In both Eskimo and Aleut there are -t- causatives, whose relationship is pointed out in Bergsland (1959: 177). It is found in all
the main dialects of Eskimo, from Siberian Yupik -ta- to Greenlandic
-ti-. In Alaskan Yupik, Jacobson (1984: 569) gives the meaning of
-te as 'to act on one so as to cause it to . . . ' (e.g. tuqu- 'die,'
tuqu-t-aa 'he killed it'). In Aleut we find -ti. In Menovshchikov's
(1968) description of Siberian Aleut, there are two causatives, one
in -sa (see No. 50), the other in -ti. The former is called a transitivizer, whereas -ti is said to be resultative, with a more concrete
goal orientation, e.g. qaka-ti 'to dry,' from qaka- 'to be dry.' The
existence of it in Kamchadal as an auxiliary verb suggests that the
ultimate source of the t causative was the verb 'to make,' found in
Old Turkish with the variants et- and it- (Räsänen 1969: 52).

50. Causative S

A less widely distributed causative involves a suffix -s. In Indo-
European, on the basis of (1) contrasts within Indic (e.g. Avestan
tačati 'runs, flows' [tač < *tak], takšati 'make run'; Sanskrit bhī 'to
fear,' bhīṣā- 'frightening'), (2) inter-branch comparisons in which
forms with and without -s appeared, e.g. Homeric Greek deidō 'I
fear' (< *de-dwoi-a, a perfect form remodeled into a present) and
Sanskrit dviṣ- 'hates, shows hostility', and (3) instances in which -s
appeared as a 'root determinative,' Brugmann (1897–1916, II.3.1:
338ff) deduced that the meaning of this 'root determinative' -s was,
in some cases at least, causative (see Persson 1891).

Gonda (1959) devoted an entire study to the Rigveda Sanskrit
verb bhūṣ- 'to strengthen, add power to' (later Sanskrit 'to adorn').
He concluded that the s- of bhūṣ-ati "has evidently a causative meaning. The presence of this -s- is not unknown . . . " Gonda also
gives additional examples of the sort mentioned above. The simplex
is bhav-ati 'is.' The etymological connection has been generally accepted without, however, necessarily positing a causative link (see
Mayrhofer 1956–76, II: 515–16).

With the discovery of Tocharian, the existence of -s as a productive causative affix was documented for the first time. Tocharian A
has -s as its normal causative. In Tocharian B it occurs after -k (and
in a few other instances), but the usual formation is -sk (see No. 53).

Some scholars have considered Tocharian A -s a variant of this -sk affix, but the latter has a distinct distribution in Indo-European, and in Eurasiatic as a whole, as well as a distinctive original function. Even if one discounted Tocharian -s as a variant of -sk, the other evidence for the Indo-European causative -s would remain.

In the two extant forms of Yukaghir, there is a causative -se- in the Tundra dialect (e.g. tire-se- 'to drown' [transitive] vs. tire- 'to drown' [intransitive]) and -š- in the Kolyma dialect (e.g. modo-š- 'to cause to sit' vs. modo 'sit').

Menges (1968: 161) discusses a general Turkic denominative -sy ~ -si, which is of relatively rare occurrence and generally has the meaning 'to pretend to do X,' e.g. Old Uighur qyl-ym-sy-n- 'to feign doing' (derived from the verbal noun qyl-ym). He compares this with the Mongolian formation -m-ši-ja-, seen, for example, in ünä-m-ši-jä- 'to take for truth' (cf. ünä-n 'truth'). There are instances, however, in which there is a simple denominative meaning, for example, Old Turkish amig 'breast,' am-si 'to suck.' What appears to be the same suffix occurs in South Tungus, for example, Gold naj-si- 'to consider someone a man,' mapa-si- 'to take for, or mistake for a bear,' Oroch amta-si- 'to consider tasteful.' In Ulch there are examples that appear to be ordinary denominatives, such as enu- 'sickness,' en-si 'be sick' (Sunik 1989: 49). In Sunik (1962: 110–13) there is an extended discussion of this formative in Tungus in which the construction found in Gold is equated with Manchu -si, which is used with phonesthemes (e.g. tuk-si 'to knock,' cf. tuktuktuk 'sound of knocking'), and is connected, following Ramstedt, with the verb se- 'make, do,' itself equated with Korean ha(-ta) 'make, do' which is used similarly. Whether these latter are connected with the forms in Gold, Oroch, and Ulch I consider doubtful and would, in any event, leave the resemblances of the Tungus forms to Turkic and Mongolian unaccounted for.

A causative -sa also exists in Ainu, e.g. pira 'open' (adjective), pira-sa 'to spread open.' The simplex is found in Batchelor (1905) only in Hokkaido. However, the form pira-sa is found in Sakhalin (Dobrotvorsky, Hattori) and in most Hokkaido dialects (Hattori). The example cited here is clear enough, but the formation is unproductive and I have not found any other examples. A prefixed si- is reported in Simeon (1968: 55) to form transitive verbs from some intransitive verbs, but he gives no examples.

In Japanese and the language of the Ryukyu Islands, -s is the normal causative. In Japanese there are numerous instances of the productive contrast -r- (intransitive) (see No. 17) and -s- (transitive, causative), e.g. noko-r-(u) 'to remain,' noko-s-(u) 'to leave behind.' There are a few instances of a contrast between -y- (intransitive) and -s- (causative), as well as some cases in which -as- is added to the simplex, e.g. ugok-(u) 'to move' (intransitive) vs. ugok-as-(u) 'to move' (transitive). Miller, however, derives this Japanese s from Altaic l_2, so that the contrast here would rather be $*l_1 > r$ and $*l_2 > s$ (1971: 122ff). I believe Miller is correct in maintaining that $*l_2$ becomes s in Japanese, but there is an independent Japanese s that would accord better with the other instances of causative s in other Eurasiatic languages.

In Eskimo the s causative is found in Sirenik -səχ-. In Siberian Yupik the causative marker -sta of Chaplino is analyzed by Emel-janova (1982: 157) as consisting of -s- causative and -ta transitivizer. The so-called "half-transitive" in -si- found in West Greenlandic and other Eskimo dialects (the term is Kleinschmidt's, in modern termi-nology it is called "antipassive") may belong here. When added to an instrumental base it allows it to take an object in the instrumen-tal case. In Aleut, -sa- derives transitive from intransitive verbs, for example, in the Siberian Aleut of Bering Island we find contrasts such as ukaγa-kuχ 'he gives' vs. ukaγa-sa-kuχ 'he brings.'

51. Causative K

The Finno-Ugric languages have a causative in *-kt in addition to the formation in *-t (No. 49). Szinnyei (1910: 130) considers this to be a compound form containing causative -t preceded by -k and Räsänen (1965) connects this genetically with the Turkic causative in -k. Ramstedt (1912: 14) notes that causatives in -ka are found in a great variety of Turkic languages and must therefore be consid-ered Proto-Turkic. Moreover, Turkic *-ka is, as he notes, obviously related to Mongolian -ka with the same function. Among the numer-ous examples cited by Ramstedt are Turkish ya-q- 'to burn' (transi-tive) (cf. ya-n- 'to burn' [intransitive]) and Teleut (Turkic) tär-gä 'to collect' (transitive), which is cognate with Old Turkic tir-, tär- 'to assemble.' In Mongolian this is a common and productive method of

derivation, e.g. *bol-ya-* 'cause to be, make,' from *bol-* 'be, become';
buča-ya 'make turn back, return' (transitive), from *buča-* 'return'
(intransitive). This formation is also found in Tungus, for example,
Evenki *-gā*, which forms transitives from intransitives, and Solon
tati-gā 'to teach,' derived from *tati-* 'learn' (Poppe 1973: 123–28).

Korean also has a causative in *-ki-*, *-ku-* (Ramstedt 1939: 133),
e.g. *kam-ki-ta* 'to bathe' (transitive), from *kam-ta* 'to take a bath.'
It is a striking point of agreement between Ainu and Mongolian that
this causative appears to be derived in Ainu from *ki* 'to make, to
do' (Dettmer 1989: 604). For Mongolian one may cite Poppe (1964:
67), where we find onomatopoeic verbs in *-gi*. In both languages,
among its various uses, is this use in onomatopoeic expressions. It
appears that in Ainu one must distinguish *ke* ~ *ki* 'to do,' used
in onomatopoeic expressions as in Mongolian, and the *-ke* ~ *-ka*
causative suffix, though they could be ultimately related. In Ainu
both *-ke* and *-ka* form transitive verbs from intransitives. The choice
between the two is lexical. Examples include *rai-ke* 'to kill' (from *rai*
'to die') and *nin-ka* 'to decrease' (transitive) (from *nin* 'to decrease'
[intransitive]). In Sakhalin Ainu *-ke* ~ *-ka* is found in this function,
for example, *asin* 'go out,' *asin-ke* 'take out'; *kotuk* 'adhere,' *kotuk-
ka* 'stick on' (Majewicz and Majewicz 1983–85). Korean also has a
denominal *-k* that perhaps also belongs here, e.g. *mul* 'water,' *mul-k-*
'be watering.'

In classical Japanese there is a suffix *-gu* that forms verbs from
nouns, e.g. *tuna* 'rope,' *tuna-gu* 'to tie' (Aston 1904: 93). As noted
by Street and Miller (1975: 72), in a number of cases Japanese has
a velar root-extension to a verb found in Altaic. Furthermore, they
suggest that "it may become possible to relate these systematically
to the Altaic causative."

In Amur Gilyak the usual causative morpheme is *-ku*. Krejnovich
(1934: 210) notes that in the dialects of Sakhalin this takes the form
-k rather than *-ku*. He believes that *-ku* is itself a compound form
that contains *-u*, an accusative marker. In fact, *-u* does occur as
both a denominative and a transitivizer/causative in the Gilyak of
the Amur region and in Sakhalin (Saval'eva 1970: 535). Examples of
-k used as a denominative are found in Glehn's material, reported
in Grube (1892), e.g. *er-x-(enč)* 'to flow,' from *eri* 'river.' This is
evidently the same as the petrified denominative marker *y* reported

in Panfilov (1962–65, II: 19). Here y is a regular alternate of k in the Gilyak system of consonant gradation. An example cited by Panfilov is *ruńy-d'* 'to point to,' derived from *tuń* 'finger,' with the initial continuent alternant found in Gilyak transitive verbs. In the same discussion Panfilov reports another unproductive suffix, *ke* ~ *ki*, e.g. *jes* 'trade' (noun), *jes-ki-* 'carry on trade,' to which he assigns the following meanings: 1. activities carried out with the object denoted by a verb stem; 2. activities as the result of which an object results or is produced. This is of course suggestive of the Mongolian use of *ki* 'to do, make' as a formative element and it also reminds one of Korean *-ki-*.

In Aliutor, a language of the Koryak subgroup of Chukotian, there is a denominative *-tku*, which corresponds to *-ttu* in Kerek (a language of the same subgroup) by the regular assimilation of *-kt* to *-tt*. Since *-t* occurs as a denominative and/or causative throughout Chukotian (see No. 49), this suffix may be analyzed as $t + ku$. It probably also occurs in Kamchadal as the suffixed marker of the second class of transitive verbs. This is a small class of verbs, all with a transitive meaning formed by suffixing *-xk-* or *-ki*, the latter in all probability being the original form (Volodin 1927: 150).

In Siberian Yupik *-ka* ~ *-qa* forms transitive verbs from stems that designate emotional states, for example, *qavaŋu-* 'have a dream,' *qavaŋu-qa-* 'sees something in a dream'; *aliŋa-* 'be afraid,' *alika-qa* 'fear something' (Emeljanova 1982: 75).

Considering the common use of the same marker for both denominative and causative, it is possible that Yukaghir *-ga-j*, *-ge-j*, *-ga-t*, *-ge-t* (Krejnovich 1968: 447), which forms verbs from adjectives (e.g. 'to become long, short, etc.'), may contain the causative, sometimes denominative, formant discussed in this section.

52. Future S

Indo-European has a variety of futures and desideratives formed by *-s-*, *-sy-*, and the like. These include the Greek future in *-s-*, the Latin type *faxō* 'I shall make,' the Baltic future in *-si-* (e.g. Lithuanian *duosiu* 'I shall give,' the Sanskrit future in *-sy-* (e.g. *bhavi-ṣy-āmi* 'I shall be') and the reduplicated desideratives in *-s* of the same language (e.g. *jighāṁ-s-āmi* 'I desire to strike'). Old Irish builds futures in *-s-*

from six verbs and also has a formation that appears to correspond to the Indic desiderative. Stang (1966: 441-42) sees in Old Prussian *-sei, -sai* a desiderative form composed of future *-s-* and optative *-ei.*

Some Indo-Europeanists consider all these connected; Meillet (1964: 215) posits an originally desiderative meaning for all these forms. Other scholars, such as Szemerényi (1978: 366), distinguish three types: (1) Latin *faxō* and other forms in *-s* analyzed as subjunctives of *-s-* aorists, (2) futures in *-sy-*, and (3) desideratives in *-s* with reduplication, and do not consider the first, at least, to be genetically related to the second and third types (see No. 46).

There are a number of similar futures or desideratives in Altaic. Menges (1968: 161) notes the common Turkic desiderative in *-sa* that is usually denominative, e.g. Kirghiz *suu-sa-* 'be thirsty,' from *suu* 'water.' Sometimes, however, the formation starts from a verbal stem and the examples include very old ones. In the Turkish of the Orkhon inscriptions one finds *ber-sä-* 'wish to give' (Tekin 1968: 116). A number of Turkic languages also have a future participle in *-asï-*, described by Kissling (1960: 234) for Turkish as "an old future participle only found now in fixed expressions (wishes and curses)." An example is *adï batasï* 'may his name be destroyed.' The desiderative meaning is obvious here. There is also a Chuvash future participle in *-as* that has been equated historically by Levitskaja (1976: 86-87) to the Turkish participle just mentioned. A nominalized form in *-sï-k* (see No. 23) also occurs in Orkhon Turkish, where it is described as a future necessitative. In addition to all these formations there is an optative marker **-su*, seen in Turkish and many other Turkic languages in the third-person hortative *-su-n*, Yakut *-ty-n*. Ramstedt (1952, II: 84) asserts that all these forms are connected and represent an old optative in **-su*. It is also possible that the Turkish negative aorist *gel-me-z* 'he/she does not come,' Chuvash *gel-me-s*, contains an old future verbal noun in *-s* (Benzing 1952). In some Turkic languages it is clearly future in meaning, e.g. Baraba *-mas-myn* 'I will not . . . ,' in which *-myn* is an affixed first-person singular pronoun. The *ma-, me-* of the cited form is, of course, the common Eurasiatic negative in *m* (see No. 57).

A nominalized form is also found in Mongolian *-sa-k*, which, when suffixed to a noun, indicates a penchant or desire for the thing signified. Mongolian likewise has a suffix *-se-* that forms desideratives from nouns, e.g. *nojir-se* 'to be sleepy,' from *nojir* 'sleep.' There is also a verbal optative in *-su* that is found in all branches of Altaic (Ramstedt 1952, II: 84–85). This includes the Common Turkic (but not Chuvash) third-person singular imperative in *-su-n* and Mongolian desideratives such as *ide-sü* 'would like to eat'; it is found more rarely in Tungus, e.g. Manchu *bi-su* 'let it be.'

Ramstedt also points to the relation of these Altaic forms with the Korean optative in *-se, -si*, e.g. *ka-se* 'I should like to go.' This comes from an earlier *-*säi* or *-*sui*. It is not clear whether Ramstedt considers the Turkish and Mongolian forms in *-sa* to be related to those in *-su*. The Turkic conditional *-sa* seems to come from earlier *-sar* (Menges 1968: 132) and its origin is not agreed on. Menges believes, however, that it derives from an aorist verbal noun that contains the element *-s-* or *-sa-*, which is "probably, not necessarily, identical with that of the desiderative aspect." Note also Kamchadal *si-* 'to wish' (Worth 1969).

In the Yupik Eskimo of Siberia there is a desiderative in *su ~ ju* and there is also the Sirenik suffix *-saχ* indicating a request to carry out the act signified by the verb. In Aleut (Geoghegan 1944) there is a verbal suffix *sa-* 'to go and do something,' which possibly also belongs here. What is evidently the same suffix is defined by Menovshchikov as causative habitual, e.g. *haqa-sa-* 'bring,' from *haqa-* 'go.'

We may note that in Altaic, as in Indo-European, there is a variety of similar constructions involving *-s* and differences of opinion among specialists as to whether they represent one or several original formations.

53. Conative SK

There is a common Indo-European verb suffix, *-ske ~ -sko*, that shows a great variety of meanings, sometimes within a single language. Thus, Pierre Chantraine (1945: 258) says, in regard to Classical Greek, that "it is hard to define its original sense." It is well known from Latin, where it is typically inceptive, e.g. *senescō* 'I become old,' *obdormiscō* 'I fall asleep.' This inceptive sense is generally agreed to be a late development, as are similar Greek formations such as *gēráskō* 'I become old.' In Greek it is sometimes iterative, as in the Ionic-Homeric imperfect. In Hittite it has an intensive-durative meaning and some scholars have considered this to be the fundamental meaning (Meillet 1964: 221, Szemerényi 1996: 273). In Tocharian B this suffix forms causatives (alongside of s in a few instances), whereas in Tocharian A only s is found. There is general agreement that this causative meaning is a late development.

I believe the proposal of Walter Porzig (1927), which connects this suffix with the Tocharian A verb *skai* 'to attempt' (Tocharian B *ske*), best accounts for both the internal Indo-European and the comparative Eurasiatic evidence. This suggestion was also adopted by Schwyzer (1939–50, I: 707), who states that "a connection with Tocharian A *skē* (Tocharian B *ske*) 'to try, attempt' makes good sense."

From the basic conative meaning of 'attempt, try' it is easy to derive frequentive, desiderative, as well as the admittedly late Indo-European causative. For this latter connection compare the causative meaning of the Arabic second conjugation and the corresponding Hebrew Pi'el, which involve reduplication of the second radical consonant and fundamentally denote plural action. Regarding the Hebrew Pi'el, Gesenius (1898: 145) noted that "the eager pursuit of an action may also consist in urging or causing others to do the same."

It is a widespread view among Indo-Europeanists, which can be traced at least to the first edition of Brugmann's *Grundriss* (1892–1900: 1029), that *-ske* ∼ *-sko* is a composite of *s-* and *-k-*. Under this *s* are included the aorist *-s* (No. 46), the causative *-s* (No. 50), not yet so interpreted by Brugmann, and the future and desiderative *-s*, *-sj* (No. 52). Brugmann admits these various *-s* formants cannot be shown to be identical but considers it probable, whereas "the *-s-* of *-s-ko* can be considered a different extension of *-s-jo*." In the second edition of his work (1897–1916, II.3: 336) Brugmann goes even further: "We can assume that *sko* arose from extension of *s-* stems by means of *-ko*." The compound nature of *ske* ∼ *sko* has been fairly generally accepted, e.g. Szemerényi (1978: 351) and Ivanov (1959: 29–31). Ivanov and others have emphasized the coexistence of *-s-* and *-sk-* causatives in Tocharian, although they vary interdialectally. Here, as in certain other languages, *-sk-* has been extended from the present system through the entire verbal inflection, and in Tocharian functions productively to form a second main category of the verb alongside the simple non-causal form. None of the advocates of this view have assigned any function to the -k- extension and the causal meaning of -sk- is generally assumed to be a late development.

In Finno-Ugric, Szinnyei (1910: 125) reconstructed Proto-Finno-Ugric *śk, without positing a meaning. In the second edition of his work (1922) he posited *sk for the same element, that is, without the palatalized ś. The number and identity of Proto-Finno-Ugric sibilants has been one of the difficult points of phonological reconstruction in this family. The meaning of this affix in Finno-Ugric languages includes, in addition to frequentative, intensive (e.g. Udmurt kur- 'ask,' kuriśk- 'pray') and conative (e.g. Vogul al- 'kill,' al-əš-l 'hunt, fish'). In this last example -l is frequentative (see No. 55) and the same combination is found in Finnish ui-ske-le 'swim about' (< ui- 'to swim'). In Finnish it never occurs except in combination with other verbal derivative elements. It is well-known that the sequence -sk- is particularly subject to metathesis. Hakulinen (1957: 197) considers it quite likely that Finnish -ksi derives in this way from -sk. It, also, is frequentative. In Veps, a Baltic-Finnic language, it occurs in its unmetathesized form with inceptive meaning as -ška- (Kham'al'ainen 1966: 92), thus paralleling in its semantic development a meaning dominant in Latin and found sporadically elsewhere.

In the Permian branch of Finno-Ugric, Udmurt -śk has developed into a present tense inflection, from its original iterative-durative meaning, in the first and second persons of a large class of verbs, and has also spread secondarily to the first person of the past tense, e.g. siĺüśko 'I stand,' siĺüśkod 'thou standest.' Khelimskij (1982: 74) points out a remarkable example of parallel historical development in the Romance languages, e.g. Italian finisco 'I finish.' The -s found in a number of common irregular verbs in Hungarian probably also derives from *śk, e.g. ves-em 'I take,' but ve-tte-m 'I took.'

For Proto-Tungus, Benzing (1955: 1068) reconstructs *-ksi with the conative meaning postulated as original. He also notes that *ksi- must come from earlier *ski-, involving a regular metathesis in pre-Proto-Tungusic, as shown by comparing Tungus -ksa with Mongol -ska, both meaning 'skin of an animal.' I am inclined to consider the

Old Turkic verb *saki-* 'be wont to, consider doing' and Mongol *sag* 'care, foresight' as possibly coming from the same root (see Räsänen 1969: 395–96).

In Chukchi there is a common suffix on verbs, *sk-iw* ~ *sk-ew* (Skorik 1961–77, II: 116, 190), that means 'to prepare to, go to do something,' thus being very close to the hypothesized conative meaning. Skorik also observes that *-iw* ~ *-ew* is a separate morpheme added to transitive verbs to express intensity of action.

In Alaskan Yupik *-ska-* is a desiderative, e.g. *miki-ska-ka* 'I want it small' (Barnum 1901: 180). Jacobson (1984: 557) describes *-sqe-*, *-sqa-* as meaning 'want one to, ask one.' The discrepancy between Barnum's *k* and Jacobson's *q* may simply be due to Barnum's lack of phonetic skill, but Hinz (1944), who seems more reliable in this respect, gives Yupik *-sk-* as occurring both transitively (*-skaa* 'wants him to') and intransitively (*-sk-uq* 'wants to'). Emeljanova (1982) finds it in Siberian Yupik (Chaplino) suffixed to verb stems with the meaning 'order to, ask to.' The suffix in question also occurs in Aleut *-čχi-* 'ask someone to' (Menovshchikov 1968: 400).

54. Reflexive U/W

A reflexive element, **w* before vowels and **u* before consonants, is found either prefixed or suffixed in a number of branches of Eurasiatic. Its original meaning is assumed to be reflexive but, as is well known, reflexive verbs frequently become reciprocals or passives, e.g. Slavic *-sja*, North Germanic *-sk*.

There is a common Uralic **w* that is suffixed to verbs as an intransitivizer, middle or passive (Collinder 1960: 281). Examples include Finnish *kuulu-* 'to be heard' (cf. *kuule-* 'to hear'), Saami *oidnu-* 'to be seen, appear' (cf. *oiaidne-* 'to see'), Vogul *tota-we* 'be brought' (cf. *toti* 'brings'), and Yurak Samoyed *sido* 'to awaken' (intransitive) (cf. *sid'e* 'to awaken' [transitive]). Collinder's examples are all passive or intransitive, but the same formative appears also as a reflexive in some Uralic languages, e.g. Mordvin *-v-* and Estonian *-u*.

Collinder (1940: 46–47) relates these Uralic forms to Yukaghir *-u*, which is found in both modern dialects, e.g. Tundra *jedu-* 'get untied' (cf. *jete-* 'to untie'), Kolyma *vietu-* 'get untied' (cf. *viete-* 'to unloose, untie'). It has also been reported in the extinct Chuvan dialect as -u ~ -o 'passive, state' (Tailleur 1962: 89).

Räsänen (1957) discusses reflexives in -u (< *bu) in Turkic. These are sometimes denominal and sometimes deverbal. An example is Middle Turkish kiŋü 'become disseminated, spread,' which is derived from kaŋ ~ kiŋ 'far.' A passive in -w- also occurs in the Tungus branch of Altaic (Menges 1968: 127).

Patrie (1982: 109) compares Ainu u 'reciprocity, mutuality' with Old Japanese u- with the same meaning. In Ainu u- is a common prefix on verbs with reciprocal meaning, e.g. onnere 'to know,' u-onnere 'to know each other.' The Japanese example cited by Patrie is ukara 'common descent group,' kara 'family.' Korean suffixes -pu- or -p- to form passives (Ramstedt 1939: 128). Since Korean has no w phoneme this is the phonologically expected reflex. Actually -w- does appear phonetically between vowels, e.g. kikkə-w-ətta 'was happy' (i.e. 'made to rejoice'). Ramsey (1978: 43) notes -Wo ~ -Wu with both causative and passive meaning in early texts and o ~ u in all later texts. He derives these from *βu, ultimately a fricativized intervocalic *-pu- (with vowel harmony variant *-po-).

Gilyak is very similar to Ainu in that it prefixes w- (Sakhalin) or v- (Amur) to form the reciprocal of the verb (Krejnovich 1979a: 313), e.g. Sakhalin w-or-nt, Amur v-or-d' 'to meet each other' (cf. or- 'to meet someone' in both dialects). In Amur v is the alternant of basic p in the consonant gradation system; there is no w, but the w of Sakhalin shows that v has a twofold source in Amur Gilyak, *p and *w, and in this case it is *w. Furthermore, in the form of Sakhalin Gilyak studied by Robert Austerlitz the reciprocal is u- and Vovin (1993: 45) posits the Proto-Gilyak reflexive *u ~ *o in the northeastern Sakhalin dialect.

Skorik (1961–77, II: 157) discusses a relatively infrequent Chukchi suffix, -ew ~ -aw, which forms intransitive verbs from substantives and adjectives, e.g. nə-korgə-qin 'happy,' -korg-aw- 'to rejoice.' This meaning is expressed reflexively in many languages, e.g. German sich erfreuen, Russian radovatsja. It also occurs in other Chukotian languages. In Muravjova's list of grammatical elements, the Chukchi form is equated with Koryak -ev and Aliutor -av, both of which are described as verb-forming suffixes.

55. Incompletive ALA

Räsänen (1965: 164) compares the Finnish frequentative in -*ala* with Turkic -*ala* with a similar meaning. Szinnyei (1910: 121) reconstructs **-ala* ~ **-ele* as Proto-Finno-Ugric. The most common meanings are 'continual' and 'frequentative.' Collinder (1965b: 118–19) considers it to be Uralic since it is also found in the Samoyed languages, e.g. Selkup -*ăl*, -*ol* 'plurality of action' and Enets -*ro*, -*lo* 'inchoative.' Collinder (1960: 275) describes its meaning in Finnish as follows: "Finnish -*le*- occurs in verbs that usually imply that the action is thought of as not being completed; some of these derivatives are iterative or reflexive."

When we examine the various meanings of this formative in Uralic, it appears that the basic meaning is incompletive. From this we can derive not only the very common iterative meaning, but also the notion of diminutive action or action for a short time or slowly. Thus, as noted by Collinder, Finnish *tappele*- 'to fight,' when compared to the simplex *tappa*- 'to kill,' "shows that it can be softened to bit by bit." In Cheremis we find *əle*- 'to live' and *əl-älä* 'to live a short time,' and in the Permian languages -*l*- has a diminutive-iterative as well as a plurative and continuative function. In Udmurt *myn-yl* 'to go on the road slowly' is derived from the simplex *myn*- 'to go.' Similar semantic developments have taken place in the other subgroups of Eurasiatic in which **-ala*- is found.

As mentioned above, Räsänen connected the Finnish forms of this suffix with Turkic. Ramstedt (1912: 8) noted that in the Turkic languages there are scattered (but genetically diverse) instances of **-ala*. Examples I have noticed include Crimean Tatar *sijpa-la*- 'to stroke from time to time,' Turkmen -*ala*- ~ -*ele* (-*la*- ~ -*le*- after vowel stems) with frequentative and intensive meaning, and Yakut -*ïalaa*- (frequentative). For Chuvash, Levitskaja (1976: 55–56) discusses an intensive form -*ala* (-*la* after vowels) that is less common than the complex form -*kala*, which is widespread in the Turkic family. According to her, -*ala*- is found in Chuvash, Turkish, Azerbaijani, Turkmen, Kirghiz, and Tatar.

Ramstedt (1912: 5) connects Turkic -*ala*, -*la* with Mongol -*l*, which is no longer productive but has the meaning of intensive or iterative and, secondarily, of sudden or violent action. An example is Mongolian *dusu-* 'fall (of a drop),' *dusul* 'to drip' (Poppe 1964: 64). This suffix also occurs in Tungus, outside of Manchu, as *-l-*, *-il-*, *-ili-* with inchoative meaning (Ramstedt 1952, II: 167).

In the Chukotian family we find Kamchadal *-ala-* which, when suffixed to a verb stem, indicates that the action is carried out to a small extent. It is thus parallel in meaning to that found in a number of Uralic languages.

56. Negative N

Indo-European has two common indicators of negation, **ne* and **mē*. Of these, the first is found in every branch of Indo-European, not only as a sentence negation, but also as a negative prefix before verbs (e.g. Latin *ne-sciō* 'I do not know') and nouns, usually with reduced grade n̥ (e.g. Greek *án-udros* 'waterless'). In contrast, *mē* occurs primarily as a negation of the imperative in Indic, Greek, Armenian, and Albanian.

In Uralic the particle of negation is likewise reconstructed as **ne* and was compared with Indo-European **ne* by Collinder (1965a: 125). Kertész (1933: 190), in a general discussion of negation in Finno-Ugric, states that although there is a negative verb **e-*, there are numerous negative adverbs and pronouns in *ń-* and *n-*, especially the latter. Yukaghir has a negative *ńe-*, *ńo-*, *ń-*, *ne-* that is for the most part used redundantly with interrogatives and the number 'one' in the meaning 'not any,' e.g. *ńe-xaŋide el xonlek* 'don't go anywhere' (literally, 'not-where don't go'). Collinder (1940: 68), after first considering the possibility that it might be a borrowing from Russian, indicates a further use (which he noted in Jochelson's texts) that considerably reduces the possibility of borrowing; the formative in question occurs within the verb complex as *-ne-* after the stem, but before the inflection of the potential mood.

In Turkic the only indication of an *n* negative is Chuvash *an* (prohibitive), which has been compared with *en* in the Permian (Uralic) languages, from which it may be a borrowing (Levitskaja 1976: 78). Others have derived it from the negative verb stem *e* followed by a suffix, either *-ŋ* (imperative) according to Ramstedt or as a participle in *n* of the same verb (Kononov). In Tungus there is a widespread form *ana*, found in Oroch, Orok, and Ulch, that typically negates adjectives, for example, Orok *asi-la ana nara* 'a man without a wife' ('wife-possessing not man'; Petrova 1968: 177).

Ainu has a privative suffix *-nak* that is used with nouns, e.g. *sik-nak* 'blind' (literally, 'eyes-without'). The final *-k* is perhaps the Eurasiatic absolutive (No. 23). Korean has a negative verb, *ani* 'not to be,' which may be compared with classical Japanese *ani*, a particle found initially in sentences that expect a negative reply. The classical language also has a negative conjugation (e.g. attributive *-nu*), most of whose forms consist of *n* followed by a vowel. Concerning this vowel, Lewin (1959: 187) says "At any rate, the paradigm of an archaic negative suffix beginning with a nasal and taking four grades, *-na, -ni, -nu, -ne*, may be deduced." A related root is the negative existential suffix *-nasi*, presumably the source of the modern negative existential *nai*, as in *mizu ga nai* 'there isn't any water' and *tabe-nai* 'does not eat,' etc. In addition, the negative imperative in the classical language is expressed by suffixed *-na*, e.g. *yuku-na* 'don't go.' In Old Japanese the same morpheme may be prefixed to the conjunctive form, e.g. *na-wabi* 'don't be upset.' The construction *yuku-na* has survived into modern colloquial Japanese (Lewin 1959: 99). In Ryukyuan also, *-na* forms the negative imperative.

In Uhlenbeck's comparisons of Indo-European and Eskimo (1935, 1942–45), he included Eskimo negatives in *n-*. For example, he adduces such forms as Greenlandic *naqqa* 'not,' and other adverbs in various forms of Eskimo, as well as the Greenlandic and Labrador *-na-* in the negative gerundive, Alaska *-na-* in the negative imperative, and prefixed *na-* in Labrador as in *na-sar-puq* 'not fast' vs. *sar-puq* 'fast.' Hammerich (1936: 69–70) posits *-na-* as the general mark of negation in the Eskimo gerund.

The Aleut adverb *naŋa* 'no, not' (Jochelson 1934: 147) seems directly comparable with Greenlandic Eskimo *naqqa* and similar forms in other dialects, e.g. Eastern Arctic *nakka* (Thibert 1970). In his reconstruction of Proto-Eskimo-Aleut, Mudrak (1989b) includes a negative morpheme **na* 'no.'

57. Negative M

Forms corresponding to Indo-European prohibitive **mē* are found in Turkic (including Chuvash), but probably not in the rest of Altaic. It takes the form *ma ~ me* and is part of the verbal complex preceding tense and person/number markers. Examples include Turkish *gel-me-di-m* 'I did not come' and Chuvash *muta-m-ăp* 'I will not praise' (cf. *mutăp* 'I shall praise'). Manchu, a Tungus language, has lost the negative verb *e* (No. 58); it has, however, a prohibitive form *ume*, without sure cognates in other Tungus languages, that may belong here (Benzing 1955: 146). It is perhaps also found in the Ainu negative existential verb *isam* 'not to be,' which we may compare with *isu* 'to be.' The form *isu* is only found in Batchelor, but the negative *isam* is well attested both in Batchelor and in other sources. In Simeon's (1968: 34) dissertation on a Hokkaido dialect there is a verb *isam-ka* 'to annihilate' with *-ka* (causative) (see No. 51) and in Pfizmaier (1851: 45) we find the phrase *teke isamu* 'without hands' (i.e. 'hands are-not'). Prohibitive *mā* (< *mawu* < *mao*) may occur in Korean (Martin 1992: 680).

58. Negative E/ELE

Two indicators of negation, **e* and **ele*, are so closely related, often by suppletion, that they are treated together both by Collinder (1940: 61) and Tailleur (1959b: 417) in their comparisons of Uralic and Yukaghir. The situation in Finnish is similar to that in other Finno-Ugric languages. There is an inflected negative verb stem that precedes the main verb, which ends in an aspirate (deriving from **k*), e.g. *e-n tiedä'* 'I don't know,' literally, 'not-I know.' However, in the second-person singular of the negative imperative we have rather *älä, älä anna'* 'don't give.' In the literary language the prohibitive marker is *älä*, but "the imperative of the verb of negation is in some dialects *elä* . . . and its relation to the verb of negation is then more apparent" (Whitney 1956: 103). In Finnish the third-person singular of the negative form is *ei*, not **e* as would be expected, and the third-person plural is *ei-vät*. The form with final *-i* is also found in Yukaghir. For Uralic the negative verb is reconstructed as **e* and the negation of the imperative derives from **elä*.

In Yukaghir both of these forms recur, but the functional division is different than in Uralic. In Yukaghir all verbs (with one important exception) prefix *el* to form the negative. But the verb *le* 'to be' prefixes instead *oi-*, which is in vowel harmonic alternation with *ei* and is thus to be identified with the Uralic variant form *ei* of the negative verb *e*. In nineteenth century recordings of Kolyma Yukaghir (Schiefner 1871–72), we find *ei-ažukei* 'mute' ('not speaking') and *ei-meginingei* 'dear' ('not-cheap'). This *ei-* is identical in form with the third-person singular of the negative verb in Finnish and has been generalized to all persons and numbers in Estonian. One may conjecture that the *-i* of *ei* is the general Eurasiatic third-person singular pronoun (see No. 18), which survives in Uralic as a verb subject marker only in the verb of negation. Uralicists, however, generally analyze Finnish *e-i* as deriving from **e-pi* (cf. the third-person plural *ei-vät* 'they are not'). Chuvan has the full form of the negative in *ai ele* 'not yet' and *alla* 'not' (Tailleur 1962) and Omok has a negative *alla* (Tailleur 1959a).

As we have just seen, the Yukaghir verb 'to be' is *l'e*, a form that has cognates in other Eurasiatic languages. The theory tentatively suggested to account for this and other intricate facts is that there was a Eurasiatic negative verb **e(i)* that, when combined with the positive verb 'to be' *le*, formed a negative existential verb **e-le* that in some instances lost either its initial or final vowel.

Both of these forms are encountered in Altaic and their relationship to Uralic has been noted by Collinder (1955, 1965a) and others. The existence of a negative verb *e-* is accepted by Altaicists for all three branches of Altaic (Ramstedt 1924a, Poppe 1960). The negation *ele* occurs as *ülü* in Classical Mongolian, with similar forms in other Mongolian languages.

The negative *e* possibly occurs in Sakhalin Ainu *e . . . sah* 'without' (Dettmer 1989: 122), e.g. *e-kema-sah aynu* 'a man without a foot,' since *sah* is cognate with Hokkaido *sak* 'without.' However, *e* might simply be an emphasizing demonstrative (see No. 8) rather than an additional negative. Of course the use of multiple negative markers to express a single negation is common across languages.

The existence of a negative *e* in early Japanese was first noted by Sansom (1928: 161). In an extended discussion, which cites the subsequent literature, Miller (1971: 281–85) further specifies the basic meaning as negative potential and identifies it with Altaic *e*. The meaning of potential negative fits well with regard to the Gilyak verb stem *ali* 'to be unable,' which may be considered to represent the full form of the negative existential **ele*.

Both forms are found in the Chukchi-Koryak group of Chuko-tian. In Chukchi there are two constructions involving $e \sim a$ as a prefix, accompanied by a suffix -ke $\sim$ -ka or by -ki $\sim$ -ke (Skorik 1961–77, I: 339–40). The vowel prefix is lost if the stem begins with a vowel; only the first of these is productive. With a noun stem it means 'without,' e.g. a-qora-ka 'without a reindeer.' With a verb stem it forms the negative infinitive, which cannot be combined with tense or person/number affixes. The subject is a personal pronoun or a noun, e.g. *yəm omlav-ka* 'I am not warm.' Here the vowel (e- $\sim$ a-) is lost and the stem is a qualitative verb 'to be warm.' To express other tenses one of a number of auxiliary negative verbs occurs with the negative infinitive. The other Chukchi form ($e \sim a$ . . . $ki \sim$ ke) is used to form substantives from substantives, active verbs, and adjectives. It shows a greater variety of meanings as compared to $e \sim a$ . . . $ke \sim ka$, but it is not productive. Examples include *e-telp(ə)-ki* 'endlessness' (cf. *telp-ək* 'to be finished'), a-val'om-ke 'one who disobeys' (cf. *val'om-ək* 'to obey'), and a-čača-ke 'taste-lessness' (cf. *nə-čača-qen* 'tasty').

In the Koryak group reflexes of *ele form sentence negations or are equivalent to English 'no!,' a natural use for a negative existen-tial. Examples are Palana Koryak *elle* and Kerek a*la* 'not.' Kerek has lost its vowel harmony system through merger so that a is the expected reflex of *e. Aliutor has gone through similar phonetic changes and has a*l*, a*lla* 'no!, not.'

In addition, for prohibitives Kerek uses the imperative of a neg-ative auxiliary verb *illa-*, which follows the negative infinitive, e.g. a-jikja-ka q-illa-tək 'don't cry!' (plural). In this example q . . . tək is the regular second-person plural imperative of the positive form. We find here a parallel to the Finnish distribution of the e and ele forms.

Languages of the Koryak group also have the negative prefix e- or its expected phonetic outcomes. Examples include the Kerek negative infinitive noted above, a-jikja-ka 'not to cry' (cf. *jikja-k* 'to cry'). With a nominal root a . . . ka means 'not having . . . .' Aliutor has the same formation, a . . . ka, which may be predicated, e.g. a . . . ka-yəm 'I don't have . . .' Palana Koryak predicates el-, e.g. *yuttin el-emelkə-l?i-n* 'this is not a good man' (for -l?i-n see No. 40).

Eskimo also has a form corresponding to the *el(e)* negative. Hammerich (1936: 92) summarizes the evidence for negation in Eskimo in the following terms: "The most important and widespread morpheme of negation is a suffix whose oldest form is probably *-il-*."

Finally, Hittite has a negative imperative *lē* as in *lē istamas-ti* 'do not hear!,' in which the verb has the inflection of the second-person singular. This form is isolated in Indo-European (see Kronasser 1956: 160) so here, as in other instances, Anatolian languages turn out to retain forms inherited from Eurasiatic that are not attested in the other branches of Indo-European. Rosenkranz (1950) and Čop (1979) have identified the Hittite prohibitive *le-* with the Uralic verb of negation *elä*. Croft (1991) has shown, on the basis of a diachronic typological survey of negation, how a marker of negation, combining with an existential verb 'to be,' may be reinterpreted as a simple negation to form a cycle of negation. The Eurasiatic developement *e* 'not' plus *le* 'to be' into *ele* as a marker of negation—with the subsequent phonetic decay that normally accompanies grammaticalization—is a variant of this process.

59. Negative LAKA

The usual marker of negation in the Aleut verb complex is *-laka* or *-laga*, used both in the indicative and the imperative. Examples are *su-laga-da* 'do not take!,' *adaɣi-laka-qiŋ* 'I have no father' (Geoghegan 1944: 69). Tailleur (1960: 127) compared the Aleut negative with the Gilyak negative existential verb *liɣi*, which may also be used after a noun to indicate 'without,' e.g. *mu liɣi-d'* 'without a boat' (literally, 'a boat is not'). Here *-d'* is the indicative marker discussed in No. 44. Tailleur also compares these with Chukchi *loŋ-* 'not,' which is prefixed to the verb, e.g. *loŋ-ipawalin* 'not having drunk.'

60. Interrogative K

An interrogative in *k* is found in every branch of Eurasiatic. In addition to this breadth of distribution, there are several further indications that we are not dealing with an accidental convergence. One of these is that *k-* is essentially personal, unlike *j-* (No. 61) and m- (No. 62), the other two most widely found interrogatives, which are practically always non-personal. In Indo-European k- is both personal and non-personal, distinguished by inflections, e.g. Latin qui-s 'who?,' qui-d 'what?' The extension to the non-personal category is due to the fact that, of its chief rivals, j- has become a relative pronoun and m- survives only marginally in interrogative adjectives and adverbs, mainly in Hittite and Tocharian. Further, there is a consistent difference in vocalism in the k- interrogative, depending on its functions. It is followed by i ∼ e as an interrogative pronoun, but e ∼ a (Indo-European e ∼ o) in other uses. Finally, as noted in No. 22, it occurs in many languages, from Uralic to Eskimo, with a suffix -na whose function is not clear, e.g. Udmurt (Uralic) kin, Mongolian (Altaic) xen, Eskimo kina, all meaning 'who?' Forms in ku- also appear. Indo-European centum languages have, of course, labiovelars in such forms, but it is noteworthy that even in a satem language like Sanskrit we find kuha 'where?,' kutra 'whither?,' etc.

The Indo-European use of k- as a relative pronoun, as for example in Latin quī, is clearly a later innovation in those languages that have it. In some Indo-European branches (e.g. Indic), it is rather j- (No. 61) that functions as a relative. Whether, in view of this, Indo-European had a relative pronoun is a much discussed question (see No. 61). At any rate, outside of certain branches of Indo-European, no Eurasiatic language employs k- as a relative pronoun.

An expected function of interrogative pronouns is to serve as a base for interrogative adjectives and adverbs such as 'which?' and 'where?' This is commonly found with k-. Furthermore, it is usual for interrogatives to be used as indefinites, particularly with negatives and in conditional clauses. In addition to this, we find k- with vocalism *e ∼ *a suffixed to an interrogative, e.g. Latin quisque 'whoever, anyone' and Japanese dare-ka 'somebody' (cf. dare 'who?'). Sometimes the interrogative has little more than an emphasizing function, which may lead to its finally becoming an empty marker. (For -ka as an emphasizer in Japanese see Aston [1904: 65].)

A less common development is for interrogatives to be used as coordinating or alternating conjugations. Already Brugmann (1892–1900, II.2: 39) pointed out the connection of the coordinating conjunction *-k^we with the *k^w- interrogative, citing the indefinite general meaning "any at all" (jeder beliebige) as the source of the coordinating conjugation. The common etymological origin of the interrogative and coordinating enclitic has been generally accepted by Indo-Europeanists, although they have not all expressed the semantic connection in the same terms. Thus Szemerényi (1978: 272) derives the meaning from 'like, how,' e.g. *pətēr mətēr-kʷe 'the father like the mother.' However, the interrogative does not by itself mean 'how?' I believe that Brugmann's general notion is correct, but it can be made more specific by analyzing examples such as Italian chi . . . chi . . . 'who? . . . who? . . . ' Duranti (1986) gives the following example: Chi la chiama Maria chi la chiama Francesca. This is in reference to a girl with a double first name, Maria Francesca. We may translate it literally as 'Some call her Maria and some call her Francesca,' but we could also translate it as 'She is called Maria and Francesca,' generalizing over the situations, or as 'She is called Maria or Francesca,' individualizing the occurences. A parallel development occurs with the interrogative j- (No. 61), which in Hittite and outside of Indo-European is also a coordinating or alternating conjunction. This parallel was noted by Watkins (1963: 16).

By a further development, not found in Indo-European, k- becomes a sentence interrogative particle, such as Japanese ka. How this can occur is shown in the discussion and examples given in Martin (1962a: 193–94). With the meaning 'or' discussed earlier we find examples such as asitá ka ásatte iku desyoo 'I expect he'll come either tomorrow (asitá) or the day after (ásatte). By a natural extension we get instances like oča ka kohii ga suki desu ka 'Do you like tea or coffee (either one)?,' literally, 'Tea ka coffee ga (subject) is pleasing ka.' From this the transition to the common use of sentence final ka in Japanese for yes-no questions is simple, e.g. ikimasu ka '(Are you) coming (or not)?'

In the remainder of this section, each branch of Eurasiatic will be discussed in turn, following the order of the preceding exposition: (1) interrogative pronoun, (2) interrogative adjectives and adverbs, (3) indefinite pronouns, (4) coordinating or alternating conjunctions, (5) sentence interrogative markers.

The existence of the first four of these five in Indo-European has been discussed in the foregoing sections and elsewhere in the present chapter and need not therefore be documented further. The existence of an interrogative k- in Uralic and its relation to Indo-

European has been adduced in every comparison of Uralic and Indo-European since Anderson (1879). It occurs in Uralic as a personal interrogative pronoun 'who?,' sometimes with the -n(a) suffix (No. 22), e.g. Finnish ken, Udmurt, Komi-Zyrian kin, sometimes without -n, as in Hungarian ki. A variant ku-, ko- also occurs (reminding us of the Indic forms), e.g. ku-ka, Hungarian hol 'where?' (h < *k). Numerous interrogative adjectives and adverbs are found in Uralic languages, e.g. Yurak Samoyed hu-na 'where?' (for -na, see No. 30), Mordvin ko-damo 'which?, what sort of?' The indefinite use of -ka is found clearly in Finnish jo-ka 'every, which (relative),' in which it has been added to the interrogative in j- (No. 61). It is also added to ku- itself in ku-ka, a variant of ken without any discernible difference of meaning, and to mi- in mi-kä 'what?' The same construction of the interrogative j- with indefinitizing k- is found in Saami juokke 'each' and with the k- interrogative in Udmurt (Permian) kin-ke 'someone' (cf. kin 'who?'). There are many more instances of the indefinitizing use of the k- interrogative, in the form -ke or -ka, in the Uralic languages. In Finnish, -ko is an enclitic, usually added to the verb to form a yes-no question, e.g. puhutte-ko te suomea 'Do you speak Finnish?' (literally, speak-ko you Finnish?). In the form -kä it is cliticized on the conjugated negative verb (Hakulinen 1957: 170), e.g. et-kä tiedä 'don't you know?' (literally, 'not-you-kä know?'). Similar constructions are found in other Baltic Finnic languages, e.g. Estonian ka-s, which introduces a question (for -s, cf. ke-s 'who?', mi-s 'what?,' with -s confined to the nominative), and Karelian -go, an enclitic used in yes-no questions, e.g. hiän-go t'ämän šano 'Did he say that?' (literally, 'he-go that said?').

Because of the variety of vowels that follow k-, Rédei, in his comparative Uralic dictionary, reconstructs *ke (ki) 'who?' and ku (ko) 'who?, which?, what?' (Rédei 1988: 140, 191). Collinder (1960: 406) reconstructs *ke ~ *ki, a striking agreement with the alternation in Indo-European (e.g. Latin qui-s 'who?,' but que-m 'whom?').

The variation in reconstructed meanings reflects the fact that in adverbial forms, particularly of place, and in relative uses back vowel forms predominate, as in Indo-European. For the Samoyed branch of Uralic, Janhunen (1977) reconstructs *ki- ~ *kɨ- 'who?' and *ku- 'what?, which?' For the former he also reconstructs *kim ~ *kimä, which is very similar to Turkic kim 'who?'

In Yukaghir k- provides the base for the personal interrogative pronoun and a number of interrogative adverbs. Examples from the Kolyma dialect are ki-n 'who?,' xamun 'how many?,' and xon 'where?' Here x derives from *k before a back vowel.

The k- interrogative is found in all three branches of Altaic. Starostin (1991: 11) reconstructs Proto-Turkic *ke/*ki 'who?,' with the same alternation as in Uralic and Indo-European. In non-Chuvash Turkic the personal interrogative is *kim, in Chuvash, käm. There are numerous interrogative adjectives and adverbs whose stem is ka-, e.g. Kumyk kajsï 'what kind of?,' kanša 'how many?,' Azerbaijani hara (< *kara) 'whence?' Many Turkic interrogatives have a base kaj, as seen in the Kumyk example above. Without an additional suffix kaj sometimes occurs with the meaning 'which?' (e.g. Karaim). This may be a crossing of the interrogatives ka and ja (No. 61) such as that posited for Korean ka-ja, which exists alongside both ka and ja (Ramstedt 1939: 165). Vilhelm Thomsen (1916: 46) notes the Turkic interrogative enclitic -gu ~ -gü, which occurs rarely in non-Chuvash Turkic, but whose antiquity is confirmed by the Turfan texts.

Perhaps Turkic kim 'who?' also represents a crossing between the interrogatives k and m (No. 62). The similar Samoyed forms mentioned above are either borrowings from Turkish or have developed internally in the same way as a crossing. Mongolian has ke-n 'who?' and a considerable number of interrogative adjectives and adverbs with the stem ka- or ke-, e.g. ka-na 'where?,' ke-r 'how?' (see Nos. 29 and 30).

In Tungus the k- interrogatives survive in adjectives and adverbs, e.g. Ulch, Nanai (Southern Tungus) xadu 'how much?' In North Tungus *k > *x > 0, so that the corresponding form is adi in Even. Benzing (1955: 1062) reconstructs Proto-Tungusic *xa- as the "most widely distributed base for interrogatives." Many languages of the Tungus group have -ka 'but, and.' As regards the phonetic difference between k and the x- of the interrogative, it appears that *k has x as a positional variant, especially between vowels, in some Tungus languages and consequently the reflexes of *k and *x are often difficult to distinguish (see the discussion in Benzing 1955: 976). As a sentence interrogative, -gu (cf. Mongolian) is found in some forms of Tungus (e.g. Even) in alternating questions. The indefinitizing function of *ka* is found in Manchu *ja-ka* 'anyone, who?' (Hauer 1952).

Menges (1968: 125) compares Altaic interrogatives in *k-* with those of Indo-European and Yukaghir, and Räsänen (1965: 164) connects them with Uralic *k-* forms, as does Collinder (1955). By implication Collinder also connects them with Yukaghir since he compares the same Uralic forms to those of Yukaghir.

In Ainu all interrogative pronouns, adjectives, and adverbs are based on *n-* (see No. 64), but *-ka* survives as the regular method of forming indefinites from interrogatives, in striking similarity to Japanese *-ka*, Uralic *-ka*, and Indo-European *-kwe*. Examples include *ene-ka* 'anyhow, somehow,' *nen-ka* 'someone' (cf. Japanese *nanika*). It also occurs as a coordinator *ka . . . ka*, following each of the constituents, e.g. *kuani ka sinuma ka* 'both I and he.' Hattori (1964: 321) voices his suspicion that Ainu *ka* might be borrowed from Japanese.

The interrogative *k-* occurs in two forms in Korean, as an enclitic and as a coordinating conjunction. For the most part yes-no questions are indicated by intonation in Korean; however, *-ka* is used with the future participle *-l* (No. 45) in the form *-lkka* to indicate a future question, often, but not necessarily, in the first person, with a semantic nuance of hesitation or intention, e.g. *na-to mur-il čom kirə julkka* 'Should I draw water for you?' (literally, 'I-also water-accusative some draw-*lkka*?'), *na-hago kyəŋču halkka* 'Will you make a bet with me?' (literally, 'me-with bet make-*lkka*?') (Lewin 1970: 88). It is also found in the interrogative form of the non-future indicative *-mnikka* (< *-pnikka*), with which we may contrast the indicative *-mnida*. According to Lewin (1970: 165), this is a very frequent form and, furthermore, the strengthening of *-k* to *-kk* is regular in all verb forms (Lewin 1970: 55). An interrogative *ko* (with variant *ku* in some dialects) also occurs and there is a by form *-ko* which may appear dialectally as *-ku* (Lewin 1970: 88, 102). The interrogative *-ja* is sometimes suffixed to *ka-*, producing *ka-ja*, as noted earlier (Ramstedt 1939: 165). Interrogative *ka* in Korean is related to Japanese *ka* by Kanazawa (1910: 38) and Martin (1991: 286). Korean *ko* forms a coordinating gerund with the meaning '(is or does) and also' (Martin, Lee, and Chang 1967: 133). It is related to the Indo-European coordinating enclitic *-kwe* by Koppelman (1928: 223).

In Japanese and Ainu k- does not survive in interrogative pronouns, adjectives, or adverbs. It is, however, the usual method in Japanese of forming indefinites from interrogatives, e.g. *dare ka* 'someone,' *itu ka* 'some time' (cf. *itu* 'when?'). It is also used as an alternating conjunction, *ka . . . ka,* meaning 'either . . . or' (whichever you want). It also functions as a sentence particle in yes-no questions, e.g. *wakarimasu ka* 'Do you understand?' (literally, 'understand [polite] *ka*?' Ryukyuan uses largely parallel those of Japanese, forming indefinites such as *tā-ga* 'someone' (for *tā* 'who?' see No. 63) and functioning as a sentence final interrogative. Use of *k* as an interrogative pronoun, however, may survive in Ryukyuan *ča* 'what?' This may be hypothesized as arising from **kia* (cf. *čaku* 'guest,' corresponding to Japanese *kyaku*, a Chinese loanword).

In Ainu *-ka* forms indefinites from interrogatives. Examples include Hokkaido *nep-ka* 'something, something or other' (Batchelor), to be analyzed as *nep* 'what?' = 'which thing?' + *ka* 'indefinitizer,' *nen-ka* 'somebody, some one or other' (cf. *neni* 'who?') and corresponding to Sakhalin *nex-ka* 'something' (Majewicz and Majewicz 1983–85) in which x derives from **p.* The Moshiagusa also has *nepka* ~ *nipka* 'something.' It is also found as a sentence interrogative in some of the Hokkaido dialects in the form *ka,* varying with *ya* in other dialects (Hattori 1964: 326). For example, in sentences such as 'Will you go?,' the Horobetsu and Nayoro dialects have the final interrogative particle *ya,* whereas the Obihiro and Soya dialects have *ka.*

According to Krejnovich (1934: 200), Gilyak *-ka* is an interrogative particle "used when someone has forgotten to take something or is not certain whether he has it or not." Gilyak also has a coordinating conjunction *-ke . . . -ke* that is used only with animates, for example, *ir-ge er-ge* 'the mother and the father' (Panfilov 1962–65, I: 166).

As an interrogative pronoun, *k* occurs in Kamchadal *k'e* 'who?' (genitive *k'en*). In Chukchi and Koryak the *k* interrogative may survive in forms involving crossing with other interrogatives, e.g. Chukchi *mik-* ~ *mek-* 'who?' (for *mi-* see No. 62) and *req-* ~ *raq-* 'what?,' with corresponding forms in other languages of the Chukchi-Koryak group. Koryak *qej . . . qej* 'either . . . or' may involve a contamination of the interrogative *k* with *j* (No. 61), similar to that of Turkic *qaj* and Korean *ka-ja*. Its difference in meaning and the absence of other instances of Turkic influence on the the Chukchi-Koryak group both suggest parallel development. We thus have three examples of the same development, but the meanings are different in each case (interrogative adverb and adjective base in Turkic, alternating conjunction in Koryak, and sentence interrogative in Korean), making it likely that these are three independent instances. A similar process, but with the opposite order of components, is probably found in another language of the Koryak group, Kerek *jaq* 'who?, what?'

In the glossary to his Koryak texts Bogoras (1917: 131) gives *kur* as the stem of an interrogative verb in the Palana dialect, but without textual citations. It could then be 'to be who?' or 'to be what?' We shall encounter similar interrogative verbs in Altaic and Gilyak with regard to interrogative *j* (No. 61). In Western Kamchadal the mysterious variant *kim* (cf. Sanskrit, Samoyed, Turkic) occurs in the form *kin-kim* 'everyone' (i.e. 'whoever?'; Worth 1969: 40).

In all dialects of Eskimo the personal interrogative is *ki-na* (nominative singular; for *-na*, see No. 22). In addition there are numerous interrogative adverbs such as Greenlandic *qaŋga* 'when?,' Greenlandic *qanuq* 'how?,' and Siberian Yupik *qafsina* 'how many?' In Alaskan Yupik *-ka* is a question particle similar in its uses to Japanese *ka* (Hinz 1944: 55). This is probably identical to *-qaa*, described in Jacobson (1984: 623) as an enclitic "used with the indicative mood to form 'yes-no' questions; also occurring independently as an exclamation meaning 'really?, is that so!'" In their grammar of Alaskan Yupik, Reed et al. (1977) simply state that it indicates a yes-no question.

The Aleut personal interrogative and relative is *ki-n*, with the *-n* reinterpreted as part of the stem so that we have *kin-ku-x* (dual) and *kin-ku-n* (plural). In addition, Aleut has a whole series of interrogatives in *qa-* that show the same alternation as Eskimo between *ki-* with a high vowel for the personal interrogative, and *qa-* for the others. These include *qata* 'where?, whither?, what?,' *qanangun* 'where?,' *qanayam* 'when?,' *qanagan* 'whence?' (Geoghegan 1944). These examples are from the Unalaska dialect; similar forms could be cited from other dialects. Marsh and Swadesh (1951: No. 129) reconstruct **qa-* as an interrogative root in Proto-Eskimo-Aleut.

61. Interrogative J

Next to k- (No. 60), j- is the most widespread interrogative root in
Eurasiatic. Indo-European, the only branch with grammatical gender, uses *je ~ *jo, with differing gender markers, to indicate both
persons and non-persons. Elsewhere it is clear that j- is non-personal
in contrast to personal k-. Furthermore, except in Indo-European
and Uralic, the meaning is clearly interrogative rather than relative,
and from this it undergoes many of the same developments as k-, for
example, into coordinating or alternating conjunctions or sentence
interrogative particles. These are discussed in the same order as in
the preceding section dealing with interrogative k-.

In Indo-European, *jo ~ *je is a relative pronoun in Indic and
Greek, whereas *kw- has a similar function in other branches such
as Italic and Germanic. Watkins, in particular, has noted the neat
parallel between the use of *kw as an interrogative and coordinating
conjunction and that of *jo in the same two uses, the latter of which
has only become known with the discovery of Hittite (Watkins 1963:
16). As he puts it, "ya 'and' is related to the relative (anaphoric)
pronoun *yo of Indo-European in exactly the same way as -$k^w e$ is
related to the relative (anaphoric) pronoun *$k^w o$."

However, *k^w- is interrogative in Indo-European and never anaphoric, much less demonstrative, which is the common source of
anaphoric pronouns. The parallelism suggests rather that *je ~
*jo was originally an interrogative that in certain branches of Indo-
European took on the functions of a relative pronoun, just as in other
branches it was *$k^w i$ ~ *$k^w e$ 'who?' that assumed these functions.
The interrogative function of *je ~ *jo, which is clearly primary
where it occurs in Eurasiatic, has shifted to that of relative in both
Indo-European and Uralic.

On this view, Indo-European would have had no relative pronoun, a characteristic of SOV languages where noun modifiers typically precede the noun. Japanese, for example, has no relative pronoun. In modern Japanese hito kuru means 'the man comes' and
kuru hito, 'the man who comes' (literally, 'come man'). The abundant use of participles to express relatives is common in older Indo-
European languages. It cannot be accidental that it is precisely
Indo-European and Uralic, both of which have generally become

SVO, that have developed relative pronouns and, as it happens, from the same source. Thus, in the final analysis, Winfred Lehmann (1974) is supported by the wider comparative data of Eurasiatic, in that Proto-Indo-European was probably not an SOV language like Turkish or Japanese, but, rather, like Hungarian, had shifted from strict SOV order while still retaining many SOV characteristics.

There is a tradition in Indo-European studies, beginning at least with Brugmann (1892–1900, II: 771), that the identity of relative *jo- and demonstrative *i was not to be doubted. According to Gonda (1954: 2), the issue is simply "Was IE i̯o- . . . originally used as a demonstrative and anaphorical pronoun, or are there sufficient reasons for believing the relative function to be more or less original?" Meillet (1934: 438), moreover (and others influenced by him), as well as Stang (1966: 233), a leading Balticist, have maintained the separateness of the demonstrative and the relative.

Given the phonetic similarity of je ~ ja and i ~ e, there are of course examples whose origin on purely formal grounds is doubtful. Thus, regarding Lithuanian jì-s 'he,' Stang (1966: 233) is certain that it goes back to the demonstrative and anaphoric *i- (Latin i-s 'he,' Sanskrit i-d-am 'this, that') and has acquired its j- from the oblique cases of the relative pronoun (cf. Old Church Slavic jego 'him,' a stem that appears as a relative elsewhere). Regarding the Old Church Slavic relative pronoun i-že I concluded that i- here was the interrogative and not the demonstrative i-, a conclusion previously arrived at by Illich-Svitych (1971–84, I: 142). It follows that the supposed connection of Old Church Slavic relative pronoun i-že with demonstrative i- (Pokorny 1959: 383) is, as Illich-Svitych put it, "erroneous." The development of interrogative *je to i- also occurs in Japanese, Kamchadal (Chukotian), and some forms of Tungus, e.g. Solon ī 'what?' (from the Proto-Tungus interrogative reconstructed as *jā by Benzing [1955: 1062]). Of course relatives may have both demonstratives and interrogatives as their source. Moreover, a relative can be used as an anaphoric, as is often the case in Classical Latin, but the development from a relative to a demonstrative I consider to be very unlikely.

The use of -ya as a coordinating conjunction 'and' is found in Hittite. It varies with -a, the general rule being that -a follows consonants and -ya, vowels. Kronasser (1956: 153) treats a as primary and asserts that -y- after vowels is a transitional sound. However, Watkins (1969: 48) notes that a Hittite form with -ya after a consonant has been discovered: *memal-ya* 'and the grits.' The same rule is found in Palaic: *ja* after vowels and -a after consonants (Carruba 1970: 49). Mel'chuk (1959: 159) and others identify the Tocharian A instrumental case ending -yo as deriving from a coordinating enclitic related to Hittite -ya; the meaning 'and' and 'with' are expressed by the same morpheme in many languages (e.g. Hausa *da*).

Collinder (1934: 57) identifies Uralic **jo-*, a frequent relative and indefinite, with the Indo-European relative pronoun **jo*. In Uralic there is a problem similar to that of Indo-European in distinguishing between demonstrative *i ~ e* and relative *jo*. The question was discussed in some detail by Paasonen (1906), who came to the conclusion that they are distinct, though he also believes that **jo-* too originally had a demonstrative meaning.

All branches of Altaic have **j-* as an interrogative and Räsänen (1949: 14) relates it to the Uralic relative. In Turkic it survives as an interrogative only in Chuvash, e.g. *je-ple* 'how?, what sort?' (cf. *a-pla* 'such'). It is widely attested in Turkic as the alternating conjunction 'or,' e.g. Karakalpak, Kazakh *ja*. As noted in No. 60, some scholars have interpreted the Turkic interrogative stem *kaj-* as the result of a crossing of the k- interrogative with *ja*. It is common in Mongolian, e.g. *jaγun* 'what?,' *jambar* 'which?,' and the verb stems *je-ji*, *jaγa-ki*, and *je-ki*, all meaning 'to do what?' In Monguor *jä-ma* 'something,' Moghol *je-ma* 'something,' etc., it is followed by the m interrogative (see No. 62) used as a marker of indefiniteness. It is also common in Tungus, e.g. Manchu *ja* 'who?, what?,' *ja-de* 'where?,' and Even *jādu* 'why?,' *jā-* 'to do what?' The Manchu reduplicated form *jaja* means 'whatever' (cf. Latin *quidquid* 'whatever' for a similar semantic development in the k- interrogative). It may also occur as a coordinator, as in, for example, Oroch *mama-ja mapa-ja* 'an old man and an old woman' (Avrorin and Lebedeva 1968: 187).

In Sakhalin Ainu -a, -ya means 'or' and for the Hokkaido dialect Batchelor gives *ya . . . ya* 'whether . . . or.' It is also used as a sentence-final interrogative in the same dialect, e.g. *oman ya* 'Has he gone?' In the Hokkaido dialect studied by Simeon (1968: 51) it is used in alternating questions, e.g. *ek ya somo ya* 'Has he come or not?' (literally, 'come *ya* not *ya*'). It may survive in -ya-k 'that (complementizer), if,' to be analyzed as the relative *ya* followed by locative *-k* (No. 26). Of similar structure are Sakhalin *ya-ko* 'when' and *ya-kuna* 'when, if.' For the construction we may compare Latin *cūr* 'why?,' which is a locative of the *k-* interrogative. Ainu may also have *i* as a reduced form of *ya* in *i-ta* 'when' (relative) (for locative *-ta* see No. 32) and in *i-ne* 'where?' (see No. 30).

In Korean, along with the *ka* discussed in the preceding section, there is a sentence interrogative particle *ja*. Sometimes we find *ka-j(a)* (Ramstedt 1939: 80). Presumably this combination developed independently in Turkic *-kaj*, where it is not a sentence interrogative particle. Compare also, in Tungus, Nanai *haj* and Ulch *xaj* 'what?'

In Japanese there is a series of interrogatives in *i-*; Old Japanese examples include *ika* 'what?,' *itu* 'when?,' *iduku* 'where?,' *iduti* 'in which direction?,' and *idure* 'which of two things?' Miller (1971: 180) relates these forms to the Altaic interrogatives in *ja-*. Japanese also has an interrogative particle *ya*, which was connected with Ainu *ya* by Kanazawa (1910: 38). In contrast to *ka*, *ya* tends to be used more often in rhetorical questions or exclamations, but purely interrogative uses occur. Examples are Old Japanese *ari ya nasi ya* 'Is there or is there not?,' *uresi ya* 'how glad (I am)' (Aston 1904: 140). Used as a coordinator, *ya* can be translated as 'and' in incomplete enumerations (Martin 1962a: 192). A modern example is *hón-ya de wa hón ya zasši ya simbun o utte imásu* 'In the bookstore (*hón-ya*) they sell books, magazines, newspapers, et cetera.' The use of *ya* as a sentence interrogative in non-rhetorical and non-exclamatory sentences has declined since Middle Japanese, in favor of *ka* (Lewin 1959: 98). Martin (1991: 286) relates Korean and Japanese *ya*.

In Gilyak, *ja-* is the base for non-personal interrogatives such as *jayo* 'what sort of?,' *jayoṇa* 'since when?,' *jaɣr(t)*, *jaŋr(t)* 'why?' Normally 'what?' is expressed by the verb stem *ja-*, as in Mongolian. Thus 'what is it?' is simply *ja-* with a third-person singular subject.

I have not included in the preceding discussion Koryak *jaq* 'what?' (and other similar forms such as *jaqaŋ* 'why?') on phonological grounds since Koryak *j-* corresponds to Chukchi *r*, which I believe arose from a palatalized *r*. However, the *ja-* interrogative does apparently survive in the Kamchadal adverb *i-t'e* 'when?' Moreover, in the Koryak group Kerek *jaq* 'who?, what?' shows a different correspondence than the *n* usually found where Chukchi has *r* and

Koryak *j*, and may therefore be an example of interrogative *j-*. It is also possible that the *-q* of this and other Chukchi-Koryak interrogatives (like that of Even [Tungus] *jāk* 'what?, which?,' similar forms in Tungus languages, Mongolian *jaγun* 'what?,' and Gilyak *jaγo* 'what sort of?') may all involve crossing with interrogative *-k* (No. 60).

At first glance the interrogative found in Greenlandic Eskimo, *su(-na)* 'what?,' in which *-na* is the absolutive (see No. 22), would seem unpromising as an example of the interrogative *je ~ ja*. However, in Sirenik (a Yupik language spoken in Siberia) the dual is *sa-k* and the plural, *sa-t*. The evidence for *a* as the vowel of this interrogative is strengthened by Yupik *chau* 'be something,' *cha* 'do what?' Even more importantly in Yupik initial *y-* appears as a variant of initial *ch* in Jacobson's dictionary (1984), e.g. *yuk, chuk* 'a human being,' with initial *ch-*, *y-* corresponding to *s-* in Inuit and some Yupik dialects. Furthermore, in the Eskimo system of consonant alternations, which is typologically similar to that of Finnish, *-s-* and *-y-* have the same strengthened alternant, **-ts-*. These facts indicate that **s* and **y* had merged in initial position in Proto-Eskimo so that Alaskan Yupik *cha* 'to do what?,' deriving from **ya*, can be directly compared with Gilyak and Mongol *ya* with the same meaning. Thalbitzer (1904: 256) notes that Greenlandic often has *s* where Alaskan Inuit has *j* and that it is reasonable to assume that *j* is primary.

The merger of *s-* and *y-* must go back to Proto-Eskimo-Aleut. Marsh and Swadesh (1951) reconstruct only medial **-y-* and its reflex in certain phonetic environments is the same as that of **-s-* in Eastern and Central Aleut.

62. Interrogative M

Old Irish *má* 'if' and Middle Breton *ma* 'what' (relative) remained isolated within Indo-European until the discovery of Tocharian and the Anatolian languages. In Tocharian B we find *mä-k-su*, an interrogative and relative pronoun. In this form the last element (*-su*) is clearly the common suppletive Indo-European demonstrative *s-/t-* (see Nos. 11 and 12). It is this combination that allows it to take on both impersonal and personal meanings. Elsewhere it is either

impersonal or a general sentence interrogative marker. We also find
Tocharian B *mänt*, Tocharian A *mant*, meaning 'how (relative)' in
both languages. These Tocharian interrogatives and relatives are obviously related to Hittite *masi-s*, *mesiyant-*, *masiwant-* 'how large?,
how many?,' *maḫḫan*, *mān* 'how?,' the latter of which is also used
as a relative. Elsewhere in Anatolian we find Hieroglyphic Hittite
mana 'if,' *mank* 'somehow,' and Luwian and Palaic *man* 'if.'

Collinder (1965a: 113) noted the connection of the Indo-European interrogative and relative with the numerous instances of similar
forms in Uralic. Examples include Finnish *mi-kä* 'which?, what?,'
Saami *mī* 'what?,' Vogul *män* 'which,' Hungarian *mi* 'what?,' and
Enets *mi?* 'what?' In Kolyma Yukaghir *me-* is prefixed to interrogatives to form indefinites, for example, *me-kin* 'someone,' *me-neme*
'something,' *me-qabun* 'a certain amount' (Krejnovich 1968: 442).

In non-Chuvash Turkic, *-mi* as a sentence question enclitic is
found virtually everywhere, e.g. Turkish *gelir-mi* 'Does he/she come?'
In Chuvash we find rather, as in Indo-European and Uralic, a series of interrogative pronouns, all nonpersonal, e.g. *měn*, *měsker*
'what?,' *miśe* 'how many?,' *měnle* 'what kind of?' Ramstedt (1952,
II: 79) also finds *m* in the Mongolian sentence interrogative *-ū* (< *wu*
< *mu*). Whether or not this analysis is accepted, there are other in-
terrogative pronouns in South Mongolian languages such as Monguor
amu, *ama* 'what?'

In addition, Kotwicz (1936: 67) pointed out that in all branches
of Altaic one finds *-ma* added to interrogatives as generalizers, a very
common function of interrogatives, e.g. Mongolian *jayu-ma* 'whatever,' Tungus *ēku-ma* 'whatever,' Turkish *nä-mä* 'something.' He
cites Deny as considering it probable that the indefinitizer-generalizer
ma is connected with the sentence interrogative *-mi* of non-Chuvash
Turkic.

In Ainu we find *mak*, *makanak* 'what,' and *makan* 'what kind?'
The latter form is strikingly close to Hittite *maḫḫan* 'how?' Korean
mjət 'how many?,' *muəs* 'what?,' and Old Korean *mai* 'why?' are
compared in Ramstedt (1952, II: 79) with similar forms in Altaic.
Although the *m* interrogative does not occur in Japanese proper, it
is found in Ryukyuan *mī* 'what?' and in the sentence interrogative
enclitic *-mi* of the same language (cf. non-Chuvash Turkic).

The m- interrogative is common in Chukotian, where it has replaced the k- personal interrogative found elsewhere. It is thus used both personally and non-personally, e.g. Chukchi mikin 'who' (interrogative and relative), mi-k 'where?,' Kamchadal min 'which?, what sort?,' ma-nke 'whither' (-nke is a locative suffix).

I have found evidence for interrogative m in Eskimo in Alaskan Yupik -mi, glossed in Jacobson (1984) as 'on the other hand, how about?,' as in kaigtua. elpet-mi 'I am hungry. How about you?' (see also Reed et al. 1977: 38). As an indefinitizer -mi is present in Naukan (Siberian Yupik) kina-mi 'someone' (cf. kina 'who?'), navək-mi 'to some place' (cf. navək 'whither?'). It is also found in the Imaklik dialect of Inuit, spoken on the Bering Strait Islands, in forms like kina-mi 'someone' (Menovshchikov 1980: 83). Recapitulating this and other evidence, Fortescue et al. (1994: 411) reconstruct a Proto-Eskimo enclitic *mi 'what about?,' with forms from Inuit, Yupik, and Sirenik. As can be seen, the use of m- in non-personal forms, often contrasting with personal k- (e.g. Uralic), is widespread throughout Eurasiatic.

63. Interrogative TA

Old Japanese ta 'who?' occurs in our oldest document, the Kojiki. In the Genji Monogatari we find tare along with ta, Modern Japanese dare (for the -re substantivizer see No. 13). Ryukyuan tā agrees with Old Japanese ta. The Ryukyuan long vowel is automatic in all monosyllables. To these corresponds Ainu taa 'what?' The same interrogative t- may occur in Korean či (North Korean ti) (called by Martin, Lee, and Chang [1967: 1522–23] "suspective"), which is sometimes employed as a sentence-final particle with meanings such as 'I suppose he is eating' or 'He's eating, isn't he?' It can also be used non-finally to mean 'whether.' Ramstedt (1939: 40) calls it a question particle, but derives it from či, ti 'thing, fact,' which is treated as a homonymous entry by Martin, Lee, and Chang (1967). Ramstedt (1949: 30) later rejected his earlier view and compared it to the Tungus interrogative-dubitative particle ti. The Tungus meaning is very similar to that of Korean ti, for example, amin-mi eme jen-di 'Is my father coming today?' ('father-my today come-perhaps?'; Ramstedt 1949: 30).

The same interrogative is found in Gilyak, where there is a whole series of interrogatives based on r̥a- in the Amur dialect and tʻa- in eastern Sakhalin. These two consonants alternate within the Gilyak system of consonant mutation, with r̥- occurring mostly after vowels (which are, however, in some instances lost). In the Amur dialect we have r̥a 'which?' (adjective), r̥a-dʹ 'which?' as a substantive (-dʹ in this latter form is No. 44 functioning as a substantivizer), r̥ag ∼ r̥aŋg 'where?,' r̥aŋs 'how many?,' r̥ain 'where?,' r̥atx 'whither?'

In Palana Koryak (Zhukova 1980) the interrogative 'what?' is tənne in the absolutive and has the stem taq- in the oblique cases. However, there is a very common correspondence, usually given as Chukchi r ∼ Koryak j ∼ Aliutor t ∼ Kerek n, that appears to derive from an earlier palatalized r (= Altaic r$_2$) and which generally occurs in the Chukchi-Koryak subgroup of Chukotian as the initial consonant of the pronoun 'what?' In this correspondence Koryak j refers to the Chavchuven dialect (the closest to a "standard" dialect of Koryak). Palana Koryak in such instances shows r, as does Chukchi. Hence Palana t- cannot be explained in this way. However, there is Chukchi tʼer 'how many?' so it is possible that an interrogative with initial t does occur in the Chukchi-Koryak group.

Yakut, which occupies a somewhat isolated position within non-Chuvash Turkic, has interrogatives in t, e.g. tuox 'what?,' toyo 'what for?' The only other support for the t- interrogative in Altaic appears to be the previously mentioned Tungus interrogative-dubitative particle ti.

64. Interrogative N

The common non-personal interrogative in non-Chuvash Turkic may be reconstructed as *ne (Miller 1971: 187). In addition to its fundamental form *ne 'what?,' it is the basis for numerous adverbs deriving from oblique case forms or petrified elements suffixed to ne, e.g. Kumyk nege 'why?,' neče 'how many?' Although this element is usually ne, it shows some vowel variation, e.g. Shor noo 'what?' There is also a variant with suffixed -mV that appears in Uzbek nima, Baraba ne, neme, Bashkir nəmə, Khakas nime, and Kirghiz nemne, emne, ne, all meaning 'what?' In all probability Kirghiz nemne arises from contamination of the form with the -m extension (*nem) with ne, and emne from the dissimilation of the initial n- of nemne. Such variants in -m, alongside of ne by itself, must be old since we find Old Uighur nemen 'how?,' and in the Orkhon inscriptions ne occurs as 'what?'

In Chuvash, where the n interrogative does not occur as such, the extended form with n in nimən-de 'nothing' may be interpreted in two ways. Either it contains the Turkic interrogative or ni- is borrowed from Russian or Persian, in both of which it is contained in negative pronouns, e.g. Russian ni-kto 'no one.' Räsänen (1969: 353) found himself unable to decide between these two alternatives.

The variant with -mV is very similar to Tundra Yukaghir neme- (ŋ) 'what?,' neme-ya 'where?,' and in the Kolyma dialect numun 'what sort of?' (see Menges 1968: 125). The Yukaghir interrogatives in n- are compared with some hesitation to Kamassian Samoyed nar 'what?,' which seems to be isolated within Uralic, by Collinder (1940: 73).

Kazár (1980: 292) compares Hungarian né- and Vogul ne-, which form indefinites such as Hungarian né-hány 'some, a few' ('né-how many?'), with Japanese. However, these forms do not occur outside of Ugric.

Outside of Turkic, the n non-personal interrogative does not seem to occur in Altaic. In Tungus there are forms meaning 'who?' that are reconstructed by Benzing as *ŋüi. In some Northern Tungus languages these appear as ni (e.g. Negidal, Even). In Even ŋi appears along with ni. Ramstedt (1952, II: 78) derives ŋi from *gi (and ultimately *ki) so that it would be a variant of the common Tungus personal interrogative in k- (No. 60). In Old Turkish neŋ 'any' (Tekin 1968: 356), we find an indefinitizing use similar to that cited below in the Ugric branch of Uralic.

The n- interrogative is prominent in the group of languages consisting of Ainu, Korean, and Japanese. In Ainu, ine and na-k mean 'where?' (for k see No. 26). In Sakhalin Ainu, Dettmer (1989: 305) cites ney 'where?, when?' from Kindaichi (see No. 31). In nen, neni 'who?' we have a form strikingly similar to Japanese nani 'what?' The -n, -ni of Ainu is, however, the same as the personal numeral classifier -n, which seems to be a shortened form of niu 'person,' as can be seen in the contrast with ne-p 'what?' ('what?-thing,' cf. Ainu pe 'thing'; see also No. 21). In Old Japanese both na and *nani* meant 'what?,' but modern Japanese retains only the latter. In addition, Old Japanese had *nado* and *naso* 'why?,' modern *náze*. In Ryukyuan *nū* and *nūndi* are 'what?,' *nū-nči* 'why?,' and -*nā*, when suffixed to individual nouns or to the conclusive form of the verb, is a general question word. In Korean, Martin (1992: 702) describes a suffix -*na* that is used in the familiar style to indicate a question, for example, *čup-na* 'Is it cold?' ('cold-*na*?'). There is also a variant -*ni* 'is it?, does it?' (Martin 1992: 714) seen in *mek-ni* 'Does one eat?' ('eat-*ni*?'). There is also Korean *nu* ~ *nuku* 'who' which was already compared by Aston in 1879 to the Japanese interrogatives in *n*-. In Sakhalin Gilyak *nar* means 'who?' and *nud*, 'what?'

An interrogative in *n*- is general in Eskimo, with the basic meaning 'what?' In Greenlandic one only finds *naa* 'where is it?,' but in Labrador it forms a series of adverbs that includes *na-kit* 'whence?' (see Nos. 26 and 33) and *na-mut* 'whither?' The first form (with the usual change *-t > -n* that characterizes Alaskan Yupik) corresponds exactly to Kuskokwim *nakin* 'whence?' Other Kuskokwim forms are *na-ni* 'where?' (see Nos. 30 and 31), *nagun* 'whereby?,' and *natmun* 'whither?' From Siberian Eskimo one may cite Chaplino *na-liq* 'which?,' Sirenik *nani* 'where?,' *namu* 'whither?,' *natsəχ* 'which?,' and *načəχ* 'how many?'

It is noteworthy that everywhere, except in Korean, in the easily explainable *na-ni* of Ainu, and in Sakhalin Gilyak (where different forms of the same root are used for persons and non-persons), the *n*- interrogative is non-personal.

65. Ordinal MT

Sinor (1988) has assembled the basic evidence for reconstructing an ordinal suffix *-mt* that may be added to cardinal numbers in both the Uralic and Altaic families. This original *-mt* has developed into *-nt* in Finno-Ugric, Turkic, and Mongolian, but is retained in Samoyed and, to some extent, in Tungus. The existence of such a suffix provides a possible explanation for the final -*m* in the Indo-European numeral 'seven' (Latin *septem*) and 'ten' (Latin *decem*). It may also appear in 'nine,' which is reconstructed by some as *newn̥* and by others as *newm̥*. Since -*t* (possibly akin to the Indo-European *t* participle) also appears in numerals (Latin *quīntus* 'fifth'), forms like Proto-Indo-European *dek̂m̥t-os 'tenth' could be reanalyzed as dek̂m̥-tos, thus forming stems in -m for some cardinal numbers. I am not aware of any earlier attempt to explain this -m in Indo-European.

66. Indefinite WEL

From Latin vel-le 'to wish' (Proto-Indo-European *u̯el; Pokorny 1959: 1137), there is derived an affix -vīs 'you wish' which, when added to interrogatives, makes them indefinite, for example, quī-vīs 'whoever you wish, anyone.' From what is possibly the same Eurasiatic root we find in Yukaghir an optative -uol, as in al-uol 'desire to do' ('do-optative'; Jochelson 1905: 126). The same construction is found in the extinct Omok dialect of Yukaghir, for example, lang-ol 'wish to drink' ('drink-optative'; Tailleur 1959a: 98). In Northern Tungus a similar suffix gives the verb an indefinite meaning, much as in Latin, e.g. Even ŋi-vəl 'whoever?,' Evenki ŋīdū-val 'to someone,' and Negidal ni-wel 'someone.'

In Kamchadal there is a desiderative suffix -al' ~ -a (the -a alternant only occurs before s). There is also a future tense that is homonymous with this suffix and probably of the same historical origin. They are distinct, however, in that both may occur in the same verbal form, but in different positions in the verbal complex.

67. Absolutive L

The assumption was made in No. 25, in the discussion of Indo-European oblique -n, that the distribution nominative -r vs. oblique -n was an instance of suppletion in which the two elements had no previous historical connection. The situation is parallel to that of Chukotian, in which there are a number of absolutive formants that contrast with an agentive case for actors in an ergative system. This agentive is an oblique (frequently instrumental) case and oblique cases often have the marker -n. In Chukchi itself we find for absolutive, in addition to reduplication of the root, the suffixes -ŋə, -ən, and -lγən, with similar forms in other languages of the group. Of these, lγən, which is quite frequent, seems to be analyzable as l- (absolutive) plus -γən (collective).

In Indo-European there seems to be just one root that has *l/n* rather than *r/n* suppletion, Proto-Indo-European *$s\underset{\circ}{u}el$ ~ *$s\underset{\circ}{u}en$ 'sun' (Pokorny 1959: 881). The tendency, as with *r/n* stems, is to generalize one or the other, as seen in Latin *sol,* English 'sun.' Avestan, however, retained the original suppletion, and in Sanskrit there are four nouns (all neuters) in which the nominative has *-i* and oblique cases *-n* (e.g. *ásthi/asthnás* 'bone').

The *-l* absolutive may occur in Yukaghir. In the Tundra dialect the nominative of the third-person singular pronoun is *tude-l,* but the locative is *tude-γa,* and similarly for other oblique cases (Krejnovich 1958: 106). However, with the logical accent as the subject of a transitive verb the *-l* is absent (e.g. *tude wie* 'he did (it)'). Similar phenomena are found in the third-person plural pronoun *titte(l)* 'they.' The Omok dialect has *tati* 'he' without the *-l.* In the Kolyma dialect there are a number of nouns in *-l* which lose the *-l* in third-person possessive forms (e.g. *noi-l* 'leg,' *noi-gi* 'his, her leg'). This happens much less frequently in the Tundra dialect. In Raiskij's material on Kolyma Yukaghir (collected by Maydell in the nineteenth century), we find *šoi* 'stone' as compared with *šeul* in Jochelson's texts (Angere 1957).

An additional clear example of *l/n* suppletion (discussed in No. 9) is the common Turkic third-person pronoun *o-l/*a-n.* A more intensive search might reveal further instances of connections among various absolutives, perhaps in Chukotian which has a series of such formatives. As we have seen, however, the case for absolutive *-l* seems the most cogent, occurring as it does in Indo-European, Yukaghir, Turkic, and probably Chukotian.

68. Reduplication in the Verb 'Give'

In Indo-European partial reduplication involving the initial consonant is a common way of forming the stem of the present tense of the verb. One of the verbs in which this takes place in several branches of Indo-European is 'to give,' for example, Greek *didō-mi* 'I give,' Sanskrit *dadā-mi* 'I give,' and Russian *dadi-m* 'we give.' In both the Kolyma and Tundra dialects of Yukaghir, the stem of the verb 'to give' (restricted to third-person receivers) is *tadi.* There is virtually no evidence for Proto-Indo-European–Yukaghir contact, so an intimate borrowing of this sort is highly unlikely.

69. Accusative GI

In both Proto-Turkic and Proto-Mongolian the accusative marker was *-yi in stems ending in vowels, and *-iyi in those ending in consonants (Poppe 1955: 191). In the Old Turkish of the Orkhon inscriptions the final -i is lost so that the forms are -y and -iy. In Classical Mongolian we have -ji after vowels and -i after consonants, but -g survives in modern dialects such as Khalka, in which we find -īg after consonants and short vowels, and -g after long vowels and diphthongs. Old Mongolian had -gi. This accusative does not appear in Tungus, in which the old nominative and accusative have generally fallen together, nor does it appear, to my knowledge, elsewhere in Eurasiatic.

70. Reflexive M

Tungus and Mongolian agree in their reflexive markers, Proto-Mongolian *-βen and Proto-Tungus *mēn. These are compared by Doerfer (1985: 20), probably the leading figure among the group of scholars who deny the relationship of the Altaic languages, but even he admits that this item "gives the impression of genetic relationship." One might perhaps compare the Eskimo marker of reflexive possession for nouns in the relative form, -mi/-mi-k (singular/plural), but the m- here may rather be the singular relative case marker, which functions as a base for the oblique case.

71. Denominative LA

A denominative suffix -la is found in all three branches of Altaic (Tenishev 1984: 424). In Turkic it is found in every Turkic language for which we have data, and is highly productive since it can form verbs from any noun, for example, Turkish baš 'head,' baš-la-mak 'to begin,' av 'hunt,' av-la-mak 'to hunt.' With regard to Mongolian, Poppe (1955: 75) cites Mongolian, Monguor, Khalkha -la and Dagur -laa- with essentially the same functions as in Turkic. For Tungus,

Benzing (1955: 116) gives the form *lā* and states that it indicates that some action is carried out with the object in question. Furthermore, it is very frequent in all Tungus languages (e.g. Evenki *āpu(n)* 'cap,' *āpu-lā-* 'put a cap on the head'). In addition to these Altaic forms, the same suffix appears to be present in Uralic, for example, Ostyak *kät-* 'hand,' *kät-l-* 'seize.'

72. Dative A ~ E

In No. 26 a dative in *-ka* was described which is found in Turkic, Mongolian, and elsewhere. In Turkic there is an alternative nominal dative in *-a* that is found particularly in the Oguz or southwestern group that includes Turkish. Its antiquity in Turkic is guaranteed by the fact that virtually everywhere this *-a* is found in the pronoun (e.g. Turkish *ban-a* 'to me'), and with the personal possessive suffixes (e.g. Turkish *baba-m-a* 'to my father').

As Poppe (1964: 198) notes, in Mongolian a suffix *-a* is commonly used in preclassical literary texts (Old Mongolian), for example, *gajar-a* 'to the country,' more rarely in the classical and modern literary language. In the classical dative-locative case suffix *-ača* we have an obvious combination of this *-a* dative with the ablative *-ča* that is found in the preclassical language (Poppe 1964: 75). This *-a* suffix also survives in classical adverbs such as *mayu̧* 'bad,' *mayu̧-a* 'badly' (Poppe 1964: 57).

There are three possible cognates elsewhere in Eurasiatic, all of which I would consider rather doubtful. One is in Kamchadal, in which *kiste-n-k* 'in the house' contrasts with *kesta-n-ke* 'into the house.' However, the *-e* suffixed here for an allative-dative belongs to the "dominant" set in the Kamchadal vowel harmony system, as can be seen in its lowering effect in the form *kesta-n-ke* above, and therefore belongs to the *i ~ e* alternant set rather than to the *e ~ a* set, as would be expected if the hypothesis of the connection with Altaic *-a* were valid.

Another possible connection is with Indo-European. In Old Hittite a case commonly called the "directive" (Laroche 1970: 22–49), which was replaced later by the *-i* locative-dative, was used to indicate 'motion towards' with verbs such as 'come, go, return,' etc. It also occurs in some adverbs (e.g. *sara* 'upward'), as well as in the verbal noun in -*atar* from which it forms an infinitive in -*anna* (< *at-na*), for example, *akuwanna* 'to drink.' Luwian has a corresponding form in -*una*. The -*a* directive also occurs in Palaic and Lycian (Rosenkranz 1978: 54) and Laroche concludes that it is Proto-Anatolian. It does not occur in any other branch of Indo-European. Those who believe that Hittite is a separate branch of Indo-European coordinate with the remainder of the family (the "Indo-Hittite" hypothesis) will be more inclined to posit a Proto-Indo-European *-*a* directive case. If it is not to be accepted as Proto-Indo-European, then it is confined to Altaic. Finally, Ainu prefixes *e-* to verbs to indicate a sort of indirect object, e.g. *e-mik* 'to bark at.' This *e-* may, however, be the transitivizer discussed in No. 8.

Appendix

Ainu Vowel Alternations

The genetic position of the Ainu language has long been considered a great puzzle in comparative linguistics. Even the Nostraticists—perhaps because of the absence of the otherwise diagnostic first-person *m* and second-person *t/s*—have refrained from drawing any conclusions on this topic. As we saw in Chapter 1, the two chief theories have been a connection with Altaic, which in the present context would make it Eurasiatic (Miller, Patrie), or with Austric (Vovin, Bengtson), or perhaps a mixture (Murayama). The body of grammatical evidence adduced here, and, it may be added, the lexical evidence to be published in the second volume, are, I believe, decisive in relation to a northern Asiatic connection. In this regard, as noted earlier, dual *k(i)* and plural *t(i)* are themselves decisive since this pattern, recognized long ago by Rask for Uralic and Eskimo, is to my knowledge diagnostic. By a diagnostic resemblance one means not that it is found everywhere in Eurasiatic. After all, particular etymologies found in every branch of Indo-European are extremely rare. What is meant is that it is found *only* in Eurasiatic. It was such diagnostic, but not universal, etymologies that furnished the proof for Hrozný that Hittite was Indo-European.

The conclusions presented here are also in consonance with the genetic conclusions drawn virtually unanimously by experts in physical anthropology. Laughlin and Harper (1979: 6–7) note that "the Ainu of Japan fit comfortably into the Mongoloid-American Indian portion of humanity" and that this conclusion is firmly founded on many traits as well as definitive dentition. Luca Cavalli-Sforza et al. (1994: 232), in what is up to now the most complete study of gene frequencies in populations of the world, found that the Ainu are in most respects northern Mongoloids and are fairly closely related to all populations of Northeast Asia. In a tree of world populations the Ainu show shortest distances from Tungus, Japanese, and Korean. Furthermore, all dialects of Ainu have the word *kotan* 'town, village,' which must be a loanword from Mongolian. There may, of course, be others. This contact with Mongolian must have taken place west of the historically attested location of the Ainu in recent times. Likewise the striking resemblance between Ainu and Mongolian in the construction of *ki* 'make, do' plus an onomatopoeic root is quite possibly a linguistic contact phenomenon.

As noted in the discussion in Chapter 2 on vowel alternations, Gilyak exhibits the final stages of a vowel harmony system in which the surviving—and no longer systematically functioning—alternating pairs of phonemes appear in fossilized form as variants between dialects, or within the same dialect as free variants or semantically differentiated doublets. In the case of Gilyak we still have a partially functioning system whose former general existence in the language as a fully developed system is recognized by all specialists.

We saw in Chapter 2 that in the Amur dialect of Gilyak the third-person possessive nominal and object pronominal prefix *i-* ∼ *e-* still follows a vowel harmonic rule with *i-* before *i*, *y*, and *u*, and *e-* before *e*, *a*, and *o*, respectively. Furthermore, this system survives in some instances in the numeral classifier system. However, the vowel harmony system does not function elsewhere in Gilyak. What we do find is that where there was formerly a variation between pairs of vowels—one harmonizing with high vowels, one with low vowels in the rest of the word—we now find these pairs of vowels only surviving in a random manner as either interdialectal or intradialectal variants, sometimes with semantic differentiation. For a fuller account of the Gilyak situation see Chapter 2. Thus we find Amur *tyf*, Sakhalin *taf* 'house,' but Amur *park* and Sakhalin *pyrk* 'only.' In most instances, however, the two dialects agree. As an example of intradialectal variation with semantic specialization, we may cite Amur *vi-d'* 'to go, to walk,' *ve-d'* 'to run (of animals).'

The final stage of vowel harmonic systems, also illustrated in Chapter 2, is found in the Chinese dialects of Mongolian, in which no functional alternations remain, though sporadic variation within and between dialects survive along with occasional semantic differentiation. This final stage is exemplified in Ainu.

There is unanimous agreement that all dialects of Ainu have a system of five vowel phonemes: *a, e, i, o* and *u*. As will be exemplified copiously in this Appendix, these arrange themselves in a system very similar to that of Chukotian, Gilyak, and Korean, and they exhibit the types of alternation and occasional semantic differentiation just mentioned. The Ainu system of alternations—*i* ~ *e, e* ~ *a*, and *u* ~ *o*—is shown in Table 8.

Table 8. The Ainu Vowel System

High	i	e	u
Low	e	a	o

In Vovin's (1993) important monograph on Ainu he recognizes the existence of an *i* ~ *e* alternation in the specific instance of the third-person object and nominal possessive prefix, and notes its coincidence in both sound and meaning with the same alternation in Gilyak. He is not aware, however, of its widespread occurence in the Eurasiatic family, as documented in Chapter 3 (No. 8). Although this alternation occurs in a number of other etymologies cited in his book (e.g. *sita* ~ *seta* 'dog'), these are nowhere discussed or accounted for. As for the *e* ~ *a* alternation, he ignores it entirely, probably because it is relatively infrequent and its most conspicuous examples are grammatical (e.g. causative *-ke* ~ *-ka* [after consonant stems]) and Vovin does not consider grammar in his book. He does note a number of *u* ~ *o* alternations, but to account for them he posits a separate phoneme with irregular reflexes. A fuller discussion will be given in the section on that alternation below.

In the following sections the alternations *e* ~ *a, i* ~ *e,* and *u* ~ *o* are discussed in that order with numerous examples. However, before dealing with these alternations a brief discussion of two related topics is in order, the first on the phonetics of the Ainu vowel system and the second on our sources for Ainu and how they are used here.

The Phonetics of the Ainu Vowel System

Phonetic descriptions of the Ainu vowel system are infrequent. The five Ainu vowels are sometimes described as basically identical with the corresponding vowels of Japanese and, of course, this may be at least partly due to the influence of Japanese bilingualism, which was prevalent in the final stages of this now presumably extinct language. The chief reason for the following discussion is that in the case of the frequent $u \sim o$ alternation there is mention in some sources that Japanese observers had difficulty in distinguishing u and o. Both are frequently described as unrounded, or with weak lip rounding, in Ainu. Japanese u is usually unrounded, but o is not. Hence Japanese speakers tend to identify Ainu o with their u because of the unrounding or weak rounding of Japanese u.

From the relatively few phonetic descriptions of Ainu I have chosen several that represent dialects that are genetically and geographically about as distant as one can find within Ainu. The first is a dissertation based mainly on a dialect of southern Hokkaido (Simeon 1968). The second (Piłsudski 1912) derives from the author's fieldwork in southeastern Sakhalin. A third is Murasaki's grammar of Sakhalin Ainu (1978).

George Simeon was a linguistically well-trained American and he states unequivocally for the three Hokkaido dialects he studied that they use five determinate vowels, a, o, e, u, and i (1968: 13). Murasaki, whose description is based on the Raychishka dialect of Sakhalin, describes i, e, and a as identical with the corresponding Japanese vowels. Ainu o is a little more front and narrow than Japanese o and Ainu u is slightly more rounded and front than Japanese u.

Piłsudski's description is similar to that of Simeon, but does not mention unrounding of u. Asai (1974), a Japanese linguist, does mention the difficulty of distinguishing u and o. However, we have abundant materials from Russian, Polish, Danish (Refsing), American, and other non-Japanese sources. Moreover, our major source for Ainu dialect forms, the Ainu dialect dictionary edited by Shirō

Hattori (1964), was overseen by an accomplished Japanese linguist and the recordings in this dictionary have been unanimously praised. There is, moreover, consistency between these recordings and those from other sources. Recent Japanese work has also been carried out by linguistically well-trained observers such as Asai and Tamura. There is agreement among these various sources regarding the existence of certain Ainu words with *u* in recordings from whatever source, and others that always have *o*.

A remarkable instance that gives us confidence in this respect is that Dobrotvorskij (1875), who worked in Sakhalin in the nineteenth century, states that *aynu* 'person' takes the form *ayno* in the vocative (a unique instance of this as a separate grammatical category in Ainu). In Hattori's dialect dictionary (which has no accompanying grammar), although the ordinary word for 'person, man' is *aynu* and is found in all of the dialects he recorded, there is a clearly exclamatory vocative form *ayno ayno* (334: 13) in the Yakumo dialect, spoken in the extreme southwest of Hokkaido, that is translated as 'hey!' in 'hey, excuse me' (literally, 'man! man!'). This coincidence in perhaps the genetically and geographically most distant Ainu dialects can hardly be accidental. Moreover, this is just one more indication of the remarkable accuracy of Dobrotvorskij's observations on Sakhalin Ainu. Finally, it is possible to find minimal pairs such as *mem* 'lake, spring,' *mim* 'meat of fish'; *ko* 'meal, flour,' *ku* 'drink' (Sakhalin *koo* and *kuu* reflecting Proto-Ainu long vowels); and *kem* 'blood,' *kam* 'flesh, meat.'

Sources on the Ainu Language

Map 3 provides a key to the identification of the dialects cited and their geographical location. The two basic sources for the information in this map are the glottochronological study of 19 dialects by Hattori and Chiri (1960) and the Ainu dialect dictionary of Hattori (1964). This latter work contains the fullest documentation that we possess on Ainu dialects, but uses just nine of the 19 dialects found in the former source and only the ninth dialect (Raychishka) was spoken on Sakhalin. As a tenth source, in order to include the Kurile Islands, Hattori used the word lists in Ryûzô Torii's ethnological study of 1903. In the word lists in this Appendix, citations

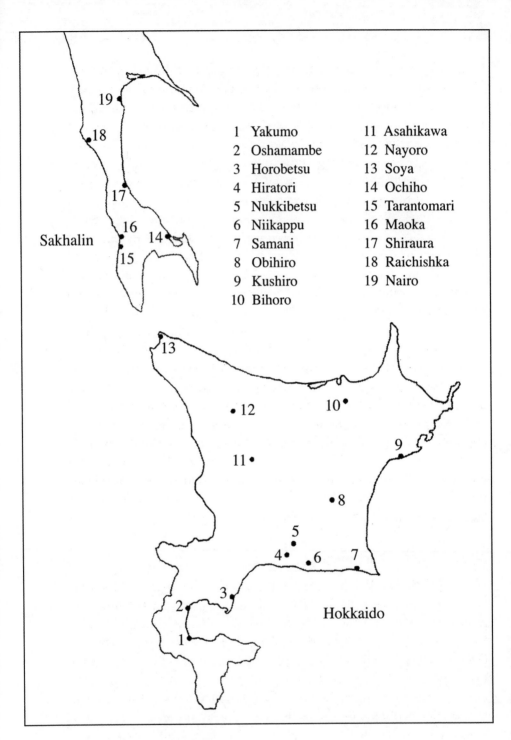

1 Yakumo
2 Oshamambe
3 Horobetsu
4 Hiratori
5 Nukkibetsu
6 Niikappu
7 Samani
8 Obihiro
9 Kushiro
10 Bihoro

11 Asahikawa
12 Nayoro
13 Soya
14 Ochiho
15 Tarantomari
16 Maoka
17 Shiraura
18 Raichishka
19 Nairo

Sakhalin

Hokkaido

Map 3. Ainu Dialects

from Hattori-Chiri follow the numbering of the dialects in Map 3 as follows: 1. Yakumo, 2. Oshamambe, 3. Horobetsu, 4. Hiratori (also called Saru), 5. Nukkibetsu, 6. Niikappu, 7. Samani, 8. Obihiro, 9. Kushiro, 10. Bihoro, 11. Asahikawa, 12. Nayoro, 13. Soya, 14. Ochiho, 15. Tarantomari, 16. Maoka, 17. Shiraura, 18. Raychishka, 19. Nairo. In citing Hattori I use his numbering 1–10, as found in his dialect dictionary.

The names of these dialects, with their numerical equivalents in Hattori-Chiri, are as follows: 1. Yakumo (HC 1), 2. Horobetsu (HC 3), 3. Saru (HC 4), 4. Asahikawa (HC 11), 5. Obihiro (HC 8), 6. Bihoro (HC 10), 7. Nayoro (HC 12), 8. Soya (HC 13), 9. Raychishka (HC 18), 10. Northern Kuriles (not in Hattori-Chiri).

The most detailed study of the classification of Ainu dialects is found in Asai (1974), where the basic division is between those of Sakhalin and the remainder. This latter grouping is in turn divided into those of Hokkaido, the northernmost of the main Japanese islands, and those of the Kuriles. All our data on the Kuriles come from the northernmost islands close to Kamchatka. In all probability the southwestern part of Kamchatka was occupied by Ainu speakers in the eighteenth century. A subclassification of Hokkaido dialects, and those of Sakhalin, is also found in Asai (1974: 49), who suggests that Sakhalin dialects can be divided into South-Western and North-Eastern, and Hokkaido into South-Western and North-Eastern, with each of the latter subdivided into South and West, and East and North, respectively.

Our sources can thus be divided into those from three major areas: Hokkaido, the Kuriles, and Sakhalin, to be discussed in that order. As noted above, our major source for Hokkaido is Hattori's dialect dictionary, eight of whose dialects are from Hokkaido. Next comes the glottochronological list of Hattori-Chiri, which also includes a number of Sakhalin dialects. Additional modern sources include Refsing (1986), based on her doctoral dissertation concerning the Shizunai dialect of southern Hokkaido, and Simeon's doctoral dissertation (1968) and a series of articles based on it. Simeon worked on three very similar dialects of southern Hokkaido, namely, Horobetsu, Hiratori, and Higashi Shizunai (closest to Niikappu). Even among these three closely related dialects, he noted two forms for 'dog,' *sita* and *seta*, in different dialects.

The most important source for Hokkaido, after Hattori's dialect dictionary, is the dictionary of Batchelor (1905), a British missionary who worked in southern Hokkaido. He gives numerous variant forms, but without stating their location. His work has been vigorously criticized by some modern Japanese scholars. However, Simeon (1968: 3) interviewed several Ainu who had been Batchelor's informants and found Batchelor's data to be accurate. There are a fair number of entries in Batchelor that are not in Hattori's dictionary, but which reappear in Sakhalin and/or the Kuriles, thus attesting to their genuineness.

In addition to the dialects in Hattori, the Hattori-Chiri glottochronological list contains forms from some Hokkaido dialects not found in Hattori's dictionary. These are, unfortunately, items confined to the 200+ items on the glottochronological list. Among earlier sources for Hokkaido is Summers (1886), which consists mainly of items from the Saru dialect, with additional entries from other sources.

By far the most interesting and important pre-modern source, however, is a Japanese one, the *Ezo hōgen moshiogusa* (i.e. Yezo [modern name Hokkaido] dialect miscellany), by Uehara Kumajirō. This work contains numerous dialect variants, but their provenience is not stated. I used the modern reprinting with introduction by Kyōsuke Kindaichi (1972). The Ainu words are rendered in the Japanese kana syllabary. From the accompanying map, which contains place names from western Hokkaido for which there are no modern sources as well as several small islands off the western coast of Hokkaido, it is clear that a very large area was investigated. Dialect variants not found in other sources reappear in Sakhalin or the Kuriles and are thus very likely to be genuine. Although I am inclined to trust these recordings—simply because of their large number—citations from the *Moshiogusa* have not been included in this Appendix if they are not contained in any other source. The most important modern sources are Simeon's dissertation, noted above, and Refsing (1986), based on the Shizunai dialect. A final source, Asai (1974), contains material on the Chitose dialect.

In addition to the materials on the Raychishka dialect in Hattori, and those of the glottochronological list in Hattori-Chiri covering other dialects from Sakhalin, there are two major sources on

Sakhalin Ainu. One of these is Dobrotvorskij (1875), a Russian doctor who lived four years in Sakhalin and not only collected an extensive vocabulary of his own, but also collated virtually all earlier sources on the Ainu language. Unfortunately he did not give the provenience of the specific Sakhalin dialect variants contained in his work. The other major source is the folkloristic and personal narrative texts in Piłsudski (1912), who gives the name of the informant and the location in Sakhalin where each text was collected. His work is further enhanced by the fact that a Polish couple (Majewicz and Majewicz 1983–85) compiled a complete index of the linguistic forms contained in Piłsudski's texts.

Unfortunately there is no modern professional linguistic study of the dialect or dialects of the Kurile Islands. Our most recent material is contained in the ethnographic study of Torii (1903), whose word list is, as noted earlier, reproduced in Hattori. The earliest material is that of Krasheninnikov (1972, originally published in 1755–56); the most extensive is that of Dybowski, collected in 1879–83 and edited by Radliński (1891–94). His vocabularies include one from Shumshu Island in the northern Kuriles, very close to Kamchatka. Asai (1974) published the vocabulary of Pinart, which was collected in Alaska about 1872 from an Aleut who had learned the dialect of the Paramushir and Limushir Islands, also close to Kamchatka. The original was Russian–Ainu, but Asai published an English version in which the vocabularies were rearranged alphabetically according to the Latin alphabet. In addition, Vovin appended to his work on the reconstruction of Proto-Ainu (1993) a vocabulary of Voznesenskij on Kurile Ainu (dialect not specified) that could not have been collected later than 1843. A most useful work in Japanese is Murayama's *Kita chishima ainugo,* that is, "The Ainu language of the Kurile Islands," which reproduces the earlier sources in the original languages and translates the material into Japanese, adding valuable comments.

The *e* ∼ *a* Alternation

I will now list and discuss examples of the *e* ∼ *a*, *i* ∼ *e*, and *u* ∼ *o* alternations in that order. In regard to each, variants in grammatical elements will be considered first, followed by the lexical evidence.

The most conspicuous grammatical example of the *e* ∼ *a* alternation is the causative -ke ~ -ka, which is suffixed to verb stems ending in a consonant. The choice between these is quite arbitrary and normally lexically determined. For example, in Hattori (243: 58) we have *san* 'to exit, go out' in dialects 1, 2, and 9, whereas we find *san-ke* 'put it out, take it out' in all dialects (243: 59). However, corresponding to *mom* 'to float away' is *mom-ka* 'to set it floating away' in dialects 1, 3–6, and 9 (142: 94). Nowhere do we find either **san-ka* or **mom-ke*. This is the usual situation. However, examples of interdialectal variation between -ke and -ka are found. For example, we find *een-ke* 'to shave it, whittle it' in dialects 1–4, 6 and 7, but *een-ka* in dialect 5, and in dialect 1, in addition to *een-ke*, we also find *een-ka* with the Japanese gloss *togorasu* 'to sharpen,' entered with a query (137: 61). If valid it shows a semantic differentiation in this instance between -ke and -ka.

Another example is *res-ka* ~ *res-ke* 'to raise or keep animals'; the first form is found in dialects 1–8 and the latter in dialect 9 (Ray-chishka in Sakhalin) (21: 184). This same word is found elsewhere in Hattori (28: 3) with the gloss 'to bring up, rear,' with *res-ka* in dialects 5–8 and *res-ke* in 9. The form *res-ke* 'brought up' is also found in Batchelor (Hokkaido), and Dobrotvorskij reports *(t)reske* in Sakhalin. The variant *res-ke* is also found in Piłsudski's Sakhalin texts in several instances. Once again the reality of a variant form in Batchelor is supported by data from Sakhalin with which he could not have been acquainted.

An interesting case of intradialectal variation occurs in Tamura's extremely detailed description of the Saru dialect where, as reported in Dettmer (1989: 606), both *sat-ke* and *sat-ka* are found. These data (and much more could be cited) are enough to show that the alternation -ke ~ -ka existed in Proto-Ainu, with -ka in certain words and -ke in others, but with alternative forms in -ka or -ke in a few instances in the same word.

Another grammatical morpheme with the *e* ~ *a* alternation is the general Eurasiatic locative -te ~ -ta, discussed in Chapter 3 (No. 32). In Hattori's work, which is not a grammar, oblique forms rarely occur, but Patrie (1982: 102) cites the general Ainu variation -te ~ -ta in the locative.

A third grammatical suffix, -ne ~ -na (No. 42 in Chapter 3), corresponds to the past passive participle of Indo-European and related forms in other languages. Examples from Batchelor, cited by Naert (1958: 102), include *mak-na* 'opened up' as against *taku-ne* 'agglomerated'; and the variants *kun-ne* ∼ *kun-na* 'black' (< **kur-ne* ∼ **kur-na*). Hattori (252: 55) has the sentence *sir kunne* 'it gets dark,' in which *sir* means 'the world,' but he also reports *kunna-no* 'early' (253: 60, dialect 6), in which -*no* is the usual Ainu adverbial suffix.

The following are lexical items that exhibit an -*e* ∼ -*a* alternation.

1. Bald (be).   Hattori (2: 5) reports two forms, *kap-ke* and *kep-ne*. Both -*ke* and -*ne* are well attested derivational suffixes. Dialect 1 has *kap-ke*, *ekep-ne*; 2 has *kap-ke* and *kep-ne*; and 4, 6, and 7 have *kep-ne* only. For 'bald head' (2: 6) dialect 6 has *kep-sapa*, in which -*sapa* is a widespread Ainu word for 'head' (cf. American English 'skin-head'). Without the suffix -*ke*, *kap* is the common Ainu word for 'skin, fur' (180: 9); it appears in Sakhalin as *kah*, with the usual syllable-final change of *p*, *t*, *k* > *h*, and is also found elsewhere in Eurasiatic (e.g. Proto-Uralic **kopa* 'skin, bark' and Japanese *kapa* 'bark'). Also of interest in Hattori (89: 34) is *tontone kap* 'processed leather' in dialect 1. Batchelor has *kep* 'skin,' *kep* 'to peel, to bark,' and *kepuru* 'bare, hairless as leather.'

2. Fox.   Hattori (186: 47) gives *sumari* for dialects 3, 7, 8, and 9. Piłsudski has *sumar* and *sumari* and other sources also have -*a*- in the second syllable, sometimes, as in the *Moshiogusa,* with the *e* ∼ *i* alternation in the last syllable, e.g. *sumare.* However, Langsdorff (1812), who published a number of word lists from different Ainu regions, reported *sumeri* in Hokkaido and southern Sakhalin.

3. Joint of the body.   Hattori (20: 169) gives *ikre* for dialect 3 and *ikra* for 4, 5, and 6. This word also occurs in 'knuckle' in the compound *tek-ikre* 'hand joint' (dialect 3). These forms agree with the simplex 'joint,' but in addition dialect 7 has *tek-ikre*. Batchelor has *ikra* and *ikura*. This word is apparently not found in Sakhalin or the Kuriles. Summers (1886) reported the Saru form *ikke* 'a joint,' with assimilation of -*r*. Thus forms in both final -*e* and -*a* are well attested in Hokkaido.

4. Light (be), thin. Hattori (290: 17) gives both *pan* and *pene* in dialects 1 and 3, and *pene* 'to be brittle' in dialect 7 (292: 30). Batchelor records *pan* 'weak, flavorless' as in *pan wakka* 'fresh water' and *pene* 'watery.' This last form is doubtless to be analyzed as *pe-* 'water' + *-ne* (adjective formant), but as seen above Hattori has *pene* 'light, thin' and in dialect 6 he gives *pene* '(fish or meat) is rotten' (97: 53). Possibly *pene* ~ *pan* 'weak' is homonymous with *pe-ne* 'watery' (see No. 8 below).

5. Like, similar. Batchelor has *sem* 'like, the same,' which may be compared with his *sam-pa* 'side' and *sama-ta* (with locative *-ta*) 'by the side of, again, besides this.' The same variation is reported in Sakhalin by Piłsudski: *sem* 'like, alike,' *sama-ke-ta* 'side of, near,' and *sam-pa-ta* 'at the side of.' In his dialect dictionary Hattori lists *sam* 'near by, close to' in dialects 1–3 and 5–8. Summer's Saru dialect form *sama-ta* 'also, again' is clearly the same word as Batchelor's *sama-ta* and shares with it the meaning 'again.'

6. On, above. We begin here with the term for 'shin,' which in some dialects is a compound consisting of *nisap* and *mekka* ~ *makka* (Hattori 17: 140). Vovin reconstructs Proto-Ainu *nisap 'shin.' However, it appears that *nisap* simply means 'knee' and *mekka* ~ *makka* means 'above, on.' For 'shin' we find in dialects 5 and 6 *nisapmakka*, but in dialect 8 we have *kemamekkaske*, in which *kema* is the common Ainu word for 'foot.' In addition we find *mekka* 'on, above' in dialect 3 (239: 39). It would seem that *mekka* ~ *makka* 'above' shares the same initial element as the verbs *makam, makan, maka-pan, maka-pam* 'go up, come up' encountered in Piłsudski's Sakhalin texts.

7. Shoulder blade, scapula. In Hattori (10: 80) we find *tapera* in dialects 1, 4–7, and 9, but *tapere* in dialect 3. Batchelor gives *tapere* and *tapera* as variant forms, whereas Dobrotvorskij gives *tapera pone* in his Sakhalin recordings, in which *pone* (~ *poni*) is the common Ainu word for 'bone.'

8. Up-river (vs. down-river). In what is probably a homonym to No. 4, we find a contrast between *pena* 'up-river' (216: 28) and *pana* 'down-river' (216: 29), e.g. *pena* and *pana* respectively in the Yakumo dialect. This opposition reappears in Murasaki's material on Sakhalin Ainu (1978: 37) in the forms *pen-ke* 'upstream,' *pan-*

ke 'downstream.' Here *-ke* is a locative suffix. These forms possibly exemplify the sound symbolism discussed in Chapter 2, with *pen-* 'weak, small amount of water upstream' vs. *pan-* 'strong, large amount of water downstream.'

9. Woman. In addition to the common Ainu word *mat* 'woman,' we find *met-ke* 'aunt' in Torii's transcriptions from the Kurile Islands (cited in Hattori [43: 43]). The genuineness of this form is supported by an early citation of *met-ke* 'grandmother' in Klaproth's *Asia Polyglotta* (1823), also from the Kuriles. The original transcription was *mätkäh*.

The *i* ~ *e* Alternation

We turn now to the *i* ~ *e* alternation. We saw earlier that Vovin admits the existence of variants *i* and *e* for the third-person possessive pronoun and the third-person verbal object; he also recognizes its identity with the Gilyak vowel harmony variants *i* ~ *e* with the same meaning. There are, however, additional alternations of this type in Ainu in other grammatical formatives, as well as in a considerable number of lexical items. These will be outlined below.

The verbal suffix *-ke* varies with *-ki* in certain instances. According to Refsing (1986: 188), the verbal suffix *-ke* is used with a small number of verbs expressing violent activity in order to express intransitivity. Among the examples she gives from the Shizunai dialect of Hokkaido are *rewe* 'to bend' (transitive), alongside *rew-ke* 'to bend (intransitive), be bent'; and *pere* 'to split, break,' but *per-ke* 'to break (intransitive), be broken.' However, in other instances *-ke* is fairly frequent, varies with *-ki,* and is transitive. It appears to be distinct from the causative *-ka* ~ *-ke,* but because both are transitivizers and have very broad and frequently specialized meanings, it is often difficult to assign *-ke* to one or the other. In a few instances, naturally enough, this gives rise to a triple alternation *-ka* ~ *-ke* ~ *-ki.* The occurrences of the *-ke* ~ *-ki* alternation are given as individual items in the following list.

Another grammatical morpheme involving this alternation is the prohibitive 'don't!' In Hattori, it appears both in 'don't!' (327: 56) and the sentence 'No! no!, don't do that' (334: 12), where it takes the form *itekke* in dialects 1, 3, 4, and 7; *itek* in 2; *iteki* in 3 and 7; and *ečiki* in 6. The initial *i-* or *e-* in these forms is the third-person object 'it,' and in *ečiki* the change **t > č* before *i* is automatic. The sequence **ti* does not occur in Ainu.

The following is a list of Ainu lexical items that show inter-dialectal variation between *e* and *i*. The numbering follows that of the preceding section on the *e* ~ *a* alternation.

10. Attack (verb). Hattori (51: 14) records *ko-čoraw-ki* in dialect 1, *čoraw-ki* in 6, but *čioraw-ke* in 5 and *čoraw-ke* in 7.

11. Bad. The term for 'bad' is *wen* in all 10 of Hattori's dialects and it is the same for Piłsudski's texts from various dialects in Sakhalin. However, two sources give *win* for the Kuriles. One is Krasheninnikov, with *win kamui* 'the devil' (i.e. 'bad spirit'), and the other is the expression for 'rain' found in Torii, *siri-win* (literally, 'weather [is] bad').

12. Bark (verb). Vovin reconstructs **mE=k* ~ *mi=k* for this word, without mentioning the vowel variation or attempting to explain it. This stem is found in Hattori (183: 2) under the meaning 'cry, sing.' In dialects 1–3 we have *mik*; in 4–8, *mek*; and for 9 (Raychishka in Sakhalin), *mek* ~ *meh*. Simeon (1968: 18) agrees with southwestern Hokkaido *mik*. The variant *meh* (< **mek*) for Sakhalin is confirmed by *mex* in Piłsudski's texts and by Dobrotvorskij's *mex* and *e-mex*, all meaning 'to bark.' Dybowski reports *mek* for the Shumshu dialect (northern Kuriles), but Voznesenski, in material also from the northern Kuriles, but quite possibly from a different island, gives *mik-va* 'barks.'

13. Bone. In Hattori (8: 58, 13: 106, 20: 167) we find *poni* ~ *pone*, either as the simplex 'bone' or in compounds such as 'cheek bone.' In these entries all of the Hokkaido dialects (1–8) have *pone*, but the Raychishka dialect of Sakhalin has *poni*. In the other Sakhalin dialects reported in Hattori-Chiri *poni* likewise occurs, as well as in Dobrotvorskij. It is also found in Dybowski's material from Shumshu Island in the northern Kuriles.

14. Born (be). Vovin (1993: 88) reconstructs **gik* ~ **gek*, with initial **g* for forms with initial *s* or *h*. Hattori (28: 1) has *hekatu* 'to be born' in dialects 1 and 2, *siko* in 6–8, and *sikah* in 9. Batchelor has, as usual, the southern Hokkaido form, in this case *hekatu*, as does Simeon (1968: 33). Dobrotvorskij's form, *sikax* '(to) grow, grow up,' is clearly the equivalent of Hattori's Raychishka form from Sakhalin, as is Piłsudski's *sikax* 'be born, emerge, appear.' This word appears in the form *higatsi* 'child' in Klaproth's Sakhalin vocabulary.

15. Bridge. This word exhibits the common Ainu metathesis *iw* > *uy* in which the forms in *-iw* alternate with those in *-ew*. In Hattori (67: 25) dialects 1–3 and 5 have *ruyka*, 9 (Sakhalin) has *riwka*, and 8, *rewka*. Dobrotvorskij, as would be expected, agrees with the Sakhalin form (*triuka* ~ *riuka*), as does Piłsudski (*riuka*). Batchelor reports *ruika* for southern Hokkaido.

16. Butterfly. Hattori (192: 98) gives *marewrew* in dialects 3–7, but *kata riwriw* in dialect 8.

17. Cold. This root shows variation between suffixal *-ke* and *-ki*. In addition to the material from Hattori's dictionary, there is also the glottochronological list of Hattori-Chiri, containing a number of additional Sakhalin dialects. In Hattori (225: 94) dialects 1–3 and 6–8 have *meray-ke*, 9 (Raychishka) has *meray-ki*, and 10 (Kuriles), *meray-kiri*. In Hattori-Chiri (No. 94), the Sakhalin dialect Shiraura has *meeray-ki*, whereas the other Sakhalin dialects (Ochiho, Tarantomari, and Maoka) have *meeray-ke*. The word is not found in Piłsudski's Sakhalin texts; Dobrotvorskij records *meray-ki* 'to freeze.'

18. Count (verb). Here, as in the preceding entry, we find variation between suffixed *-ke* and *-ki*. Hattori (260: 1) records *pis-ki* in dialects 1–4 and 6, but *pis-ke* in 5 and 7–9. Summers' Saru dialect likewise has *pis-ke*, rather than the *pis-ki* we would be expect from Hiratori's *pis-ki* (dialect 3 in Hattori). The *Moshiogusa* has *pis-ki*. Two other sources from Sakhalin, Dobrotvorskij and Piłsudski, report *pis-ke*, in accord with Hattori's Raychishka dialect. In the northern Kuriles, Torii has *ipisiks* and thus gives no evidence regarding the vowel following *k*.

19. Dangle. This is another verb with the *-ke* ~ *-ki* suffix, followed by the transitive-causative suffix *-re*. All of the dialects in Hattori's entry 'to dangle (it)' have -*ki*, but dialect 3, in addition to *rat-ki-re*, also has *rat-ke-re*.

20. Dog. Hattori (186: 45) has *seta* in dialects 1–3 and 6–9, but *sita* in 4 and 5. Torii (Hattori, No. 10) reports both *seta* and *sita* in the northern Kuriles. That mishearing is unlikely to be involved is shown by the fact that Torii transcribes *shita* with non-phonemic palatalization that is absent in *seta*. Batchelor, as is generally the case, has the southern Hokkaido variant *seta*. Simeon (1968: 14), who worked on three neighboring dialects in southern Hokkaido, also gives *seta* for Hiratori (another name for Saru), for which Hattori has *sita*, thus showing intradialectal variation. Additional Hokkaido dialects with *sita* are found in Hattori-Chiri (No. 21), namely, Samani and Kushiro. Dobrotvorskij's Sakhalin form *seta* agrees with Hattori's dialect 9 from Raychishka in Sakhalin. The *Moshiogusa* once more shows its reliability in giving both Hokkaido variants, *seta* and *sita*.

21. Eat. The most common word for 'to eat' is *e* or *i-pe*. It is clear that *i-pe* is a denominalized verb form from *i-pe* 'food,' which contains the common nominalizer *pe* 'thing.' The nominal meaning is shown in Hattori (184: 34) in the word for 'bait, food,' where we find *epi* in dialect 1, *ep* in 3–5 and 7, *epi-hi* (the "possessing form") in 6, and *ipe* in 9 (Kuriles). Thus we find the *e* ~ *i* alternation in both *e* ~ *i* 'to eat' and *pe* ~ *pi* 'thing.' A further bit of evidence for *e* 'to eat' is found in the word for 'rice,' given in a sentence in Hattori (152: 17), in which dialect 2 has *a-e-p* as against the usual word for 'food,' *i-pe*, in dialect 1. Likewise Summers gives *e-pi* 'to eat' for the Saru (Hiratori) dialect, alongside of the more usual form *i-pe*, as a variant in the same dialect.

22. Fat, butter. For 'oil (as food)' Hattori (93: 11) gives *ke* in dialects 7 and 8, *kee* in 9 (Sakhalin), and *čep-ke* 'fish oil' in 10 (Kuriles). However, a variant *ki* occurs in Langsdorff's southern Sakhalin list (*kiie*), where the Sakhalin long vowel in monosyllables corresponds regularly to short vowels elsewhere. The existence of a *ki* variant in Sakhalin is confirmed in Piłsudski's Sakhalin texts (*ki* 'fat'). However, in a text from Tarajka (Bay of Patience) *ke* is found.

23. Finger, hand, five. A semantic differentiation occurs here. We find *aske* 'hand' in dialect 2, *aske-pet* 'finger' in dialects 3–8, the metathesized form *aspeket* in dialect 2, and *asikipit* in dialect 10 (Kuriles; Hattori 11: 82). For 'five' Vovin (1993: 81) reconstructs **aski* and **asik* 'five,' "possibly related to **askE* 'hand.'" *E* is Vovin's symbol for a protophoneme that gives *e* in all the dialects. Dybowski's form from the Kuriles, *askipit* 'finger,' is basically similar to *asikipit* of Torii, cited above.

24. Fire. Hattori has *ape* in all dialects except the Kuriles. In Torii's material from that area we find *api* and *apoi*. The same source also has *apoi* 'fireplace.' Batchelor notes that *ape* 'fire' is sometimes pronounced *api*. Krasheninnikov and Dybowski both give *api* for the Kuriles. Vovin reconstructs **apE* as possibly derived from *apOy*. However, this does not account for the form *api*. This word clearly presents phonological problems.

25. Flick it (to), flip it. Here Hattori (134: 41) has various forms with prefixes and suffixes, but the stem is clearly *pit* in dialects 1, 2, 4, 6, 7, and 9, but *pet* in dialect 5. The only instance of an entry in other sources that could be found was (possibly) Batchelor's *pit-ke* 'be subject to fits.'

26. Fondle, pet, love. In this case the alternation is between *-ke* and *-ki*, a morpheme to which it is difficult to assign a specific meaning. In Hattori (72: 19) dialect 4 shows *ekatarotke* and dialect 7, *ekatay-rotke*, but dialect 6 has *ekataratki*. This is evidently the same word as Batchelor's *ekataiirotke* 'to like, be fond of, love.'

27. Foot. For 'foot' Hattori (17: 144) has either *ure* or *para-ure*, the latter more properly 'instep' (cf. *para* 'broad' and *para-tek* 'hand' vs. *tek* 'hand, arm'). In dialects 1–8 one or both of these is recorded. In Hattori-Chiri we find *para-uri* 'foot' in the Ochiho dialect of Sakhalin.

28. Footwear. Hattori (87: 19) reports *ker* for dialects 1–7, but *kiro* in 8 and 9. This word evidently has the same stem as Batchelor's *kero-p*, in which *-p* is the common Ainu nominalizer deriving from *pe* 'thing.' Simeon has *ker* (1968: 18). The Sakhalin form *kiro* 'shoes' is also found in Piłsudski's texts and his *kere* 'leg' may belong here and would thus show the existence of both *ker-* and *kir-* on Sakhalin. Summers has forms with both *e* and *i* from different dialects on Hokkaido, *keri* 'Ainu snow shoes' in Usu, but *kiro* 'leather shoes' in Saru. The only instance from the Kuriles I have noted is Krasheninnikov's *kir*.

29. For some time. Hattori (257: 88) here has *setakko* for dialect 3, but *sitakkaneko* for dialect 4. The *Moshiogusa* shows the same variants, *setakko* and *sitakko*. Batchelor also has *setakko* with the meaning 'for a long time.' This form is apparently confined to a limited area in southern Hokkaido.

30. Forehead. In Hattori (3: 9) we find *kiputur* in dialects 1–4, 6, and 7, but *keputur* in 5. Batchelor has *keputuru*. Klaproth's Kamchatka word list has *kiputur*, as does Dybowski from the northern Kuriles (Shumshu). This word is apparently not found in Sakhalin.

31. Gather. A stem with the fundamental meaning 'gathering together' or 'both,' when accompanied by 'hand, foot,' or 'side,' takes the form *ekare* ~ *ekari*. The basic data are to be found in the following entries in Hattori: 'gather' (70: 2), 'flock together' (183: 27), 'get cloudy' (i.e. 'clouds gather together'), 'assemble' (234: 6), 'both sides' (236: 23), 'both hands' (268: 90), and 'both legs' (268: 9). In all of these examples the part that means 'gather, associate, both' is *ekare* or *ekari*. The former is found consistently in dialects 1, 6, and 7, and the latter in 2 and 8.

32. Glare at. Hattori (3: 16) reports *ker* in dialects 1, 3, 4, and 6, but *kir* in dialect 3. This verb is usually preceded by *sik* 'eye' and may be further preceded by *ko-* 'to, toward.'

33. Gnaw. This was only found in Batchelor, with two variants: *kere-kere* and *keri-keri*.

34. Good for (to be too), be regrettable. The only examples found were in Hattori (168: 48), with *čikari* in dialects 3 and 4, and *čikare* in 8.

35. Gray. The word often has the nominal meaning 'instrument for hunting whales.' Are these homonyms? At any rate, Dobrotvorskij recorded *mare* and *mari* on Sakhalin, with both meanings. In Hattori (282: 5) we find *maare* 'gray' in the Raychishka dialect of Sakhalin. Batchelor's dictionary gives *marek* 'a hook used in spearing fish.'

36. Hit. In this term we have variation in the suffix -*ki* ~ -*ke*. Hattori (72: 18) has *sitay-ke* only in Soya in extreme northwestern Hokkaido, a dialect that often resembles those of nearby Sakhalin. In the Hattori-Chiri glottochronological list, in addition to Soya, we find *sitay-ke* in Ochiho, Tarantomari, and Maoka. However, in the northernmost dialect (Nairo) they report *sitay-ki*. The form with final -*i* is also found in Piłsudski, who worked in eastern Sakhalin including probably Nairo in the northeast. Batchelor, who usually agrees with southern Hokkaido, here has *sitay-ki*.

37. Hot (water). The entry 'hot water' is found in Hattori (95: 27), sometimes as a phrase whose second member is *wakka* 'water.' For 'hot water' we find *sesekka* or the like in dialects 1, 5, 8, and 9. However, for the northern Kuriles, Torii has *sesiki-pe*, in which -*pe* is an alternative word for 'water.' The *Moshiogusa* gives *seseku* ~ *sesika* for 'to heat water' and Batchelor has *asesekka* 'to heat, make hot' and *aseika* 'to steep in hot water, scald.' We see then that the common alternation is *sesek* ~ *sesik*. Initial *se*- may be a reduplicative syllable that is absent in Batchelor's form, *aseika*.

38. Hot (to be), boil, warm (of weather). The Ainu form *pop-ke* is found in all the Hokkaido dialects, usually preceded by the word *sir* 'world, atmosphere, weather.' In dialect 1 *pop-ke* can occur without *sir* with regard to a person feeling warm. In the Kuriles, however, Torii records *siripoki*. Elsewhere, however, the root *pop*, which shows no alternation, may occur without the suffix -*ke* ~ -*ki*, e.g. in the *Moshiogusa siri pop* 'heat of the sea.' The same root, with a different causative suffix, is found in Dybowski, *pop-ti* 'bring to a boil,' but Hattori (97: 48) gives *pop-te* for dialects 1–3, 6, and 7, and *poh-te* for 9.

39. Important, valuable, heavy (to be). Hattori (293: 39) gives two entries for what in most dialects is the same root, *pasi* ~ *pase*. For 'important, valuable' (293: 39) we find *pasi* in dialect 1 and *pase* in dialect 2. For 'heavy' (272: 14) there is *pase* in all eight Hokkaido dialects and *paase* in Raychishka (Sakhalin). Thus dialect 1 (Yakumo) appears to have semantically differentiated *pasi* 'important' and *pase* 'heavy.' Batchelor gives *pase* 'heavy, true, important,' and Dobrotvorskij has *pase* 'heavy' for Sakhalin. The *Moshiogusa* has the variant forms *pasi* and *pase*, both meaning 'heavy.'

40. Jump. Yet another word with the variable suffix *-ki* ∼ *-ke* is found in the form *ter-ke* in all the Hokkaido dialects reported in Hattori (22: 186) and Torii gives *teri-ke* for the Kuriles. Vovin here reconstructs **tEr-kE*. However, Dybowski's word list from Shumshu (northern Kuriles) contains *ter-ki*. The same verb, with the meaning 'to run,' is found in the *Moshiogusa* as *tere-ke*, but *teri-ki* occurs with the meaning 'to jump.' Inasmuch as the same term is used for 'run' and 'jump' in many languages, we possibly have here a semantic distinction between the *i* and *e* variants.

41. Kill. From *ray* 'to die' a causative *ray-ke* 'to kill' is found generally in Ainu. This is no doubt an example of the lexicalized causative alternation *-ke* ∼ *-ka* discussed earlier. However, in this particular verb Hattori (29: 10) reports the form *ray-ki* in Sakhalin (Raychishka). A similar form from Sakhalin is found in Hattori-Chiri (No. 62), namely, Nairo *tay-ki*. Other more southerly Sakhalin dialects (Ochiho) have *ray-ke* like Hokkaido. However, in Piłsudski's Sakhalin texts there are a fair number of occurrences of *ray-ki* and no occurrences of *ray-ke*. As noted earlier, since *e* alternates with both *a* and *i*, it is understandable that *i* might be introduced in instances in which *e* alternates with *a*. With the reciprocal prefix *u-*, we find *u-ray-ke* 'to make war.' Here also forms in *-ke* are found in Hokkaido dialects 1, 5, 7, and 8 (Hattori 51: 13), but in Sakhalin (Raychishka) and in Torii's data from the Kuriles we find *-ki*.

42. Kindle. A verb with the basic meaning 'to rub firesticks in the hand to produce fire' is found in Batchelor in the form *kes* or *kisa*. In the same source we find the nominal compound *ape-kes*, "pronounced by some as *ape-kis*," with the meaning 'firebrand' (*ape* 'fire'). This stem is apparently not found in Hattori's Ainu dialect dictionary, but the *Moshiogusa* has *kes-ke* 'to set on fire' and Dobrotvorskij gives the verb *kisa* 'to drill, bore a hole' for Sakhalin.

43. Late (be), come late. This is another word with the variant suffix *-ki* ∼ *-ke*. In Hattori (253: 64) we find *oraw-ke* in dialects 1, 4, 5, and 7, and *oraw-ki* in 3 and 8. In Batchelor's dictionary there is *oraw-ki* ∼ *oraw-ke* 'late, to miss, to be too late' (adverb and intransitive verb). What seems to be the same stem occurs in the *Moshiogusa* as *orauka* 'behind, in the last place,' probably connected with *rauke* 'bottom, depth.'

44. Left (hand). Both *har-ki* and *har-ke* are found, generally compounded with following *sam* 'side' or *tek* 'hand.' The form *har-ke* occurs in dialect 1; *har-ki* in 2–7; and *hari-ki* in 8–10. The form in -*i* is also found in Batchelor (*hari-ki*) and in Dobrotvorskij (*hare-ki*). Vovin reconstructs **gar-ke*. As can be seen, the variants *hari-* ~ *hare-* are also found in some instances along with the suffix -*ki* ~ -*ke*.

45. Middle. The basic variants *nos-ke* and *nos-ki* are also found in the words for 'midnight' and 'noon.' In Hattori (236: 20) we find *nos-ki* 'middle, center' in all the Hokkaido dialects, but in Raychishka in Sakhalin we have *noske-ke* and *noski-ke*, and in the northern Kuriles, *si-nosi-ke*. The form in -*ke* is further attested in Batchelor's *an-nosi-ke* 'midnight,' *nos-ke* ~ *nosi-ke* 'middle,' and in Dobrotvorskij's *an-nos-ke* 'midnight.' The *Moshiogusa* has both forms, *nos-ki* ~ *nos-ke* 'in the middle,' as well as *nosketa an* 'in the middle,' with locative -*ta*. Evidence of variation within Sakhalin is found in Piłsudski's texts, *nos-ke-ta* 'in the middle,' but *an nos-ki* 'midnight.'

46. Near (be). This is another form with the suffix -*ki* ~ -*ke*. Vovin reconstructs **gan-kE* and it is true that all the citations in Hattori (235: 11) have -*ke*. However, he has no entry for the Kuriles. Moreover, in Piłsudski's Sakhalin texts both *han-ke* and *han-ki* are found and the *Moshiogusa* also contains both -*ki* and -*ke* as variants. The suffix -*ki* also occurs in Klaproth's Kurile vocabulary as *gan-gi-ta* 'near,' with the locative suffix -*ta*.

47. Necessary, useful. Hattori (294: 40) has phrases containing *iwan-ke* in dialects 3–7 and 9. Dobrotvorskij has a noun *ivan-ki* 'necessity,' followed by *ivan-ke* in parentheses. The *Moshiogusa* gives *yuwan-ki* and *yuwan-ge*.

48. Needle. Hattori (123: 72) has *kem* in dialects 1–7, but for Soya in northwestern Hokkaido he gives *kim*. Dobrotvorskij, Batchelor, Dybowski, Vosnesenskij, and Summers all have *kem*, but Klaproth has *kim* in his Sakhalin vocabulary.

49. Now. In this word there is variation between *tane* and *tani*. It is to be analyzed as demontrative *ta-* + locative *-ne* ~ *ni*. Hattori (246: 27) has *ta-ne* in dialects 1–8, but *ta-ni* in 9 and 10. We also find *tani* 'today' in Krasheninnikov and both *tane* and *tani* in the *Moshiogusa*. As would be expected, Batchelor has forms with *-ne*, as does Summers, both from Hokkaido.

50. Put (it), place (it). Hattori has examples of the verb *ari* ~ *are* under a number of different headings, as follows: 'put it, place it' (140: 77), 'make (a fire)' (105: 52), 'make (a light)' (106: 61), and 'set (a trap)' (112: 22). Possibly 'to leave it, leave it over' (151: 13) also belongs here. Summarizing the material from the above entries, we find that *are* occurs in dialects 1, 2, and 4–8, and with the expected long vowel (*aare*) in dialect 9 (Sakhalin). In dialect 3 we find *ari*. Dybowski's material from the Kuriles also shows *ari*. In Piłsudski's Sakhalin texts both *are* and *ari* are found. It is plausible to conjecture that *a-re* ~ *a-ri* is the causative of *a* 'to sit' since the usual causative of stems ending in a vowel is *-re*. If this hypothesis is valid, then the causative *-re* ~ *-ri* would be an additional instance of a grammatical formative with the *e* ~ *i* alternation.

51. Raise. In this case we have a causative of *rikin* 'to go up.' Hattori (241: 48) has the usual *-ka* ~ *-ke* alternation, *rikin-ka* in dialects 2, 3, and 5, but *rikin-ke* in 7–9. Piłsudski, as would be expected, has *rikin-ke* 'go up.' However, a form in *-ki* is found in the *Moshiogusa*. This word provides another example of the triple alternation *-ka* ~ *-ke* ~ *-ki*, discussed above under No. 41 'kill.'

52. Round. The basic meaning of the stem *kari* ~ *kare* seems to be 'circular,' from which comes the meaning 'empty,' as in a circular hole, and then 'ignorant.' The following entries in Hattori are considered here: 'eddy, whirlpool' (217: 33), 'full moon' (from its circular shape) (223: 7), 'circle' (275: 15), and 'be round' (275: 16). From a comparison of these entries we find *kari* in dialects 1–4 and 6–8. However, dialect 8 has *kare* in *wakka si-kare* 'water circles,' in which *si-* is a reflexive prefix, and the *Moshiogusa* has the phrase *i-ramu-s-karé*, with the variant *i-ramu-s-kari*. The meaning here is *i-ramu* 'his/her mind' and *s-kare* 'is empty.' Interesting also is Batchelor's form, *si-kari*, with two meanings, (1) 'round,' (2) 'without, not having, i.e. empty' (cf. black hole). Possibly the forms meaning 'empty' are borrowed from Japanese *kara* 'empty, vacant' and are homonymous with those meaning 'circular.'

53. Run. Corresponding to *cas* in dialects 5 and 9 of Hattori are two of Torii's terms from the Kuriles, *cashi* [casi] and *case*.

54. Seagull. We find in Hattori (189: 78) *kapiw* in dialects 1–4 and 6–9, but *kapew* in 5. Batchelor has *kapiu* and Krasheninnikov gives *pon-gapif*.

55. Shave. Hattori's entry '(to) split it, tear it lengthwise' (136: 52) must, in spite of the difference in meaning, be the same root as that for 'shave' in other sources. Hattori records *mim* in dialects 3, 6, and 7. Voznesenskij has both *e-mim-ki* 'to shave' and *e-mem-ki-epira* 'razor' (cf. *epira* 'knife'). Batchelor likewise has the variant in *e*, namely *mem-ke* 'to shave,' the same form given by Simeon (1968: 18)

56. Shine, glitter, sparkle. Hattori (224: 17) has *imeru* and *mermer* in dialect 3. In the Kuriles, Dybowski has *imir* 'lightning' and *api-miriri* 'sparks,' in which *api-* means 'fire.' Batchelor has forms both in *mer-* and *mir-*, including *meri* ~ *miru* 'a bright flash of light or fire,' *meri-at* ~ *miru-at* 'to sparkle,' *merimeri* 'a spark,' *miru* 'to twinkle as a star, to sparkle,' and *mirumiru* 'sparkle, shine, twinkle.' For Sakhalin, Dobrotvorskij gives *miro* 'a flint to strike fire,' which is presumably the same root.

57. Shrimp, lobster. Hattori (193: 16) records *paki* in dialect 3, but his two informants from dialect 6 gave *paki* and *pake*, respectively. Hattori's *paki* from dialect 3 agrees with Summers' data from the same dialect, as well as with Batchelor's form. In the *Moshiogusa* we find *pake* 'crawfish claw,' presumably the same word and supporting the existence of a variant in final *-e*.

58. Smash. Hattori has *poče-ka* for dialect 4, but *poči* for 9. Batchelor gives *poči* 'to crush' and in Dobrotvorskij's Sakhalin material we likewise find *poči* 'to crush.' Since Batchelor's data are from southern Hokkaido, his form *poči* indicates that forms with final *-i*, not elicited from Hattori's informants, once existed on Hokkaido as well.

59. Split (to), break (intransitive).   The stem of this verb is *pere* ∼ *peri*. It often occurs with the suffix *-ki* ∼ *-ke*, here an intransitivizer. Hattori's entry 'break it, destroy it, damage it' (134: 44) contains *pere* in dialects 3, 5, 6. His entry '(to) break or split into two or more pieces (intransitive)' (134: 56) has *pere* in dialects 1, 2, and 4–7. The same root occurs with the intransitive suffix *-ki* ∼ *-ke* (135: 47). For the Kuriles, Torii reports *perike* and in one instance Hattori gives *pereke* and *periki*. Though the vowel variation in Torii, an ethnologist, might be attributed to lack of linguistic training, the *Moshiogusa* has both *pereke* and *periki*.

60. Squat (to).   Related forms for this stem are found in Hattori (23: 193) as follows: in Hokkaido, *hopicinas* (1), *hopicine'a* (3), *opecinas* (4), and in Sakhalin, *hopicinasaa kii* (*kii* 'to make'). Thus in the second syllable two Hokkaido dialects and Sakhalin have *i*, but one Hokkaido dialect (4) has *e*.

61. Stop (to), stand.   The form *ros-ki* is found in Hattori's entry 'halt, stop' (65: 14) and in 'stand' (24: 195). Under the former head we find *ros-ki* in dialects 1, 3, and 4, and under the latter, also *ros-ki* in 1–6. However, in the sentence 'There is a house over there' (i.e. 'stands over there') dialects 4 and 6 have *ros-ki*, but dialect 8 has *ros-ke*. The same distribution is found in the sentence 'There is a man over there' (150: 4).

62. Three.   In almost all sources (e.g. Hattori 260: 6) we find *re-* 'three,' usually followed by a numeral classifier. However, the initial prevocalic element clearly derives from *tr-*, e.g. Nairo *t-* (Sakhalin), Dobrotvorskij *tr-*, and is so reconstructed by Vovin. A variant *tri bzhi* is found in Pinart; *bzhi* (= *pis* is a common numeral classifier). The form in Pinart is interesting not only because of the final vowel, but because it shows in the Kuriles the survival of the initial *tr-* cluster, posited correctly by Vovin. Another example of *tr-* in the Kuriles is *trek* 'beard' in Krasheninnikov, as compared to *rek* in Hattori's dialects 1–9. In the modern recording by Torii for the Kuriles we find *reki* without the *tr-* initial found in Krasheninnikov.

63. Tired (to get).   Here once more we find the triple alternation *-ka* ∼ *-ke* ∼ *-ki*. In Hattori (29: 14) we have *sin-ki* 'to get tired' in dialects 1–7; *sin-ke* in 8; and *sin-ka* (Japanese gloss 'intransitive') in dialect 9. This latter form, from Sakhalin, is also found in Piłsudski, with the meaning 'tired, tiredness, with difficulty.' This verb stem should be paired with Hattori's entry for 'to rest' (29: 15), *sini* in dialects 1–7, but *siine* in 9. There is thus evidence for *i* ~ *e* in both the stem and suffix.

64. Tray. The stem variants -*čiki* ~ -*čike* are found in Hattori under the entries 'tray' (117: 11) and 'low dinner table' (117: 12). For 'tray' we have *ni-o-čiki* in dialect 1, and for 'low dinner table, *o-čiki* in dialects 1 and 8, *o-čike* in 2 and 3, and *oh-čikeh* in 9. Batchelor has *očike* 'tray' and Dobrotvorskij, *očiki*. The initial *o-* in these forms is a locative prefix.

65. Up. The stem *ri* ~ *re*, sometimes with locative -*k*, is found in a number of entries in Hattori. One of these, '(be) high, tall,' is *ri* in dialects 1–7 and 10, *o-ri* in 8, and *o-rii* in 10. In Hattori's entry for 'up' (239: 40), a form containing locative -*k*, we find *ri-k* in dialects 1 and 3, *ritta* (< **ri-k-ta*) in 4, and *ri-k-wa* in 8. However, besides these forms with a radical *ri-*, we find in dialect 1 *herekas* and the same form is reported in Oshamambe by Hattori-Chiri. There is thus in Yakumo and Oshamambe an alternation between *ri-* 'to be tall' and *re-k* 'above.' Other sources uniformly show forms in *ri*, e.g. Batchelor *herikasi* 'upwards,' *rikita* 'above,' and Dobrotvorskij *trikin* 'above, upwards, to ascend.'

66. Water, liquid. There are two common roots for 'water' in Ainu, though usually not in the same dialect, *wakka* and *pe*. The latter usually takes the form *pe*, but *pi* occurs both independently and in compounds. Krasheninnikov and Langsdorff have *pi* 'water.' In the term for 'tear' (= 'eye-water'), Hattori (5: 29) gives *nu-pe* in dialects 1–8, *nuu-pe* in 9, but from Torii (northern Kuriles), *nu-pi*. Dybowski, likewise from the northern Kuriles, gives *nu-pi* 'tear.' Moreover, the *Moshiogusa* (all of whose recordings are from Hokkaido) has *itu-pi* 'mucus' (i.e. 'nose-liquid').

67. Wet (to get). In Hattori (139: 71) the word *teyne* 'to get wet' is found in dialects 1–8. Our earliest source for the Kuriles (Krasheninnikov) and our most recent (Torii) agree in having *teyni-toy* 'mud,' in which the second part means 'earth, soil.' This form appears in all 10 dialects of Hattori (209: 13) as 'earth, soil.' Thus 'mud' in the Kuriles is *teyni-toy*, i.e. 'wet earth.'

68. Which?   Interrogative and relative 'which' are found in Hattori (313: 44) and (313: 46), respectively. The form is *inki-* in dialects 4–6 and 8, but *inke-* in 1–3 and 7.

The existence of quite numerous instances of the alternation *i* ~ *e* is certainly established by the above examples, which are by no means exhaustive. There are far more numerous instances, not cited here, in which all sources agree in *e*, or all in *i*.

The *u* ~ *o* Alternation

The last alternation we consider is that between *u* and *o*. Here Vovin recognizes the existence of a number of instances in which some dialects (as given in Hattori) have *u* and some have *o* as distinct from other instances in which all dialects have *u*, or all have *o*, for the same word. He tries to account for this by positing an additional protophoneme *O* that is represented by *u* in dialect 1 (Yakumo), but *o* in dialect 8 (Soya). The other dialects have "broken reflexes," that is, either *o* or *u* may occur depending on the specific word. But "broken reflexes" is merely a euphemism for irregular sound correspondences. It is not necessary to posit these.

There is current among comparativists, outside of Indo-European, an oversimplified version of the comparative method that does not agree with what we have known for over a century, since the time of the Neogrammarians. All we need is the succession of two of the most common types of linguistic change—conditioned sound change and the operation of analogy—to produce a system of random alternations that may sometimes be used to distinguish grammatical categories or may produce variants that are semantically differentiated between synonyms. A third factor often present is the merger of the conditioning sounds. Examples of such resulting alternation in Indo-European are qualitative vowel ablaut and German umlaut. Allowing such alternations, which are quite normal, does not open the door to loose speculations or the equation of any sound with any other any more than does the admission of Indo-European qualitative ablaut *e* ~ *o*, without which Indo-European etymological studies would be reduced to shambles. The alternation is that of certain specified and usually phonetically similar sounds.

There are in fact even more examples of the $u \sim o$ alternation than appear in Vovin's book and some are clear violations of Vovin's rule, described above. In compiling the following list, a special word should be said about the *Moshiogusa*. This work contains numerous instances of variant forms in *u* and *o*. I have not included any examples that are attested solely by the *Moshiogusa*. It is quite likely that all of these are valid, especially since Uehara investigated many areas, including western Hokkaido and offshore islands, for which there are no modern descriptions. There are two reasons for excluding these examples. One is that they are so numerous. The other is that as a Japanese speaker it is possible, for reasons discussed above, that he had difficulty in distinguishing Ainu *o* and *u* consistently.

There are two instances of the the $u \sim o$ alternation in grammatical markers. One is the formative *-nu* ~ *-no*, which primarily derives adverbs from adjectives. It is also found in many examples in which it is difficult to assign it a definite meaning. It occurs frequently as an adjective formant after *-as-*, e.g. *way-as-nu* ~ *way-as-no* 'clever, bright.' What is probably the same formant is found in examples like *kem-nu* 'to bleed' (cf. *kem* 'blood'). Words in *-nu* ~ *-no* are listed as separate items in the list of lexical items given below.

The second grammatical marker is the demonstrative stem *tu* ~ *to* that was discussed in Chapter 3 (No. 11). We might note that it violates Vovin's rule in that it occurs as *to* in Yakumo and as *tu* in Soya, instead of *tu* and *to*, respectively (see Hattori-Chiri, No. 5 'that' and No. 108 'there').

Listed below are lexical items that show the $u \sim o$ alternation.

69. Alive. In Hattori-Chiri's glottochronological study we find *sik-nu* in dialects 3–9, 11, and 12, *sit-nu* in dialect 10, and *sis-nu* in dialects 14 and 16–19. As discussed in Chapter 3 (No. 14), *sis-* and *sit-* are originally singular and *sik-* dual. This word is really 'eye-possessing,' as noted by Refsing (1986: 149). In dialect 13 in Hattori-Chiri (Soya) we find *sik-no*, but in Hattori's dictionary (28: 198) we have *sik-nu* '(to) be alive, live.' We also find *sis-nu* in Piłsudski's texts.

70. Arise, project.   Patrie (1982: 80) cites *tuk* ~ *tok* 'to extend up-ward, to arise, come up, protrude,' but he does not indicate the provenience of the two alternants. Hattori (8: 62) has several entries containing this root; for example in dialect 8 we have *rek tukka* 'to grow (of a beard)' (i.e. 'beard projects'). The stem also occurs in Hattori's entry for '(to) bud, put forth buds or shoots' (198: 19). Combining these two entries we find *tuk* in dialects 1–7. In dialect 8 (Soya) we find a variation between *rek tukka* 'beard sprouts' and *e-tok* 'to bud, put forth sprouts.' I consider this to be intradialectal variation, a common occurrence in ablaut type alternations. Accord-ing to Vovin's rule only *tok* should occur in this dialect. Batchelor gives both *tok* and *tuk*. Vovin's rule takes no account of the con-ditions for the *u* ~ *o* variation in Sakhalin, where Dobrotvorskij reports *tokoki* 'small sedge creeping out of the ground.' The *Mosh-iogusa* contains *tuku* 'come forth, sprout.'

71. Arm.   In Hattori (11: 82) there is a word *mon* 'hand, arm' in dialect 2 that in other dialects only occurs in compounds. One exam-ple, from Raychishka in Sakhalin, is *mon-peh* 'finger' (11: 93). Do-brotvorskij records the variant forms *mumpe* ~ *mompe* 'finger,' also in Sakhalin. Batchelor has a series of compounds containing *mon* 'hand,' e.g. *mon-sutu* 'beat, strike with the hand,' *mon-us* 'busy,' and *mon-saure* 'not busy, not much to do.' The same stem may also be contained in 'forearm,' which is *amunnin* in dialect 1 and *amunin* in 2–4 (Hattori 11: 85). A form corresponding to the Sakhalin word for 'finger,' cited above, is reported by Summers for the Saru dialect of Hokkaido as *mompets* 'finger, toe.' It probably occurs as *mono* 'work' in the same dialect, e.g. *mon-rayke* 'work, job, to work' in dialects 1–8, *mon-rayki* in 9 (Hattori 110: 1, 2). Dobrotvorskij also gives *mon-rayki* 'to work.' These last forms (*mono*, etc.) might, how-ever, be borrowings of Japanese *mono* 'thing, business,' as suggested by Dobrotvorskij.

72. Black.   A stem with the basic form *kur* ~ *kor* occurs in Ainu in *kunne* 'black' (< *kurne*), and probably also as *kur* in the word for 'shadow.' All the citations of this common root, including those in Hattori-Chiri for a number of Sakhalin dialects, go back to *kur*, except that we find in Raychishka *e-koroku* 'black.' Forms with *kor-* are also reported by Dybowski for the Kuriles in *ekorok-piy* and *ekorok-tay*, both meaning 'black,' but Krasheninnikov has *ekuroko*.

73. Bosom. Vovin reconstructs *opsOr. His *o* is the one which alternates with *u*, whereas *O* is a constant *o*. In Hattori (86: 49), the word for 'bosom' is *upsor* in dialects 1–4, *ussor* in 5–7, *osorin* in 8, and *uhsoro* in 9. Piłsudski gives *ussoro*. Thus we find that *u* in the initial syllable is reported by both Hattori and Piłsudski for Sakhalin. For the meaning 'inside,' Hattori (240: 44) likewise gives *upsor* in dialect 1, and Batchelor has *upsoro* 'bosom, inside.' In the second syllable *o* is found consistently.

74. Buttocks. For this word Vovin reconstructs *OsOr*, with a constant *o* in both syllables. However, under this entry in Hattori (14: 121), though we do find *osor* in all the Hokkaido dialects (1–8), for Raychishka, in Sakhalin, we find *us-kuy*, in which *kuy* means 'urine.' With the shorter form *us* we may compare in Piłsudski *os* 'behind, back' and *osi* 'behind, backwards' in the *Moshiogusa*. In Batchelor we find *oso-ma* 'feces' and *osoro-ka* 'from the posteriors, from behind.' Similar forms are found in the Saru dialect reported by Summers: *osiuro* ~ *osioro* 'anus' and *oso-ma* 'excrement.'

75. Clever (be), bright. For this entry Hattori (296: 56) gives *wayasno* in dialect 1 and *wayasnu* in dialect 2. This is an adjectival derivative from *waya* 'wisdom, ability,' reported by Batchelor, who also gives *waya-asnu* 'wise.' Hattori (296: 57) has the same stem in *waya-sap* 'foolish' (i.e. 'sense-lacking'). The *Moshiogusa* has both *wayasino* and *wayasinu* 'wise, sensible.' This etymology contradicts Vovin's rule in that in dialect 1 (Yakumo) we find *o* rather than the posited *u*.

76. Dig. A verb with the root *ur* ~ *or* is usually preceded by the locational prefix *o*-. In Hattori (137: 64) this stem occurs in the shape *ouri* in dialects 1–7. However, in dialect 2, alongside *ouri*, is found *ohori*. This word does not seem to occur in Sakhalin, and since it is not recorded in Soya (dialect 8), it does not test Vovin's rule.

77. Dirt. Hattori (19: 161) has *tur* in dialects 1–8 and *turu* in 9 and Batchelor records *turu* 'dirt, filth,' but Piłsudski has *tori-ma* 'rubbish' (-*ma* is a suffix that seems to mean 'a deposit') and the *Moshiogusa* gives *toru-us* 'dirty, unclean.'

78. Early (be). Hattori (253: 60) has *kunnano* in dialect 6, a form which may be compared with Torii's recordings from the Kuriles, *konon* and *kongo*. The existence of a variant stem *kon* is further supported by Dybowski's *koŋka* and Klaproth's *koŋka*, both from the Kuriles.

79. Earth.   For this word Hattori gives *toy* in all ten dialects in his dictionary (209: 13). The glottochronological list of Hattori-Chiri likewise has *toy*, or the reduplicated form *toytoy*, in all the dialects reported there.   However, *tuy* was recorded in Sakhalin by both Langsdorff and Klaproth and it is also found in the *Moshiogusa*.

80. Earth worm.   Hattori (194: 125) has *tonin* in dialect 1 and *tunin* in dialects 2 and 3, which contradicts Vovin's rule. Batchelor and the *Moshiogusa* both have *tonin*.

81. Flour, meal.   Hattori (93: 17) gives *irup* for dialects 1, 4, 6, and 7, but *irop* in 8. I have not found this word in any other source. It does not contradict Vovin's rule.

82. Fly (noun).   Hattori (192: 105) has *mos* in dialects 2 and 4–7, *mossi* in 8, but *mus* in 3, and *too-mus* in 9. Dobrotvorskij's *tomus* from Sakhalin approximates Raychishka (dialect 9 in Hattori), also in Sakhalin. Batchelor has *mos*, as would be expected. Two sources from the Kuriles (Klaproth and Voznesenskij) have *mos* in agreement with most of Hokkaido.

83. Forehead, temple.   Hattori's entries for 'forehead' and 'temple' (3: 9, 10) have *noyporo*, or more complex expressions which contain it, in dialects 3, 5, and 8, but *noypuru* in 6, exhibiting the *u* ~ *o* alternation in both syllables. Dobrotvorskij has *noyporo* 'forehead' in his Sakhalin vocabulary.

84. Frame for a fireplace.   Hattori (105: 50) gives *inunpe* in dialects 1–4, 6, 7, and 9, but *inonpe* in 8, conforming to Vovin's rule. In dialect 5 we find *iunpe*. Batchelor, Dobrotvorskij, and the *Moshiogusa* all have forms in *u*.

85. Frost.   The forms found in Hattori (231: 64) are *taskor* in dialects 1–5, *taskuru* in 6, *taskur* in 8, *taskoro opas* (*opas* 'snow') in 9, and *tasukuru* in 10. This word violates Vovin's rule in two ways since we find *o* in dialect 1 and *u* in dialect 8. The Sakhalin variant in *o* is supported by Dobrotvorskij's *taskoro* 'hoar frost,' but

Vosnesenskij's *taskor* 'hoar frost' as against Torii's *tasukuru*, shows variation in the northern Kuriles.

86. Give birth. The basic stem is *kur* ~ *kor*. The forms recorded in Hattori (28: 2) include instances in which *po* 'child' (Sakhalin *poo*) is prefixed. Dialects 1 and 3–9 have *kor*, but dialect 3, in addition to *kor* and *po-kor*, also has *ikururu*. Batchelor parallels these latter two with *pokor* 'to bear' and *ikururu* 'pangs of childbirth.' Piłsudski reports *po-koro* in Sakhalin and Dybowski gives both *pokuri* and *pokori* in the northern Kuriles. The stem *po* ~ *pu* 'small, child' is discussed below in No. 106.

87. Go to sleep (of a foot). Hattori (21: 178) has *tukunne* in dialects 1–5 and 7–8, but *tokunne* in 6. It violates Vovin's rule because dialect 8 has *u*.

88. Grease, fat. This etymology shows variation between *kir(i/u)pu* and *kir(i/u)po*. There is *i* ~ *u* variation in contact with the labial *p*-. Hattori (93: 10) gives *kirpu* in dialects 1–3 and 8, alongside *kirupu* in 9. There is also in Hattori's dictionary a term for 'oil' (93: 11) that is transcribed as *kirpo* in dialects 6 and 7. This word clearly violates Vovin's rule in that we find *u* in dialect 8 (Saru) instead of the predicted *o*. Additional examples of this word are found in Hattori-Chiri's glottochronological list (No. 32). Of particular interest here are the additional Sakhalin dialects, which in two cases disagree with Raychishka in having final -*o* rather than -*u*. These are dialects 15 and 16 with *kiripo*. Dobrotvorskij's Sakhalin rendering is *kiripu*, which is the same as Dybowski's form from the northern Kuriles. In this instance the *Moshiogusa* agrees with dialects 6 and 7 in Hokkaido, having *kiripo*, but Batchelor has *kiripu*, agreeing with the most common form in southern Hokkaido dialects.

89. Hiccup (verb). For this verb Hattori (10: 75) gives two variants, *yo(m/n)kor* and *yo(m/n)kur*, which follow Vovin's rule. Vovin reconstructs **yOmkor*; Hattori lists *yonkur* in dialects 1, 3, and 4, *yomkor* in 6 and 7, *yonkor* in 2, 5, and 8, and *yonkoro* in 9. I have not found this verb in any source besides Hattori.

90. Hole. In Hattori (274: 8) we find *puy* in dialects 1–5 and 9, and Vovin reconstructs **puy*. There is, however, evidence for an alternative form *poy* in the *Moshiogusa,* which gives both *puy* and *poy.* For the Kuriles, Dybowski gives *poy* 'hole,' *poyti* 'dig a hole,' but Voznesenskij has *puy.*

91. Husband. In Hattori (45: 60) all the entries are *hoku* or *oku.* I have found no data from the Kuriles, but a number of Sakhalin dialects reported by Hattori-Chiri (No. 145) have *hoko.* Moreover, Piłsudski has both *hoku* and *hoko* in his Sakhalin texts, proving that *hoko* is well attested in Sakhalin.

92. Inside. Hattori (240: 24) has *tum* in dialects 1 and 3, *čise-tuman* 'in the house' in dialect 8, *tun-keke* in 9, but *tom* in dialect 7. Refsing (1986: 125) notes both *tom* and *tum* 'inside, in the middle of' in the Shizunai dialect of Hokkaido. This word violates Vovin's rule in that *tuman* occurs in dialect 8 rather than *tom-.* The forms thus far cited are all from Hokkaido. For the Raychishka dialect in Sakhalin Hattori gives *tun-keke* with a query. However, the variant with *-u-* is attested in Piłsudski's texts in the form *tumu-ke-ta* 'among, in, inside.' Vovin (1993: 45) says that it is clear that *tom* and *tum* are variants of the same word.

93. Island. Hattori (212: 7) gives *mosir ~ mosiri* 'island,' which is a compound of *mo-* 'land, island' + *-sir(i)* 'place, world.' However, the *Moshiogusa* has both *mosiri* and *musiri,* and Klaproth gives the phrase *musiri kamui* 'island prince' in his Sakhalin vocabularies.

94. Kill. In Ainu a number of verbs have forms indicating plural action. One of these is 'to kill' with singular *ray-ke ~ ray-ka ~ ray-ki,* discussed in No. 41 above. The plural is *ronno ~ ronnu.* In Hattori (29: 10) we find *ronnu* in dialects 1–3, 6, and 7, but *ronnu* in 4, 5, and 9. Batchelor states that the plural of *ray-ke* is *ronnu,* but the *Moshiogusa* has both *ronno* and *ronnu.* Piłsudski gives *ronno* 'kill, kill many times.' Its apparent absence in Hattori's dialect 8 does not allow us to test Vovin's rule.

95. Man. The word *aynu* 'person, man,' the source of the ethnic name Ainu, occurs as *aynu* in Hattori's dialects 1–9, but as *ayno* in dialect 10 (Torii's Kurile form). The form *ayno* is also found in Pinart and in Dybowski's Shumshu dialect in the northern Kuriles. However, Voznesenskij gives the phrase *aynu kur,* in which *kur* means 'person,' for the northern Kuriles. In the earlier literature, based on initial Russian contacts in Kamchatka and the Kuriles, the ethnic term is frequently *ayno*. Dobrotvorskij asserts that *ayno* is the vocative of *aynu* and this is supported by the phrase *ayno, ayno* in Hattori's dialect 1 in southwestern Hokkaido, which is translated as 'Hey!' (literally, 'man! man!').

96. Mother. All of the Hokkaido examples in Hattori (39: 14) have *hapo* with final *-o*, but *hapu* is reported by several sources from Sakhalin (Langsdorff and Klaproth) and from Hokkaido also (Balbi). Krasheninnikov also gives a form with final *-u* from the northern Kuriles. The existence of final *-u* in some areas of Hokkaido is suggested by the *Moshiogusa*, which has variants with both final *-o* and *-u*. This word no doubt contains the diminutive *-po* ~ *-pu*.

97. Mouth. This word has a *paro* ~ *paru* alternation. It also contains the peculiar Ainu interdialectal variation *p-* ~ *č-*, deriving from an earlier **pr-* according to Vovin. For this word Hattori (6: 40) gives *par* ('belonging form' *paro*) in dialects 1–3, *čar* ('belonging form' *čaro*) in dialect 4, *čaro* in 5, and *paroho* (historically a 'belonging form') in 6. All of these have *-o*, but dialect 9, Raychishka in Sakhalin, has *čaru*. In the Kuriles, Torii records both *čaru* and *čaro*. Hattori-Chiri, in addition to *čaru* in dialects 18 and 19 in Sakhalin, has *čara* in 16 and 17, and Dobrotvorskij gives both *čara* and *čaru*. I cannot explain the variant in final *-a*.

98. Narrow. Hattori (271: 16) gives *hut-ne* for dialects 1–4, *hup-ne* for 5–7, *o-hot-ne* for 8, *o-huhne* for 9, and *hup-ne* for 10. It is reconstructed as **gopnE* by Vovin (1993: 54) and conforms to his rule. Hattori-Chiri (No. 155) has an additional form with *o* from Sakhalin, *o-hoh-ne* in the Ochiho dialect. Dobrotvorskij reports from Sakhalin *o-huf-ne* and *huf-ne*.

99. Navel. Under the entry 'navel, belly button' Hattori (14: 116) reports *hanku* for dialects 1–3, 7, and 9, but *hanko* in 6. The form in Torii's Kurile material, *kanko*, agrees in its final vowel with Dybowski's *aŋko*, also from the Kuriles. An additional variant *hanka*, in the compound *hanka-puy* (*puy* 'hole'), is reported by Hattori for dialects 4, 5, and 8. The Raychishka dialect in Sakhalin has *hanku* ~ *hanka* ~ *hanka-puy*. Hattori qualifies the second form as *rō* 'old, archaic.' The *Moshiogusa* likewise has *hanka-puy*. Dybowski's *xanku* 'belly button' agrees with Hattori's Sakhalin recording *hanku* and Batchelor's southern Hokkaido form, also *hanku*.

100. Nettle.   This word is apparently not in Hattori's dictionary. Batchelor has both *muse* and *mose*. Dobrotvorskij gives *mose* for Sakhalin and Summers reports the same form for the Saru dialect on Hokkaido.

101. Old (be).   This word, *husk-* ~ *hosk-*, is interesting in that there has been semantic differentiation between the two alternants. The former fairly consistently means 'old' and the latter 'in old times, previous, last, before,' except perhaps in the Kuriles. Thus Hattori (247: 11) gives *husko* 'old' for dialects 1–9, but *hosko* 'in old times' for dialect 8, *hoski-no* 'originally, at first' for dialects 1, 3, and 6, and *hoski* with the same meaning for dialect 8. This distinction also appears in Batchelor, where we find *husko* 'old, ancient' and *hosike* 'previously, last, before,' and in Piłsudski, who gives *husko* 'old, antecedent, previous' and *hoski* 'previous, antecedent.' In Hattori-Chiri, under 'old' (No. 72), all dialects have *husko* and Dybowski gives *oskoyen* ~ *oskoin* 'formerly, previously.' The only important exception to the semantic differentiation noted above occurs in the northern Kuriles, where Torii gives both *hosuku* and *husiko*, both meaning 'to be old, not new.' Additional examples include *hoski* 'early, former' in Dobrotvorskij and *hoski cup* 'last month' in Hattori (249: 25).

102. Rainbow.   In Hattori (26: 48) we find *rayoči* in dialects 2–7, *raoči* in 8, but *rayuči* in 1 and *rayunči* in 10. It thus follows Vovin's rule. From Sakhalin we find *rayoči* and *rahoči* in Piłsudski, and in Klaproth's Kurile list *rayunči* agrees with Torii's *rayunči* given above.

103. Robust (be).   Under this semantic head Hattori (29: 12) has *tom-as-nu* in dialects 2 and 6, but *tum-as-no* in 1. Under the heading 'be strong' Hattori (292: 26) gives *tum-as-nu*, as does Simeon (1968: 48). This is a violation of Vovin's rule in that dialect 1 has -*o*, not -*u*. This word is obviously derived from *tum* 'strength' (20: 170).

104. Saliva. The general word for 'saliva' is *non*, but Hattori-Chiri (No. 9) give *nun* for the Kushiro dialect on the east coast of Hokkaido. The variant in *o* is also reported from the Kuriles by Dybowski in *nono*. The *Moshiogusa* has both *non* and *nun* and Klaproth's Sakhalin list likewise has *nun*. These latter forms strengthen the case for the genuineness of the otherwise deviant *nun* of Kushiro.

105. Sea otter. Under Hattori (186: 43) we find *rakko* in dialects 1 and 3, *rahko* in 9, and *rakko* in 10. However, two sources from the Ainu of Kamchatka have *raku* (Dybowski) and *rakku* (Krasheninnikov).

106. Small, child. A widespread stem *pu* ~ *po* is found in Ainu meaning 'small' or 'child'; it is frequently used as a diminutive affix or as the second member of a compound. In Hattori (40: 16) and elsewhere, *po* occurs as 'child' in dialects 1, 4, 5, 7, and 8, and *poo* in 9. Its occurrence in a compound may be illustrated by Hattori's entry for 'son' (40: 17), which is *okkay-po* in dialects 2 and 4–6, though *po* by itself can also mean 'son' in some dialects. Another compound is the word for 'daughter,' which is *matne-po* 'female child' in dialects 1–8 and *mahpoo* (< **mat-poo*) in the Raychishka dialect of Sakhalin. However, in the Kuriles we usually find *-pu*. An example in a compound is given by Krasheninnikov, *sta-pu* 'little dog,' in which *sta* (< *sita*) 'dog' is followed by the diminutive suffix *-pu*. Krasheninnikov also reports the diminutive *-po* ~ *-pu* in two additional kin terms, in one of which we find *-pu* (*k-pu-ku* 'my son'), in the other *-po* (*k-pom-machi* 'my daughter'). In the latter form *-machi* means 'female.' The postulated former agreement in vowel height is found in *-pu-ku* vs. *-po-ma-*, but this is probably accidental, as shown by *pumpu* 'descendant, young man,' *pu-mat* 'girl,' in the same source. Also in the Kuriles, Pinart gives three more examples of compounds with this stem, *ku-me-pu* 'son,' *k-ama-pu* 'daughter,' and *u-pu* 'brother' (in which *ku-* and *k-* mean 'my').

107. Snot. In Hattori (5: 34) we find *etu-čima* in dialect 1, but *eto-čima* in 2 and 3. This is a compound in which the first element means 'nose.' For the simplex 'nose' Hattori (1: 34) has *etu* in all dialects. A similar variation is found in Batchelor, *etu* 'nose,' but *eto-r* 'mucus.' This last form appears in Hattori (5: 32) under 'nasal matter,' for which he gives *etor* in dialects 1–4, 6, and 7. The case for an alternation *etu* ~ *eto* 'nose' is further strengthened by the *Moshiogusa*, which has *eto*.

108. Snow. Hattori gives *upas* in dialects 1–7, but *opas* in 8, in accordance with Vovin's rule. The form *opas* is likewise found in the Raychishka dialect of Sakhalin. For the Kuriles, Torii has *upasu* and *upasi*, and both Krasheninnikov and Pinart give *upas*.

109. Son-in-law. In most instances this word is *koko*. However, in the Kuriles Krasheninnikov and Voznesenski give *koku* and Dybowski gives *kuku*, with *u* in both syllables.

110. Spit (verb). In Hattori (7: 53) we find *tupse* in dialect 1, but *topse* in 2–9. This conforms to Vovin's rule. A variant with *o* in the initial syllable is also found in Piłsudski's Sakhalin recordings: *tohej* 'spittle.' Batchelor has *tupsi* 'to expectorate.'

111. Strong₁. Hattori (20: 171) gives *okirasno* for dialect 1, but *okirasnu* for 2 and 3. It thus violates Vovin's rule. This root seems to be a virtual synonym with *tomasno* ~ *tomasnu* 'robust.' It occurs in the Raychishka dialect of Sakhalin as *kirorokoro*, and in Piłsudski's texts as *kiror* ~ *kiroro* 'force, physical strength.' In Hokkaido it occurs as the noun *kiror* 'strength' in dialects 1–3 and 5 (Hattori 1: 3, 5).

112. Strong₂. The variation here is in the adverb and adjective forming suffix *-nu* ~ *-no*. Hattori (292: 26) has only *ruy* 'be strong' (in dialects 1 and 9), but Batchelor records *ruy-no* 'greatly, much, loudly,' and the *Moshiogusa* has both *ruy-no* and *ruy-nu* 'powerful, numerous.' Langsdorff's list from southern Sakhalin has *ruy-no* 'high.'

113. Suck. The stem of this verb is probably *num* ~ *nom*. Forms like *nun* evidently arise from reduplicated forms with *-m* assimilated to *n*. Under 'to suck, to sip' Hattori (96: 37, 38) gives *numnum* in dialect 1, *nunnun* in 2, 4, and 9, *nun* in 7, but *nonnon* in 8, in conformity with Vovin's rule. The *Moshiogusa* has the variants *nunnu* and *nonno*, the latter also meaning 'to kiss.'

114. Tail. In Hattori (181: 17) we find on the one hand *akkoci* in dialects 4 and 5, *atkoci* in 3, *atkocike* and *akkot* in 8, but *akkuci* in 6. Batchelor has *atkoci* 'fish tail.' In Piłsudski's texts we find the variant forms *oxcara* and *oxcari*, which are perhaps not cognate with the previously cited occurrences.

115. Trousers. The variant forms *omunpe* ~ *omonpe* are found in Hattori (86: 6). These forms contain the locative prefix *o-* and *-pe* 'thing,' a common nominalizer. In dialects 1–4 we find *omunpe*; in dialects 5, 7, 8, *omonpe*; and in dialect 6, *homonpe*.

116. Urine. Under the headings 'to urinate' and 'urine' Hattori (15: 126–27) gives forms with the stem *-koy-* ~ *-kuy-*. Dialects 1–4 have *-kuy-* and dialects 6 and 8, *-koy-*. In dialect 7 both are found, *o-koy-ma* 'to urinate' and *kuy-wakka* 'urine' (*wakka* 'water'). In dialect 9 (Sakhalin) intradialectal variants are also found, *o-koy-se* 'to urinate' and *on-kuy* 'urine.' In both instances *-koy-* occurs in the verb and *-kuy-* in the noun.

117. Whisper, mutter. Under 'whisper' Hattori (56: 6) gives *pinu-pinu* in dialects 1–3, *pino* and *pinu* in dialect 4, and *pinopino* in 4 and 6. Dialect 7 has *e-epinu*. Under 'mutter' (56: 8) we find in dialect 3 *yay-ko-pinupinu*, with reflexive *yay-* and dative *-ko-*. Dialects 4 and 5 have *pinopino*.

Classification of Eurasiatic Languages

The following classification of languages belonging to the Eurasiatic family includes all languages mentioned in the text. For a complete listing of languages belonging to the various branches of the Eurasiatic family (e.g. Indo-European, Uralic, Altaic, etc.), the reader is referred to Ruhlen (1991). For certain languages significant dialects are given in parentheses following the language name, e.g. Yukaghir (Kolyma, Tundra, †Omok, †Chuvan). Language families are written in capital letters, individual languages and dialects in capital and small letters (though some families consist of a single language, e.g. Yukaghir, which is not closely related to any other language within Uralic).

EURASIATIC

I †ETRUSCAN: †Etruscan
II INDO-EUROPEAN:
    A †ANATOLIAN: †Hittite, †Hieroglyphic Hittite, †Cuneiform Hittite, †Palaic, †Lydian, †Luwian, †Lycian
    B ARMENIAN: Armenian, †Phrygian
    C †TOCHARIAN: †Tocharian A (=Eastern), †Tocharian B (=Western)

  D INDO-IRANIAN:
      1 INDIC: †Sanskrit, †Vedic, †Rigveda, †Prakrit, †Old Indic
      2 IRANIAN: †Avestan, †Old Persian
  E ALBANIAN: Albanian
  F GREEK: Greek (†Attic, †Doric, †Homeric, †Mycenean, †Aeolic, †Delphic, †Elean)
  G ITALIC: †Oscan, †Umbrian, †Venetic, †Latin, French
  H CELTIC: †Old Irish, Irish, Breton, Welsh
  I GERMANIC: †Gothic, †Old High German, †Old Norse, German, †Old Saxon, English, Frisian
  J BALTIC: †Old Prussian, Latvian, Lithuanian
  K SLAVIC: †Old Church Slavic, Russian, Polish, Czech, Serbo-Croatian

III URALIC-YUKAGHIR:
  A YUKAGHIR: Yukaghir (Kolyma, Tundra, †Omok, †Chuvan)
  B URALIC:
      1 SAMOYED:
          a NORTH: Yurak (=Nenets), Enets (=Yenisei Ostyak), Tavgy
          b SOUTH: Selkup (=Ostyak Samoyed) (Tāz, Ket, Tym), †Kamassian
      2 FINNO-UGRIC:
          a UGRIC: Hungarian, Vogul, Ostyak
          b FINNIC:
              i PERMIAN: Komi-Zyrian, Udmurt (=Votyak)
             ii VOLGAIC: Mordvin, Cheremis (=Mari)
           iii NORTH FINNIC: Saami (=Lapp)(Kola), Finnish, Karelian, Veps, Votic, Estonian, Livonian

IV ALTAIC:
  A TURKIC:
      1 CHUVASH: Chuvash
      2 COMMON TURKIC: †Old Turkish (=Uighur), Turkish (Osmanli), Crimean Turkish, Gagauz, Turkmen, Azerbaijani, Uighur, Uzbek, Bashkir,

Karaim, Kumyk, Tatar, Baraba, Crimean Tatar,
Nogai, Karalkapak, Kazakh, Kirghiz, Yakut,
Khakas, Sagai, Altai, Teleut, Shor, Tuvin, Kara-
gas

B MONGOLIAN: †Classical Mongolian, Mongol, Moghol,
Dagur, Monguor, Yellow Uighur, Baoan, Kalmyk,
Buriat, Khalkha, Ordos

C TUNGUSIC:

    1 NORTHERN: Even (=Lamut), Nigidal, Evenki,
Solon, Orochon

    2 SOUTHERN: †Manchu, †Ju-chen, Nanai, Gold,
Ulch, Orok, Oroch, Udihe

V KOREAN-JAPANESE-AINU:

A KOREAN: Korean

B JAPANESE-RYUKYUAN: Japanese, Ryukyuan

C †AINU: †Ainu (Hokkaido, Sakhalin, Kuriles)

VI GILYAK: Gilyak (=Nivkh) (Sakhalin, Amur)

VII CHUKOTIAN:

A NORTHERN: Chukchi, Koryak (Chavchuven, Palana),
Kerek, Aliutor

B SOUTHERN: Kamchadal (Ukä, Sedanka)

VIII ESKIMO-ALEUT:

A ALEUT: Aleut (Bering, Unalaska, Atka)

B ESKIMO:

    1 SIRENIK: Sirenik

    2 YUPIK (=YUIT):

        a SIBERIAN: Chaplino, Naukan

        b ALUTIIQ: Chugach, Kodiak

        c CENTRAL: Kuskokwim, Nunivak, Ekog-
miut

    3 INUIT (=INUPIAQ): Inuit (St. Lawrence Island,
Norton Sound, Kangianermiut, Seward Penin-
sula, Imaklik, Sigluit, Mackenzie, Hudson Bay,
Southhampton Island, Labrador, Greenlandic)

References Cited

The following abbreviations are used in the References:

BB	*Bezzenberger Beiträge.*
BSLP	*Bulletin de la Société de Linguistique de Paris.*
FUF	*Finnisch-Ugrische Forschungen.*
IF	*Indogermanische Forschungen.*
IJAL	*International Journal of American Linguistics.*
JIES	*Journal of Indo-European Studies.*
JNSSSR	*Jazyki Narodov Sojuza Sovetskix Sotsialesticheskix Respublik,* 5 vols. 1966–68. Moscow: Nauka.
JSFO	*Journal de la Société Finno-Ougrienne.*
MSFO	*Mémoires de la Société Finno-Ougrienne.*
PTF	*Philologiae Turcicae Fundamenta,* Jean Deny, Kaare Grønbech, Helmuth Scheel, and Zeki Velidi Togan, eds. 1959. Wiesbaden: Franz Steiner.
UAJ	*Ural-Altaische Jahrbücher.*
VJ	*Voprosy Jazykoznanija.*
ZfVS	*Zeitschrift für vergleichende Sprachforschung.*

Adelung, J. C., and J. S. Vater. 1806–17. *Mithridates,* 4 vols. Berlin.
Adrados, Francisco R. 1989. "Etruscan as an IE Anatolian (but not Hittite) Language," *JIES* 17: 363–83.

Anderson, Nikolai. 1879. *Studien zur Vergleichung der Ugrofinnischen und Indogermanischen Sprachen.* Dorpat: Laakmann.

Angere, Johannes. 1957. *Jukagirisch-Deutsches Wörterbuch. Zusammengestellt auf Grund der Texte von W. Jochelson.* Stockholm: Almqvist and Wicksell.

Ard, Josh. 1981. "A Sketch of Vowel Harmony in the Tungusic Languages," in Bernard Comrie, ed., *Studies in the Languages of the USSR,* Edmonton, Linguistic Research, 123–43.

Asai, Tōru. 1974. "Classification of Dialects: Cluster Analysis of Ainu Dialects," *Bulletin for the Study of North Eurasian Cultures* 8: 45–138.

Aston, William G. 1879. "A Comparative Study of Japanese and Korean Languages," *Journal of the Royal Asiatic Society of Great Britain and Ireland,* 317–64.

———. 1904. *A Grammar of the Japanese Written Language,* 3rd ed. London: Luzac.

Austerlitz, Robert. n.d. Mss.

———. 1990. "Typology in the Service of Internal Reconstruction: Sakhalin Nivkh," in Winfred Lehmann, ed., *Language Typology 1987. Systematic Balance in Language,* Amsterdam, John Benjamins, 17–34.

Avrorin, V. A., and E. P. Lebedeva. 1968. "Orochskij jazyk," *JNSSSR* V: 191–209.

Baldi, Philip. 1983. *An Introduction to Indo-European Languages.* Carbondale: Southern Illinois University Press.

Barnum, Francis. 1901. *Grammatical Fundamentals of the Inuit Languages as Spoken by the Eskimo of the Western Coast of Alaska.* Boston and London: Ginn.

Bartholomae, Christian. 1889. "Arisches," *BB* 15: 1–43, 185–247.

Baskakov, N. A. 1966. "Altajskij jazyk," *JNSSSR* II: 506–22.

Batchelor, John. 1905. *Ainu-English-Japanese Dictionary (including a Grammar of the Ainu Language),* 2nd rev. ed. London: Kegan Paul, Trench, Trubner.

Bazin, Louis. 1961. "Y a-t-il en turc des alternances vocaliques," *UAJ* 33: 12–16.

Bechtel, Friedrich. 1921–24. *Die griechischen Dialekte,* 3 vols. Berlin: Weidmann.

Beckes, Rob. 1982–83. "On Laryngeals and Pronouns," *ZfVS* 96: 200–32.

Behagel, Otto. 1923–32. *Deutsche Syntax, eine geschichtliche Darstellung,* 4 vols. Heidelberg: Winter.

Beke, Ö. 1928. "Zur Kasuslehre des Finnischugrischen und Indogermanischen," *IF* 46: 230–47.

Benedict, Paul K. 1990. *Japanese/Austro-Tai.* Ann Arbor: Karoma.

Benveniste, Émile. 1935. *Origines de la formation des noms en indo-européen.* Paris: Adrien Maisonneuve.

———. 1959. "La forme du participe en luwi," in R. von Kienle, et al., eds., *Festschrift Johannes Friedrich,* Heidelberg, Winter.

———. 1962. *Hittite et indoeuropéen: Études comparatives.* Paris: Adrien Maisonneuve.

Benzing, Johannes. 1952. "Der Aorist im Türkischen," *UAJ* 24: 130–32.

———. 1955. "Die tungusischen Sprachen. Versuch einer vergleichenden Grammatik," *Abhandlungen der Geistes- und Sozialwissenschaftlichen Klasses,* No. 11, Mainz, 947–1099.

Bergsland, Knut. 1951. "Aleut Demonstratives and the Aleut-Eskimo Relationship," *IJAL* 17: 169–79.

———. 1956. "Aleut and Proto-Eskimo," *Proceedings of the 32nd International Congress of Americanists,* Copenhagen, 624–31.

———. 1959. "The Eskimo-Uralic Hypothesis," *JSFO* 61: 3–29.

Blažek, Václav. 1992. "Kartvelian Materials in the Nostratic Lexicon: New Etymologies II," in Vitaly Shevoroshkin, ed., *Nostratic, Dene-Caucasian, Austric, and Amerind,* Bochum, Germany, Brockmeyer, 129–48.

Boas, Franz. 1894. "Der Eskimo-Dialekt von Cumberland-Sundes," *Mittheilungen der Anthropologischen Gesellschaft in Wien* 24: 97–114.

———. 1911. "Introduction," in *Handbook of American Indian Languages,* Part I, Washington, D.C., Smithsonian Institution, Bureau of American Ethnology, Bulletin 40, 1–84.

Bobé, Louis Theodor Alfred. 1925. "Egede, Hans Poulsen Relationer fra Grønland, 1721–36, og Det gamle Grønlands ny perlustration, 1741," *Medelelser om Grønland* 54.

Bogoras, Waldemar. 1917. *Koryak Texts.* Publications of the American Ethnological Society, Vol. 5. Leiden: Brill.

———. 1922. "Chukchee," in Franz Boas, ed., *Handbook of American Indian Languages,* Part II, Washington, D.C., Government Printing Office, 631–903.

——. 1934. "Luoravetlanskij (chukotskij) jazyk," in E. A. Krejnovich, ed., *Jazyki i pis'mennost' paleoaziatskix narodov,* Part III, 5–46.

——. 1937. *Luoravetlano-russkij (chukotsko-russkij) slovar',* ed. by S. N. Stebnitskij. Moscow: Uchpedgiz.

Boller, Anton. 1857. "Nachweis, dass das Japanische zum uralaltaischen Stamme gehört," *Sitzungsberichte der Kaiserlichen Akademie der Wissenschaft, Phil. hist. Klasse,* 393–481.

Bomhard, Allan R. 1988. "The Prehistoric Development of the Athematic Vowel Endings in Proto-Indo-European," in Yoël L. Arbeitman, ed., *A Linguistic Happening in Memory of Ben Schwartz: Studies in Anatolian, Italic, and Other Indo-European Languages,* Louvain, Peeters, 113–40.

——. 1992. "The Nostratic Macrofamily (with special reference to Indo-European," *Word* 43: 61–83.

——. 1994 [revised]. *Lexical Parallels between Proto-Indo-European and Other Languages.* Charleston, South Carolina: Signum.

Bomhard, Allan R., and Jerome Kerns. 1994. *The Nostratic Macrofamily: A Study in Distant Linguistic Relationship.* Berlin: Mouton de Gruyter.

Bouda, Karl. 1952. "Die Verwandschaftsverhältnisse der tschuktschischen Sprachgruppe," *Acta Salamanticensia Filosofia y Letras,* Tomo V, No. 6.

Bourquin, Theodor. 1891. *Grammatik der Eskimo-Sprache.* London: Moravian Mission Agency.

Brockelmann, Karl. 1954. *Osttürkische Grammatik der islamischen Litteratursprachen Mittelasiens.* Leiden: Brill.

Brugmann, Karl. 1904. *Die Demonstrativpronomina der indogermanischen Sprachen.* Leipzig: Teubner.

——. 1910. "Adverbia aus d. mask. Nom. sg. prädikativer Adjectiva," *IF* 27: 233–78.

Brugmann, Karl, and Berthold Delbrück. 1892–1900. *Grundriss einer vergleichenden Grammatik der indogermanischen Sprachen,* 1st ed. Strassburg: Trübner.

——. 1897–1916. *Grundriss der vergleichenden Grammatik der indogermanischen Sprachen,* 2nd ed. Strassburg: Trübner.

Brugmann, Karl, and Albert Thumb. 1913. *Griechische Grammatik* (4th expanded edition). Munich: Beck.

Buck, Frederick Holden. 1955. *Comparative Study of Postpositions in Mongolian Dialects and the Unwritten Languages.* Cambridge: Harvard University Press.

Budenz, J. 1879. *Über die Verzweigung der ugrischen Sprachen,* Separat-Ausdruck aus der Festschrift Benfey, ed. by Leo Meyer, et al. Göttingen: Peppmüller.

Burrow, T. 1954. "The Sanskrit Precative," in Johannes Schubert and Ulrich Schneider, eds., *Asiatica (Festschrift Waller),* Leipzig, Harrassowitz, 35–42.

———. 1965. *The Sanskrit Language.* London: Faber and Faber.

———. 1979. *The Problem of Shwa in Sanskrit.* Oxford: Clarendon Press.

Campbell, Lyle, and Marianne Mithun. 1979. *The Languages of Native America.* Austin: University of Texas Press.

Carruba, Onofrio. 1970. *Das Paläische. Grammatik. Lexikon,* Studien zu Baghazköy-Texten 10. Wiesbaden: Harrassowitz.

Castreń, Matthias Alexander. 1957. *Versuch einer Koibalischen und Karagassischen Sprachlehre,* ed. by Anton Schiefner. St. Petersburg: Kaiserliche Akademie der Wissenschaften.

Cavalli-Sforza, Luca, Paolo Menozzi, and Alberto Piazza. 1994. *History and Geography of Human Genes.* Princeton: Princeton University Press.

Chamberlain, Basil Hall. 1889. "A Vocabulary of the Most Ancient Words of the Japanese Language (assisted by M. Ueda)," *Transactions of the Asiatic Society of Japan* 16: 225–85.

———. 1895. *Essay in Aid of a Grammar and Dictionary of the Luchuan Language,* Supplement to *Transactions of the Asiatic Society of Japan* 23.

Chantraine, Pierre. 1945. *Morphologie historique du grec.* Paris: Klincksieck.

Chejka, M., and A. Lamprecht. 1984. "Nostratichnata ipoteza, sŭstojanie i perspektivi,' *Sŭpostavitelno Ezikoznanie* (Sofia University) 9: 86–92.

Cherkasskij, M. A. 1960. "Voprosu o genezise singarmonicheskix variantov i parallelizmov v tjurkskix jazykax," *VJ* 4: 53–61.

Clauson, G. 1969. "A Lexicostatistical Appraisal of the Altaic Theory," *Central Asiatic Journal* 13: 1–23.

Collinder, Björn. 1934. *Indo-Uralisches Sprachgut.* Uppsala: Alm-qvist and Wiksell.

———. 1940. *Yukagirisch und Uralisch, Uppsala Universitets År-skkrift,* Vol. 8.

———. 1955. *Fenno-Ugric Vocabulary: An Etymological Dictionary of the Uralic Languages.* Stockholm: Almqvist and Wicksell.

———. 1960. *Comparative Grammar of the Uralic Languages.* Stock-holm: Almqvist and Wicksell.

———. 1964. *Sprachverwandtschaft und Wahrscheinlichkeit, Språk-vetenskapliga Sällskapets Forhandlingar.* Uppsala.

———. 1965a. "Hat das Uralische verwandte? Eine sprachvergle-ichende Studie," *Acta Universitatis Upsaliensis,* N.S. 1: 4.

———. 1965b. *An Introduction to the Uralic Languages.* Berkeley: University of California Press.

Comrie, Bernard. 1980. "Inverse Verb Forms in Siberia: Evidence from Chukchee, Koryak, and Kamchadal," *Folia Linguistica Europaea* 1: 61–74.

Čop, Bojan. 1979. "Indogermanisch-Anatolisch und Uralisch," in Wolfgang Meid and Erich Neu, eds., *Hethitisch und Indoger-manisch,* Innsbruck, Innsbrucker Beiträge zur Sprachwissen-schaft, 9–24.

Cowley, Arthur Ernest. 1910. *Gesenius' Hebrew Grammar,* edited and enlarged by Kautzsch, 2nd English edition. Oxford: Claren-don Press.

Croft, William. 1991. "The Evolution of Negation," *Journal of Linguistics* 27: 1–27.

Cuny, A. 1937. "Chamito-sémitique et indo-européen: Histoire des recherches," in *Mélanges de linguistique et de philologie offerts à Jacq. van Ginneken,* Paris, Klincksieck, 141–47.

Dall, William H. 1897. *Alaska and Its Resources.* Boston: Lee and Shepard.

Décsy, Gyula. 1965. *Einführung in die Finnisch-Ugrische Sprach-wissenschaft.* Wiesbaden: Harrassowitz.

———. 1969. "Finnougrische Lautforschung," *UAJ* 41: 33–75.

Dening, Walter. 1881. "A Vocabulary of Ainu Words and Phrases," *The Chrysanthemum* 1, No. 9, Yokohama.

Dettmer, Hans A. 1989. *Ainu-Grammatik.* Wiesbaden: Harras-sowitz.

Diakonov, Igor M. 1965. *Semito-Hamitic Languages.* Moscow: Nauka.

Dixon, J. M. 1883. "The Ainu Language," *The Chrysanthemum* 3: 67–71, 110–13.

Dobrotvorskij, Mikhail Mikhailovich. 1875. *Ajnsko-russkij slovar'.* Kazan: University of Kazan.

Doerfer, Gerhard. 1970. Review of *Altaistica. Sonderdruck aus der Wissenschaftlichen, Zeitschrift der Humboldt-Universität zu Berlin Jahrgang* 18: 244–50.

———. 1972. "Das Krimosmanische," *PTF,* 272–80.

———. 1985. *Mongolo-Tungusica.* Wiesbaden: Harrassowitz.

Dolgopolsky, Aaron B. 1964. "Gipoteza drevnejshogo rodstva jazykovyx semej severnoj evrazii s verojatnostnoj tochki zrenija," *VJ* 1964, No. 2, 53–63.

———. 1965. "Metody rekonstruktsii obshcheindoevropejskogo jazyka i sibiroevropejskaja gipoteza," *Etimologia 1964,* 259–70.

———. 1984. "On Personal Pronouns in the Nostratic Languages," in Otto Gschwantler, et al., eds., *Linguistica et Philologica. Gedenkschrift für Björn Collinder,* Vienna, Wilhelm Braumüller, 65–112.

Duranti, Alessandro. 1986. "Language in Context and Language as Context." Handout, Stanford, April 29, 1986.

Eckardt, Andre. 1965. *Grammatik der koreanischen Sprache, Studienausgabe,* 2nd rev. ed. Heidelberg: Groos.

Eckmann, János. 1959. "Das Chwarezmtürkische," *PTF,* 113–37.

Egede, Poul Hanson. 1760. *Grammatica Grönlandica Danico-Latina.* Copenhagen: G. F. Kisel.

Ehrlich, Hugo. 1910. *Zur indogermanischen Sprachgeschichte.* Königsberg: Beiträge zur Jahresbericht des altstädtischen Gymnasiums Ostern.

Emeljanova, N. M. 1982. *Klassy glagolov v eskimoskom jazyke, chaplinskij dialekt.* Leningrad: Nauka.

Erman, Adolf. 1848. *Reise um die Erde durch Nord-Asien und die beiden Oceane in den Jahren 1828, 1829, und 1830,* vol. 3. Berlin: Reimer.

Fortescue, Michael. 1984. *West Greenlandic.* London: Croom Helm.

Fortescue, Michael, Steven Jacobson, and Lawrence Kaplan. 1994. *Comparative Eskimo Dictionary.* Fairbanks: Alaska Native Research Center, University of Alaska.

Friedrich, Johannes. 1952. *Hethitisches Wörterbuch.* Heidelberg: Winter.

———. 1960. *Hethitisches Elementarbuch,* 2nd ed. Heidelberg: Winter.

Frisk, Hjalmar. 1960–70. *Griechisches etymologisches Wörterbuch,* 2 vols. Heidelberg: Winter.

Gabain, Annemarie von. 1950. *Alttürkische Grammatik,* 2nd ed. Leipzig: Harrassowitz.

———. 1959. "Das Alttürkische. Old Turkic," *PTF,* 21–45.

Gamkrelidze, T. V., and V. V. Ivanov. 1984. *Indoevropeskij jazyk i indoevropejtsi.* Tbilisi: Tbilisi State University.

Geoghegan, Richard Henry. 1944. *The Aleut Language.* Washington, D.C.: U. S. Government Printing Office.

Georgiev, Vladimir Ivanov. 1964. "Etruskisch und Späthetitisch," *Die Sprache* 17: 54–70.

———. 1985. "Das Medium: Funktion und Herkunft," in Bernfried Schlerat, ed., *Grammatische Kategorien, Funktion und Geschichte,* Wiesbaden, Ludwig Reichert, 218–28.

Gesenius, W. 1898. *Hebrew Grammar,* edited and enlarged by E. Kautsch, translation from the 25th German edition, edited by G. W. Collin. Oxford: Clarendon Press.

Golovastikov, A. N., and Aaron B. Dolgopolsky. 1972. "Rekonstruktsija chukotsko-korjatskix kornej i nostraticheskie etimologii," in *Konferentsija po sravitel'no-istoricheskoj grammatike indoevropejskix jazykov,* Moscow, Nauka, 27–30.

Gonda, J. 1954. "The Original Character of the Indo-European Relative Pronoun ịo-," *Lingua* 4: 1–41.

———. 1959. *Four Studies in the Language of the Vedas.* The Hague: Mouton.

Greenberg, Joseph H. 1959. "The Origin of the Masai Passive," *Africa* 29: 171–76.

———. 1963. *The Languages of Africa.* Bloomington: Indiana University.

———. 1978. "How Does a Language Acquire Gender Markers?," in Joseph H. Greenberg, ed., *Universals of Human Language,* Vol. 3, Stanford, Stanford University Press, 47–82.

———. 1981. "Nilo-Saharan Movable -k as a Stage III Article (with a Penutian Parallel)," *Journal of African Languages and Linguistics* 3: 105–12.

———. 1987. *Language in the Americas.* Stanford: Stanford University Press.

———. 1990. "The Prehistory of the Indo-European Vowel System in Comparative and Typological Perspective," in Vitaly Shevoroshkin, ed., *Proto-Languages and Proto-Cultures,* Bochum, Germany, Brockmeyer, 77–136.

———. 1997. "The Indo-European First- and Second-Person Pronouns in the Perspective of Eurasiatic, Especially Chukotian," *Anthropological Linguistics* 39: 187–95.

Groenbech, K., and John R. Krueger. 1955. *An Introduction to Classical (Literary) Mongolian.* Wiesbaden: Harrassowitz.

Groot, Gerard. 1940. "Besonderheiten der Ryûkyûsprache," *Monumenta Nipponica* 3.1: 302–13.

Grube, Wilhelm. 1892. *Linguistische Ergebnisse; Part I: Giljakisches Wörterzeichnis, nach dem originalaufzeichnungen von Leopold von Schrenk und P. Glehn und mit grammatischen Bemerkungen von dr. Wilhelm Grube.* Anhang zu Schrenk's *Reisen und Forschungen im Amurlande,* Anhang zum III Band, part 1. St. Petersberg: Kaiserliche Akademie der Wissenschaft.

Güntert, Hermann. 1916. *Indogermanische Ablautprobleme.* Strassburg: Trübner.

Gusmani, Roberto. 1964. *Lydisches Wörterbuch.* Heidelberg: Winter.

Hajdú, Péter. 1981. *Az uráli nyelvészet alapkérdései.* Budapest: Tankönyvkiadó.

———. 1992. *Introduzione alle lingue uraliche.* Turin: Rosenberg and Salier.

Hakulinen, Lauri. 1957. *Handbuch der finnischen Sprache,* Vol. 1. Wiesbaden: Harrassowitz.

Hammerich, L. L. 1936. "Personalendungen und Verbalsystem im Eskimoischen," *Det Kongelige Danske Videnskabernes Selskab. Historisk-filologiske Meddelelser* XXIII, 2, Copenhagen, Munksgaard.

Hamp, Eric. 1982. "Indo-European Substantives in *-mo-* and *-mā,*" *ZfVS* 96: 172–77.

Hattori, Shirō. 1964. *An Ainu Dialect Dictionary.* Tokyo: Iwanami Shoten.

Hattori, Shirō, and Mashiho Chiri. 1960. "Ainugo shohōgen no kiso goi tōkeigakuteki kenkyū" ("A Lexicostatistical Study of the Basic Vocabulary of Various Ainu Dialects"), *Minzokugaku kenkyū* 24: 307–42.

Hattori, Takesi. 1962. "Versuch einer Phonologie der Südostgiljakischen," *Journal of Hokkaido Gokugei University,* Section I-A: 67–96.

Hauer, Erich. 1952. *Handwörterbuch der Mandschusprache.* Wiesbaden: Harrassowitz.

Hayata, Teruhiro. 1975. "A Note on Vowel Harmony in Korean," *Gengo Kenkyū* 68: 104–18.

Hermann, Eduard. 1934. "Alte Probleme aus dem Gebiet des Personalpronomens," *IF* 52: 214–16.

Hinz, John. 1944. *Grammar and Vocabulary of the Eskimo Language as Spoken by the Kuskwokim and Southwest Coast Eskimos of Alaska.* Green Bay, Wisc.: Reliance.

Hirt, Hermann A. 1895. "Über die mit *m*- und *bh*- gebildeten Kasussuffixen," *IF* 5: 251–55.

———. 1913. "Fragen des Vokalismus und der Stammbildung im Indogermanischen," *IF* 33: 209–318.

———. 1921–37. *Indogermanische Grammatik,* 7 vols. Heidelberg: Winter.

Hoffmann, J. B. 1950. *Etymologisches Wörterbuch des griechischen.* Munich: Oldenbourg.

Hübschmann, Heinrich. 1885. *Das indogermanische Vokalsystem.* Strassburg: Trübner.

Hyogmyon Kwon. 1962. *Das koreanische Verbum verglichen mit dem altaischen und japanischen Verbum (Zur Typologie des Koreanischen).* Seoul: H. Kwon.

Illich-Svitych, Vladislav M. 1964. "Drevnejshie indoevropejskie-semitiskie jazykovyje kontakty," in *Problemy indoevropejskogo jazykoznanija,* Moscow, Nauka, 3–12.

———. 1967. "Materialy k sravnitel'nomu slovarju nostraticheskix jazykov," *Etimologija 1965,* 321–73.

———. 1971–84. *Opyt sravnenija nostraticheskix jazykov,* 3 vols. Moscow: Nauka.

Imré, Samu. 1988. "Geschichte der ungarischen Sprache," in D. Sinor, ed., *The Uralic Languages: Description, History and Foreign Influences,* Leiden, Brill.

Iskhakov, F. G., and A. A. Pal'mbakh. 1961. *Grammatika tuvin-skogo jazyka.* Moscow: Izdatel'stvo Vostochnoj Literatury.

Itkonen, Erki. 1954. "Zur Geschichte des Vokalismus der ersten Silbe im Tscheremissischen und in den permischen Sprachen," *FUF* 31: 149–345.

Ivanov, V. V. 1959. "Toxarskije jazyki i ix znachenije dl'a sravnitel'-no-istoricheskogo issledovanija indoevropejskix jazykov," in V. V. Ivanov and A. Mel'chuk, eds., *Toxarskije jazyki*, Moscow, Izdatel'stvo innostranoj literatury, 5–37.

Jacobson, Steven A. 1984. *Yup'ik Eskimo Dictionary.* Fairbanks: Alaska Native Language Center, University of Alaska.

Janhunen, J. 1977. *Samojedischer Wortschatz. Gemeinsamojedische Etimologien.* Helsinki: Castrenianumin Toimieitta 17.

Jochelson, Waldemar. 1905. "Essay on the Grammar of the Yuka-ghir Language," *Annals of the New York Academy of Sciences* 16, 5: 97–154.

———. 1912. "The Aleut Language and its Relationship to the Eskimo Dialects," *Proceedings of the 18th International Congress of Americanists, London,* Part I, 96–104.

———. 1934. "Unaganskij (aleutskij) jazyk," in Ja. P. Al'kor, ed., *Jazyki i pismennost' narodov severa,* Part I. Moscow-Leningrad: Uchpedgiz.

Johansson, Karl Friedrich. 1889. "Morphologische Studien I," *BB* 14: 151–63.

———. 1890. 'Morphologische Studien III," *BB* 16: 121–69.

Joki, Aulis J. 1971. "Über das Element *n* in der samojedischen Deklination," *FUF* 39: 1–17.

Jurafsky, Daniel. 1996. "Universal Tendencies in the Semantics of the Diminutive," *Language* 72: 533–78.

Kammenhuber, Annalies. 1969. "Hethitisch, Palaisch, Luwisch und Hieroglyphenluwisch," in *Handbuch der Orientalistik,* Erste Abteilung II, Band 1 und 2, Abschnitt Lieferung 2, Leiden, Brill, 119-357.

———. 1980. "Zum indogermanischen Erbe im Hethitischen," *ZfVS* 94: 33–63.

Kanazawa, S. 1910. *The Common Origin of Japanese and Korean.* Tokyo: Sanseido.

Karpov, V. G. 1966. "Khakasskij jazyk," *JNSSSR* II: 428–45.

Kazár, Lajos. 1980. *Japanese-Uralic Language Comparison: Locating Japanese Origins with the Help of Samoyed, Finnish, Hungarian etc. An Attempt.* Hamburg: Lajos-Kazár-Tsurusaki.

Kerns, John C. 1967. *The Eurasiatic Pronouns and the Indo-Uralic Question.* Privately printed.

Kert, G. M. 1966. "Saamskij jazyk," *JNSSSR* III: 155-71.

Kertész, M. 1933. "Zur Frage der finnisch-ugrischen Verneinung," *MSFO* 67: 190-99.

Kham'al'ajnen, M. M. 1966. "Vepskij jazyk," *JNSSSR* III: 81-101.

Khelimskij, E. A. 1982. *Drevnejshije vengersko-samojedskije jazykovije paralleli.* Moscow: Nauka.

Kim Boo-Kyom. 1959. *Gehört die koreanische Sprache zu den altaischen Sprachen?* Sternberg-See: Schraml.

Kindaichi, Kyōsuke, ed. 1969. *Ezo hōgen moshiogusa kaisetsu* [Commentary on the Ezo Dialect Miscellany], by Uehara Kumajirō, 1804]. Tokyo: Kobunkan.

Kissling, Hans Joachim. 1960. *Osmanisch-Türkische Grammatik.* Wiesbaden: Harrassowitz.

Klaproth, H. J. 1823. *Asia Polyglotta.* Paris: I. M. Eberhart.

Kleinschmidt, Samuel. 1851. *Grammatik der grönländischen Sprache.* Berlin: Reimer.

Kolesnikova, V. D., and O. A. Konstantinova. 1968. "Negidalskij jazyk," *JNSSSR* V: 109–28.

Komai, Akira. 1979. *A Grammar of Classical Japanese.* Chicago: Culver Press.

Koppelmann, Heinrich. 1928. "Die Verwandschaft des koreanischen und der Ainu-Sprache mit den indogermanischen Sprachen," *Anthropos* 23: 199–234.

———. 1933. *Die eurasische Sprachfamilie: Indogermanisch, Koreanisch und Verwandtes.* Heidelberg: Winter.

Korsakov, G. M. 1939. *Nymylansko (korjaksko)-russkij slovar'.* Moscow: Gosudarstvennyj Izdatel'stvo Slovarej.

Kortlandt, Frederik. 1987. "Archaic Ablaut Patterns in the Vedic Verb," in George Cardona and Norman H. Zide, eds., *Festschrift for Henry Hoenigswald,* Tübingen, Gunter Narr, 215–23.

Kotwicz, Władysław. 1936. *Les pronoms dans les langues altaiques. Polska Akademia Umiejętnośći, Prace Komisji Orientalisticznej,* No. 24, Kraków.

——. 1962. *Issledovanija po altajskim jazykam.* Moscow: Izdatel'stvo inostrannoj literatury.

Krasheninnikov, Stepan P. 1972. *Explorations of Kamchatka, 1735–1741,* translated with introduction and notes by E. A. P. Crownhart-Vaughan. Portland: Oregon Historical Society.

Krause, Scott Russell. 1980. "Topics in Chukchee Phonology," Ph.D. dissertation, University of Illinois.

Krause, Wolfgang. 1956. "Bemerkungen zu dem nominalen *nt*-Suffix in Hethitischen und Tocharischen," in H. Kronasser, ed., *Gedenkschrift Paul Kretschmer* I, Wiesbaden, Harrassowitz, 189–99.

Krause, Wolfgang, and Werner Thomas. 1960. *Tocharisches Elementarbuch, Band 1. Grammatik.* Heidelberg: Winter.

Krejnovich, E. A. 1934. "Nivxskij (giljakskij) jazyk," in Ja. P. Al'kor, ed., *Jazyki i pismennost' narodov severa,* III, Moscow, Uchpedgiz, 181–221.

——. 1937. *Fonetika nivxskogo jazyka.* Moscow-Leningrad: Uchpedgiz.

——. 1958. *Jukagirskij jazyk.* Leningrad: Akademia Nauk, Leningradskoje Otdelenije.

——. 1968. "Jukagirskij jazyk," *JNSSSR* V: 435–52.

——. 1976. "Ob odnoj tjurksko-paleoazijatskoj jazykovoj paralleli," in Klashtornyj, et al., eds., *Turcologica* (Kononov Festschrift), 94–100.

——. 1979a. "Nivxskij jazyk," in *Jazyki aziji i afriki* III, Moscow, Glavnaja Redakcija Vostochnoj Literatury, 295–329.

——. 1979b. "Jukagirskij jazyk," in *Jazyki aziji i afriki* III, Moscow, Glavnaja Redakcija Vostochnoj Literatury, 348–82.

——. 1982. *Issledovanija po jukagirskomu jazyku.* Leningrad: Nauka.

Kretschmer, Paul. 1891. "Indogermanische accent- und lautstudien," *ZfVS* 31: 326–472.

Kronasser, Heinz. 1956. *Vergleichende Laut- und Formenlehre des Hethitischen.* Heidelberg: Winter.

Krueger, John Richard. 1961. *Chuvash Manual.* Bloomington: Indiana University.

Kuryłowicz, Jerzy. 1932. "Les désinences moyennes de l'indoeuropéen et du hittite," *BSLP* 33: 1–4.

——. 1956. *L'apophonie en indo-européen.* Wrocław: Polska Akademia Nauk.

La Terza, E. 1936–37. "I pronomi personali dell'indo-europeo," *Rivista Indo-Greco-Italica* 20: 49–64, 21: 54–66.

Ladefoged, Peter. 1968. *A Phonetic Study of West African Languages,* 2nd edition. Cambridge: Cambridge University Press.

Ladefoged, Peter, and Ian Maddieson. 1996. *The Sounds of the World's Languages.* Oxford: Oxford University Press.

Lamb, Sydney M., and E. Douglas Mitchell, eds. 1991. *Sprung from Some Common Source. Investigations into the Prehistory of Languages.* Stanford: Stanford University Press.

Lange, Roland A. 1973. *The Phonology of Eighth Century Japanese.* Tokyo: Sophia University.

Langsdorff, G. H. von. 1812. *Bemerkungen auf eine Reise um die Welt in den Jahren 1803 bis 1807,* 2 vols. Frankfurt am Mein: Wilmans.

Laroche, E. 1958. "La comparaison du louvite et du lycien," *BSLP* 53: 159–97.

——. 1962. "Un 'ergatif' en indo-européen d'Asie Mineure," *BSLP* 57: 23–43.

——. 1970. "Études de linguistique anatolienne III," *Revue Hittite et Asianique* 28: 22–71.

Laughlin, William S., and Albert B. Harper. 1979. *The First Americans.* New York: G. Fischer.

Lee, Honsol H. B. 1989. *Korean Grammar.* Oxford: Oxford University Press.

Lehmann, Winfred P. 1974. *Proto-Indo-European Syntax.* Austin: University of Texas Press.

Lejeune, Michel. 1972. *Phonétique historique du mycenien et du grec ancien.* Paris: Klinksieck.

Leskien, August. 1909. *Grammatik der altbulgarischen (altkirchenslavischen) Sprache.* Heidelberg: Carl Winter.

——. 1910. *Handbuch der altbulgarischen (altkirchenslavischen) Sprache,* 5th edition. Weimar: H. Böhlau.

Levitskaja, L. S. 1976. *Istoricheskaja morfologija chuvashskogo jazyka.* Moscow: Nauka.

Lewicki, Marian. 1930. *Przyrostki przystówkowe -ra, -rä, -ru, -rü,*

-* rɨ*, -*ri w językach altajskich*. Wilno: Zakładu Nauk Oriental-istycznych Uniwersitetu Jana Kazimierza w Lwowie.

Lewin, Bruno. 1959. *Abriss der japanischen Grammatik, auf der Grundlage der klassischen Schriftsprache*. Wiesbaden: Harras-sowitz.

———. 1970. *Morphologie des koreanischen Verbums*. Wiesbaden: Harrassowitz.

———. 1976. "Japanese and Korean: The Problems and History of a Linguistic Comparison," *Journal of Japanese Studies* 2: 389–412.

Li, Bing. 1996. *Tungusic Vowel Harmony: Description and Analysis*. Amsterdam: University of Amsterdam.

Lindau, Mona. 1975. "Features for Vowels," *UCLA Working Papers in Phonetics* 30: 23–43.

Lukoff, Fred. 1982. *An Introductory Course in Korean*. Seoul: Yonsei University Press.

Lytkin, V. I. 1974. "Obshchije svedenija o finno-ugorskix jazykax," in V. I. Lytkin, et al., eds., *Osnovy finno-ugorskogo jazykoz-nanija*, Vol. I, Moscow, Nauka, 18–28.

Macdonnell, A. A. 1910. *Vedic Grammar*. Strassburg: Trübner.

Majewicz, Alfred B., and Elżbieta Majewicz. 1983–85. *An Ainu-English Index Dictionary to Bronisław Piłsudski's Materials for the Study of the Ainu Language and Folklore*. Poznań, Sapporo, Osaka: ICRAP Research Project.

Majtinskaja, E. E. 1966. "Vvednije: pribaltijsko-finskije jazyki," *JNSSSR* III: 9–25.

———. 1974. "Vengerskij jazyk," in V. I. Lytkin, ed., *Osnovy finno-ugorskogo jazykoznanija*, Vol. 1, Moscow, Nauka, 342–414.

———. 1979. *Istoriko-sopostavitel'naja morfologia finno-ugorskix jazykov*. Moscow: Nauka.

Mariès, M. L. 1930. "Sur la formation de l'aoriste et des subjonctifs en -ç- en arménien," *Revue des Études Arméniens* 10: 167–82.

Marsh, G., and Morris Swadesh. 1951. "Eskimo-Aleut Correspondences," *IJAL* 17: 209–16.

Martin, Samuel E. 1961. *Dagur Mongolian. Grammar, Texts, Lexicon*. Bloomington, Ind.: Indiana University.

———. 1962a. *Essential Japanese,* 3rd revised edition. Rutland, Vermont: Tuttle.

———. 1962b. "Phonetic Symbolism in Korean," in N. Poppe, ed., *American Studies in Altaic Linguistics,* Bloomington, Indiana University, 177–89.

———. 1966. "Lexical Evidence Relating Korean and Japanese," *Language* 42: 185–251.

———. 1987. *Japanese through Time.* New Haven: Yale University Press.

———. 1991. "Recent Research on the Relationships of Japanese and Korean," in Sydney M. Lamb and E. Douglas Mitchell, eds., *Sprung from Some Common Source,* Stanford, Stanford University Press, 269–92.

———. 1992. *Korean Reference Grammar.* Rutland, Vermont: Tuttle.

Martin, Samuel E., Yang Ha Lee, and Sungun-Chang. 1967. *A Korean-English Dictionary.* New Haven: Yale University Press.

Martinet, André. 1955. "Le couple *senex–senatus* et le 'suffixe' -*k*-," *BSLP* 51: 42–56.

Matsumoto, Nobuhiro. 1928. *Le japonais et les langues austroasiatiques, étude de vocabulaire comparé.* Paris: Geuthner.

Mayrhofer, Manfred. 1956–76. *Kurzgefasstes etymologisches Wörterbuch des Altindischen,* 3 vols. Heidelberg: Winter.

———. 1987. *Indogermanische Grammatik,* Vol. 1. Heidelberg: Winter.

Meillet, Antoine. 1932. "Sur le type de gr. μαινόλης," *BSLP* 33: 130–32.

———. 1934. *Le slave commun,* ed. by A. Vaillant. Paris: Honoré Champion.

———. 1964. *Introduction à l'étude comparative des langues indoeuropéenes,* 8th edition. Tuscaloosa: University of Alabama Press.

Mel'chuk, Igor A. 1959. "Kratkij ocherk morfologiji toxarskix jazykov," in V. V. Ivanov, ed., *Toxarskije jazyki,* Moscow, Izdatel'stvo Inostrannoy Literatury, 158–202.

Mel'chuk, Igor A., and Elena N. Savvina. 1978. "Toward a Formal Model of Alutor Surface Syntax: Predicative and Completive Construction," *Linguistics* (Special Issue), 5–39.

Mel'nichuk, A. S. 1979. "O genezise indoevropejskogo vokalizma," *VJ* 5: 3–16, 6: 3–16.

Menges, Karl H. 1952. "Zu einigen Problemen der tungusischen Grammatik," *UAJ* 24: 112–21.

——. 1968. *The Turkic Languages and Peoples. Ural-Altaische Bibliothek*, Vol. 15. Wiesbaden: Harrassowitz.

——. 1975. *Altajische Studien II. Japanisch und Altaisch.* Wiesbaden: Franz Steiner.

——. 1995. *The Turkic Languages and Peoples*, 2nd revised edition. *Veröffentlichungen der Societas Uralo-Altaica*, Vol. 42. Wiesbaden: Harrassowitz.

Menovshchikov, G. A. 1961–77. *Grammatika chukotskogo jazyka*, 2 vols. Leningrad: Nauka.

——. 1962–67. *Grammatika jazyka azijatskix eskimosov*, 2 vols. Moscow-Leningrad: Akademia Nauk.

——. 1964. *Jazyk sirenikskix eskimosov.* Moscow-Leningrad: Nauka.

——. 1968. "Aleutskij jazyk," *JNSSSR* V: 386–406.

——. 1975. *Jazyk naukanskix eskimosov.* Leningrad: Nauka.

——. 1980. *Jazyk eskimosov beringa proliva.* Leningrad: Nauka.

Meyer, Leo. 1890. *Handbuch der griechischen Etymologie.* Leipzig: S. Hirzel.

Miller, Roy Andrew. 1967. *The Japanese Language.* Chicago: University of Chicago Press.

——. 1971. *Japanese and the Other Altaic Languages.* Chicago: University of Chicago Press.

——. 1974. "The Origins of Japanese," *Monumenta Nipponica* 29: 93–102.

——. 1983. Book Note on James Patrie, *The Genetic Relationship of the Ainu Language, Language* 59: 447–48.

——. 1991a. "Japanese and Austronesian," *Acta Orientalia* 52: 148–68.

——. 1991b. "Genetic Connections among the Altaic Languages," in Sydney M. Lamb and E. Douglas Mitchell, eds., *Sprung from Some Common Source. Investigations into the Prehistory of Languages,* Stanford, Stanford University Press, 293–327.

——. 1991c. "Anti-Altaists *contra* Altaists," *UAJ* 63: 5–62.

——. 1991d. "How Many Verner's Laws Does an Altaicist Need?," in William G. Boltz and Michael C. Shapiro, eds., *Studies in the Historical Phonology of Asian Languages,* Amsterdam, John Benjamins, 176–204.

Moll, T. A. 1957. *Chukotsko-russkij slovar'*. Leningrad: Gosudarstvennoje Uchebno-Pedagogicheskoje Izdatel'stvo Ministra Prosvechenija RSFSR, Leningradskoje Otdelenije.

Möller, Hermann. 1906. *Semitisch und Indogermanisch*. Hildesheim: Georg Olms.

Moravcsik, Edith. 1974. "Object-Verb Agreement," *Working Papers in Language Universals* 15: 25–140. Stanford: Linguistics Department, Stanford University.

Morris, Ivan I. 1966. *Dictionary of Selected Forms in the Japanese Literary Language*. New York: Columbia University Press.

Mudrak, Oleg. 1989a. "Kamchukchee Roots," in Vitaly Shevoroshkin, ed., *Explorations in Macrofamilies*, Bochum, Germany, Brockmeyer, 90–110.

———. 1989b. "Reconstructing Eskaleutian Roots," in Vitaly Shevoroshkin, ed., *Reconstructing Languages and Cultures*, Bochum, Germany, Brockmeyer, 112–24.

Müller, Friedrich. 1876–88. *Grundriss der Sprachwissenschaft*, 4 vols. Vienna: Hölder.

Murasaki, Kyoko. 1978. *Sakhalin Ainu*. Tokyo: Tokyo Foreign Language University.

Muravjova, Irina Anatol'jevna. 1979. "Sopostavitel'noje issledovanije morfologii chukotsogo, korjakskogo, i al'utorskogo jazykov," Ph.D. dissertation, Moscow.

Murayama, Shichirō. 1957. "Vergleichende Betrachtung der Kasus-Affixe im Altjapanischen," in *Festschrift Poppe*, Wiesbaden, Harrassowitz, 126–31.

———. 1966. "Mongolisch und Japanisch—ein Versuch zum lexikalischen Vergleich," *Asiatische Forschungen* 17: 153–56.

———. 1971. *Kita Chishima Ainugo*. Tokyo: Yoshikawa Kōbunkan.

———. 1976. "Tungusica-Japanica," *UAJ* 48: 186–87.

Myrkin, V. Ja. 1964. "Tipologija lichnogo mestoimenija i voprosy rekonstrukciji jego v indoevropejskom aspekte," *VJ* 13.5, 78–86.

Naert, Pierre. 1958. *La situation linguistique de l'ainou I. ainou et indoeuropéen*. Lund: Lund universitets Årskrift, New Series, Section 1, Vol. 53, No. 4.

Nikolaieva, Irina Alekseevna. 1988. "Problema uralo-jukagirskix geneticheskix svjazej," Ph.D. dissertation, Institute of Linguistics, Academy of Sciences of the U.S.S.R.

Novikova, K. A. 1960. *Ocherki dialektov evenskogo jazyka. Part 1: ol'chskij dialekt.* Moscow-Leningrad: Akademija Nauk Sovjetskix Sotsialesticheskix Respublik.

Ōno, Susumu. 1970. *The Origin of the Japanese Language.* Tokyo: Kokusai Bunka Shinkokai.

Ōno, Susumu, et al. 1974. *Iwenami kogo-jiten.* Tokyo: Iwanami Shoten.

Paasonen, Heikki. 1906. "Die finnischen Pronominalstämme *jo-* und *e-,*" *FUF* 6: 114–17.

———. 1907. "Zur Frage von der urverwandschaft der finnischugrischen und indoeuropäischen Sprachen," *FUF* 17: 13–31.

Palmaitis, Mykolas L. 1981. "The New Look of Indo-European Declension (Thematic Stems)," *IF* 86: 71–95.

Panfilov, Vladimir Zinovievich. 1962–65. *Grammatika nivxskogo jazyka,* 2 vols. Moscow-Leningrad: Akademija Nauk.

———. 1973. "Nivxsko-altajskije jazykovije svjazy," *VP* 5: 3–12.

Patkanow, S., and D. R. Fuchs. 1910. "Laut- und Formenlehre der südostjakischen Dialekte," *Keleti Szemle* 11: 57–138.

Patrie, James. 1982. *The Genetic Relationship of the Ainu Language.* Honolulu: University Press of Hawaii.

Pedersen, Holger. 1903. "Türkische Lautgesetze," *Zeitschrift der deutschen morgenländischen Gesellschaft* 57: 535–61.

———. 1908. "Die idg.–semitische Hypothese und die idg. Lautlehre," *IF* 22: 341–65.

———. 1931. *Linguistic Science in the Nineteenth Century.* Cambridge: Harvard University Press. [Translation of *Sprogvidenskaben i det Nittende Aarhundrede,* 1924]

———. 1933. "Zur Frage nach der Urverwandschaft des Indoeuropäischen mit dem finno-ugrischen," *MSFO* 67: 308–25.

———. 1935. "Il problema delle parentele tra i grandi gruppi linguistici," *Atti del Congresso Internazionale dei Linguisti, Rome, 1933,* Florence, Felice de Monnier, 328–33.

———. 1938. *Hittitisch und die anderen indoeuropäischen Sprachen.* Copenhagen: Levin and Munksgaard.

Persson, Per. 1891. *Studien zur Lehre von der Wurzelerweiterung und Wurzelvariation.* Uppsala: Uppsala Universitets Årsskrift 1891, Filosofi, språkvetenskap och historiska vetenskaper, 4.

Petrova, T. I. 1968. "Orokskij jazyk," *JNSSSR* V: 172–90.

Pfizmaier, August. 1851. *Kritischer Durchsicht der von Dawidow verfassten Wörtersammlung aus der Sprache der Aino's*. Vienna: Hof- und Staatsdruckerei.

Piłsudski, Bronisław. 1912. *Materials for the Study of Aino Language and Folklore*. Kraków: Spółka Wydawnictwo Polska.

Pisani, V. 1976. "Zum armenischen Pluralzeichen -k'," *ZfVS* 89: 94–99.

Pokorny, Julius. 1959. *Indogermanisches Etymologisches Wörterbuch*, Vol. 1. Bern and Munich: Francke.

Polivanov, Evgenii Dimitrievich. 1968. *Statji po obshchemu jazykoznaniju*. Moscow: Nauka.

Poppe, Nikolaus. 1924. "Beiträge zur Kenntnis der altmongolischen Schriftsprache," *Asia Major* I: 668–75.

———. 1953. Review of D. Sinor, *On Some Altaic Plural Suffixes*, *FUF* 31: 26–31.

———. 1955. *Introduction to Comparative Mongolian Studies*. *MSFO* 110.

———. 1959. "Das Jakutische (einschliesslich Dolganisch)," *PTF*, 671–84.

———. 1960. *Vergleichende Grammatik der Altaischen Sprache, Teil I. Vergleichende Lautlehre*. Wiesbaden: Harrassowitz.

———. 1964. *Grammar of Written Mongolian*. Leipzig: Harrassowitz.

———. 1973. "Über einige Verbalstammbildungssuffixe in den altaischen Sprachen," *Orientalia Suecana* 21: 119-41.

Porzig, Walter. 1927. "Zur Aktionsart indogermanischen Präsensbildungen," *IF* 45: 152–67.

Prellwitz, Walther. 1905. *Etymologisches Wörterbuch der griechischen Sprache*. Göttingen: Vandenhoek and Ruprecht.

Pritsak, Omodjan. 1959. "Das kiptschakische," *PTF*, 87–112.

Pröhle, Wilhelm. 1916. "Studien zur Vergleichung des Japanischen mit den Uralischen und Altaischen Sprachen," *Keleti Szemle* 17: 147-83.

Pulleyblank, Edwin G. 1993. "The Typology of Indo-European," *JIES* 21: 63–118.

Pultr, Alois. 1960. *Lehrbuch der koreanischen Sprache*. Halle: Niemeyer.

Radliński, J. 1891–94. *Slownik narzeczy ludów kamczackich*. Rozprawy Widzialu filolocznego Akademii Umiejętnośći w Krakowie, Polska Akademia Umiejętnośći.

Radloff, W. 1882. *Phonetik der nördlichen Türksprachen.* Leipzig: Weigel.

Ramsey, Samuel Robert. 1978. *Accent and Morphology in Korean Dialects: A Descriptive and Historical Study.* Seoul: The Society of Korean Linguists.

Ramstedt, G. J. 1904. "Über mongolische pronomina. Mit einer Nachtrage über die turkischen possessivsuffixe," *JSFO* 23: 3.

———. 1912. "Zur Verbalstammbildungslehre der mongolischen-türkischen Sprachen," *JSFO* 28.3: 1-86.

———. 1924a. "Die Verneinung in den altaischen Sprachen. Eine semasiologische Studie," *MSFO* 52: 196–215.

———. 1924b. "A Comparison of the Altaic Languages with Japanese," *Transactions of the Asiatic Society of Japan,* 2nd series, 41–54. [Reprinted in *JSFO*, 1951]

———. 1939. *A Korean Grammar. MSFO* 82.

———. 1945. "Das deverbale Nomen auf -*i* in den altaischen Sprachen," *Studia Orientalia* 11.6.

———. 1949. *Studies in Korean Etymology. MSFO* 95.

———. 1950. "Das deverbale Nomen auf -*m* in den altaischen Sprachen," *MSFO* 98: 225–64.

———. 1952–57. *Einführung in die Altaische Sprachwissenschaft,* 2 vols. *MSFO* 104.

Räsänen, Martti. 1949. "Zur lautgeschichte der türkischen Sprachen," *Studia Orientalia* 15: 14–16.

———. 1957. "Materialien zur Morphologie der türkischen Sprachen," *Studia Orientalia* 21.

———. 1965. "Über die ural-altaische Sprachverwandschaft," *Sitzungsberichte der finnischen Akademie der Wissenschaften 1963,* Helsinki, Verlag der finnischen Akademie der Wissenschaften, 161–72.

———. 1969. *Versuch eines etymologischen Wörterbuchs der Türksprachen.* Helsinki: Finnische Literaturgeselschaft.

Rasmussen, Knud. 1888. *Grønlandske Sproglære.* Copenhagen: A. Rosenberg.

———. 1941. "Alaskan Eskimo Words," *Report of the Fifth Thule Expedition 1921–24,* Vol. III.4. Copenhagen: Gylendalske Boghandel.

Ravila, Paavo. 1941. "Über die Verwendung des Numeruszeichens in den uralischen Sprachen," *FUF* 27: 1-136.

Rédei, Károly. 1988. *Uralisches Etymologisches Wörterbuch,* Vol. 1. Wiesbaden: Harrassowitz.

Rédei, Károly, and Istvan Erdély. 1974. "Sravnitel'naja leksika finno-ugorskix jazykov," in *Osnovy finno-ugorskogo jazykoznanija,* I, Moscow, Nauka, 397–438.

Reed, Irene, et al. 1977. *Yup'ik Eskimo Grammar.* Fairbanks: Alaska Native Language Center, University of Alaska.

Refsing, Kirsten. 1986. *The Ainu Language: The Morphology and Syntax of the Shizunai Dialect.* Aarhus: Aarhus University Press.

Rosén, Haiim B. 1978. "*amamini* und die indogermanischen Diathesen- und Valenzkategorien," *ZfVS* 92: 143–78.

Rosenkranz, Bernhard. 1950. "Hethitisches zur Frage der Indogermanischen-Finnisch-Ugrisch Sprachverwandtschaft," *Archiv Orientalní* 18: 439–43.

——. 1966. Review of B. Collinder, *Hat das Uralische Verwandte?, Bibliotheca Orientalis* 23: 204–06.

——. 1978. *Vergleichende Untersuchungen der altanatolischen Sprache.* The Hague: Mouton.

Ruhlen, Merritt. 1991. *A Guide to the World's Languages,* Vol. 1: Classification. Stanford: Stanford University Press.

Sansom, G. B. 1928. *An Historical Grammar of Japanese.* Oxford: Oxford University Press.

Saukkonen, Pauli. 1964. "Die Verwendung des nominativischen und illativischen Infinitivs im Mordwinischen," *FUF* 35: 88–115.

Saussure, Ferdinand de. 1879. *Mémoire sur le système primitif des voyelles dans les langues indo-européennes.* Leipzig: Teubner.

Sauvageot, Aurelien. 1924. "Eskimo et ouralien," *Journal de la Société Américaniste de Paris* 16: 279–316.

Saval'eva, V. N. 1970. *Nivxsko-russkij slovar'.* Moscow: Sovetskaja Entsiklopedija.

Savchenko, A. N. 1960. "Problema isxozhdenija lychnyx okanchanij glagola v indoevropejskom jazyke," *Lingua Posnaniensis* 8: 44–56.

Schiefner, Anton von. 1871. "Über baron Gerhard von Maydell's jukagirsche Sprachproben," *Mélanges Asiatiques* 6: 373–99.

———. 1871–72. "Beiträge zur Kenntnis der jukagirischen Sprache," *Académie Royale des Sciences de Saint-Pétersbourg, Bulletin* 5.3, 16, 373–400.

Schmalstieg, William R. 1980. *Indo-European Linguistics.* University Park: Pennsylvania State University Press.

Schmidt, Johannes. 1889. *Die Pluralbildung der indogermanischen Neutra.* Weimar: Böhlau.

———. 1899. "Die Kretischen pluralnominative auf -εν und verwandtes," *ZfVS* 36: 400-16.

Schmidt, Rüdiger. 1981. *Grammatik der Klassisch-Armenischen mit sprachvergleichenden Erläuterungen.* Innsbruck: Institut für Sprachwissenschaft der Universität.

Schmitt-Brandt, Robert. 1973. *Die Entwicklung des indogermanischen vokalsystems,* 2nd revised ed. Heidelberg: Gross.

Schott, Wilhelm. 1849. *Über das Altai'sche oder Finnisch-Tatarische Sprachengeschlecht,* Philologische und historische Abhandlungen der Königlichen Akademie der Wissenschaften zu Berlin.

Schwyzer, Eduart. 1939–50. *Griechische Grammatik auf der Grundlage von Karl Brugmanns Griechische Grammatik.* Munich: Beck.

Sebestyén, Irene M. 1970. "Zur juraksamojedischen Konjugation," *FUF* 38: 137–225.

Senn, A. 1966. *Handbuch der litauischen Sprache,* Vol. 2. Heidelberg: Winter.

Serebrennikov, B. A. 1964. *Osnovyje liniji razvitija padezhnej i glagolnej system v uralskix jazykax.* Moscow: Nauka.

Serebrennikov, B. A., and N. Z. Gazhdieva. 1986. *Sravnitel'no-istoricheskaja grammatika tjurkskix jazykov,* 2nd ed. Moscow: Nauka.

Setälä, E. N. 1887. "Zur Geschichte der Tempus- und Modusstammbildung in den finnisch-ugrischen Sprachen," *JSFO* 2: 1–184.

Shevoroshkin, Vitaly, and Alexis Manaster Ramer. 1991. "Some Recent Work on the Remote Relationships of Languages," in Sydney M. Lamb and E. Douglas Mitchell, eds., *Sprung from Some Common Source,* Stanford, Stanford University Press, 178–99.

Shibatani, Masayoshi. 1985. "Passives and Related Constructions: A Prototype Analysis," *Language* 61: 821–48.

———. 1990. *The Languages of Japan.* Cambridge: Cambridge University Press.

Shields, Kenneth. 1982. *Indo-European Noun Inflection: A Developmental Study.* Paris and London: Pennsylvania State University Press.

Shimkin, D. B. 1960. Review of Bergsland, *Aleut Dialects of Atka and Attu, American Anthropologist* 62: 729–30.

Sihler, Andrew L. 1995. *New Comparative Grammar of Greek and Latin.* Oxford: Oxford University Press.

Simeon, George John. 1968. "The Phonemics and Morphology of Hokkaido Ainu," Ph.D. dissertation, University of Southern California.

———. 1969. "Hokkaido Ainu Phonemics," *Journal of the American Oriental Society* 89: 751–57.

Sinor, Denis. 1952. "On Some Ural-Altaic Plural Suffixes," *Asia Major* II: 203–30.

———. 1968. "La langue mandjou," in *Handbuch der Orientalistik,* I: 5, 3, Leiden, Brill, 257–80.

———. 1988. "The Problem of the Ural-Altaic Relationship," in Denis Sinor, ed., *The Uralic Languages. Description, History and Foreign Influences,* Leiden, Brill, 706–41.

Sköld, Hannes. 1927. "Indo-Uralisch," *FUF* 18: 216-31.

Skorik, P. Ja. 1961–77. *Grammatika chukotskogo jazyka,* 2 vols. Moscow: Akademija Nauk.

———. 1968. "Chukotskij jazyk," in *Jazyki narodov Sovetskix Socialesticheskix Respublik,* V: 248–70.

Smith, Lawrence E. 1977. *Some Grammatical Aspects of Labrador Inuttut.* Ottawa: National Museum of Canada.

Solmsen, Martin. 1899. "Etymologien," *ZfVS* 15: 463–84.

Sommer, F. 1947. *Hethiter und Hethitisch.* Stuttgart: Kohlhammer.

Sommer, F., and A. Falkenstein. 1938. *Die hethitisch-akkadische Bilingue des Hattušiliš.* Abhandlungen des bayrischen Akademie der Wissenschaft, Phil.-hist. Abteilung, NF 16.

Spahn, Mark, and Wolfgang Hadmitzky. 1996. *The Kanji Dictionary.* Rutland, Vermont: Charles Tuttle.

Spalding, A. E. 1960. *A Grammar of the East and West Coasts of Hudson Bay.* Ottawa: Queen's Printer.

Specht, F. 1932. "Beiträge zur griechischen Grammatik," *ZfVS* 59: 31–131.

Speirs, A. G. E. 1984. *Proto-Indo-European Laryngeals and Ablaut.* Amsterdam: Hakkert.

Stang, Christian S. 1966. *Vergleichende Grammatik der baltischen Sprachen.* Oslo: Universitätsverlag.

Starostin, Sergei A. 1975. "K voprosu o rekonstruktsii prajaponskoj fonologicheskoj sistemy," in *Ocherki po fonologii vostochnyx jazykov,* Moscow, Nauka, 271–80.

———. 1984. "Gipoteza o geneticheskix svjazax sinotibeticheskix jazykov s enisejeskimi i severnokavkazkimi jazykami," in *Lingvisticheskaja rekonstruktsija i drevnejshaja istorija vostoka,* Moscow, 19–38.

———. 1990. "A Statistical Evaluation of the Nostratic Macrofamily," in Richard Dawkins and Jared Diamond, *Evolution: From Molecules to Culture,* Cold Spring Harbor, Cold Spring Harbor Laboratory, p. 33.

———. 1991. *Altajskaja problema i proisxozhdenije japonskogo jazyka.* Moscow: Nauka, Glavnaja Redakcija Vostochnoj Literatury.

Stebnickij, S. N. 1934. "Itel'menskij (kamchadal'skij) jazyk," in E. A. Krejnovich, ed., *Jazyki i pismennost' narodov severa,* Part III, Leningrad, Gosudarstvenoje Uchebno-Pedagogicheskoje Izdatel'stvo.

Steinitz, Wolfgang. 1950. *Geschichte des ostjakischen Vokalismus.* Berlin: Akademie Verlag.

Street, John. 1974. *On the Lexicon of Proto-Altaic: A Partial Index to Reconstructions.* Madison, Wisc.: privately printed.

———. 1978. *Altaic Elements in Old Japanese,* Part 2. Madison, Wisc.: privately printed.

———. 1982. Review of James Patrie, *The Genetic Relationship of the Ainu Language, Journal of the Association of Teachers of Japanese* 17: 192–204.

Street, John, and Roy Andrew Miller. 1975. *Altaic Elements in Old Japanese.* Madison, Wisc.: privately printed.

Sturtevant, Edgar H. 1932. "The Development of Stops in Hittite," *Journal of the American Oriental Society* 52: 1–12.

———. 1933. *A Comparative Grammar of the Hittite Language.* Philadelphia: University of Pennsylvania.

Summers, James. 1886. "An Aino-English Vocabulary," *Transactions of the Asiatic Society of Japan* 14: 186–231.

Sunik, O. P. 1962. *Glagol v tunguso-man'churskix jazykax.* Moscow-Leningrad: Akademija Nauk.

———. 1968a. "Ul'chskij jazyk," *JNSSSR* V: 149–71.

———. 1968b. "Udegejskij jazyk," *JNSSSR* V: 210–32.

———. 1968c. "Tunguso-man'chzhurskije jazyky," *JNSSSR* V: 53–67.

———. 1989. *Ul'chskij jazyk.* Leningrad: Nauka.

Swadesh, Morris. 1952. "Unaaliq and Proto-Eskimo IV. Diachronic Notes," *IJAL* 18: 166–71.

Syromiatnikov, Nikolai A. 1972. *Drevnejaponskij jazyk.* Moscow: Institut Vostokovedenija, Akademija Nauk SSSR.

———. 1981. *The Ancient Japanese Language.* Moscow: Nauka.

Szemerényi, Oswald. 1967. "The New Look of Indo-European Reconstruction and Typology," *Phonetica* 17: 65–99.

———. 1978. *Introducción a la linguistica comparativa.* Madrid: Gredos.

———. 1990. *Einführung in die vergleichende Sprachwissenschaft,* 4th ed. Darmstadt: Wissenschaftliche Buchgesellschaft.

———. 1996. *Introduction to Indo-European Linguistics.* Oxford: Clarendon Press.

Szinnyei, Josef. 1910. *Finnisch-ugrische Sprachwissenschaft,* 1st edition. Leipzig: Göschen.

———. 1922. *Finnisch-ugrische Sprachwissenschaft,* 2nd edition. Leipzig: Göschen.

Tailleur, Oliver Guy. 1959a. "Les uniques données sur l'omok, langue éteinte de la famille youkaghire," *Orbis* 8: 78–108.

———. 1959b. "Plaidoyer pour youkaghir branche orientale de la famille ouralienne," *Lingua* 8: 403–23.

———. 1960. "La place du ghiliak parmi les langues paléosiberiennes," *Lingua* 9: 113–47.

———. 1962. "Le dialecte tchouvane du youkaghir," *UAJ* 34: 55–99.

Takahashi, Morio. 1952. *Romanized Japanese-English Dictionary.* Kobe: Taisedo.

Tekin, Talat. 1968. *A Grammar of Orkhon Turkish.* The Hague: Mouton, Uralic and Altaic Series, No. 69.

Tenishev, E. R. 1984. *Sravnitel'no-istoricheskaja grammatika tjurkskix jazykov: morfologija.* Moscow: Nauka.

Thalbitzer, William. 1904. *A Phonetical Study of the Eskimo Language. Medelelser om Grønland* 31.

———. 1911. "Eskimo," in *Handbook of American Indian Languages,* Vol. 1, Washington, D.C., Government Printing Office, 971–1069. Bureau of American Ethnology Bulletin 40.

Thibert, Arthur. 1970. *Dictionary English-Eskimo Eskimo-English.* Ottawa: Canadian Research Center for Anthropology, Saint Paul University.

Thomas, Werner. 1952. *Die tocharischen Verbaladjecktive auf -l, eine syntaktische Forschung.* Berlin: Adakemie-Verlag.

Thomsen, Vilhelm. 1916. "Turcica. Étude concernant l'interprétation des inscriptions turques de la Mongolie et de la Sibérie," *MSFO* 37.

Thumb, Albert. 1958–59. *Handbuch des Sanskrit,* 3rd ed., revised by Richard Hauschild, 2 vols. Heidelberg: Winter.

Tittel, H. 1922. "Die Sprache der Ainu von Sakhalin," *Mitteilungen der deutschen Gesellschaft für Natur- und Völkerkunde Ostasiens* 17: 70–89.

Todaeva, Buliash Khoichevna. 1964. *Baoanskij jazyk.* Moscow: Nauka.

Toivonen, Yrjö Henrik, ed. 1955–83. *Suomen kielen etymologinen sanakirja,* 7 vols. Lexica Societatis Finno-Ugricae XII, 1.

Torii Ryûzô. 1903. *Chishima ainu* [Ainu of the Kurile Islands]. Tokyo: Kokawa Kōbunkan.

Tsintsius, V. I. 1975–77. *Sravnitel'nyj slovar' tunguso-man'chzhurskix jazykov,* 2 vols. Leningrad: Nauka.

———. 1982. *Negidal'skij jazyk.* Leningrad: Nauka.

Uhlenbeck, C. C. 1907. *Ontwerp van eene vergelijkende vormleer der Eskimotalen. Verhandelingen der koninklijke Akademie van Wetenschappen te Amsterdam,* Afd. Letterkunde Nieuwe Reeks, Deel 8, No. 3.

———. 1935. *Eskimo en Oer-Germaansch. Mededeelingen der Koninklijke Akademie van Wetenschapen,* Deel 77, Serie A, No. 6.

———. 1942–45. "Ur- und altindogermanische Anklänge im Wortschatz des Eskimos," *Anthropos* 37–40: 113–48.

Unger, James Marshall. 1975. "Studies in Early Japanese Morphophonemics," Ph.D. dissertation, Yale University.

Vaillant, André. 1950–66. *Grammaire comparée des langues slaves,* 3 vols. Lyon: IAC.

Vértes, Edith. 1967. *Die ostjakischen Pronomina.* The Hague: Mouton.

Vladimirtsov, B. Ja. 1929. *Sravnitel'naja grammatika mongol'skogo pismennogo jazyka: xalxaskogo narechija.* Leningrad: Izdanija Leningradskogo Vostochnogo Instituta imeni A. S. Enukidze.

Volodin, Aleksandr Pavlevich. 1976. *Itel'menskij jazyk.* Leningrad: Nauka.

Vos, Fritz Philipp Franz von. 1993. "Siebold and the Ainu Language," in Josef Kreiner, ed., *European Studies on Ainu Language and Culture,* Munich, Judicium, 63–80.

Vovin, Alexander. 1993. *A Reconstruction of Proto-Ainu.* Leiden: Brill.

———. 1994. "Long Distance Relationships, Reconstruction Methodology, and Origins of Japanese," *Diachronica* 11: 95–114.

Wackernagel, Jacob. 1909. "Attische Verstufen des Itazismus," *IF* 25: 326–337.

Wackernagel, Jacob, and Albert Debrunner. 1896–1930. *Altindische Grammatik,* 3 vols. Göttingen: Vandenhoek and Ruprecht.

Walde, Alois. 1938–54. *Lateinisches etymologisches Wörterbuch,* 2 vols., 3rd revised ed. by J. B. Hofmann. Heidelberg: Winter.

Walde, Alois, and Julius Pokorny. 1928–32. *Vergleichendes Wörterbuch der indogermanischen Sprachen,* 3 vols. Berlin and Leipzig: De Gruyter.

Watkins, Calvert. 1962. *Indo-European Origins of the Celtic Verb I. The Sigmatic Aorist.* Dublin: Institute for Advanced Studies.

———. 1963. "Preliminaries to a Historical and Comparative Analysis of the Celtic Verb," *Celtica* 6: 1–49.

———. 1969. *Indogermanische Grammatik,* III.1. Heidelberg: Winter.

———. 1990. "Etymologies, Equations, and Comparanda: Types and Values and Criteria for Judgement," in Philip Baldi, ed., *Linguistic Change and Reconstruction Methodology,* The Hague, Mouton de Gruyter, 289–304.

Wenck, Günther. 1954–59. *Japonische Phonetik,* 4 vols. Wiesbaden: Harrassowitz.

Whiteman, John. 1990. "A Rule of Medial *-r- loss in pre-Old

Japanese," in Philip Baldi, ed., *Linguistic Change and Reconstruction Methodology*, Berlin, Mouton de Gruyter, 511–45.

Whitney, Arthur H. 1956. *Finnish.* Seven Oaks: Nodder and Stoughton.

Whitney, William Dwight. 1879. *A Sanskrit Grammar.* Leipzig: Breitkopf and Härtel.

Wiklund, Karl Bernard. 1906. "Finnisch-ugrisch und indogermanisch," *Le monde orientale* (Uppsala) 1: 43–65.

Windekens, A. J. 1944. *Morphologie comparée du tocharien.* Louvain: Muséon.

Winter, Werner. 1950. "The Reduplication Type *bharībharti/bharibhrati* in Greek," *Language* 26: 532–33.

Woodhuizen, Fred C. 1991. "Etruscan and Luwian," *JIES* 19: 733–50.

Worth, Dean. 1969. *A Dictionary of Western Kamchadal. University of California Publications in Linguistics* 59.

Yoshitake, S. 1930. "History of the Japanese Particle *-i*," *Bulletin of the School of Oriental and African Studies* 5: 889–95.

———. 1934. *The Phonetic System of Ancient Japanese.* London: Royal Asiatic Society.

Zajtseva, M. I. 1981. *Grammatika vepsskogo jazyka.* Leningrad: Nauka.

Zhukova, A. N. 1972. *Grammatika korjakskogo jazyka.* Leningrad: Nauka.

———. 1980. *Jazyk palanskix korjakov.* Leningrad: Nauka.

Zimmer, H. 1888. "Keltische studien," *ZfVS* 30: 1–292.

Indexes

Semantic Index

General Index

No attempt has been made in the following index to list every citation of every language—or even every language family—mentioned in this book. Such an index would have been excessively long, cumbersome, and of very little use to most readers. In fact, since each section of Chapter 3 deals with a specific grammatical formative, even the Semantic Index provides a rough outline of the book. The present index is limited to some of the more important references to languages and language families, as well as to general topics and certain authors.

Library of Congress Cataloging-in-Publication Data

Greenberg, Joseph Harold
    Indo-European and its closest relatives : the Eurasiatic language
family / Joseph H. Greenberg.
        p.   cm.
    Includes bibliographical references and index.
    Contents: v. 1. Grammar.
    ISBN 0-8047-3812-2 (v. 1 : alk. paper)
    1. Indo-European languages. 2. Ural-Altaic languages.
3. Hyperborean languages. I. Title.
    P569.G74   2000
    410—dc21   99-41501

⊗ This book is printed on acid-free paper.

Original printing 1999
Last figure below indicates year of this printing:

08 07 06 05 04 03 02 01 00 99

Designed and typeset by Merritt Ruhlen with the TEX typesetting
language.

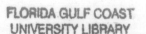